The Metropolis

A History of American Life

PAUL LAUNE

THE GREAT CRUSADE
AND AFTER
1914-1928

A HISTORY OF AMERICAN LIFE

To complete the series there will appear subsequently Vol. IV by Evarts B. Greene covering the period 1763-1790; and Vol. V by Dixon R. Fox covering the period 1790-1830.

THE GREAT CRUSADE
AND AFTER
1914-1928

vol XII

BY

PRESTON WILLIAM SLOSSON

ASSOCIATE PROFESSOR OF HISTORY, UNIVERSITY OF MICHIGAN

With an editorial foreword by
ARTHUR M. SCHLESINGER
and DIXON RYAN FOX

New York
THE MACMILLAN COMPANY

Set up and electrotyped by J. J. Little & Ives Co.
Printed in the United States of America

What we demand in this war, therefore, is nothing peculiar to ourselves. It is that the world be made fit and safe to live in; and particularly that it be made safe for every peace-loving nation which, like ourselves, wishes to live its own life. . . .

WOODROW WILSON, "Address to Congress, January 8, 1918," *Congressional Record*, LVI, pt. i, 680.

Upon us [in 1917] devolved the herculean work not only of meeting the special military requirements of ourselves and our allies, but of meeting the large alimentary deficits of the allied world and to some extent of the neutrals, besides seeing to it that our own people were adequately fed, fueled, and clothed. Our problem of industrial mobilization and application was thus vaster and more complex than that of any of the other nations at war. And it was thrust upon a people less prepared, by tradition, training, economic struggle, political organization and control, and by forethought, to undertake it than was any other.

GROSVENOR B. CLARKSON, *Industrial America in the World War* (Boston, 1923), 7.

The United States has evolved from a country of political experiment, a debtor to Europe, a radical disturber of established government, the hope of the oppressed and an inspiration to all men everywhere who wished to be free; into a wealthy and conservative country, the world's banker and stabilizer, the most powerful enemy to change and revolution. American residence, once the right of the "poorest child of Adam's kin," has become a jealously guarded privilege. Americans have obtained a degree of comfort and a sense of security beyond the dreams of departed philanthropists. In this process many of the old rugged virtues have been lost; but much of the old neighborliness and concern for social welfare have lasted. . . .

SAMUEL ELIOT MORISON, *An Hour of American History* (Phila., 1929), 155-156.

CONTENTS

ILLUSTRATIONS
(By the Editors)

A view of New York from Governor's Island. From an etching by Anton Schutz. The tallest tower, that of the Bank of the Manhattan Company, was not actually completed until 1930, though it was planned in 1928 and 1929. The artist, born and educated in Germany and after his arrival in this country an instructor in the Art Students' League in New York City, made his reputation as one of America's most successful etchers largely on the basis of his views of city buildings.

The report in the *New York Tribune*, May 8, 1915, of the sinking of the *Lusitania* eight miles off the Irish coast, while on its way from New York to Liverpool, by a German submarine the previous afternoon. Actually 1152 persons, 114 of them Americans, lost their lives.

From a painting by Walter De Maris, entitled "The Liberty Loan, 1918," owned by the *American Bankers' Association Journal*, by whose permission it is here reproduced. The scene will be recognized as in Wall Street, New York City, looking past the Subtreasury Building toward Trinity Church.

(a) A cartoon entitled "Our own yard is enough to worry about," by William Ireland (1880-   ). It was published in the *Columbus* (Ohio) *Dispatch*, March 4, 1924, with which newspaper Mr. Ireland became associated in 1899. The opinion here represented was widespread throughout the Middle West, though, of course, there were other reasons for refraining from world cooperation besides the one here indicated. On the other hand, many of those in the East who favored joining the League of Nations were bitter critics of corruption and inefficiency in the federal government. This certainly had been the official attitude of the Democratic party.

ber 29, 1929. It is stated in the accompanying text that all these models originated in Paris. Incidentally this sample illustrates the modern tendency in advertisements to be "educational" rather than merely to describe and recommend wares.

(a) The opening purse. From *Financing Philanthropy*, III (1928), 33, a publication issued by Marts and Lundy, Inc., directors of campaigns for financial purposes. Such organizations, at least in their great development, resulted largely from the "drives" of war time. Undoubtedly by their administrative aid and advice they stimulated the habit of giving for public purposes.

(b) The changing cost of living. From the *Survey Graphic*, XIV (1928), 121, for which it was drawn by Helen B. Phelps from a chart by the National Bureau of Economic Research.

(a) The power-driven machine supplants the horse. From an advertisement (here showing the top third only) in the *Country Gentleman*, LXXXV, no. 13 (March 27, 1920), 71. This picture is interesting not only because of the motor cultivator indicated and the legend below, but also because of the idealized type of American farmer, especially in the figure at the left, a type persisting in virtually all farm journals of the time.

(b) Governor Lynn Frazier (center) visiting a North Dakota farmer and his wife. Faith in the propaganda of the Nonpartisan League was maintained by such personal visits as well as by party journalism and mass meetings. This kind of farmhouse, a combination of sod and wood construction, was still to be found in many places in the north prairie country throughout the period. From Charles Edward Russell, *The Story of the Nonpartisan League* (N. Y., 1920).

Henry Ford and his son Edsel, in May, 1927, standing at Dearborn, Michigan, beside their fifteen-millionth Ford automobile, a Model T, while they contemplate "Old Number One," the first car produced by Mr. Ford in 1903. The contrast in efficiency was greater than that in size; were there space to show the first little shed-roof shop side by side with the immense plant, an infinitesimal portion of which forms the background here, it would be striking indeed. Copyright by the Wide World Photo Co.

        (a) Interracial courtesies. The officers of the Colored
Benevolent and Protective Order of Elks meeting to the
number of 80,000 in their twenty-sixth annual convention
in Richmond, Va., late in 1925, photographed with Governor E. L. Trinkle, Mayor E. F. Bright and others who
have just welcomed them to the city. Never before had
such a large number of Negroes visited a Southern city.
It was feared that the parade, five miles long, might lead to
some expression of racial animosity; circumspect behavior
on both sides, however, was mutually appreciated and the
occasion was remembered with satisfaction by all. The
picture is from *Collier's*, LXXVII, no. 6 (Feb. 6, 1926),
23.

        (b) A typical North Carolina upland road about 1914.
Mud was the farmer's greatest obstacle to profit.

        (c) A typical North Carolina upland road a decade
later. Conservatism in the legislature gave way in 1921
and at Governor Cameron Morrison's behest the sum of
$50,000,000 was appropriated to build 6200 miles of
roads, a large part of them hard finished; a little later
$15,000,000 was added. A tax on gasoline contributed
much to meet the cost. This and the companion picture
are from the *American Review of Reviews*, LXVIII
(1923), 630.

        (d) The Industrial Rayon Corporation factory at Cov-
ington, Alleghany County, Va. This plant, built at the
end of the period, testified not only to the vogue of artificial silk, but to the advantage of location in the Southern
highlands with reference especially to cheap power and
labor. The land, too, being cheap, the main building (337
x 727 ft.) was designed with only one story. It was provided with a siding on the railroad and connection with
a stream for its filtration apparatus. Near by, as usual,
were planned 300 bungalows to house the workers brought
in from the mountains. Reproduced from the *Textile
World*, LXXVII, 699 (Feb. 1, 1930).

        (a) A football game at the University of Illinois sta-
dium, October 18, 1924. The stadium, built as a memorial to the 184 Illinois men who died, and others who had
served, in the World War, was the gift of 21,111 alumni
averaging $100 each. This game with the University of
Michigan, attended by 67,205 spectators, was the first after
the edifice was finished; it resulted in a victory of 39 to 14
for the home team, largely through the runs of Harold
("Red") Grange. The U. of I. band of 170 pieces and
the U. of M. band of 100 entertained the crowd before

the game. The Illinois Central had recently completed a new station at Urbana-Champaign, moved partly by the realization of the added passenger traffic which the stadium would bring. Seventeen special trains carried many of those coming from Chicago to this game. A few weeks later the Illinois team went to the University of Minnesota to play the dedication game in the new $700,000 stadium at that institution. From the *Illinois Alumni News*, III, no. 3 (December, 1924).

(b) and (c) Players in the game. The figure on the left is "Red" Grange. Details from an illustration in the same, III, no. 2 (November, 1924); a *Chicago Tribune* photograph.

EDITORS' FOREWORD

It was once maintained by respectable critics that "contemporary history" was a contradiction in terms, that no one could estimate events without knowing what they led to. In this plausible reasoning it was overlooked that many, hailed as great historians from Thucydides down, have written of their own times. Professor Slosson's chapters will illustrate how a historian can write of such events with just detachment, handling the abundant source material and written comment with the same technique that he would use in chronicling the life and way of any previous generation. Attempting by imagination to divine the verdict of the future, he strictly keeps the past tense in writing of transactions whose echoes are still ringing. In the same historical spirit he seeks the wide and balanced view that one would get in such perspective. Since within these limits come nearly all the varied interests of Americans, the readers of this volume, for the most part, will have the engaging opportunity to see themselves as the data of history. The author in presenting the case for this generation expects, it appears, a sympathetic judgment from posterity. Fully aware of foibles and follies and, here and there, deep injustice, nevertheless his buoyant narrative is a wholesome antidote to much that has been written of these years, accounts conceived in irritation, hopelessness and shame.

The year 1914 revealed the community of mankind in the modern world. A shot was fired in a Balkan province and its reverberations broke the peace of shepherds on the hills of Colorado. Many years before, a European crisis

had been profoundly felt by our young nation, but in
1789 there was at the same time a new constitution, with
attendant problems of domestic policy, and a new trans-
Alleghany West beckoning to adventure; one cannot isolate the factors. In 1914, for the first time since the
Revolution, an epoch opened in American history almost
entirely through causes in the world without. With sur-
prise and some vexation many learned that it was but
one world and that we were part of it.

Then began those difficult years for thoughtful Americans, trying to choose a wise and honorable course while
beset on all sides by organized persuasion. Having led
the reader through the valley of decision, Professor Slosson reviews the war that followed, the lift of common
resolution, the incidence of tragedy, and sudden, swift
efficiency streaked with bungling. But it is a war seen
from the private's bunk, the housewife's kitchen, the
business man's desk. The entire population being mustered into service, war, more than ever before, became
social history; the armies at the front were but the cutting edge of a weapon wielded by a nation. It was a great
crusade in which those who worked at home played a
part as well as those who were sent.

War is so abnormal an experience of civilization that
it gets back but slowly to old ideals of peace. The title
of the book *The Great Crusade and After* suggests sar-
donically the moral slump which followed when the
tumult and the shouting died—the blunted conscience,
the overwrought nerves, the growth of intolerance,
standards unsettled by the recent prodigality, just as in
the days of reconstruction after the Civil War. While
tracing the sad results in many quarters, Professor Slosson also points out the artificial and illusory nature of
economic prosperity under war conditions. As far as the

average American was concerned, the fifteen years which began in 1913, divide themselves into two parts: the first, to 1923 or 1924, when with mounting prices the consumer's hand could scarcely reach the things he needed to consume, and the second, when with readjusted income he met the new scale with more comfort than he had enjoyed for many a year, the farmer and some others being marked exceptions in both periods. The spectacle of abundant wealth on almost every side, the report of scandal in high places which destroyed the faith of youth, a multiplicity of new laws like that prohibiting the sale of intoxicating liquors which could profitably be circumvented and the easy means of attack and escape afforded by the ubiquitous automobile—these made for lawlessness and violent crime in such degree as to bring chagrin to the nation.

Noting all these shadows, the author still sees a picture brightened by idealism if not sweet reasonableness. He hails the final victories of women in establishing an equal status in American society, the colossal effort to carry a great population into the opportunities of higher education, the bold experiment that wiped out the saloon, and the rising level of life for Negroes. The chapter on the services of science and invention to the common life, contributed by Dr. Edwin E. Slosson, but supplements his evidence. Whether Henry Ford's economic philosophy that consumption makes prosperity is sound or not, it seemed the ideal of this generation that goods should be distributed to everybody. In what previous time, here or elsewhere, was a bricklayer's bride so luxuriously dowered as in this? Skeptics might demur and say that scholars and gentlemen must suffer if bricklayers' brides were so astonishingly prospered, but such sentiments commanded little credit. Bentham, if his bones in Bloomsbury could come to life again, would read Professor Slosson's book with much satisfaction, for few societies, if any, have more dearly cherished his idea of the greatest happiness of the greatest number.

A. M. S.
D. R. F.

THE GREAT CRUSADE
AND AFTER
1914-1928

THE GREAT CRUSADE
AND AFTER

CHAPTER I

BETWEEN PEACE AND WAR

IN counting the annual rings that tell the life story
of a fallen tree the forester can sometimes distinguish
narrow, crowded lines that testify to years of stress and
drought. If trees had memory we can be sure that they
would reckon events as they befell before or after the
"hard times." The World War of 1914-1918 marked
five such bands of waste and suffering across the life of
nearly every nation in the world. No other recorded
human disaster, not even the Black Death of the fourteenth century, so intimately touched each race of mankind or created so general a brotherhood of suffering.
Even the few neutral nations which did not contribute
to the casualty lists were shaken profoundly by the economic repercussions of the European conflict. For America, as for Europe, it closed one age and began another.

Yet there was a difference. The war came to Europe
as illness comes to a man of advancing years and weak-
ened constitution, a disaster native to the system. The
war came to the United States from without, from causes
for which the United States had little responsibility.
The American people have never really accepted it as
a part of their national tradition. Ten years after its
close they remained still irritated and bewildered by it,
rarely viewing it with that sentimental reminiscent fondness that inwrapped 1776 and 1861, although there

were relatively far more American "Tories" in the former year and Northern "copperheads" in the latter than "pro-Germans" in 1917. In many European countries which suffered more deeply than the United States the revulsion from the war took a positive form, such as radical socialism or a militant and uncompromising pacifism. The average American felt rather that, while his government could perhaps not have avoided the war, the war ought somehow to have avoided America; that it was most unpleasant for a quiet gentleman who happened to be the spectator of a street fight suddenly to be forced to use his fists to protect his own head.

The United States of 1914 certainly presented as unwarlike a spectacle as the sun ever shone upon. The problems of politics were economic problems, concentrating in the "quest for social justice," not questions of foreign policy.[1] The president, Woodrow Wilson, was a student and teacher of history, a "scholar in politics," and therefore an anomaly in American political life. He was believed to be strongly a pacifist and had resisted considerable newspaper clamor for a military occupation of Mexico, then in the throes of a revolution which jeopardized local American interests. His secretary of state, William Jennings Bryan, was avowedly a crusader for world peace and a foe of "imperialism." The Democratic party, in power by virtue of a split in the Republican camp, had been, at least since 1860, the party of "no foreign entanglements." Alone among the Great Powers the United States had neither alliances nor morally binding *ententes* with other nations. The permanent diplomatic policy of the nation, based on the principles of Washington, Jefferson and Monroe, was that of nonintervention in European affairs combined with a

[1] H. U. Faulkner, *The Quest for Social Justice* (*A History of American Life*, XI).

watchful guardianship of American countries from European intrusion. If some exceptions to this policy had been made, particularly in the administration of Theodore Roosevelt, no one supposed that they would be repeated while Wilson occupied the White House.

The first reaction of the American public to the European tragedy was one of sheer humanitarian horror. It seemed incredible that the peace of western Europe, unbroken since 1871, should be so abruptly terminated. Of the diplomatic controversies which led to the crisis only the professionally informed—diplomats, journalists, historians—were aware. American newspapers before August, 1914, gave relatively less space to foreign affairs than the newspapers of any European country. They duly recorded, without special emphasis, the assassination of an Austrian archduke, but the baseball season was in full swing and the relative importance of events seems to diminish with distance. For those who took any interest in the doings of diplomacy, President Wilson's difficulties with Mexico seemed far more disturbing than the rise of another war cloud in the Balkans. But the swift interchange of threats among the Great Powers in the last week of July and the outbreak of hostilities in August brought the European crisis to the front page. The *New York Times* in particular distinguished itself by printing in full the official British correspondence, running to more than a hundred documents, as soon as the British government made it public. From the outbreak of the war till the entrance of the United States made necessary a sort of military censorship, the American press continuously laid before its readers the fullest account of current events which could then be obtained anywhere in the world. Eagerly the reading public pored over the newspaper maps, measuring off the gains reported by each side, attempting in vain to reconcile the optimistic German accounts of rapid advance in Belgium and France with French and British statements minimizing every gain. French military terms and the names of Polish towns became more or less pronounceable. The study of geography was resumed by many who had hoped to lay it by forever upon graduation from the grammar school.

But this avalanche of current information left the public hungrily curious for interpretation. America had to go to school to the historians as well as to the geographers, learn the meaning of "triple alliance" and "triple entente," estimate the significance of the Bagdad Railway project, study the national aspirations of conquered peoples from Alsace to Bosnia, discover from past wars why France was so hot a foe of Germany, and Italy so cold a friend to Austria. Even after the United States had been a belligerent for almost a year, the *Dial* commented editorially on the unabated thirst for knowledge about the European situation.[1] "We have an eagerness to learn the political and historical background of the war, as well as to read the more intimate personal descriptions, which would be regarded with astonishment in any of the European capitals. . . . We shall probably end by being better informed about the war than those who live next door to it." If this prophecy was not altogether fulfilled, the reason lay in no insufficiency of the quantity of information but in its extraordinarily streaky quality. The war books varied in merit all the way from such scholarly and impartial surveys as Charles Seymour's *Diplomatic Background of the War* (1916) and Bernadotte Schmitt's *England and Germany* (1916) to shamelessly mendacious propaganda or the highly dubious confessions and "revelations" of self-alleged European spies. There was partic-

[1] *Dial*, LXIV, 305 (March 28, 1918).

ular demand for books that interpreted Germany or her ruler, and Roland G. Usher's *Pan-Germanism*, printed only a few months before the outbreak of the war, came just in time to ride on the crest of the wave. As in England, there was demand for translations and discussions of the strangely assorted trio, Nietzsche, Treitschke and Bernhardi, as alleged fomenters of the German militarist spirit.

From the outbreak of the war till the sinking of the *Lusitania*, American public opinion may fairly be described as neutral, though this neutrality was not that of indifference but rather a balance of contending forces. The official neutrality of the government forced the individual citizen to reach his own conclusions. And the prize of American sympathy was worth winning, even when all Europe took for granted that the United States would not interfere. As the most powerful of the nations at peace, perhaps the only neutral free from foreign intimidation which might limit her freedom of action, the United States could make her influence strongly felt. She could permit a continuous supply of the credits, money, raw materials and manufactured goods needed for the prosecution of the war, to flow towards France and Britain (geographical position and naval blockade limited aid to Germany, Austria-Hungary and Russia) or, conversely, place a ban on the export of all sorts of munitions of war. She could perhaps influence the peace settlement and, in any case, the diplomatic and commercial contests after the war. Moreover, many Europeans felt that the verdict of American opinion would in itself be a moral victory, not that Americans were wiser than other men but because neutrals could approach the issues more impartially than any belligerent and might anticipate the ultimate decision of history.

The strong foundation stone of German propaganda was the fact that, next to the British Isles, Germany had made the largest contribution to the American population. The greater number of German Americans were of the second or third generation, men whose fathers or grandfathers had entered the country between the forties and the nineties of the last century. They were not considered as "foreigners" in the same sense as the later immigrants from Italy, Poland and the Balkans. They had acquired citizenship, become assimilated to the ways of American life, and exercised no little political influence. After the United States entered the war they were loyal and patriotic with but very few exceptions, but in the days of neutrality they could see no reason for restraining their sympathies. The German-American Alliance, the numerous local *bunds, vereins* and vernacular newspapers, frankly sided with the Central Powers. Dr. Bernhard Dernburg, formerly colonial secretary of the German Empire, now arrived and set himself to the task of organizing and mobilizing this inchoate sentiment.[1] A large crop of ephemeral periodicals, such as George S. Viereck's *Fatherland*, and still more ephemeral societies, such as the curiously misnamed American Neutrality League and the American Independence Union, devoted themselves to active propaganda for any measure that might help the Central Powers or embarrass the Entente Allies.

The following extract from a letter by Alexander Konta to Dr. Bernhard Dernburg in reference to the proposed purchase of a New York newspaper in the German interest is typical of the methods employed. The date is of March 31, 1915, and the alien-property

[1] See "Pan-Germanism in the United States: Dr. Dernburg and his Publicity Bureau," *World's Work*, XXX (1915), 135-137; One of the War Propagandists (*pseud.*), "War Propaganda," *Sat. Eve. Post*, CCI (1929), no. 50 and later issues.

custodian declared it to be the earliest record of the scheme to purchase newspapers in English for German propaganda.[1]

Prohibition is seriously occupying the minds of the brewers and distillers of this country. . . . A paper that would not be hostile to the personal liberty of the citizen . . . could count upon the powerful sympathy of the brewers and distillers, who command almost illimitable capital, and what is more, means of giving the paper in question a circulation large enough to attract advertisers. Add to this a discreet appeal to every German society in the country for support by its members and we could easily count upon a national daily circulation of 500,000 copies. This to be sure would be a circulation among Germans and German Americans, whereas what is wanted is native American readers, but if this German circulation is built up discreetly as I suggest, the men in the street will be impressed by numbers. . . . Politically the transaction would have to be handled with the utmost delicacy. No suspicion of the influence behind it should be allowed to reach the public.

But the German Americans were far from being the only element in the country to favor the Central Powers. Many Jews had good cause for hating their step-fatherland of Russia. The Irish Americans had a feud seven centuries old with England. They, too, had a press and an array of nationalist societies, and they were more active in politics than the Germans. Some Americans of purest English descent shared this dislike because of inherited prejudices and schoolbook accounts of the Revolution,[2] the War of 1812 and the subsequent dip-

[1] *N. Y. Sun,* Sept. 20, 1918. The *New York Evening Mail* was purchased to aid the German cause, but missed its effect by being as over-cautious as Viereck's *Fatherland* was overblatant.

[2] Charles Altschul, *The American Revolution in Our School Text-books* (N. Y., 1917), analyzes the treatment of the Revolution in nearly a hundred school histories in use twenty or more years before. The

lomatic controversies, or because of temperamental clashes between self-assured Briton and sensitive American.[1] The most respectable pro-German element consisted of a very small but influential group of university men who had received their schooling in Germany, or had traveled there, and had fallen in love with all the nobler aspects of German civilization.

As active American aid to Germany was out of the question, friends of the Central Powers concentrated their attention on two main objects: to keep the United States out of the conflict, and to prevent the export of munitions of war to the Entente Powers. On both these points, though from widely different motives, the pacifist was perforce in alliance with the pro-German. "Let us place an embargo on the munitions export," said the latter. "We cannot send aid to Germany and it is unneutral, at least in spirit, to aid one combatant alone." "By all means let us do so," rejoined the pacifist, "but not to help or hinder either side; merely to end this infernal profiteering in the weapons of murder." This combined sentiment, flowing from two such different sources, resulted in sharp congressional debates on the embargo proposal, which was brought forward as a threat whenever the Entente encroached too greatly on American interests.

A curious early expression of pacifist sentiment was the crusade of the peace ship *Oscar II* which sailed for Europe at the beginning of December, 1915, "to get the boys out of the trenches by Christmas." Henry Ford, the automobile manufacturer, was the backer of the expedition, having been misled into the belief that the belligerent nations which had rejected the official medi-

attack on the newer textbooks, more favorable to England after the war, is discussed in chap. xi of the present volume.

[1] Owen Wister, *The Ancient Grudge or a Straight Deal* (N. Y., 1920), gives many amusing contemporary examples of such misunderstandings.

ation of the United States would welcome the unofficial good offices of American citizens. The voyage had, as might have been expected, no other effect than to give war-weary Europe a comic interlude in the midst of the great tragedy.[1]

The Entente Allies maintained propaganda every whit as active as the German and, on the whole, with greater skill. Much of the German publicity went to the foreign-language press, which the average American never reads, and much was wasted on specially subsidized periodicals which reached only those who already agreed with their views. English propaganda, and England was the most active of the Entente nations in the matter, was directed straight at the periodicals of highest repute and the men of widest influence. Sir Gilbert Parker has told the story.

> Among other things, we supplied three hundred and sixty newspapers in the smaller states of the United States with an English newspaper which gave a weekly review and comment on the affairs of the war. We established connection with the man in the street through cinema pictures of the army and navy, as well as through interviews, articles, pamphlets, etc. . . . We advised and stimulated many people to write articles; . . . we had reports from important Americans constantly, and established association by personal correspondence with influential and eminent people of every profession in the United States. . . .[2]

Add to this the facts that the American and British publics, whatever their past quarrels, could be reached through the medium of the same language, that the cable and mail routes were controlled by the Entente (though

[1] The story is told in L. P. Lochner, *Henry Ford—America's Don Quixote* (N. Y., 1925).

[2] Sir Gilbert Parker, "The United States and the War," *Harper's Mag.*, CXXXVI (1918), 522.

the Germans were able to make some use of the wireless), and that many traveled Americans possessed French or British sympathies, and the ground was prepared for intervention if the German government should commit acts hostile to American rights and interests.

The greatest personal asset on the side of intervention was ex-President Theodore Roosevelt, the most influential private citizen in the nation. In the first days of the war he had written editorials for the *Outlook* in mild approval of neutrality. But within a few months he had come to view the war as a campaign in the eternal struggle between right and wrong. He complained that the administration was "pussyfooting," that President Wilson conducted himself like a "Byzantine logothete," and that "hyphenated Americans" were converting the country into a "polyglot boarding house." [1] He compared the popular pacifist song "I didn't raise my boy to be a soldier" with "I didn't raise my girl to be a mother," and contended that a nation which shrank from righteous war in defense of the oppressed was already effete. Only a few public men before 1917 stood with Roosevelt, but among them were some of much influence. Robert Bacon, once Roosevelt's secretary of state, sought election to the Senate as an "avowed unneutral." Walter Hines Page, American ambassador to London, while neutral in his public activities was ardently sympathetic with the Entente in his private advices to the president. [2] Henry James, possibly the most famous American novelist of his day, became a British subject as a personal expression of his sentiment about the war.

From a survey of the American press at the beginning

[1] Roosevelt's views were expressed in his *Fear God and Take Your Own Part* (N. Y., 1916).

[2] See B. J. Hendrick, *Life and Letters of Walter Hines Page* (Garden City, 1922-1925), II, 20-25, and *passim*; III, 132 ff.

of hostilities it appeared that, out of a total of 367 editors, 105 admitted favor for the Allies and 20 for the German cause, the other 242 disavowing any preference. The feeling of the communities represented was given as pro-Ally in 189 cases, pro-German in 38, divided in 140. The expression of war-time sentiment was partly sectional. In both cases the Middle West was more favorable towards the German cause than the East, the Far West, or the South.[1] This was particularly true in states with a large German population, such as Wisconsin, or in cities with an important German element, such as Cincinnati and St. Louis. Even among the Americans of English stock, however, interventionist sentiment decreased with distance as one moved west from the Atlantic Coast. Lack of contact with European affairs, preoccupation with local economic issues, and an idealistic pacifism, well typified by William Jennings Bryan of Nebraska, the chief foe of intervention in the cabinet, all predisposed the West to view with distrust the growing war sentiment. Sharp comment by Eastern newspapers on the pacifism of the Mid-West provoked a corresponding sensitiveness, an exchange which brought an amusing sequel when, after the United States entered the war, Western editors could show that recruiting proceeded most rapidly in the "pacifist" states.[2] The shoe was now on the other foot—a great relief to toes too often stepped on.

The economic effects of the war on neutral America were important but diverse. In some ways serious injury was done to foreign trade. European demand for luxury manufactures ceased at once. The cotton trade also was badly hit by the interruption of normal trade with Ger-

[1] *Literary Digest*, XLIX, 939 (Nov. 14, 1914).
[2] "Patriotism, East and West," *Literary Digest*, LIV, 1486 (May 19, 1917).

many, although Great Britain out of deference to American opinion long refrained from placing cotton on the list of absolute contraband. To help out the distressed cotton belt, Americans were asked to make purchases within the home market to balance the temporary loss of foreign export trade. "Buy a bale of cotton" became the watchword of the day. There was much unemployment in the winter of 1914 and many gloomy forecasts that so great a war must mean the shattering of the financial structure of modern civilization the whole world over.

But better times came as war orders arrived from the Entente nations. Even cotton rose to more than the normal price. European demand for wheat and other food products enabled many Western farmers to pay off their mortgages. But the relative importance of agricultural exports diminished. Urgent as was the need in France and England for American pork and flour, the need for steel, copper and explosives took precedence. By 1916 the neutral United States had become the principal foreign munition depot for the Entente. The iron and steel exports of the United States more than doubled from 1914 to 1916 and almost doubled again by 1918. The export of explosives increased from $6,272,197 in 1914 to $467,081,928 in 1916.[1] It has been claimed that the Du Pont powder factories "saved the cause of the Allies in 1915."[2] When the war broke out they were producing twelve million pounds a year; when it ended, more than four hundred million pounds.

Certain American industries were stimulated indirectly by the cessation of German competition in the home market. For many years the United States had been

[1] Isaac Lippincott, *Economic Development of the United States* (N. Y., 1927), 722-723.
[2] W. S. Culbertson, *Commercial Policy in War Time and After* (N. Y., 1919), 55.

content to import the cheap and excellent German dyes;
by March, 1915, the supply was completely cut off by
the blockade. "The world was searched for reserve supplies of coal-tar dyes. Light shades became common in
many lines of goods. Designs were changed, especially in
calicoes and ginghams. Small figures were printed on
white backgrounds. Natural dyes, such as logwood and
fustic, came into more common use," and the American
dye industry, which "can hardly be said to have existed
in 1914," was exporting to foreign countries by 1919.[1]
The finer grades of optical glass, an industry whose
world center was Jena, Germany, were also lacking, and
in some cases astronomers had to wait till the war ended
for their expected telescope lenses. Drugs and chemicals
of various sorts, some of them covered by German patents, were hard to obtain. During the war period (1914-
1919) the value of the annual output of coal-tar chemicals in the United States increased from $13,492,453
to $133,499,742,[2] and the value of drugs from
$176,747,080 to $418,221,150.[3] At the expense of the
consumer the United States had become a self-dependent
nation for nearly every manufactured necessity.

Domestic manufacturers seized the opportunity to
launch a "made-in-America" campaign, supported
partly by the patriotic argument that the good citizen
should patronize his own national industries, partly by
the practical consideration that it was awkward to depend for industrial needs on a foreign production that
might at any time be interrupted by war. They claimed
also that American products were not really inferior to
European; only tradition, prestige and social snobbishness gave a fictitious value to the foreign label. "If

[1] Culbertson, *Commercial Policy*, 37, 43.
[2] "Reports for Selected Industries," *U. S. Fourteenth Census* (1920).
X, 630.
[3] "Reports for Selected Industries," 676.

women could be made to realize that the country which
has produced the best machines," wrote an advocate of
the movement, "can show equal superiority in making
almost everything else, they would be as proud of home
products as are the patriotic women of France." [1]

The war reversed the financial relation of the United
States to Europe. There had long been an excess of exports over imports, but this "favorable balance of trade"
was increased from five to tenfold by war conditions.
Moreover, in times past this had been offset by less
visible but equally important assets of Europe: the payment of freight charges to European shipowners, the
payment of interest and profits to foreign investors in
American enterprises, the remittances of immigrants to
their relatives in the mother country, and the free spending of American tourists abroad. But now the huge dis-
proportion of exports to imports could no longer be met
by such assets. Britain, France and the other purchasers
of American goods had to send gold to the United States
in unprecedented quantities. Even so, they could not pay
for all they needed and were forced to buy on credit or
liquidate the American securities held by their citizens. [2]
These included not only the bonds and stocks of every
important railroad and industrial company, but literally
hundreds of the old underlying subsidiary lines out of
which the great modern systems grew. President
L. F. Loree of the Delaware and Hudson Company estimated that in the eighteen months ending July 31,
1916, there were returned to this country $1,288,773,-
801 of railroad securities, mainly held in Great Britain. [3]

For the closing of the Central Europe market the

[1] "The 'Made in the U. S. A.' Campaign," *Literary Digest*, XLIX,
876-877 (Nov. 7, 1914).
[2] See esp. A. W. Atwood, "Paying off the Mortgage on the United
States," *World's Work*, XXXIII (1917), 243-250, 399-403, 651-655.
[3] Atwood, "Paying off the Mortgage on the United States," 653.

United States obtained partial compensation not alone
from the war orders of western Europe but also in the
opportunity to capture neutral markets which both
belligerent groups were now forced somewhat to neglect.
Prior to the war Britain and Germany had been far
more active than the United States in establishing banks
and branch commercial houses in Latin America, in
studying the language and customs of the people, and
in pushing their manufactures by carefully laid campaigns of salesmanship. Germany and Italy, moreover,
had sent immigrants to temperate South America as
well as to the United States; Paris was in many ways
the cultural capital of all the southern republics, and
Spain and Portugal were brought close to them by ties
of language and historic tradition. A certain fear of the
United States, too close and powerful a neighbor to be
altogether trusted, had induced many Latin Americans
to deal by preference with Europe. But, in spite of the
fact that both export and import trade with Latin
America doubled in value from 1914 to 1917, it cannot
be said that full advantage was taken of the new opportunities. The American salesman was too impatient
as a rule to make allowance for the leisurely cere-
moniousness of the Latin-American merchant, and from
ignorance he was apt to make such tactical blunders as
sending circulars printed in Spanish to Portuguese Brazil.
From 1917 to 1928 the actual increase in the trade with
Latin America was inconsiderable.

In selling munitions to the belligerents and in temporarily replacing them in neutral markets the United
States profited to some extent from the misfortunes of
Europe, a fact which did not add to the popularity of
America abroad. Too often foreign critics forgot the
other side of "war prosperity": the dislocation of prices,
the decreased buying power of people with fixed in-

comes, the fall in the value of bonds and railroad shares, the frequent strikes for higher pay as the trade unions bent themselves to the task of keeping wage levels above the rising cost of living.[1] There can be little doubt that the economic condition of the nation as a whole would have been better in the long run if the World War had never taken place. Prices took their first sharp upward turn in 1916 and continued to rise till the latter part of 1920, but as early as April, 1917, the pinch of distress was beginning to be felt by competent and thrifty salaried folk. "My professional salary of $2000," testified a public employee in New York City, "has been increased only fourteen per cent in fourteen years. . . . We have denied ourselves every luxury and some things regarded as necessary, but there is hardly enough money for doctor, dentist, and oculist. . . . The excessive cost of meat must be paid from the cost of breakfast eggs. The excess cost of potatoes to satisfy the children's hunger must be paid from oranges conducive to health." [2] "I am a successful doctor's wife," wrote a woman in Sapulpa, Oklahoma, "yet when we meet high taxes, rent, fuel, water, lights, groceries, meats, and dry goods for our family of six we find ourselves too near the red unless we cut out milk (at 15 cents a quart), butter (at 55 cents), use meat only once a day," and dispense with eggs at fifty-five cents a dozen. During the entire period from 1916 to 1920 the professional classes, salaried clerks, civic officials, police, and others whose income was fixed by law or custom were worse off relatively, and in some respects absolutely, than at any time since the Civil War.

Labor troubles, as always in a time of rapidly changing prices, were frequent and serious. In the autumn of

---

[1] For price trends in general, see chaps. vi and vii.
[2] *Independent,* XC, 65 (April 7, 1917).

1916 even the dairy farmers struck for better prices from
the distributing companies, shut off a third of New
York's milk supply for several days, and forcibly
dumped the milk cans of nonunion dairymen who per-
sisted in making deliveries. In 1916 the railroad brotherhoods threatened a tie-up of all the principal lines in the
country unless they were granted a basic eight-hour day
with extra pay for overtime work. Congress passed the
Adamson act in September, conceding the principal demands of the railwaymen.[1] President Wilson was much
criticized by his political opponents for yielding to demands which, however just in themselves, were forced
on the government by the threat of a general railroad
strike. The general attitude of the Wilson administration was favorable to labor.[2] The president had favored
legislation exempting trade unions from antitrust laws,
guaranteeing the rights of merchant seamen, and forbidding the interstate transportation of products made
by child labor. He was on friendly terms with the leaders of the American Federation of Labor, and the majority of his appointments, notably the choice of Louis
Brandeis and John H. Clarke to the Supreme Court,
pleased liberals as much as they displeased conservatives.

Though in these early years the American may have
viewed the war too much as a mere interested spectator,
unaware of the danger that his own nation might also
become involved in a conflict that already extended from
Japan to Portugal, at least he was a sympathetic spectator. The case of Belgium, obviously innocent of any
fault except that of lying across a road which the German army wished to take, appealed especially to Ameri-

[1] W. Z. Ripley, "The Railroad Eight-Hour Law," *Am. Rev. of Revs.*,
LIV (1916), 389-393; E. J. Clapp, "The Adamson Law," *Yale Rev.*,
VI (1916-1917), 258-275.

[2] F. A. Ogg, *National Progress* (A. B. Hart, ed., *The American Nation: a History*, N. Y., 1905-1917, XXVII), chap. v.

can sentiment. Herbert Clark Hoover, a mining engineer
of Quaker stock, born in Iowa and educated in California, had been consulting engineer for more than fifty
mining companies scattered about the world in Mexico,
China, Australia, South Africa, India and many parts of
Europe. Setting aside a technical career which had already made him a wealthy man, he undertook the chair-
manship of the Commission for Relief in Belgium. From
that moment forward his life was claimed by public
service, as federal food administrator during the war,
secretary of commerce and president after it.[1] To the
Belgian people America was able to make two great
gifts: the direct present of money and goods, and the
organizing ability that made them available. The United
States contributed over thirty-four million dollars to
Belgian relief, the British Empire over sixteen million
dollars, and other countries over one million in voluntary charity, besides the still greater amount obtained
from formal loans and subsidies from the American,
French and British treasuries.[2]

The magnitude of the administrative task required
what was almost the construction of a special government. "Food had to be secured in a limited and disor-
ganized market, vessels had to be chartered to proceed
across the mine-strewn North Sea through the naval
blockade, and, finally, the relief supplies had to be transshipped in barges and towed through 133 miles of ob-
structed waterways, passing the German lines, to Brussels. Naval and military authorities, bound to be unsympathetic in the circumstances, foretold certain failure

[1] His associate on the commission, Edward Eyre Hunt, prophesied in
1916: "I am not a prophet or the son of a prophet, but I know that
the public service of Herbert C. Hoover has just begun. . . . as soon as
the war is over and Belgium is free, his own country will have need of
him." *War Bread* (N. Y., 1916), 197-198.
[2] G. I. Gay, *Statistical Review of Relief Operations* (Stanford Univ.,
1925), 64-69.

of the unprecedented undertaking." [1] Soon the commission was feeding over nine million people. Established as a neutral organization, but with recognized diplomatic rights and obligations and flying its own flag, the unusual status of the commission was characterized by a famous Allied diplomat as a "piratical state organized for benevolence." Belgian relief was the largest task of American charity until the end of the war opened up opportunities for aid in Poland, Russia, Austria, Hungary, Serbia, Armenia and Greece. During the actual fighting it was not easy for substantial aid to reach these more distant countries, yet something was done to fight the typhus epidemic in the Balkans. Fashionable society organized fairs and "benefits" for all sorts of special charities: Christmas toys for European children, aid for blind and crippled soldiers, ambulances for Italy, succor for missionary schools in Turkey.

As the most important neutral nation the United States had thrust upon her the duty of championing the principle of the "freedom of the seas," implying the right of neutrals to trade with oversea customers as freely in time of war as in time of peace, except that contraband goods intended directly for belligerent use might be captured and that merchant ships might be barred from a port held in a close and effective blockade. But neither the Entente Allies nor the Central Powers could enforce a blockade in the strictest legal sense. Germany could trade overseas across the Baltic and overland with Switzerland, Denmark and the Netherlands in spite of every effort of British, French and Russian patrols. German submarine warfare, on the other hand, established no blockade whatever, as even in the worst of times the great majority of ships reached British ports in safety.

[1] Gay, *Statistical Review*, 5.

Contraband proved an even more slippery concept than blockade. The neutrals tried to confine the word to munitions in the most limited sense: explosives, arms, cavalry horses, and the like; the belligerents tried to extend it to every class of goods useful to a nation in war time: oil, cotton, copper, fats, meat, grain, etc. The fact that Germany placed the entire food supply of the nation under public regulation gave the Entente Allies a pretext to put foodstuffs on their contraband lists since it was no longer easy to distinguish civilian from military supplies. Still another difficulty arose when neutral states neighbor to Germany resold or transshipped goods bought from abroad. This placed the Entente naval authorities in the embarrassing dilemma of high-handedly "rationing" neutral trade or else permitting Germany to import all she needed by the simple process of bringing it into the country through Dutch or Danish ports.

The American government had frequent occasion to protest at the way in which the Entente Powers, and more especially the British navy, invaded neutral rights by arbitrary extension of contraband lists, the interruption of mails, the blacklisting of neutral firms trading with the enemy, the misuse of neutral flags to protect belligerent merchant ships, and the curtailment of shipments to European neutrals. But the German declaration of a war zone around the British Isles in which ships might be sunk without further warning constituted a far graver problem. On February 10, 1915, President Wilson warned the German authorities that they would be held to "strict accountability" for acts endangering the lives of American citizens. Attacks on the American vessels *Cushing* and *Gulflight* and the killing of an American citizen on the British liner *Falaba* challenged the American position, but they were speedily forgotten in

the general horror aroused over the sinking of the
Lusitania.

On May 7, 1915, the British passenger liner *Lusitania,* carrying munitions of war but not (as was alleged
at the time) armed for combat, was torpedoed off the
Irish coast. Nearly twelve hundred of the passengers and
crew were drowned, among them one hundred and fourteen American citizens. The fact that the German embassy had officially warned intending passengers by
newspaper advertisement that they were in peril, and
that a medal was struck commemorating the event,[1]
made the act seem a particularly deliberate affront. For
the first time in the course of the war the American
public began to consider armed intervention as a possibility.[2] Historians have often stated that in the anger
and agony of the first news President Wilson, had he
so desired, could have obtained a declaration of war from
Congress.[3] But when the president contented himself
with a solemn reiteration of his former warning the
greater part of the press seemed relieved. The typical
view of the Mississippi Valley states was expressed by the
St. Louis Globe-Democrat, which, on May 11, 1915,
denounced the submarine outrage but added, "The
United States is happily outside that maelstrom of murder. We will not be drawn into it if we can, with honor,
avoid it." But the president's phrase, "There is such a
thing as a man being too proud to fight," spoken at a
meeting of newly naturalized American citizens, was
widely misinterpreted as an unconditional peace-at-any-
price utterance which cost him much popularity.

[1] J. S. Bassett, *Our War with Germany* (N. Y., 1919), 43-45.
[2] "We shall be at war with Germany within a month," declared Colonel
E. M. House, the president's confidential adviser, when he heard the news
in London. Hendrick, *Life and Letters of Walter Hines Page,* II, 2.
[3] See, for example, L. B. Shippee, *Recent American History* (N. Y.,
1924), 410.

From that time onward there was a war party in the United States, small at first but growing with each unlawful sinking, till the destruction of the *Sussex* in March, 1916, brought an ultimatum from Washington and a promise from Berlin that henceforward merchant ships would not be sunk without warning or attempt to save the lives of passengers, unless they offered flight or resistance.[1] Germany reserved the right, however, to withdraw this pledge if necessity arose, and thus the war cloud still hung over the United States. An abiding bitterness against Germany remained after the *Lusitania* sinking and editors noticed that a newspaper sold better in the streets if the day's news headlined a victory of the Entente than if it were so worded as to seem a German success.[2] Neither the people nor the government were as yet convinced of the need of war, but it is significant that early in 1916 Congress tabled resolutions, strongly supported by pacifists and pro-Germans alike, warning American citizens not to take passage on armed merchantmen, and that in the same year Congress undertook the task of building a greater army.

Nineteen hundred and sixteen will probably be remembered in American annals as the "preparedness" year. The political atmosphere of the time was curiously unreal. Though most persons realized that the United States stood on the verge of war, care was taken not to state the danger in so many words. One talked, rather, of "preparedness" at large or discussed the abstract beauties of pacifism. Serial magazine stories and moving pictures —such as "The Fall of a Nation"—narrated imaginary invasions of the United States, but rarely called the invaders Germans, even when they appeared on the film in

[1] Woodrow Wilson, *The New Democracy* (R. S. Baker and W. E. Dodd, eds., N. Y., 1926), II, 147-152, 422-424.

[2] "The Partiality of the Press," *Independent*, LXXXIV, 44-45 (Oct. 11, 1915).

LXXV.......No. 25,010.

New York Tribune

First to Last—the Truth; News : Editorials : Advertisements

SATURDAY, MAY 8, 1915.

PRICE ONE CENT

WEATHER:

FAIR TO-NIGHT AND TO-MORROW

1,300 Die as Lusitania Goes to Bottom; 400 Americans on Board Torpedoed Ship; Washington Stirred as When Maine Sank

CAPITAL AROUSED,
SITUATION GRAVEST
YET FACED IN WAR

Washington Determined That Germany
Shall Not Be Allowed to Shirk
Responsibility for Deaths.

GREATLY FEARS LOSS OF AMERICANS

President Shows Nervousness as Bulletins of Disaster Come In—Strongest Protest Yet Made
Planned Even if No U.S. Citizens Were Lost

THE LUSITANIA, SUNK BY GERMAN TORPEDO, WITH HEAVY LOSS OF LIFE.

Dying and Injured Brought In with Other
Survivors to Queenstown—Two Torpedoes Fired, Says Steward.

FEW FIRST CLASS PASSENGERS SAVED

Attack Made About Eight Miles from Irish Coast in
Broad Daylight and in Fine Weather—Survivor Tells of Bravery of Cunard Officers.

GERMANS TOAST
'VICTORY' AMID

U. S. OWES IT TO SELF-RESPECT TO ACT,
SAYS ROOSEVELT; 'PIRACY ON VAST SCALE'

MANY NOTED
NEW YORKERS

Germany's Challenge

spiked helmets. If the average champion of preparedness were asked why the country must arm, he usually replied with such generalities as, "We must be strong enough to maintain American rights," or "Universal military training is an excellent school for democratic citizenship." If you pressed him further, he would say something about Mexican raids along the southwestern border—no votes could be lost by denouncing Mexicans. The Republican and Democratic parties during the campaign of that year strangely resembled two little children quarreling in a cage containing a sleeping tiger, but scolding in an undertone so as not to wake the sleeper.

Certainly if danger there were, whether or not it could wisely be mentioned, the United States was wise to overhaul the armory. At the outbreak of the World War the United States had the smallest army among important nations, and the national guard, which supplemented it, varied in equipment and discipline with the standards of each state. The great majority of Americans were without any military experience whatever and not even accustomed, as past American generations had been, to riding, shooting and camping in the open. The navy was certainly inferior in strength to the British, probably to the German, and possibly to the French. In October, 1915, Congress adopted a three-year building program to bring the navy up to a strength at least comparable to that of any other nation at a cost of half a billion dollars, and the national defense act of the following June increased the size of the regular army and of the national guard and provided for an officers' reserve corps to be trained in summer camps of the Plattsburg type.[1]

The most popular and interesting aspect of the preparedness movement was the opening of summer training camps for civilians. General Leonard Wood did

[1] *U. S. Statutes at Large*, XXXIX, pt. i, 166-217.

much to initiate the plan by organizing such a camp at Plattsburg, in northern New York, in 1915.[1] Colleges and universities also laid greater stress than formerly on their courses in military science. Drill was less perfunctory to the student who now foresaw a chance of becoming an officer in actual war. From the colleges and from the summer camps came many of the officers of the volunteer and drafted levies raised during the war. Under modern conditions it takes several months' intensive training to turn a civilian into a soldier and an even longer time to fit him to be an officer. Obviously the training camps could but make a beginning, but at least they selected from the mass of men of military age those who were interested in the army and who had the physique and the qualities of leadership which fitted them for the profession. The partial mobilization of the army and the national guard for service on the Mexican border greatly increased interest in military affairs.[2] If there were no big war with Germany there might at least be a little one with Mexico.

The preparedness propaganda of such organizations as the National Security League, the American Defense Society, the Navy League and the American Rights Committee was counterbalanced by that of pacifist organizations, such as the American League to Limit Armaments, the American Union against Militarism, the Women's Peace Party, the various peace societies, old and new, and the Socialist party, committed to nonintervention in the war. A somewhat different angle of approach from either was represented by the League to Enforce Peace, founded in Philadelphia on June 17, 1915, by a committee of more than a hundred members,

[1] See Leonard Wood, "Plattsburg and Citizenship," *Century*, XCIV (1917), 49-54.
[2] Ogg, *National Progress*, 297-300.

including ex-President William Howard Taft, A. Lawrence Lowell, president of Harvard University, and Theodore Marburg, former ambassador to Belgium. As far back as September, 1914, Hamilton Holt, editor of the New York *Independent*, had advocated a league of peace to prevent war, a plan which was indorsed, in principle at any rate, by ex-President Roosevelt.[1] The idea of the League to Enforce Peace was that peace could not be obtained by mere moral crusades against war and armament, but must come as the result of international confederation to maintain peace and overawe the aggressor.[2] Woodrow Wilson's later construction of the League of Nations already existed here in blueprint.

A further cause of irritation against Germany, only second in importance to submarine warfare, was the discovery of various plots and conspiracies to hamper, by illegal means, the manufacture and export of munitions of war in the United States. Failing to accomplish their purpose of obtaining an embargo on munitions from Congress, some German agents and sympathizers fell back on more covert methods.[3] Companies were organized to purchase the machinery and supplies essential to the production of munitions, simply to keep them from the Allies; agents induced the Bosch Magneto Company to contract with the Entente for fuses and then finally to find some way of avoiding delivery. The Hamburg-American shipping line provided false manifests for vessels carrying supplies to wandering German cruisers. The Austrian ambassador, Dr. Constantin Dumba, sent an American emissary to carry dispatches to Austria, among

[1] *Independent*, LXXIX, 427 (Sept. 28, 1914); LXXXI, 13-17 (Jan. 4, 1915).

[2] Anon., "Historical Light on the League to Enforce Peace," World Peace Found., *Pamphlet Ser.*, VI, no. 6.

[3] Charles Seymour, *Woodrow Wilson and the World War* (Allen Johnson, ed., *The Chronicles of America Series*, New Haven, 1918-1921, XLVIII), chap. iv.

them plans to foment strikes in munition factories here. Dumba and two German attachés, Boy-Ed and Von Papen, were given their dismissal for activities hostile to the country in which they were guests. Most sinister of all, and most significant in its consequences (for it worked a revolution in the sentiment of the generally pacifist Southwest), was the attempt made by the German foreign secretary, Alfred Zimmermann, in the last days of American neutrality, to secure Mexico's support in case of war with the United States by offering her the opportunity of regaining New Mexico, Arizona and Texas.

Very few echoes of the war appeared in the political campaign of 1916. The Democrats contented themselves with such vote-catching slogans as, "He kept us out of war," or "War in the East; peace in the West; thank God for Wilson!" while the Republicans were divided between those, such as Theodore Roosevelt, who wished Wilson had taken a strong stand against Germany, and those, such as Senator Robert M. La Follette of Wisconsin, who feared lest he lead the nation into war. But when Jeremiah O'Leary, head of the so-called American Truth Society, denounced Wilson as too friendly to England, the president made the stinging retort: "I would feel deeply mortified to have you or anybody like you vote for me. Since you have access to many disloyal Americans and I have not, I will ask you to convey this message to them." [1] Charles Evans Hughes, the Republican nominee, carried his caution from the Supreme Court bench into the campaign and, apparently over-careful to lose no votes, won too few. The former Progressives divided, some supporting Wilson but the majority following their leader Roosevelt back into the Republican fold.

[1] *American Year Book for 1916,* 41.

The United States had known several somnolent elections, but that of 1916 is rather to be described as somnambulistic. Under other circumstances the closeness of the contest would have made it an interesting campaign, but the real mind of the nation was elsewhere. Who cared to read conventional speeches when he might read daily of the greatest battles ever fought and knew there was constant danger that they might involve America? The one touch of excitement in the campaign came in the week following election when the result hung in doubt until the final returns were heard from California. The chief significance of the election (since both parties failed to face the issues of the hour) was in the new sectional alignment. For the first time in American history the Farther West determined the outcome. The South, as was expected, remained Democratic, the East and Middle West (with the exception of New Hampshire and Ohio) went Republican, but the states beyond the Missouri, a majority of them normally Republican, rallied to Wilson almost as a unit.[1] It was an impressive demonstration of the fact that the Great West could hold the balance of power in American politics.

Fresh from his victory, President Wilson made a dramatic play for world peace. He offered the belligerents an opportunity to state the terms on which war might be concluded. The Entente outlined their terms; the Central Powers refused to state theirs but offered to enter a conference.[2] Before the Senate on January 22, 1917, the president reviewed the negotiations and urged a "peace without victory" based on the equal rights of all nations, great and small, and secured by a league of nations.[3]

[1] *American Year Book for 1916*, 42-47, 170.
[2] *American Year Book for 1916*, 97-99.
[3] Wilson, *New Democracy*, II, 407-414.

But his efforts failed either to end the war or to avert American participation in it. At the end of January the Central Powers declared a war zone around enemy coasts in which all ships, neutral or belligerent, might be sunk. The one exception permitted, which Americans took as an additional insult, was the right to send along a narrow sea lane one passenger ship a week, decorated with "zebra stripes," as the press termed them, of alternate red and white. The United States promptly severed diplomatic relations with Germany, but awaited a hostile act before declaring war. As a temporary measure the president advocated the defensive arming of American merchant ships. A pacifist minority in the Senate talked the resolution to death, but the president accomplished the same end by executive action.

Public opinion began to crystallize into war sentiment. Germany's repudiation of her former pledge to spare unarmed merchant ships, the timely exposure of various plots within the country and of Zimmermann's bid to Mexico to help herself to three American states, the German deportation of Belgian civilians, the revolution in Russia (the American press, with virtual unanimity, had been hostile to the old régime in that country), and the continued sinking of American ships in the war zone enabled the president, when the new Congress assembled, to ask for a declaration of war. Many papers which had formerly opposed intervention now thought that armed neutrality was "nothing . . . but a buckling on of a sword for a siesta in a rocking chair," [1] and applauded the formal declaration of war.

Yet there were still anti-interventionists. On the decisive vote in Congress fifty members of the House and six of the Senate held out against the action. Moreover, down to the actual declaration, a coalition of pacifist so-

[1] *St. Louis Globe-Democrat*, Feb. 27, 1917.

cieties, the Emergency Peace Federation, bombarded Congress with appeals to keep America out of Europe's quarrel. Wilson's former secretary of state, Bryan, agitated against intervention, though he had labored earnestly for Wilson's reëlection the previous year. The Socialist party, meeting in convention at St. Louis, declared it a capitalistic war and promised opposition to its prosecution,[1] a step which led to the eventual arrest of many Socialist leaders, among them Eugene V. Debs, frequently the party candidate for president, on the charge of obstructing recruiting by speaking against the war. A minority of Socialist intellectuals, however, including J. G. Phelps Stokes, Charles Edward Russell, William English Walling, W. J. Ghent and John Spargo, the men who had done most to build up American Socialism, broke with their party in the belief that the war was one of democracy against autocracy—a loss of leadership which the party could ill afford.[2]

With the actual beginning of hostilities most of the opposition ceased. The question of American participation had not been at all a party issue—it was no more a Democratic than a Republican war. The sectional alignment, such as it was, ended on April 6, 1917, and from then onward the West strove to outdo the East in war fervor. Nor was there any division of classes on the question. Pacifism was a matter of individual conviction, pro-Germanism, usually, of family inheritance, and neither proved to be of much significance. There were no draft riots such as had figured in Civil War times. Particularly commendable was the conduct of the German Americans. Though their sympathies had been vociferously for the German cause from 1914 to 1917, few hesitated when the choice became

[1] *American Labor Year Book for 1917-1918*, 373-379.
[2] See later, chap. iii.

inevitable between the land of their fathers and the land of their children. The melting pot had proved to be no idle metaphor. The many nationalities in the United States recognized themselves as a single nation.

CHAPTER II

AMERICA IN WAR TIME

WAR was a simple matter in the days when good Sir Brian could unhook his armor from the wall, mount his charger and be off in fifty minutes to answer the summons of his liege lord. Even in the eighteenth century, when war had already become a science for specialists, the army represented the nation only as a football team represents its college. The civilian could supply funds, pray for victory, cheer from the side lines, but did not take an active part in the game. The coming of the "nation in arms" in the days of Carnot, Napoleon and Scharnhorst meant hardly more—merely that the civilian might be, as an individual, brought into the ranks in case of need. Only with the twentieth century did mine and factory, farm and home, school and laboratory, become so many cogs in a single war machine. In the World War an army was not an army without transports, airplanes, motors, tanks, field telephones, intrenching tools, barbed-wire fencing, gas masks, field glasses and a thousand other accessories whose lack might give the enemy a slight but fatal margin of superiority.

To produce all that was necessary—from such major necessities as coal, oil, wheat, beef, rubber and steel down to such small details as cherry pits for gas masks and paint for camouflaged merchant ships—thousands of workingmen had to be taken from their usual peace-time tasks to the munition plants; hundreds of thousands of farmers had to alter their crop routine; and millions of men,

women and children in every walk of life had to modify
their habits of purchase and consumption. Even the
rarest, most unmilitary talents might find use in modern
war. Many expert dentists were called into service to
perform operations on jawbones broken by shrapnel.
Several artists devoted themselves to designing liberty-
loan posters. The linguist could work for the censor
and examine letters from Persia or Finland. Some college professors developed a latent talent for deciphering
the codes of enemy agents. Literary folk who sympa-
thized in any degree with the national effort could find
endless opportunities for propaganda, one of the major
weapons of modern warfare. Actresses and other en-
tertainers were in demand to keep up the morale of soldiers in cantonments or at the front. Perhaps one reason why the World War brought a relapse toward bar-
barism in the treatment of noncombatants was that,
under the conditions of the time, very few residents in
a belligerent country were really noncombatant.

To mobilize a nation instead of merely an army was
a gigantic task in any case, and in the United States one
that presented some special difficulties. Two objects had
to be kept in view, not wholly consistent with each
other: the establishment of a separate American army
and full support to the Entente Allies while it was being
organized.[1] If France, Britain and Italy had not been
largely dependent on the continuance and increase of
American commercial and financial aid, the task of 1917
would have been much simpler, the exportation of munitions could have been discontinued until the American expeditionary force was equipped, all war loans
spent on this equipment, all American shipping reserved
for troop transportation. But to have followed this

[1] T. G. Frothingham, *The American Reinforcement in the World War*
(Garden City, 1927), chap. ii.

policy, and thus have isolated western Europe from its
main external base of supplies, would have presented
a victory to Germany. On the other hand, the United
States did not consider it sufficient to float loans, build
ships, raise crops, make munitions, and then hand them
all over to the Entente Allies. The military collapse of
Russia enabled Germany to regain a slight superiority in
man power on the Western front, and special French
and British military missions urged that men were as
necessary as munitions. It is doubtful if in any case
public opinion would have sanctioned a mere war by
proxy as month after month passed with no sign of collapse from Germany.

Another difficulty peculiar to the United States was
the immense distance of the war zone from the base.
It was thought a signal feat for Great Britain to have
kept in being an army across the narrow English Channel; the United States had to send one across the Atlantic. For each soldier landed in France some fifty
pounds of supplies and equipment must be landed also
each day. The food supply alone rose to nine million
pounds a day at the end of the war.[1] The French ports
had to be enlarged and improved to make possible the
accommodation of a new army. Transportation on both
sides of the ocean was a problem second in magnitude
only to the long sea trip. The entire railway system of
the United States had to be reorganized under national
control to collect at the Atlantic ports millions of tons
of essential supplies. In France the sector of the front
held by the Americans had to be kept in touch with the
ports by American equipment on French roads and
railroads.[2] Nor was France the most distant theater of

[1] Benedict Crowell and R. F. Wilson, *The Armies of Industry* (same
authors, *How America Went to War*, New Haven, 1921, IV-V), II, 588.
[2] Frothingham, *The American Reinforcement*, chaps. xv, xxi.

American action, though certainly the largest. At one time an American force had to guard tracks in Siberia from hostile Russian bands.

A third difficulty lay in the national tradition of the American people. They were, for the most part, the descendants of Europeans who in one way or another did not fit into the ordered social life of the old continent—pioneers, adventurers, rebels, refugees, "come-outers" of all sorts.[1] Like all sons of frontiersmen they hated discipline and had little of the Teutonic willingness to obey an order simply because it was an order. War was as hateful to them because it meant loss of liberty as because it meant loss of life. Champ Clark, speaker of the House of Representatives, voiced an inveterate prejudice when he opposed compulsory military service on the ground that his mind had always classed together the conscript and the convict.[2]

Still more hateful were the inevitable interferences with civilian life in war time: food control, fuel control, regulation of private business, censorship of the news. An English officer once asserted the paradox that his people were "warlike but not military"; that is to say, they took more kindly to fighting than to drill. The same remark might have been made of the American "doughboy." We have the best of testimony, enemy testimony, that he fought as well as any European soldier; but we have also his own testimony as to how he hated his domineering sergeant, how he felt humiliated at having to salute any strange officer he might encounter in the street, how he longed to break the regulations and red tape, and how glad he was to doff the uniform and get back into civilian clothes, a symbol of

---

[1] A. M. Schlesinger, *New Viewpoints in American History* (N. Y., 1922), 1-22, 109-112.
[2] *Congressional Record*, LV, pt. ii, 1120 (April 25, 1917).

his reconquered right to "do as he darned pleased." The task of turning an industrial system organized for peace into a nation-wide munition plant was no greater than that of turning a nation of individualists into a drilled and disciplined war machine.

Yet the United States decided for compulsory service almost as quickly as for war, in marked contrast to England's reliance on volunteering until half her war had been fought. The probable reason for this difference, since prejudice against conscription was much the same in both countries, was that at the time when the United States entered the struggle it was possible to observe and benefit by the English experience with the voluntary system. It did not fail to enlist recruits in adequate numbers, but it took the wrong men—those who perhaps were more needed as expert mechanicians in the munition factories—or it took the right men at the wrong time. The real advantage of compulsory service was orderliness, the possibility of raising just the numbers who could be trained and equipped at the time and with the least disturbance to the production of war necessities.[1]

On June 5, 1917, 9,586,508 young men between twenty-one and thirty-one registered, thus placing themselves at the disposal of the army. Many were granted complete or partial exemption on the ground of physical unfitness, the support of dependent families, or their special qualifications for necessary industries. The rest were placed in a first class of enrolled men and the order of their muster into service determined by lot. No one was permitted to purchase exemption or hire a substitute; in that respect, at least, democracy had made a great advance since the Civil War. The banker's son and the

[1] E. H. Crowder, *The Spirit of Selective Service* (N. Y., 1920), is a useful study of the operation of the draft.

laborer's son stood an equal chance of being drafted into the service; indeed, if the laborer's son were needed in the shipyards and the banker's son had spent his time in play, it was the latter who went to the trenches. Each district had its quota to fill, and a single drawing of lots in Washington determined the order in which men would be summoned to the colors in each case. Regular army, national guard and the new army of drafted men were placed under uniform discipline as a consolidated national force. The offer of ex-President Roosevelt to lead a special expeditionary force of volunteers was rejected by the president, on advice from military experts, because it was feared that such an expedition would withdraw thousands of men of exceptional ability, zeal and experience from the training camps where they were needed to officer the inexperienced civilians "blown in by the draft." [1]

Life in the training camps came as a revolutionary experience to many. Sons of aliens in the big cities who had barely learned the English language, "poor whites" from isolated mountain hamlets in the South, Negro laborers from Louisiana swamp lands, boys from lonely Dakota wheat farms, all the untraveled classes of the country, were uprooted from their homes. To go to war was an adventure for everyone, but even to go to the nearest training camp was an adventure for these. Their trip to camp was often their first railroad journey, their port of embarkation their first experience in a strange city, their voyage to France their first sight of salt water.[2] Drill and discipline seemed harshly restric-

[1] Charles Seymour, *Woodrow Wilson and the World War* (Allen Johnson, ed., *The Chronicles of America Series*, New Haven, 1918-1921, XLVIII), 122-123.

[2] The story is told of a Negro from a frequently flooded district on the lower Mississippi who, peering out of a porthole on the broad Atlantic, ejaculated, "De levee is done bust fo' shuah dis time!"

tive to young Americans accustomed to be their own masters and homesickness was prevalent. But the brief hours of freedom granted to those who obtained leave to visit the neighboring towns were much enjoyed, in spite of watchful military police and officers who exacted salutes at every encounter. Hospitable civilians who did not know how else to show their interest in the tender-foot soldiery lavishly entertained them in churches, clubs and private homes. In the camp itself opportunities for social recreation were provided by civilian welfare agencies, and every cantonment had one or more newspapers of its own.[1]

Very soon the recruits adapted themselves to their new social environment. Military discipline and cantonment life, working in coöperation, tended to standardize the raw material even more effectively than a boarding school. Myriad types of drafted men tended to merge, as in a composite photograph, into a single generalized type of soldier. "You're in the army now," the older recruits told the younger at every opportunity. A certain *esprit de corps* grew up among the drafted men almost as soon as among the volunteers. At first the latter tended to look down on the former with a certain condescension as near-slackers who had to be dragged into the great game; but before long the drafted men were answering the taunt of "slacker" by the counter-stroke of "draft dodger!" The same soldier slang was repeated in the accent of forty-eight states. They all ate the same "goldfish" (tinned salmon), wore the same "tin helmets," and perhaps wagered their pay on crap games, more picturesquely styled "African golf" or "the galloping dominoes." Whether we approve and call it socialization, or disapprove

[1] A. M. Schlesinger, "The Khaki Journalists, 1917-1919," *Miss. Valley Hist. Rev.*, VI, 350-359.

and term it standardization, unquestionably this dip into cantonment life did much to make the oncoming generation more like-minded. Back in civil life once more, no longer the American Expeditionary Force, but the American Legion, they had a common background of experience that tended to modify sectional or provincial differences.

The training camps were mushroom cities. Instead of merely erecting tent colonies it was decided to build large, well-ventilated wooden barracks equipped so far as possible with water supply, electric light, sewerage systems and other "public utilities." Sixteen soldier-cities were built for the national army (the drafted men), and sixteen others for the national guard (volunteer militia). The national-guard encampments were all in the South and relied more largely on the use of tents. The cost of the cantonment cities averaged eight million dollars each for the national army, and almost a fourth as much for the national guard.[1] Construction was rushed forward with remarkable speed, for until adequate quarters were ready training could not begin. Even as things were, soldiers sometimes came to camp while their quarters were still unfinished and had themselves to take a share in the task of making them habitable. Many criticized the new barracks as needlessly elaborate and presenting too great a contrast to the hardships of the trenches, but housing experts answered that the government was well advised in sparing no pains to keep the camps clean, dry and sanitary because they were made to house civilians from superheated city flats, untempered to campaigning in wintry weather.[2] Within a few months cantonments had been built to house one

[1] Frothingham, *The American Reinforcement*, 118.
[2] John Ihlder, "Our New Cities," *Survey*, XXXIX, 88-93 (Oct. 27, 1917).

million eight hundred thousand men, equivalent to the population of Philadelphia.[1]

Physical and mental tests of the soldiers told much of the national standards in time of peace, for the drafted men represented a very fair cross section of the whole population. A new registration in the fall of 1918 comprised the age limits from eighteen to forty-five; all together about twenty-six million men were registered or entered the service before registration. In all, about three million five hundred thousand men were brought into the army, two million crossed the Atlantic, and over one and a third million took part in battle.[2] It was disconcerting to learn that about one young American in every four was practically illiterate, and about one in three physically unfit. The proportion of unfitness was still higher for the manufacturing districts and for the middle years of life.[3] New England, New York and the industrial Northeast generally had many of the unfit, and the Far West also made a poor record, presumably because the health resorts of the Rockies had attracted many men threatened with tuberculosis. But in a belt of prairies and great plains, extending continuously from North Dakota to Texas, over seventy per cent of those examined were found fit, and the South and agricultural Middle West generally made a good showing. Once more it had been demonstrated, as among British volunteers in the Boer War, that urban conditions unfit many for a soldier's life. It should be remembered, however, that a man may enjoy excellent health and be capable of steady hard work for ten hours a day in fac-

[1] Frothingham, *The American Reinforcement*, 119.
[2] L. P. Ayres, *The War with Germany* (Wash., 1919), 22, 101.
[3] "The evidence available indicates fifty to sixty per cent of the men between 31 and 46 years of age could not have passed for general military service if the physical requirements had remained unchanged." J. H. Beard, "Physical Rejection for Military Service," *Scientific Mo.*, IX (1919), 5.

tory or office and yet not pass an army test because of some minor defect such as fallen arches, bad teeth or short sight.

Mental inspection was more of a novelty in army routine than physical inspection. For several years careful experimentation had been carried on by psychologists to devise tests of alertness, memory, logical decision, and other measurable mental traits, and to some extent these methods had found application in the personnel work of large factories. But never before had they been employed to sift the wheat from the chaff in a great army. Their first use was to make a rough division between those fit for soldiers' work and the minority too dull to be of use in modern war, even in the ranks. But it was equally important to sort out superior degrees of ability among the drafted men so that they might be tried out for special service or fill vacancies among the noncommissioned officers. An "alpha" test was devised for those who could easily read and were accustomed to verbal symbols; a "beta" test for those with little education. Of course, a recruit sometimes had high intelligence and yet was ill adapted to responsible work in the army because he lacked authority, decisiveness or tact in handling other men. But this happened far less frequently than one might suppose. At Camp Meade a group of soldiers were graded into five classes according to the intelligence tests, and then separately graded by their officers on grounds of soldierly qualities such as reliability, discipline and initiative. In nearly half the cases (49.5 per cent), the men examined fell into the same class on both tests and in most of the other cases the difference was of only one grade.[1] The practical success of the army tests advertised them widely

[1] D. W. La Rue, "The Rationale of Testing Intelligence, with Special Reference to Testing in the Army," *Scientific Mo.*, VII (1918), 411.

and led to the increased use of such psychological siftings in both academic and commercial life.[1]

The training of the men was as carefully divided into stages as in any school or college. On the average, the soldier had six months of drill in the fundamentals of military life while in cantonments. Here he learned obedience—the first and hardest lesson—drill and care of equipment, and received the physical training necessary to fit him for active campaigning. He was also given special instruction in the peculiarities of trench warfare, often under the direction of experienced French or British officers who could speak directly from experience. Then he went overseas for two months more of intensive specialized instruction; then for a month into a "quiet" section of the battle front, which meant merely that he would probably not take part in a general offensive; after that, into an "active" sector and continuous battle. Though this program could not always be followed, every possible effort was made to preserve the degrees of experience, for at best eight or nine months were a short time to transform a civilian recruit into a veteran warrior.

The training of officers presented a still more difficult problem. The regular army and the national guard together had about nine thousand at the opening of the war. Capable noncommissioned officers could, of course, be raised to higher rank; and civilians who had taken military drill in school or college, or who were wanted merely as medical or administrative officials, could quickly be made useful. But the greater number, some two thirds of the two hundred thousand commissioned officers, were graduates of the training camps. The Plattsburg idea, evolved during the years of anxious neutrality, solved the most difficult personnel problem

[1] See chapter xiv.

of the army.[1] No doubt the average training-camp graduate, usually a business or professional man in civil life,
had a very superficial grounding in military science as
compared with the West Pointer. But as a rule he proved
to be an apt pupil, adaptable, energetic, and capable as
an executive. When he failed, it was less commonly from
lack of skill in his unfamiliar trade than from lack of
tact in dealing with the men whom he commanded.

The story of the campaigns of 1917 and 1918 does
not belong to this book, which is concerned with the
effect of the war on America rather than with the effect
of America on the war. But before returning to the
civilian organization behind the lines it would be appropriate to speak briefly of the experience which two
million men took back with them from Europe. The
soldier of the American Expeditionary Force faced perils
much greater than fall to the lot of the civilian, and
yet, just because of the inevitable hardships and dangers
of his task, he had to be cared for in a most paternal
fashion. Early hours are recommended to the civilian by
his doctor; the soldier was summoned to rise by bugle.
He shaved, cleaned his teeth, brushed his uniform under
inspection, and if his clothes became filthy in the trenches
he must at his first opportunity visit a "delousing" station to kill the "cooties" with live steam. If he wore out
one suit of clothes he must requisition another. He had
no choice as to his diet, though until supplies ran low
he had the privilege of deciding how many times he
would fill his plate. When travel was necessary he went
in a freight car guaranteed to hold "forty men or eight
horses" and paid no fare. If he had dependents, the government provided him with insurance. If he wanted to

[1] William Menkel, "Making Officers for Our New Army," *Am. Rev.
of Revs.*, LVI (1917), 58-62. For the Students' Army Training Corps
in the colleges and universities, see P. R. Kolbe, *The Colleges in War
Time and After* (N. Y., 1919), 69-81.

spend his leisure time in study, books and classes were provided.[1] His correspondence was carefully censored to prevent any leakage of military information. He carried an identification disk at all times so that he might not be buried as an unknown soldier. The army provided his quarters, his food, his tools, his clothes, his hair cuts, his dental and medical work, his burial costs and practically all other necessary expenses. This was less true of the officers, whose expensive outfits often outran the funds provided to buy them.[2]

This care of the soldier appeared at its best in the work of the Red Cross and the medical officers of the army. In some respects, such as the treatment of burns and the reconstruction of broken jawbones, American physicians and surgeons achieved triumphs which before the war would have been considered impossible. But in all the belligerent countries the care of the sick and wounded showed high efficiency as compared with any previous war. If soldiers wounded in battle lived to reach the base hospitals they generally recovered, and five times out of six could again enter active service. Soldiers were usually inoculated against typhoid and further guarded by rigorous sanitary regulations. During the War with Mexico, in the medical dark ages of 1846-1848, disease killed off in one year more than a tenth of the whole American army,[3] and as recently as the Spanish-American War took five lives for each one lost on the battlefield. In France, in 1917 and 1918, less than half as many Americans died from disease as died in battle.[4]

[1] See F. P. Stockbridge, "The Khaki University," World's Work, XXXVII (1919), 332-339, for a description of technical training of army men in the trades of peace.

[2] Isaac Marcosson, S.O.S. (N. Y., 1919), ably describes the multiform tasks performed by the Services of Supply.

[3] See C. R. Fish, The Rise of the Common Man (A History of American Life, VI), 306.

[4] Ayres, War with Germany, 123-130.

Typhoid, dysentery, bubonic plague, typhus, cholera and other familiar war-time scourges were almost unknown in the American army. Romance has always pictured the soldier as shot through the heart or bleeding from a sword cut; the World War was the first great conflict in which the conventional picture of a soldier's deathbed approximated the truth. For previous wars a far more accurate type of the average soldier's lot would be a sick man stretched on a tumbled hospital cot from the effects of bad diet, foul water or an infected insect bite.

Yet one terrible plague broke through all the barriers which science could erect. The influenza, inducing the even more fatal pneumonia, appeared in a particularly active and malignant phase in the autumn of 1918. World-wide in range, it took its victims indifferently from the army at the front, the recruits in barracks and the civilians at home. In mid-September, 1918, all diseases combined were taking soldier lives in the American cantonments at an average rate of five out of a thousand per year, a ratio not high even for healthy young men outside the army. One month later the death rate had risen from five a year to four a week. Fortunately, the epidemic was as brief as it had been severe. With the frosts of late autumn it diminished and with the winter almost disappeared.

Schools and churches were closed for several weeks in many cities. Men and women walking abroad covered their faces with masks to prevent infection; a stranger visiting an American city during that fatal October might have imagined that the Germans had attacked with poison gas which compelled the wearing of gas masks. The disease had an ugly habit of selecting strong young men and women in their twenties and thirties in preference to the infants or elderly folk who are the first victims of most epidemics. The result was that the influenza inflicted just the same sort of injury on the nation as the war itself, killing off many of those most fit to do the work of the world. The *Survey* editorially estimated the economic loss to the nation from sickness and death during the epidemic at "not less than three billion dollars." [1]

Next to the Red Cross, the Young Men's Christian Association was the most important welfare agency with the army. Unfortunately circumstances made its task a rather thankless one. The government had assigned to it the duty of running the official "canteens," but its resources were not equal to supplying freely the chocolate, cigarettes and other little luxuries which it handled. Many soldiers unfavorably contrasted its policy of selling these extras with the policy of the Knights of Columbus and the Salvation Army in giving them without charge, forgetting how much vaster a task had been assigned the Y. M. C. A. Moreover, the government found it impossible for military reasons to allot to the canteens all the cargo space that had been promised, so that many Y. M. C. A. huts ran short of supplies altogether. A certain defensive note has therefore crept into even the eulogies of the Y. M. C. A., though in the main its work was well performed. [2]

The most characteristically American of all the activities of the A. E. F. was the army newspaper, the *Stars and Stripes*. [3] It was no stiff, official journal for the purpose of conveying orders from headquarters and care-

---

[1] *Survey*, XLI, 194 (Nov. 16, 1918). See also G. M. Price, "Mobilizing Social Forces against Influenza," and J. P. Murphy, "Meeting the Scourge," *Survey*, XLI, 95-96, 97-100 (Oct. 26, 1918).

[2] Katharine Mayo, *"That Damn Y"* (Boston, 1920), is probably the fairest summary of the work of the Y. M. C. A. in the war.

[3] Alexander Woollcott, "The Stars and Stripes," *Sat. Eve. Post*, CC, nos. 38-39 (March 17, 24, 1929); Schlesinger, "The Khaki Journalists," 358-359.

fully censored information. The staff of editors and reporters was mainly made up of professional journalists enlisted in the army, with a total confusion of ranks. When official orders were to be promulgated they were headlined in the undignified manner traditional in American journalism. Thus the formal announcement that soldiers absent without leave would be placed in a punishment division and detained in France after other divisions had sailed for home was placed on the front page as "SKIDS GREASED FOR A. W. O. L.s" to the confusion of an English captain who asked in despair, "What are 'Skids'? And what are 'aywulls'?" But four truant soldiers out of every five reported back to their outfit within five days of the article in the *Stars and Stripes*.[1] The paper had its own way of keeping up soldier morale, one that would have filled a European high command with horror. In its cartoons and comic strips, drawn by professional caricaturists, it gently satirized all the aspects of army life which the soldiers found distasteful—the stiff uniforms, the endless saluting, the starchy officers, and even the editors of the paper itself. The soldier thus found expressed for him the irritations which military discipline did not permit him to voice himself, and many a grouch harmlessly exploded in hearty laughter.

One of the main difficulties of the American soldier was that of adjusting himself to the life and traditions of the French. The difference of language was no slight barrier. The ordinary private or, for the matter of that, the ordinary officer hardly did more than pick up a dozen phrases in half a year abroad, and, for the rest, conversed in that strange mixture of French, English and explanatory gesture which the English had already nicknamed "*entente-cordiale* language." Army balladry

[1] Woollcott, "The Stars and Stripes," 22-23.

was often written in that strange tongue, such as the
endless English verses, interlarded with French phrases,
about the "Mademoiselle from Armentières," most famous of them all.

But a greater barrier than language was that of custom. Most American soldiers had never visited Europe
before and subconsciously expected all the mechanical
aids and conveniences so abundant in the United States.
Few of them were capable of appreciating French art
and science, and few of them were imaginative enough
to make allowances for the waste and strain of four
years' warfare in making a country look slovenly and
unkempt. What they noticed was that bathtubs were
rare, the small villages dirty, the petty shopkeepers ava-
ricious, and French methods of doing business slow and
custom-ridden. Anything of French origin or manufacture took the adjective "frog," such as "frog automobile" or "frog elevator," and usually there was a
flavor of mild contempt in the phrase, an intimation
that while the French might be good fighters they could
not be expected to handle business affairs with Anglo-
Saxon efficiency.[1] There was, of course, a friendlier side
to American-French relations. The little children easily
fraternized with the soldiers and begged from them gifts
of chocolates and souvenir buttons. The better educated
officers and soldiers, especially after the armistice, made
some acquaintance with the real French civilization. But
on the whole the army was homesick, devoutly anxious
to leave a strange country and make the alliterative schedule of "Heaven, Hell, or Hoboken by Christmas!" This
impatience was much increased after the fighting was
over and some divisions were kept at dull routine army
chores in France while their more fortunate comrades

[1] "Just wait till us Angry-Saxons gets over," as one Negro soldier
said. J. B. Scherer, The Nation at War (N. Y., 1918), 63.

were already back at their old jobs in the United States. General Pershing was journalistically reported to have said on his arrival, "La Fayette, we are here!" One weary soldier in the spring of 1919 parodied it, "La Fayette, we are *still* here!"

The active and determining share of the American army as an independent unit in the World War was confined to the brief period from July to November, inclusive, 1918.[1] Many Americans had already seen action, but in small units brigaded with the more experienced French and British troops, or in relatively quiet sections of the front. The prolonged deadlock of trench warfare was, however, almost ended, and instructions to the American army, dated as early as October, 1917, had proclaimed the principle that "All instruction must contemplate the assumption of a vigorous offensive. This purpose will be emphasized in every phase of training until it becomes a settled habit of thought." [2] The Americans began their share in the counterattack at Belleau Wood (thenceforward "the Wood of the Marines") near Château-Thierry in the Marne Valley. We have a German army report [3] which best sums up the impression which the personal qualities of the American troops made at this time on their foe:

> The Second American Division must be reckoned a good one and may even perhaps be reckoned as a storm troop. The different attacks on Belleau Wood were carried out with bravery and dash. The moral effect of our gunfire can not seriously impede the advance of the American infantry. The Americans' nerves are not yet

[1] Frothingham, *The American Reinforcement*, chaps. xxx-xxxviii.
[2] J. J. Pershing, *Final Report of General John J. Pershing* (Wash., 1919), 14.
[3] Cited from Colonel de Chambrun and Captain de Marenches, *The American Army in the European Conflict* (N. Y., 1919), 153. For General Ludendorff's similar opinion, see Erich von Ludendorff, "The American Effort," *Atlantic Mo.*, CXXIX (1922), 681.

worn out. The qualities of the men individually may
be described as remarkable. They are physically well set
up, their attitude is good, and they range in age from
eighteen to twenty-eight years. They lack at present
only training and experience to make formidable adversaries. The men are in fine spirits and are filled with
naïve assurance; the words of a prisoner are characteristic—"We kill or get killed."

In September, operating independently, the Americans smashed in the salient of St. Mihiel and, in October
and November, took part in a continuous battle of forty-
seven days in the Meuse Valley and the wooded hills of
the Argonne. The latter campaign, or "Battle of the
Argonne," cost more American lives than all the rest
of the war. Colonel Leonard P. Ayres has compared it
with the somewhat similar Battle of the Wilderness in
the Civil War.[1] "Twelve times as many American troops
were engaged as were on the Union side. They used in
the action ten times as many guns and fired about one
hundred times as many rounds of ammunition. The actual weight of the ammunition fired was greater than
that used by the Union forces during the entire Civil
War. Casualties were perhaps four times as heavy as
among the Northern troops in the Battle of the Wilderness." The proportion of the western front held by the
Americans had increased from one per cent in January,
1918, to twenty-one per cent in November.[2] When the
armistice was signed on November eleventh the Americans were masters of the territory from Verdun to Sedan.
The whole German war plan from February, 1917,
onward was a huge gamble that the war could be won
before American troops arrived in sufficient numbers to
give the Entente Allies a distinct advantage in man

[1] Ayres, *War with Germany*, 112-113.
[2] Ayres, *War with Germany*, 140.

power. Germany had at least five chances in her favor in this hazard, for her object would have been equally obtained: if the submarine campaign had starved out England; if it had halted the movement of men or goods from the United States; if the transportation of the American army should interfere with the export of war material to France or Britain; if the United States failed to organize an adequate force; or if the American soldiers, nearly all of them wholly inexperienced in modern warfare, proved incompetent at the front. These questions were answered, but not in a day or a year. Nineteen hundred and seventeen was a year of preparation rather than of achievement, and the preparation was not too complete. At the opening of 1918 the United States had taken over only about six miles of intrenchment, and "quiet" sectors at that. Even a friendly French critic has pointed out that "America if left to herself, without British tonnage, without practical training by the Allied armies, would have arrived too late to play her part in the final act." [1] Almost all artillery material and ammunition used by the A. E. F. was procured in France or Britain, mainly the former.[2] The British furnished about half of the transport tonnage used in taking American soldiers to France; the Americans about forty-five per cent, including confiscated German merchant shipping, the remainder being loaned by France, Italy and other maritime states.[3] The American aircraft program was barely under way after a year of war effort and American aviators in France had to depend on European combat planes.[4]

The submarine, which had brought the United States

[1] Edouard Réquin, *America's Race to Victory* (N. Y., 1919), 198.
[2] De Chambrun and De Marenches, *The American Army*, 236.
[3] Ayres, *War with Germany*, 48.
[4] For aircraft building, see Ayres, *War with Germany*, chap. vii.

into the war, was also the greatest obstacle which the nation had to surmount. Its destructiveness could be met by building new ships faster than the old ones were sunk, by evading the submarine attacks, by protecting merchantmen and transports with armed convoy, and by actual destruction of the submarine. At first it seemed as though all these methods together might prove inadequate. In April, 1917, Germany sank 875,000 tons of shipping. Ships were being destroyed several times as fast as they were being built, and submarines built several times as fast as they were being sunk. The total tonnage of the world before the war was about 32,000,-000; the Germans and their allies had sent to the bottom over 7,500,000 tons.[1] The days were growing longer, and in the high latitudes of British waters the Germans hoped to be able to locate and strike at ships for fifteen or sixteen sunlit or twilight hours in the midsummer season.

Village inventors, confident that American ingenuity could solve any problem, badgered the navy with such proposals as walling in the whole North Sea, equipping all ships with buffers or double hulls, and deflecting the course of torpedoes by huge magnets. One device, seemingly quite as fantastic and yet proving practically useful, was the dazzle camouflage. Ordinary camouflage, such as the steel grey of a battleship, the mud-colored khaki of the infantryman and the white fur coat of the polar bear, seeks to make the object melt into the horizon. The dazzle camouflage aimed at deception rather than obscurity. Transports and cargo ships were decorated in huge zigzag designs, like so many floating cubist paintings, until American ports resembled nightmare harbors beyond the gates of ivory and horn. But the purpose was practical enough: to deceive the watching

[1] J. L. Leighton, *Simsadus:* London (N. Y., 1923), 3.

submarine commander as to the exact size, speed and direction of his target.[1]

The arming of merchant ships proved ineffective, and a convoy system was adopted instead whereby merchant ships went out in huge fleets under the protection of cruisers and destroyers. The course followed was irregular, the time of sailing rigidly concealed and all lights darkened. By autumn the monthly tonnage losses had been cut to half the April figure. Transports did not always travel with convoy. They sailed from "an Atlantic port," [2] usually New York or Norfolk, for Brest, St.-Nazaire, Liverpool or Bordeaux. They relied more on speed than on protection to take them through the danger zone and, as a rule, passed in complete safety though much discomfort, for, to economize space, the men were packed in like sardines and had to take turn and turn about in the bunks. The hunting of the submarines was carried out in various ways, in coöperation with the Allied fleets, chiefly by depth charges from destroyers or patrol boats or the use of contact mines. Some were also destroyed by machine gun fire, caught in mine nets, bombed by airplanes, rammed by warships, or lured to doom by "mystery" decoy ships, destroyers camouflaged to resemble merchant vessels.

The constructive side of the war against the submarine was to build new ships. Until 1917 most commerce and passenger traffic across the Atlantic was carried in European vessels. Of these the British had the lion's share, but France, Norway, the Netherlands and, until 1914, Germany played also important parts. Most

[1] L. R. McCabe, "Camouflage—War's Handmaid," *Art World*, III (1918), 313-318; E. C. Peixotto, "Special Service for Artists in War Time," *Scribner's Mo.*, LXII (1917), 1-10.

[2] Censorship had its humors. Though it compelled the newspapers to refer to New York merely as "an Atlantic port," it did not prevent them in some cases from telling how the "vessels steamed out from an Atlantic port past the Statue of Liberty."

shipping of United States registry was engaged in coast-
wise or Great Lakes traffic. The shipbuilding program
was for a time delayed by a controversy between the
shipping board and the emergency fleet corporation.[1]
At first Major General George Goethals, the chief builder
of the Panama Canal, directed construction, but he re-
signed on an important technical issue—should the new
ships be steel or wooden? Looking to the future, steel
ships might have been the better investment, but the
urgent need for immediate construction made it necessary to disregard the commercial viewpoint entirely
and consider only the military emergency. The new
wooden ships were supplemented by the conversion into
troop transports of confiscated German liners, the deflec-
tion of shipping from Oriental and Latin-American
trade, the leasing of Dutch, Swedish and Norwegian
steamers, and even the arbitrary commandeering of some
Dutch vessels.

Shipbuilding and other war-time industries made it
as necessary for the government to house its workmen
as to build barracks for the soldiers. "The main problem giving the country concern is no longer the housing
of its soldiers but the housing of the industrial army,"
wrote a housing expert in the summer of 1918. "We
have taken some small city of 30,000 or 40,000 population and have almost overnight doubled its population by placing contracts in the factories."[2] In many
cases the government found it necessary to erect not only
houses but "to build streets and sewers, water and lighting systems, moving picture shows, and schools and
places of amusement."[3] Hamilton Holt's description of

[1] See *The Bridge to France* (Phila., 1927) by E. N. Hurley, chairman
of the shipping board.
[2] Lawrence Veiller, "The Housing of the Mobilized Population," Am.
Acad. of Polit. and Social Sci., *Annals*, LXXVIII, 20-21.
[3] Veiller, "Housing of the Mobilized Population," 23.

Hog Island (near Philadelphia) is a good picture of these mushroom shipbuilding towns.[1]

> Here was an absolutely flat stretch of land circling back from a straight mile and a half of water front that last summer was nothing but a dismal, soggy, salt swamp inhabited only by muskrats and mosquitoes, now a beehive of industry, and one of the great manufacturing cities of the world. . . . Giant cranes were unloading huge pieces of steel and logs from the freight cars. Donkey engines were puffing. Sirens were blowing. Those titanic human woodpeckers, the compressed air riveters, were splitting the ears with their welding. A half dozen scows were dredging the river and a dozen pile drivers were descending with giant whacks upon the logs at the water's edge. . . . With begrimed faces and mud-encrusted shoes the men worked and walked along, laughing and shouting, singing, and swearing. Hog Island was alive.

For the control of American industry and its direction towards military purposes in case of war the army appropriation act of August 29, 1916, provided for the creation of a council of national defense, consisting of the secretaries of war, the navy, the interior, agriculture, commerce and labor. An advisory commission was established to coöperate with this body on technical matters: Daniel Willard, president of the Baltimore and Ohio Railroad, on transportation; Howard E. Coffin, on munitions manufacture; Bernard M. Baruch, on metals and minerals; Julius Rosenwald, on clothing and supplies; Dr. Hollis Godfrey, on engineering and education; Dr. Franklin H. Martin, on medicine and surgery; and Samuel Gompers, president of the American Federation of Labor, on labor affairs.[2] One of the most

[1] Hamilton Holt, "Hog Island," *Independent*, XCIV, 196 (May 4, 1918).
[2] Frothingham, *The American Reinforcement*, 33-42, 365-367.

important subordinate agencies of the council was the
war industries board, established in July, 1917, and
given executive power in March, 1918. "The Board set
out to prevent competition among those buying for the
war, and to regulate the use by the civil population of
men, money, and materials in such a way that civilian
needs, not merely civilian *wants*, should be satisfied." [1]
At the end of the war the board and its subordinate
agencies amounted almost to an economic dictatorship, for it could penalize producers, who would not
coöperate, by giving priority in the supply of raw materials to rival manufacturers whose work better fitted
the military need. Unnecessary building was discouraged.
When a strongly supported movement in Chicago sought
the construction of a large temporary memorial to the
soldiers, a permit was refused and the application subsequently withdrawn. Permits were similarly refused for
the building of frame tabernacles for the use of the popular evangelist, Billy Sunday. Even a large public-school
building project, involving eight million dollars, was
suspended in New York City. [2]

Price-fixing, stimulus to production, economy and
standardization, as well as the determination of priorities, became concerns of the board. Shoe manufacturers
were restricted to three colors in leather; new lasts and
heights were forbidden. Bathing caps were limited to
one style for each manufacturer. Automobile tires were
reduced from 287 types to 9; steel plows from 312 to
76; buggy wheels from 232 to 4. [3] The advantages of
standardization thus learned during the stress of war
were remembered after the peace and, as we shall see,
the simplification of styles of manufacture was greatly

[1] B. M. Baruch, *American Industry in the War* (Wash., 1921), 29.
[2] Baruch, *American Industry*, 57.
[3] Baruch, *American Industry*, 65-69.

extended under the auspices of the department of commerce during the secretaryship of Herbert Hoover. In the main, the business men of the nation needed no coercion to direct their efforts toward stimulating the production of war commodities, and many of them gave up a unique chance of private profit to serve in some administrative office for a nominal salary, usually a "dollar a year." On the other hand, the government's price-regulating policy of allowing a fixed percentage of profit above the gross costs of production placed a direct, though possibly an inevitable, premium on reckless expenditure.[1]

Priority for the needs of war over those of peace had to be obtained in transportation as well as in production. Terminal points became congested with cars as the bulk of east-bound traffic mounted, and routing them back to where they were needed was a problem requiring central control. William G. McAdoo, secretary of the treasury, became director general of the railroad administration, a dictator of traffic. With complete disregard of competing private companies the railways were organized into regional units, passenger trains were cut to a minimum, and pleasure travel discouraged. Schedules and rates were made uniform, and the use of freight for nonessential goods subordinated to the carrying of munitions. The railroad tangle interlocked with the fuel shortage in the cold winter of 1917-1918 to provoke one of the most serious crises of the war. Thirty-seven ships laden with munitions were held up in New York Harbor for lack of fuel and the coal barges were held in the

---

[1] For the business aspects of the war effort, see esp. the series edited by Crowell and Wilson, *How America Went to War* (6 vols.) : *The Giant Hand; The Road to France* (2 vols.) ; *The Armies of Industry* (2 vols.) ; *Demobilization;* and also G. B. Clarkson, *Industrial America in the World War* (Boston, 1923) ; General Johnson Hagood, *The Services of Supply* (Boston, 1927) ; and Marcosson, *S. O. S.*

grip of heavy ice in several of the most important North-eastern ports.[1]

In January, 1918, Fuel Administrator Harry A. Garfield, in order to get the coal moved to the Eastern cities and the waiting ships, took the drastic and unpopular step of closing down all manufacturing plants, not needed for the making of munitions or other essential purposes, for five days and for a series of Mondays thereafter. These "heatless Mondays" were bitterly resented but loyally obeyed; "this invasion of the rights of business which were supposed to be sacred to us, was received with the practical thought: 'Garfield did not do this to be mean; he had reasons.' "[2] The householder had to suffer, too, unless he had a cellar well stocked with coal before the shortage began. In order to conserve gasoline for motor trucks citizens were requested to keep their automobiles in the garage, especially on Sundays and holidays, unless necessity brought them out.

The civilian war agencies—the shipping board, the war industries board, the war trade board which established priorities in foreign commerce, the railroad administration, the fuel administration and the food administration—constituted in fact new branches of the federal executive, as powerful and independent as any department of the government. Yet they were not made formal cabinet offices and the old political cabinet was not changed in structure, and but little in personnel, during the war. Of all the branches of the new, unpolitical war administration which had grown up side by side with the cabinet, that which reached the greatest number of individuals was the food administration,

[1] "The Coal Crisis and 'Heatless Days,' " *Current History*, VII (1918), 473-476.
[2] Frederick Palmer, *America in France* (N. Y., 1918), 158-159.

which required the coöperation of every farmer, every housewife and, to some extent, every consumer as well.[1]

Herbert Hoover, the food administrator, found his task almost the opposite of that which had faced him in Belgium. The United States was threatened with no famine and did not require to be provisioned. The problem was rather to create a food surplus in America to relieve a food shortage in Europe. No food cards or rationing were introduced and the main reliance was on persuasion rather than compulsion. A special commission, entirely independent of the food administration's grain corporation, established a fixed price of $2.20 per bushel for spring wheat, twenty cents above the minimum guaranteed by congressional act.[2] Millers were not permitted to sell flour for more than a stipulated margin above their costs, and hoarding and profiteering were severely treated. The high and stable price offered for wheat encouraged so much planting that the 1918 crop of nine hundred and twenty-one million bushels was adequate for the needs of the war.[3] This rapid expansion of the planted area of staple grains had, as we shall see, an unfortunate recoil after the war, when the curtailment of European demand brought prices down to half the war-time figure.

The domestic aspect of the food situation was almost as important as the agricultural. Women and boys on vacation formed a "land army" to help in farm work, and the Boy Scouts planted home vegetable gardens in accordance with the slogan, "Every Scout to feed a sol-

[1] C. R. Van Hise, Conservation and Regulation in the United States during the World War (Wash., 1917), is the best comprehensive account.
[2] F. M. Surface, The Stabilization of the Price of Wheat during the War and Its Effect upon the Returns to the Producer (Wash., 1925), 13-15, 43-48.
[3] Surface, Stabilization of the Price of Wheat, 17.

dier." Just the foods in which the average American's diet was richest he was now called on to deny himself— the meats, fine flour, fats and sweets. He was willing, but needed much instruction as to how to set about it. Millers, bakers and housewives joined forces to devise more or less tempting substitutes for fine wheat bread from coarse-milled "whole wheat," corn, rye and other grains. In addition, wheatless days were advertised when patriotic Americans forewent altogether the usual slice or two of bread at dinner. Cheaper cuts of meat supplemented the traditional expensive steaks, and some restaurants catered to the national love of novelty by adding horse, rabbit and even whale meat to the menu. Meatless days were observed as rigorously as Catholic Fridays. Housewives were urged not to purchase more food than they were certain to use so that there might be the less danger of its spoiling, and the garbage cans which before the war were full of discarded fragments of food now went to the dump half empty.[1] To prevent the more conscientious from overdoing things and trying to live on nothing but hardtack and spinach, the food administration advised all to "eat plenty, wisely, without waste."

But women helped the war effort in many other places besides the kitchen; indeed one of the main effects of the war on American life was to bring them out of the kitchen. They were particularly in demand for the types of factory work which required delicate discrimination of touch. "I know a woman who has for years been the Northern agent for the woven rugs and homespun

[1] For example, the tons of raw garbage collected in Chicago declined from 12,862 during the month of June, 1916, to 8386 for the same month a year later. In some cities persons who had contracted to collect garbage for feeding purposes were forced to go out of business. Ivan Pollock, *The Food Administration in Iowa* (B. F. Shambaugh, ed., *Iowa Chronicles of the World War*, Iowa City, 1923), I, 181; II, 12.

made in a certain mountain community in the South,"
wrote one observer.

> Now she has closed up her business and is going to
> one of the base hospitals to do work in occupational
> therapy. . . . The government gas mask factory has
> proved a most interesting field for many artists, musi-
> cians, and stage women. One well-known portrait
> painter is now spending her days in turning over little
> brass disks and carefully inspecting both sides. . . .
> The aircraft factories, too, seem to have an especial ap-
> peal to women. It may be because the sewing on the deli-
> cate wings of the aircraft is something that is distinctly
> women's work. . . . Wireless telegraphy is attracting
> many women who have the necessary background of
> physics and mathematics.[1]

This movement of women into "men's jobs" at something like men's wages revolutionized the economics of
many a household. Jane Fuller was a widow who
worked as a housemaid at thirty dollars a month, and
her sixteen-year-old son did odd jobs for the butcher.
As the draft took more and more men away from industry, the boy became a machine operator at $3.50 a
day and the widow earned as much in a munition factory. "Today this mother and son—and the case is both
actual and typical—average forty dollars a week where
a year ago their total income was thirty dollars a
month."[2]

To carry the cost of war the burden was divided between taxes and loans. Both withdrew capital from ex-

[1] Norma B. Kastl, "Wartime, the Place and the Girl," *Independent*,
XCVI, 56 (Oct. 12, 1918).
[2] Blackman-Ross Company, *The Effect of the War on Business Conditions* (N. Y., 1918), 6-7. See also Harriet S. Blatch, *Mobilizing Woman
Power* (N. Y., 1918) ; Ida C. Clarke, *American Women and the World
War* (N. Y., 1918) ; and Mrs. Nevada D. Hitchcock, "The Mobilization of Women," Am. Acad. of Polit. and Social Sci., *Annals*, LXXVIII,
24-31.

penditure on the comforts and luxuries of peace and
were thus really paid in present costs, but because a loan
promises a "reward of abstinence" by repaying the bondholder at the expense of the taxpayer, it will call out
money that would hide from the taxgatherer. Five great
loans were floated, each was oversubscribed, and a total
of more than twenty-one billion dollars raised from
more than sixty-five million subscriptions. The first four
were called "liberty loans," [1] the last, coming after the
armistice, a "victory loan."

In order to insure the success of the liberty loans the
government had to embark on a new campaign of publicity, quite literally "selling the war" to the nation.
In most European countries, perhaps most notably in
France, a government bond issue sells itself as the people
are ever on the watch for a safe investment bearing a
constant rate of interest. In the United States, on the
other hand, people seem to like a touch of speculation
in their investments. The banks and the financial class
would readily have taken the new bonds, and did take
many of them, but the administration desired a wider
participation in the loan and it was consequently necessary to persuade many to invest who had never before
owned a bond or planned to buy one. To make this
easier, bonds were sold in low denominations, the fifty-
dollar issue being especially popular, and these could
be bought on the installment plan by the accumulation
of "thrift stamps" and war-savings certificates. As the
department stores had already familiarized the public
with the trading-stamp idea this method of purchase
was widely popular.

Of course, appeal was made to patriotism as well as to

[1] The habit prevailed of carrying propaganda into the names of war-
time institutions, thus "liberty bonds," the "liberty motor" of the airplane, and "liberty cabbage" to take the alien taint from sauerkraut.
Humorists proposed to rename dachshunds "liberty pups."

thrift. Buying a bond was buying a share in the war, the one best way in which the stay-at-home could help. Popular artists designed posters to bring home to the most casual bystander the urgent needs of the war, and "four-minute men" in the moving-picture theaters painted in brief words the iniquities of Germany, the hardships of the soldiers and the need for immediate aid. Some citizens' committees overdid matters and treated as suspect anyone, especially if an alien, who did not choose to buy a bond. Offenders were sometimes haled before extralegal or "kangaroo" courts, and occasionally yellow paint would decorate overnight the front door of the noninvestor.[1]

The federal organization of war work was paralleled and completed by state, county, municipal and neighborhood organizations. As a rule these were not permanent functionaries added to the state or federal civil service but volunteer committees, manned by unpaid workers though sanctioned by the state authorities. So ready and apt were the American people to improvise new administrative machinery that one of the main duties of the state councils of defense was to discourage the excessive multiplication of agencies that might get in one another's way. For instance, many charitable enterprises overlapped one another, and some were so badly managed as to waste much of the money received. An Illinois law therefore forbade the soliciting of funds for war aid or relief except from agencies approved by the state council or recognized by the federal government, and of 1499 applications for such approval only 1045 obtained it.[2] A general letter from the council of national defense on September 10, 1918, approved the

[1] C. D. Stewart, "Prussianizing Wisconsin," *Atlantic Mo.*, CXXIII (1919), 99-105; N. R. Whitney, *The Sale of War Bonds in Iowa* (*Iowa Chronicles of the World War*, Iowa City, 1923), chap. v.
[2] Illinois State Council of Defense, *Report* (Chicago, 1919), 69-70.

The Liberty Loan, 1918

simple type of local organization developed in Alabama: "You will note that it contemplates county councils consisting of all county representatives of government war work—one for each agency—and no other members. It is a perfect example of coördination wholly excluding duplication of effort." [1]

The Illinois state council of defense may be taken as typical of the organization in the larger industrial states. Certain agencies embraced the whole state, but the following were paralleled in county or town subdivisions: the women's committee, for coördinating women's activities; the publicity committee, consisting usually of the newspaper publishers in each county; the food production and conservation committee; the neighborhood committee whose "primary function was the promotion of patriotic thought and action"; the county auxiliary, for miscellaneous duties; the highways transport committee, "to promote use of public roads and relieve rail transportation"; the commercial economy administration, to promote thrift and reduce waste; and the nonwar construction bureau, to eliminate needless construction. [2]

A national bureaucracy might possibly have handled the local problems of war administration more efficiently than this spontaneous growth of local committees and councils, but it could not have enlisted an equal degree of popular enthusiasm. The fact that nearly every prominent citizen could wear some sort of button or

[1] Alabama Council of Defense, *Report* (Montgomery, 1919), 10.

[2] Illinois State Council of Defense, *Report*, 10-12. Similarly, the Connecticut state council of defense had sections on publicity, on food supply, on transportation, on Americanization (work among the foreign-born), on child welfare, on health and recreation, on industrial survey (coöperating with the federal war industries board), on commercial economy, on commercial relations, on employment, on boys' working reserve (mainly farm labor), on coal and fuel, on education, on sanitation, and a woman's division later merged with the council as a whole. Connecticut State Council of Defense, *Report* (Hartford, 1919).

badge, that homes and business houses could hang out
flags with a star for each person serving in France, that
the operation of the draft was in the hands of local civilian boards, that food-saving posters could be placed in
every kitchen window, that every child could collect
thrift stamps, made the war national as no congressional
resolution or presidential proclamation could have. Probably the wisest thing done by Washington in the war
was not to attempt to do too much, but to leave something for the initiative of "Zenith City" and "Gopher
Prairie."

The result of this neighborhood organization was
that the war seemed much nearer in 1918 than it had
the previous year. The press was urged to change the
phrases "the Allies" and "the Entente Powers" in news
headlines to "our Allies" and "we." [1] The usefulness
of this shift of emphasis is shown in the changed attitude of large portions of the press. The Hearst newspapers, which in 1917 had advocated in editorial after
editorial keeping the army and navy at home "and so
compelling Germany, if she wants to fight, to come to
us," [2] had now all come into line for the successful prosecution of the war. There was no formal press censorship, but the press was enjoined to publish no details of
military movements or shipping news without official
approval, and these directions were generally obeyed to
the letter.

An *Official Bulletin* published by the government informed the nation of such military operations as it was
not necessary to keep secret, and the committee on public information, headed by a liberal journalist, George
Creel, distributed millions of pamphlets in English and

[1] H. B. Mitchell, "Our Headline Policy," *Columbia War Papers*, ser.
1, no. 4, 4-5.
[2] *Literary Digest*, LVII, 12-13 (March 25, 1918), gives a summary
of contemporary protests against the policy of the Hearst papers.

other languages on the causes of the war.[1] This committee, however, was highly unpopular with Congress,
partly because it seemed to be an attempt to "ration"
the news and partly because of temperamental clashes
between Mr. Creel's incautious wit and the dignity of
some congressional leaders.

The government was as zealous to spread propaganda
within Germany and other enemy countries to promote
rebellion as to spread it within the United States to foster loyalty. In the summer and autumn of 1918 aviators
and floating balloons carried a hundred thousand leaflets
a day over a zone one hundred and fifty miles deep behind the German lines.[2] They stressed the war aims of
President Wilson and the clear distinction he had drawn
between the German government and the German people, and, according to Ludendorff and other German
leaders, they were among the main causes of the republican revolution in that country.[3] One ingenious method
used by the army was to circulate postcards among enemy soldiers to be delivered up and mailed in the event
of their being taken prisoner, reassuring their relatives
of good food and treatment—and, incidentally, encouraging thoughts of surrender.[4] The great American
art of publicity and advertisement was never more successfully employed than in "selling the war" to the
United States and simultaneously "selling peace" to the
enemy.

Labor troubles were among the major causes of delay
in making preparation for war. The attitude of President Gompers and nearly all other high officials of the

[1] George Creel, *How We Advertised America* (N. Y., 1920).
[2] H. D. Lasswell, *Propaganda Technique in the World War* (N. Y.,
1927), 184. This book has a useful bibliography on its subject.
[3] Von Ludendorff, "The American Effort," *Atlantic Mo.,* CXXIX
(1922), 681.
[4] Lasswell, *Propaganda Technique in the World War,* 167.

American Federation of Labor was almost aggressively loyal and few strikes of any importance were directed against the war or intentionally designed to hamper it in any way. The trouble lay in the economic sphere, not the political. With rapidly rising prices, the displacement of trained union men by nonunionists and women, and the war-time disregard of customary limitation on the hours of labor, the trade unions feared that their hard-won gains of the past were being imperiled.[1] Hence they demanded recognition of the union and a high standard of wages.

At the end of the first war year there was an unpleasant record in many important places: "The workmen of the Wheeling Steel and Iron Company went out last summer, thereby holding up work on 2,000,000 tin cans a day—material needed for packing the food supply of the soldiers. . . . The raincoat makers in New York struck for higher wages and a union shop. As they were making army slickers the employers had to yield both their demands. . . . The Holt Tractor Company, which makes the caterpillar tractors that form the basis of the 'tanks,' was held up for three months, the issue of the strike being once more unionization."[2] The worst conditions of all existed on the Pacific Coast where shipyard men, at the very moment when the whole issue of the war depended on the available shipping tonnage, refused to handle nonunion lumber or metal even when no other materials were available. Even the munition factories engaged in making the Browning machine gun, a vital necessity for the army, at one time went on strike. The administration

[1] *American Labor Year Book for 1917-1918*, 11-21.
[2] B. J. Hendrick, "England Has Industrial Peace—Why Not We?," *World's Work*, XXXV (1918), 485-486. See also Ordway Tead, "The American Labor Situation in War-Time," *Century*, XCV (1918), 354-359.

preferred to smooth out these difficulties through such agencies as the labor committee of the council of national defense and the national war labor board rather than to pass any general law against war-time strikes, but injunctions were freely and frequently used to prevent particular strikes, even after the armistice.[1]

For the repression of real opposition to the national cause the government had at hand two far-reaching laws. The espionage act of June 15, 1917, forbade false statements which might injure the prosecution of the war, incitements to disloyalty, obstruction of recruiting, and similar attempts to impede the activities of the government. The act of May 16, 1918, defined as seditious and punishable all disloyal language and attacks on the government, the army and navy, or the cause of the United States in the war. Under these statutes, and even more drastic state legislation, many agitators who denounced the war or pointed to it as the nemesis of capitalism were jailed.[2] There was strangely little opposition from German agents or German sympathizers. Judge George W. Anderson declared that, "As United States attorney from November, 1914, to October, 1917, I was charged with a large responsibility as to protecting the community from pro-German plots. . . . Now, I assert as my best judgment, grounded on the information that I can get, that more than ninety-nine per cent of the advertised and reported pro-German plots never existed."[3]

Where the Industrial Workers of the World were active in the Farther West the conflict was most acute. The I. W. W. promoted huge strikes in the copper mines and in the lumber camps, apparently less to oppose the

---

[1] Alexander Bing, *War-Time Strikes and Their Adjustment* (N. Y., 1921), 154-156.

[2] Zechariah Chafee, jr., *Freedom of Speech* (N. Y., 1920), deals critically with the government's policy from a legal point of view.

[3] "The Red Hysteria," *New Republic*, XXI, 251 (Jan. 28, 1920).

war or better their wages than to strike a blow at the capitalistic system in general. Their lawless violence was met with equal lawlessness on the other side. In August, 1917, the agitator Frank Little was lynched in Montana. In the copper region of Arizona nearly twelve hundred strikers, about a third of them members of the I. W. W., were deported beyond the state line by force. Attempts to prosecute the kidnapers failed because local sentiment was with them. During and immediately after the war, to be a member of the I. W. W. was to encounter legal penalties for "criminal syndicalism" or sedition.[1] An amusing example of the way in which official "correctness" merged into personal enthusiasm for direct action was the report of a Nevada sheriff to the governor:

> I regret to report to Your Excellency that on such and such a date, such and such a person was forcibly taken from my possession by parties unknown. He was placed on trial by an improvised tribunal and found guilty of lukewarmness toward the cause of the United States . . . whereupon (after tarring and feathering him) they instructed him to leave the country, telling him that if he ever comes back they will lynch him—and if he does, by ——, Governor, *we will!* [2]

Another type of opponent to the war was the man whose conscientious scruples forbade him to serve. Members of religious sects teaching absolute nonresistance, such as the Quakers, were exempted from military service by law, but this exemption did not cover all the cases that arose.[3] Some conscientious objectors adhered

[1] Bing, *War-Time Strikes*, 255-269.
[2] Cited from Scherer, *The Nation at War*, 121.
[3] Two excellent studies survey the field and classify the types of conscientious objectors in the war: C. M. Case, *Non-Violent Coercion* (N. Y., 1923), and N. M. Thomas, *The Conscientious Objector in America* (N. Y., 1923).

to no sect and believed in Christianity only as a general teaching of peace and good will, or regarded the particular war as unjust or "capitalistic," or merely revolted emotionally against the idea of killing anyone. Again, there was the case of Roger Baldwin, director of the American Civil Liberties Bureau, who refused to obey the draft on the individualistic plea of his "uncompromising opposition to the principle of conscription of life by the state for any purpose whatever, in time of war or peace." [1] Nor were the bewildered draft boards prepared to deal with strange religious sects who not only objected to fighting but had conscientious scruples against saluting, wearing buttons (the Amish Mennonites), donning uniforms or shaving.[2] Whether these passive resisters were cruelly or humanely treated in the prison camps depended partly on the good nature of the officers in charge, but even more perhaps on their imagination and sense of humor. Most of what careful investigations reveal about the conscientious objectors is negative.[3] They were rarely cowards, hardly ever positively pro-German, equal to the average recruit in physique and rather above him in intelligence tests. Some were, however, self-absorbed, neurotic, or otherwise temperamentally incapable of civic coöperation; many others were fanatical literalists in religion or passionate disciples of class-struggle socialism. From the point of view of the army the important thing was that the conscientious objectors of all types and classes were too few in number to make any practical difference in filling up the ranks.

One of the most ill-advised expressions of overzealous patriotism was the war on the German language.

[1] Thomas, *The Conscientious Objector*, 27.
[2] *N. Y. World*, Jan. 16, 1919.
[3] Case, *Non-Violent Coercion*, chap. xi.

Even as early as 1915 the unpopularity of the German cause had brought about a decline in the study of German in the high schools, though Spanish was more frequently substituted than French, perhaps with some thought of preparing to capture Latin-American trade.[1] During the war many states forbade the use of foreign languages as the primary medium of instruction even in private schools (usually making an exception of religious teaching), took the teaching of German out of the elementary grades by law or simply dropped German courses from the school curriculum by administrative action. Even ten years after the war German had not quite recovered its relative position in the curriculum of 1914. Some officers of the American Defense Society wanted to go further and suppress all public use of the German language during the war and even proposed a boycott of it afterwards. The number of newspapers and periodicals published in German in the United States decreased from about five hundred to three hundred and forty-four in the two war years.[2] But the feeling against the German language, and the yet more absurd objection to German music, did not long outlast the war, and practically nothing more was heard of hasty proposals to boycott goods "made in Germany" when peace came again. Cautiously, one by one, German-American restaurants and other places of business with Teutonic names resumed their former designations. Almost the only enduring influence of the passionate hatreds and enthusiasms of 1918 was an enhanced national self-consciousness with which we must deal in its place.[3]

A more important influence of the war on American

[1] *Independent*, LXXXII, 5 (April 5, 1915).
[2] E. H. Bierstadt, *Aspects of Americanization* (Cin., 1922), 74.
[3] See later, chap. xi.

life was the lesson it taught in organization. The war came to a lax, individualistic people; a year was wasted in blundering experiment and another year spent in building up a sound war machine. The full strength of the army and its equipment could not have been placed in the field until 1919, and perhaps not until 1920. The sudden, rather unexpected surrender of Germany and her allies left the government with uncompleted contracts on its hands for the expenditure of hundreds of millions of dollars, an army equally divided between training camps and trenches, factories and power plants half completed, and a nation which, having just passed through all the stages from apathy to profoundest enthusiasm, had no appropriate outlet for its emotions.

The abrupt termination of the war, while welcome in every way, was almost as hard to realize as its abrupt beginning. On armistice day or, rather, on the eve of the armistice—for the news had been prematurely announced—all business was suspended and thousands poured into the city streets, at once elated and bewildered. On their heads fell a shower of paper tape and torn scraps of telephone directories flung as confetti from office windows in the great carnival of peace. So deep was this paper snow that a few matches would have set the business districts aflame, and the fire companies remained in anxious readiness for a call. But the mass of the crowd did not want to smoke, and rarely raised a cheer or gave any other outward sign of rejoicing. It was enough to walk for miles along the city streets with ten thousand strangers, and to realize that in that moment of good news not one of them was really a stranger.

CHAPTER III

SHADOWS OF RECONSTRUCTION

"THE war," said a soldier proverb, "will last a hundred years—five years of fighting and ninety-five of winding up the barbed wire." The first days of reconstruction after any great war are at once tragic and tedious; they lack the dramatic quality that partly redeems the cruelties of battle. The patriotic unity which is called into life by war disappears with the emergency that gave rise to it and dissolves in a welter of confusion, bickerings and recriminations. The decade after Yorktown and the decade after Appomattox include many of the pages of American history which patriots would most willingly forget. The effect of the World War on the people of the United States was apparently less profound than that of either the War for Independence or the Civil War because it was briefer and because it was fought wholly on foreign soil, but the road back to normal life was rocky enough. There was a war-prosperity boom with great inflation of prices, followed by a serious depression. There was some radical discontent, reflected in a number of violent strikes during 1919, and a corresponding conservative panic leading to hasty legislation against aliens and radicals. There was a series of scandals in connection with oil leases and other public business that recalled the days of the Tweed Ring and the Carpetbaggers.[1] Certain forms of crime became, if not more common, at any rate bolder and more defiant.

[1] For the Reconstruction scandals after the Civil War, see Allan Nevins, *The Emergence of Modern America* (*A History of American Life*, VIII), chaps. i, vii, xi.

"Robbery under arms" and the almost open warfare of rival gangs of "bootleggers," "hijackers" and "racketeers" attracted alarmed attention. Some have even traced, though perhaps speculating too boldly, the effects of war on national morale in the impassioned frivolities of the younger generation and the pessimistic tone of the new realistic fiction.

In every belligerent country a part of the war's aftermath was the repudiation of the statesmen who had directed the course of the struggle. In eastern and central Europe, where conditions were most deeply disturbed, this took the form of violent revolution and experiments in socialism and radical democracy or dictatorship. In the countries of western Europe and in the United States the political reactions were registered peacefully by ballots at the polls instead of by bullets. In a revulsion of sentiment against foreign adventures and entanglements the United States reverted to an insular nationalism, rejecting the peace treaties negotiated by President Wilson, and repudiating his cherished dream of a league of nations.[1] As early as 1918 the Democratic party had lost control of Congress and in 1920 it lost also the executive branch.

During the last two years of the Wilson administration an increasingly hostile Congress was busy, in the intervals of the fight over the peace treaties, in repealing war-time legislation. The president was deprived of his special emergency powers, the boards and bureaus which he had controlled were liquidated, and the country restored to its peace-time basis. One of the most perplexing tasks in this field was the disposal of the publicly controlled railroads and the publicly owned ships. Government ownership was now an unpopular policy. The American people as a whole were in a more con-

[1] See later, chap. xi.

servative mood than they had known since the days of
Hanna and McKinley, as hostile to new ventures in
economic policy as to new commitments in foreign
affairs. The proposal for a continuation of national
management of the railroads, and the compromise
Plumb plan for the control of railroads by a copartner-
ship of representatives of the public, the managers and
the workers, met with little favor.[1] The policy adopted,
embodied in the Esch-Cummins act of 1920, provided
for the return of the railroads to their former private
ownership and control, the grant of a temporary guarantee of profits, the establishment of a railroad labor
board to supervise wage agreements, and an increase in
the powers of the interstate commerce commission.

Under private management and peace conditions there
was a considerable improvement in railroad service.[2]
The competition of motor truck and motor bus cut
heavily into the revenues of short-line railroads and
electric trolley lines. To the more powerful companies,
however, this competition was rather a stimulus to
greater efficiency. The average freight train in 1920 contained thirty-seven cars, weighed 1443 tons and made
ten miles an hour, including stops. The average freight
train of 1926 contained over forty-five cars, weighed
about 1750 tons and averaged twelve miles an hour.
There was an increase of more than forty per cent in
the amount of effective work done by the enginery of
each train hourly.[3] Fruitless, cut-throat competition was

[1] See G. E. Plumb, "Labor's Solution of the Railroad Problem,"
Nation, CIX, 200-201 (Aug. 16, 1919). This number of the Nation
contains a general symposium on the railroad question by various publicists.

[2] W. J. Cunningham, "Railroads," Committee on Recent Economic
Changes, Recent Economic Changes in the United States (N. Y., 1929),
I, 255-308.

[3] Samuel Dunn, "A Revolution in Railroading," World's Work, LIII
(1927), 425.

much reduced. In contrast to the old "trust-busting"
attitude of the public, the press and the government,
mergers and consolidations were encouraged. By 1928
six thousand lines had been, through one device or another, merged into about eight hundred, and experts
predicted that in the course of time there would be not
more than twenty distinct systems for the whole United
States.[1]

A still more difficult problem was presented by the
merchant marine.[2] The railways, after all, had been
privately established to meet the ordinary needs of peace
and it was merely a question of time and readjustment
to restore their old status after a brief interval of governmental operation to meet the exigencies of war. But
the greater part of the American transatlantic shipping
fleet had been built to fill the gaps in the world's merchant marine caused by Germany's submarine warfare
and by the need of transporting troops and munitions of
war. The shipping board now found on its hands a large
number of ships, many of them wooden vessels of hasty
construction, which were no longer needed. For lack of
business, scores of the new ships rotted at their wharves,
while the government vainly sought American buyers
willing to pay even a small fraction of their cost. An
entire fleet of more than two hundred wooden ships was
eventually sold for little more than the original cost of
building a single vessel. To the end of June, 1924, the
shipping board had acquired 2541 vessels, of which
1051 had been sold, 86 lost, 18 scrapped and 85 transferred to other departments of the government. Of the
remaining 1301, only 636 were in active service.[3] In

[1] W. G. Shepherd, "Turntable," Collier's, LXXXI, 40 (March 31,
1928).

[2] E. S. Gregg, "Shipping," Recent Economic Changes, I, 309-319.

[3] Isaac Lippincott, Economic Development of the United States (N. Y.,
1927), 733.

1928 the Jones-White merchant-marine act authorized extensive subsidies to private shipowners.

The same revulsion from war socialism that caused the rejection of a nationalized railway system and a nationalized merchant marine led also to the attempt to transfer to private operation another white elephant from the federal menagerie, the nitrate plant at Muscle Shoals, Alabama. According to Secretary W. M. Jardine of the department of agriculture, the Wilson dam and the two nitrate plants in the vicinity of Muscle Shoals cost the public treasury first and last $130,000,000.[1] Two smaller units in Ohio brought the cost of public nitrate plants up to about $150,000,000. It was hoped that Muscle Shoals would be of signal importance in providing electric power and fertilizer for the farmers; but its importance for the latter purpose had been much exaggerated, for it would have taken thirty-eight such plants to produce all the nitrogen required by the corn crop alone, not to mention other crops.[2] Henry Ford at one time seemed willing to add Muscle Shoals to his many other side lines, but he demanded such favorable terms that his offer was not accepted. The proposal of Senator George W. Norris of Nebraska for government operation, chiefly as a check on the "electric power trust," met with the approval of Congress, but fell before the veto of President Coolidge.

Compensation for the returned soldier was another reconstruction problem. The veterans of the war argued that they had voluntarily accepted, or been assigned by conscription, a disagreeable and dangerous task at a time when most of them could have made several times a soldier's pay by civilian work. Some of them had been

[1] W. M. Jardine, "The Problem of Muscle Shoals," *Current History*, XXVIII (1928), 724. Articles by Robert Stewart and Senator G. W. Norris follow.

[2] Robert Stewart, in the same *Current History* symposium, 727.

kept in service so long after the armistice that they found
their jobs taken when they were at last demobilized.
Hence arose a demand for what its advocates termed "adjusted compensation" and its adversaries the "bonus."
Both parties in Congress viewed the demand with favor,
but Presidents Harding and Coolidge, in closer touch
with the treasury officials, opposed the plan of a general
money grant to unwounded veterans. They pointed out
that the veterans' bureau was spending about half a billion dollars each year in compensation for injuries, hospital care and vocational training for the disabled, and
contended that business could never endure a continuance of high taxes to take care also of the veterans who
still enjoyed good health. Several states enacted laws
granting compensation to soldiers native to the state;
nearly half the veterans received some grant, usually
small, from this source. In 1924 Congress at last passed
a law over the presidential veto which awarded certificates of insurance in value proportioned to length of
service.[1]

Though the nation was grateful enough to spend
money lavishly for hospital care and vocational education for wounded soldiers, it was at the same time too
preoccupied with private business to make sure that all
the money voted by Congress was spent to the best advantage. Charles R. Forbes, the head of the veterans'
bureau, found the temptations of his office too much for
him. A senatorial investigation disclosed that he and his
fellow conspirators had looted the funds of the bureau
to their private advantage, and the shadow of a criminal
conviction lay across the most sacred trusteeship of the
federal government. The new chief, General Frank T.
Hines, did much to restore public confidence in the
bureau.

[1] *U. S. Statutes at Large*, XLIII, pt. i, 121-131.

The somewhat perfunctory struggle for the adjusted-compensation law was one of the few evidences of group consciousness among the ex-service men. For the most part, both soldiers and civilians seemed to want to forget the war as soon as possible. During the war there had been much talk of making military training a compulsory course in all the schools and of building the largest fleet in the world. But within a few years after the armistice the regular army and its auxiliary services were hardly larger than they had been in 1916; many schools and colleges that had introduced military training into the curriculum had abandoned it or made it optional, and bitter complaint arose from the land, sea and air branches of the national defense that their appropriations did not suffice to keep their services in efficient condition. Militarism took too much time for the busy American of the decade after the war. The American Legion, founded in 1919, flourished as a veterans' social club and benevolent society rather than as a power in politics. In 1918 an American officer made the confident prediction, based on the historical experience of all our previous wars, that "the next President of the United States is now commanding a brigade or a regiment in France." [1] But in the elections of 1920, 1924 and 1928 both major parties nominated civilians, and very few army officers were able to make any political capital of their war record.

The effects of the war on American life were unquestionably important, but most of them were disguised, indirect, rather than openly present to consciousness. For example, the indignation against Germany which mounted from the first news of the invasion of Belgium in 1914 to its climax in the final death grapple of the

[1] Major-General F. V. Greene, *Our First Year in the Great War* (N. Y., 1918), 37.

nations in 1918, had already begun to seek other channels in 1919.[1] The alien forces which menaced America
were now pictured as wearing the red cap of revolution
rather than the spiked helmet of militarism. Soviet Russia quickly replaced Germany as the villain of international politics.

The "red" panic of 1919 was indeed one of the most
curious aftereffects of the war. "No one who was in the
United States, as I chanced to be, in the autumn of
1919," declared an English Liberal journalist, "will forget the feverish condition of the public mind at that
time. It was hagridden by the spectre of Bolshevism.
. . . Property was in an agony of fear, and the horrid
name 'Radical' covered the most innocent departure
from conventional thought with a suspicion of desperate purpose. 'America,' as a wit of the time said, 'is the
land of liberty—liberty to keep in step.' "[2] In a few
cases there was, to be sure, a little real fire under the
great smoke cloud of "radical" panic. In the Pacific
Northwest the so-called One-Big-Union movement
looked towards the establishment of a universal workers'
soviet to seize industry with the weapon of a general
strike and then hold it in the name of the proletariat. An
older organization, the Industrial Workers of the World,
did not accept so completely the Russian program, but
in spirit and tactics resembled it. Both organizations believed that workingmen should unite by whole industries and not, as was the program of the American Federation of Labor, by separate crafts. Both viewed the
strike not as a weapon to gain specific concessions of
wages, hours, and the right of collective bargaining, but
rather as a means to disorganize the whole fabric of cap-

[1] See later, chap. xi.
[2] A. G. Gardiner, *Portraits and Portents* (N. Y., 1926), 13. See also
Will Irwin, *How Red is America?* (N. Y., 1927).

italistic production. The Industrial Workers of the World, however, probably never much exceeded fifty thousand active members and the One-Big-Union movement does not seem to have enlisted more than thirty thousand.[1]

In the well-organized trades these radical unions played little or no part, but they found a field for action among ill-paid, unorganized casual laborers in the lumber camps, the grain fields and the textile mills. In some cases the strikes were supplemented by sabotage, or destructive action "on the job," such as driving spikes into lumber to wreck saws, burning haystacks, spoiling machinery, and the like. In the far Northwest a number of violent conflicts attracted national attention, such as the attempted general strike of February, 1919, in Seattle, which brought Mayor Ole Hanson, who crushed it, into momentary prominence as the "strong man of the hour." On armistice day of the same year a riot between American Legionaries and members of the I. W. W. in Centralia, Washington, caused several deaths.

In the prosperous days of 1919 strikes were numerous, widespread and not infrequently violent. This was due partly to the effort to bring wages up to the new price levels and partly to the general restlessness of the period. Some four million workers were on strike at some time during the year.[2] All the fundamental industries—coal, steel, railways and textiles—suffered in turn. The strike which attracted widest attention was the result of an attempt to unionize the steel industry.

[1] "In June, 1920, forty-three delegates met in Chicago and organized the American branch of the O.B.U. They asserted that they represented 40,000 members, but in 1922 one of the organizers claimed only 30,000 members in this country." James O'Neal, "The Passing of the I.W.W.," *Current History*, XXI (1925), 531-532.
[2] Labor disputes in 1919 numbered 2665; employees involved, 4,160,-348. D. J. Saposs, "Labor," *Am. Journ. of Sociology*, XXXIV, 79.

It lasted from September, 1919, till the following January. The attempt of some of the union leaders, such as William Z. Foster, to give a revolutionary turn to the struggle resulted in creating prejudice against the strikers. The press hardly gave their side a hearing at the moment, but an investigation by a special commission of inquiry of the Interchurch World Movement showed that many of the grievances of the steel workers were very real and demanded remedy.[1] The Church had stepped in where the press failed.

One of their greatest grievances was the long working day and week. Approximately one half of all the employees of the striking mills were subject to the twelve-hour day, and one half of these in turn were subject to the seven-day week, the average week for all the employees being 68.7 hours.[2] Sometimes at the turn of a shift the steel worker would be compelled to stay on duty without relief for twenty-four hours. The methods used by the employers and managers to break up trade-union solidarity were often questionable. Spying on meetings of the union was frequent. The following letter of instructions is significant:

> We want you to stir up as much bad feeling as you possibly can between the Serbians and Italians. Spread data among the Serbians that the Italians are going back to work. Call up every question you can in reference to racial hatred between these two nationalities; make them realize to the fullest extent that far better results would be accomplished if they will go back to work. Urge them to go back to work or the Italians will get their jobs.[3]

[1] Commission of Inquiry, Interchurch World Movement, *Report on the Steel Strike of 1919* (N. Y., 1920).
[2] *The Steel Strike of 1919*, 11-12.
[3] Dated Oct. 2, 1919. *The Steel Strike of 1919*, 230.

Though the strike was a failure in its immediate objects, the twelve-hour day disappeared within a few years from the steel mills, largely as a result of the intervention of President Harding.

One of the most interesting specimens of the strike fever was the Boston police strike of 1919. The police, whose fixed salaries bore no relation to the rising cost of living, insisted on organizing in affiliation with the American Federation of Labor, and struck to secure the recognition of their union. For a few days the city was stripped of its legal protection, though university lads and others acted as temporary substitutes. No very great outbreak of crime took place, though some shops were plundered; but everyone felt the presence of a dangerous crisis. The grievances of the police were real, but a police strike, raising the classical question "who shall guard our guardians?" seemed, in Governor Calvin Coolidge's phrase, a "strike against public safety." There was a difference of opinion as to the active part played by the governor in crushing the strike, but at least he spoke out clearly against it and won national fame overnight. When he was reëlected governor on the Republican ticket, he received the congratulations of the Democratic president.

After 1919 strikes became less frequent and less associated with revolutionary dreams.[1] In contrast to the more than four million men on strike or locked out in 1919 there were about a million and a half in 1920 and about a million in 1921.[2] But they continued vex-

[1] Selig Perlman, *A History of Trade Unionism in the United States* (N. Y., 1923), chaps. xi-xv.

[2] Except in 1919, the number of strikers from 1916 to 1922 was annually between one and two million; after 1923 it decreased rapidly to between three and four hundred thousand in 1926 and 1927. Saposs, "Labor," 79. The decreasing extent of strikes reflected mainly the prosperity and comparative stability of prices which prevailed during the period 1924-1928, but in part also a decline in the strength of trade

atiously common in certain industries, such as coal mining. Everywhere in the world coal mining, for many reasons, was in an unsatisfactory condition. The work itself was dangerous and laborious, and long periods of idleness alternated with busy seasons when the miners toiled for eight or nine hours underground. Conditions of employment and rates of pay varied enormously between good fields and bad. As particular coal beds approached exhaustion and shafts had to be sunk more deeply, the costs of production increased and the profits shrank towards nothing. American miners and mine owners alike were in a better position than their European fellows, for the mines themselves were newer and richer. American miners were less insistent on government ownership as a solution than the British; their objects were to unionize the entire coal field, to secure a higher rate of pay and, by means of a shorter working week, spread production evenly through the year. In the nonunion fields, such as parts of West Virginia, the men complained also that their houses were on mining-company land and their shops company stores, so that they were altogether at their employers' mercy. Strikes were frequent in the anthracite fields of Pennsylvania, and in 1922 soft and hard-coal workers alike dropped tools to fight a proposed wage cut.

The strike of 1922 involved one terrible incident, the massacre at Herrin, Illinois, which may be selected as illustrating industrial lawlessness at its worst. The event was the more significant because of the character of the community.[1] Herrin was a prosperous and progressive town, the center of forty-four coal mines in its imme-

unionism during the immediately preceding period of depression. See later, chap. vi, for the general economic trend of the times; also Leo Wolman, "Labor," *Recent Economic Changes*, II, chap. vi.

[1] W. L. Chenery, "Why Men Murder in Herrin," *Century*, CIX (1924), 187-194, is the best account.

diate neighborhood. Its ten thousand citizens owned fourteen hundred automobiles; there were seven grammar schools, an excellent high school, several churches and a tradition of community music, the most civilizing of the arts. Moreover, nine tenths of the people in Williamson County were native-born Americans,[1] the "foreign agitator" and the socialist "red" being conspicuously absent. On the other hand, the miners were strongly organized and any attempt to break the unions was considered a threat of open war.

The mine guards and strike breakers imported into the county made themselves very unpopular with the farmers as well as with the townsfolk and the miners. One of the mine owners violated the "armistice" conditions of the strike by shipping away the coal that the strikers had permitted to be brought to the surface. On June 21, 1922, the strikers besieged the mine pits and captured them. Having no power to resist, the defenders of the mine surrendered on promise of being protected. As the prisoners marched out, however, there was some obscure shift in leadership and the mob fell under control of violent men who had made no promises. As the prisoners were released they were shot down and the wounded were butchered where they lay. No one responsible could be found; the trials that followed the twenty-five deaths resulted in the acquittal of all concerned. A legislative committee that investigated the case commented: "It appeared from the sentiment of the people in the community that it was impossible to convict anybody of these murders no matter how strong the testimony."[2]

[1] E. A. Wieck, "Bloody Williamson County," *Nation*, CXVI, 10 (Jan. 3, 1923).
[2] Chenery, "Why Men Murder in Herrin," 189. The story did not end with these unavenged murders. Violence was still in the air. In 1924 the Ku Klux Klan attempted to enforce the prohibition law by spectacular

In the days of American adolescence when industries were still on a merely local scale, the public had regarded strikes as private battles between employers and employed. But the huge twentieth-century concentrations of both capital and labor made it possible for a strike in a key industry to throw out of employment thousands of men in other industries dependent upon it. A traction strike that sent John Citizen walking to work, a builders' strike that made impossible his dream of a cheap suburban home, a walkout at the gas works that left the streets to darkness and the footpad, or a police strike that advertised to the criminal element that their time had come, all emphasized the fact that in industrial warfare there were no neutral rights. Perhaps the most daring solution brought forward during these years was the proposal of Governor Henry Allen of Kansas for an industrial-relations court with plenary powers to decide all industrial disputes that threatened the public welfare.[1] Organized labor, however, bitterly opposed compulsory arbitration on the ground that labor contracts imposed by authority and enforced by penalties amounted to slavery. The courts declared the Kansas anti-strike law unconstitutional in some of its important features.[2]

On the whole the influence of the American Federation of Labor, the Railroad Brotherhoods and other

raids. The sheriff, an enemy of S. Glenn Young, the local Klan raider, enlisted deputies, some of them reputed to be bootleggers. One of them, Ora Thomas, killed Young and was himself killed in the riot which followed. The state militia were called in to police the streets. Much pent-up emotion was drained off into safer channels when Howard S. Williams conducted a series of evangelistic revivals, bringing Ku Kluxers and their foes to the same bench of penitence. *Literary Digest*, LXXXIV, 34-40 (Feb. 21, 1925), gives a summary of press comment. See also *Literary Digest*, LXXXVI, 28-29 (Aug. 1, 1925).

[1] "The Kansas Strike Cure," *Literary Digest*, LXIV, 17 (Feb. 7, 1920).

[2] "A Blow to Compulsory Arbitration," *Literary Digest*, LXXXV, 11 (April 25, 1925).

large unions were distinctly conservative.[1] Labor unions might indorse particular candidates, but they refused to enter the political arena as an independent party. The United States was not called upon to face a general strike of all the principal unions at once, such as occurred in Great Britain in 1926. Many of the most vexatious strikes of the reconstruction period were "outlaw" strikes by small local unions, acting in disobedience to orders of the national officers, or spontaneous walkouts that had no official sanction even from a local union. In all public statements on the question the labor leaders denounced the Bolshevist movement in Russia and all attempts to emulate it in other countries, and the public noticed the curious paradox that many conservative business men advocated the recognition of Soviet Russia for commercial reasons while the chiefs of organized labor opposed it. The influence of organized labor was thrown successfully in favor of stricter limitations on foreign immigration and unsuccessfully in favor of railroad nationalization and federal regulation of child labor.

American Socialism failed to recover even the very moderate position it had held earlier. The entrance of the United States into the World War divided the party into "patriot" and "pacifist" factions on the issue of open opposition to the national military effort. Those who, from sympathy with the Entente Allies or from a feeling of national solidarity, gave support to the war, for the most part withdrew from the active Socialist movement, leaving it in the control of bitter-ender opponents of intervention. As we have seen, the hand of the law fell very heavily upon the latter; Eugene Debs, the vet-

[1] Wolman, "Labor," 481-485; E. T. Devine, "American Labor's Improved Status since 1914," *Current History*, XXVIII (1928), 804-809. Some constructive aspects of American trade unionism are discussed in chap. vi.

eran party leader, made his presidential campaign in 1920 from prison.

Another party schism took place when the Russian Bolshevist revolution divided American Socialists between a left wing which wished to affiliate with Moscow and establish a "dictatorship of the proletariat" and a more conservative group which remained loyal to the old program of democracy and social evolution. As a consequence most of the energy which should have gone into a united assault on the high battlements of capitalism was wasted on factional feuds.[1] The left-wing faction usually took the name Communist, but sometimes the communists were themselves divided on petty points of theory or practice. James O'Neal listed in 1924 no less than sixteen communist organizations of national scope which tried to wear the mantle of Lenin.[2] Most of these were very short-lived, and many of them were finally swept together into the Workers' party under the leadership of William Z. Foster, hero of the steel strike of 1919. There were only fifteen or twenty thousand members of the communistic groups and the great majority of them could not speak English, the Finns being the largest alien unit. The Workers' party dropped the former communist policy of holding secret and illegal meetings and came into the open with a regular national ticket in 1924 and 1928.

The more orthodox wing of the Socialist movement, still keeping the copyright of the Socialist party name, joined with many liberal and reformist bourgeois ele-

[1] Such Socialist dailies as the *New York Call*, and such periodicals as *Wiltshire's* and the *Appeal to Reason*, passed out of existence without leaving successors. The ever lively *Masses* (and its successors the *Liberator* and the *New Masses*) preached an esoteric and "Greenwich-Villagey" Bolshevism that appealed much more to college sophomores than to workingmen.

[2] James O'Neal, "Changing Fortunes of American Socialism," *Current History*, XX (1924), 95.

ments in supporting the presidential candidacy of
Robert M. La Follette in 1924, but acted independently
again in 1928 under the eminently respectable leadership of the Reverend Norman Thomas, pacifist writer
and Princeton graduate. All socialistic national tickets
combined cast a smaller relative vote after the war than
the Socialist party alone in 1912.[1]

The labor unrest of 1919, the communistic movement
within the Socialist ranks, lurid newspaper accounts of
Russian intrigues in the farthest ends of the earth, and
the still undischarged nerve tension of war time must all
be taken into account in explaining the hysteria of the
period. The papers, very literally, "saw red" everywhere. The word "radicalism," which had been rather
a compliment in the Bull Moose days of 1912-1916
when it implied merely a reasonable progressivism in
politics, now had an implication of dynamite. Many
states passed laws against "criminal syndicalism" sufficiently drastic to jail any man on the rolls of one of
the many more or less secret communist parties or associations. Prosecutions were especially common in California. The American Civil Liberties Union was kept
busy in defending one case after another of bewildered
immigrants whose crude political doctrines had involved
them somehow in the meshes of the law.[2] In December,
1919, the *Buford* sent back a boatload of Russian or
near-Russian communists to Soviet Russia.[3] Postmaster-

[1] The Socialist party membership declined from 1912 to 1920 from
118,000 to 26,000; its vote increased only from 897,000 to 915,000 in
spite of the enlargement of the electorate by the grant of equal suffrage
to women. O'Neal, "Changing Fortunes of American Socialism," 92.

[2] See A. G. Hays, *Let Freedom Ring* (N. Y., 1928), for a breezy
account of the activities of the Civil Liberties Union by one of the
leading participants.

[3] Some of the deported radicals on the "Soviet Ark," as the newspapers called the *Buford*, were anarchists who found in Russia a far
more stringent "police state" than America. Other emigrants, such as
William D. Haywood, the I.W.W. leader who had "skipped bail" and

General Albert S. Burleson suppressed one number of the periodical *Masses* and then, with a cruel sense of humor, refused to admit subsequent issues to the mails on the ground that, not being regularly published, it was no longer a "periodical." [1]

Attempts were even made to hold the antiwar Socialists responsible after the war for their former pacifist views. Victor Berger, chosen to represent a Wisconsin constituency in the House of Representatives, was twice debarred from taking his seat in Congress. The New York legislature, while the Lusk committee was solemnly investigating radical propaganda of all shades and considering ways and means of keeping it from the schools, decided to strike yet another blow for national security and barred five Socialists from membership on the direct charge that no Socialist could be considered loyal to the Constitution.[2] Eventually, however, most "political prisoners" held as pacifists, conscientious objectors to war, or sympathizers with revolution, were pardoned, and after 1920 there were no further attempts to keep duly elected Socialists out of office.[3]

One incident of these times, not very important in itself, threatened to become an American equivalent to the French Dreyfus case for the excitement it occasioned, the length of time it remained before the courts and the public, and the alignment of social forces it created. Nicola Sacco and Bartolomeo Vanzetti, Italians with anarchistic views, were accused of murdering a shoe-factory paymaster in April, 1920, and were convicted

fled abroad on his own account, started with more sympathy for Bolshevism, but they also seem to have suffered some disillusionment.

[1] Zechariah Chafee, jr., *Freedom of Speech* (N. Y., 1920), 107.

[2] "Albany's Ousted Socialists," *Literary Digest*, LXIV, 19-20 (Jan. 24, 1920) ; "The Socialists' Hour at Albany," *Literary Digest*, LXVII, 11 (Oct. 2, 1920).

[3] For the Ku Klux Klan and other manifestations of hypersensitive nationalism, see later, chap. xi.

on rather flimsy evidence the following year.[1] After a wait of seven years, during which the men sought in vain to get their case reheard in a higher court, they were executed in August, 1927. What gave the Sacco-Vanzetti case its special notoriety was the use of the radicalism of the accused as an argument by both friends and foes. Judge, jury and community were prejudiced against them from the start; radicals, equally prejudiced, decided that the whole charge of murder was merely a pretext to "railroad" inconvenient agitators. The evidence in the case was confused and contradictory; and even conservative-minded folk questioned whether the accused had received a fair trial. Under pressure of liberal opinion the governor of Massachusetts appointed a committee of three, among them President A. L. Lowell of Harvard University, who reported they saw no reason for advising the intervention of the pardoning power. As the day of the execution approached, bomb outrages took place in protest, not only in the United States but in distant foreign lands.[2] When the last appeal for stay of sentence was pending, huge crowds gathered in front of the American embassy at London and in front of American consulates at Plymouth and elsewhere to agitate in behalf of the accused.[3] In Latin Europe and in Latin America small riots occurred; Soviet Russia hon-

[1] Felix Frankfurter, The Case of Sacco and Vanzetti (Boston, 1927), is an acute analysis by a legal scholar. Upton Sinclair, Boston (N. Y., 1928), is a fictionized version.

[2] Jeannette Marks, Thirteen Days (N. Y., 1929), gives a sympathetic account of the last frantic efforts in Boston to stay the execution.

[3] The present writer witnessed the Plymouth gathering from the consulate. The crowd of about two hundred dock laborers and unemployed seemed moved by no special excitement, but merely to be "demonstrating" according to a prearranged program. After the execution these demonstrations ceased, though the still open question of the guilt or innocence of the accused continued to be debated by the periodical press of both continents. Friends of the men founded a monthly magazine, the Lantern, in Boston in 1928 to keep the issues presented by the case before the public.

ored them as martyrs. Even conservative newspapers in
Europe used the case as a convenient text for preach-
ments about the quality of American justice.

The dominant notes in the political life of the time
were conservatism and indifference. Evidences of the
former may be found in the already mentioned weakness of third-party movements, in the huge majorities
obtained by the Republican party in three successive elections, in the fact that both major parties consistently
nominated men who had the confidence of the world of
business, in the acceptance of the protective-tariff principle by the Democrats in 1928, and in the popular
favor accorded to very wealthy men in high political
office.[1] The genial standpatter Warren G. Harding, who
died in the midst of his term; Vice-President Calvin
Coolidge, close-mouthed, intent on economy, a typical
self-contained Vermonter, who succeeded him; and
the energetic apostle of science in business, Herbert
Hoover, represented an ascending scale of ability, but
all alike stood for what President Harding had termed
"normalcy."

The general indifference to politics was not altogether
a new phenomenon. No election after 1896 had brought
to the polls a very large proportion of the electorate.[2]
But 1920, when only about half of those eligible to vote
exercised their franchise, marked the nadir of interest
in American politics, and 1924, in spite of a vigorous
third-party fight by Robert M. La Follette, made but

---

[1] Andrew W. Mellon, secretary of the treasury; Charles G. Dawes,
vice-president during President Coolidge's elective term; Frank O. Lowden,
governor of Illinois, aspirant for the presidency and leader of the farm-
relief movement, were typical examples of the successful business man in
politics.
[2] In 1928, owing to the agitation of the prohibition question and
the outstanding personal popularity of both candidates, there was a temporary increase in the vote. For comment on that campaign, see chaps.
iv and ix.

little better showing. Several causes suggest themselves.[1]
There were no clearly defined issues in most of the contests, all party platforms being deliberately vague on the
most disputed points. The old party feeling of the Civil
War days had faded to a mere tradition, and in the
Lower South, with the virtual disfranchisement of the
Negro, a single-party system had made the section so
solid that, with the exception of 1928, the only real contests took place at the Democratic primaries. The grant
of woman suffrage increased the absolute but decreased
the relative vote since more women than men abstained
from going to the polls. But probably the most important factor was simply the pressure of competing interests. So engrossing was the complex life of business, and
so exacting the obligations of the life of pleasure, that
politics was no longer needed as a popular amusement or
topic of conversation.[2] The decline of politics is
curiously parallel to the contemporaneous decline of the
pulpit, and in both cases the fundamental cause seems
to have been simply that people in general preferred the
automobile and the movies to the affairs of church or
state.

One unfortunate effect of the popular apathy in politics was the absence of that eternal vigilance which is
the price of freedom from corruption as truly as from
tyranny. President Harding, weak, good-natured, over-
loyal to unworthy friends, was not the man to prevent
the birds of prey from hovering about the rich prizes of
the public treasury.[3] The plundering of the veterans'

[1] An excellent analysis may be found in "The Vanishing Voter," by
A. M. Schlesinger and E. M. Eriksson, New Republic, XL, 162-167
(Oct. 15, 1924).

[2] "A dynamic history of the period might give a volume or two to
the automobile and a foot-note to affairs of state." R. L. Duffus, "1900-
1925," Century, CIX (1925), 488.

[3] S. H. Adams, Revelry (N. Y., 1926), is a bitter but largely truthful
depiction of the Harding régime under a thin veil of fiction. Perhaps the

bureau by Colonel Forbes was but one of several major scandals in his brief administration.[1] Attorney-General Harry M. Daugherty, chosen rather because of his part in securing Mr. Harding's nomination than because of any legal eminence, made the department of justice a whispering gallery of sinister rumor, and was finally dismissed in March, 1924, by President Coolidge for obstructing the investigation of his department. One of Mr. Daugherty's business associates, Thomas W. Miller, alien-property custodian, was convicted in 1927 of conspiracy to defraud the government in the transactions of the American Metal Company. The election of three Republican senators—Truman H. Newberry of Michigan in 1918, Frank L. Smith of Illinois in 1926, and William S. Vare of Pennsylvania in the same year—was challenged on the ground of excessive or illegal campaign expenditures.

But the scandal which far outreached all others in the publicity which it received as well as in the important public interests involved concerned the disposal of the national oil reserves.[2] Reserve No. 1, at Elk Hills, California, was created in 1912, and Reserve No. 3, at Teapot Dome, Wyoming, in 1915. In May, 1921, only a few months after assuming office, Secretary Edwin Denby of the navy department transferred the administration of the oil reserves to the department of the interior. In charge of the latter was Albert B. Fall, ex-senator from New Mexico, a throwback to an early American type of pioneer-politician, who affected a cowboy pose and a fine contempt for reformers and conservationists. In 1922 Secretary Fall, secretly and without

best estimate of the period is by W. A. White, *Masks in a Pageant* (N. Y., 1928), 389-434.

[1] See earlier, p. 77.
[2] See M. E. Ravage, *Teapot Dome* (N. Y., 1924), and contemporary newspapers and magazines.

securing competitive bids, leased the Teapot Dome reserve to Harry F. Sinclair and the Elk Hills reserve to Edward L. Doheny. The pretext for the leases was that they were on terms advantageous to the government, that oil stored in the reserves was being lost by leakage, and that in the case of a naval emergency, such as a war with Japan, a little oil stored in available tanks would be more useful than undeveloped reserves buried in the middle of the continent.

A senatorial investigation begun by Senator Thomas J. Walsh of Montana disclosed a more sinister state of affairs than the most suspicious had expected. It was revealed that Sinclair had contributed heavily to the campaign expenses of the party in power, that in 1921 Doheny had personally "loaned" Secretary Fall one hundred thousand dollars without interest or security, and that elaborate precautions had been taken and several false tales told to hush up the whole of these transactions. The government, at last stirred to action, appointed ex-Senator Atlee Pomerene and Owen J. Roberts as special counsel to represent the national interests. The civil suits for cancellation of the oil leases were carried from court to court and finally, in 1927, the Supreme Court voided both the Elk Hills and Teapot Dome concessions as legally invalid and permeated with fraud and corruption. The criminal suits undertaken by the government were less successful. Both Doheny and Sinclair were acquitted on jury trial from charges of conspiracy,[1] but Fall was convicted in October, 1929, and sentenced to a year's imprisonment for accepting a bribe. Even the oil scandals seem to have had but little effect in weakening the party in power or strengthening the

[1] A new scandal arose from these trials when Sinclair was found to have caused jurors in his case to be shadowed by spies from the W. J. Burns detective agency. In 1929, Sinclair, many times a millionaire, served a sentence in a Washington jail for contempt of court.

Many Americans worried by domestic concerns hesitated to add responsibilities abroad;

As Sacco and Vanzetti were carried to their graves many felt that intolerance had triumphed.

The Aftermath of War

opposition, though within the Republican ranks they probably did something to discredit the "Old Guard" of professional politicians.

Private crimes attracted more attention from press and public than national scandals. No topic was more common in news and editorial columns than the "crime wave." And yet it remains an open question whether there was a crime wave, in the sense of an absolute increase in the total volume of law violation. Statistics were in such confused and unreliable condition that criminologists waged inconclusive war as to whether felonies were really becoming more common or merely remaining at their normal high American level.[1] A comparison of the homicide (murder and manslaughter) rate for the period 1914-1918 and the five following years (1919-1923) shows but little change.[2] What even the incomplete and partial statistics available demonstrate beyond dispute is the permanently low standard of public security in the United States as compared with any other country of comparable general civilization.

According to Dr. Frederick L. Hoffman, statistician of the Prudential Insurance Company, the homicide rate

[1] "There are no reliable records of the number of crimes, murders or otherwise, committed in the United States. The National Crime Commission is now working on a plan for the gathering of simple statistics throughout the country." Letter of Mr. Louis Howe of the National Crime Commission to the writer, July 23, 1928. See also F. L. Hoffman, "Murder and the Death Penalty," *Current History*, XXVIII (1928), 408-410.

[2] Average homicide rate for the registration area of the census: 1914-1918, 7.2 per hundred thousand; 1919-1923, 7.92 per hundred thousand. If the white population alone be considered, the increase is less marked and would be eliminated if the low rate of 1918 (when so much of the nation was under military discipline) be omitted. The census-bureau estimates of relatively little change are confirmed from other sources. Figures compiled by the Metropolitan Life Insurance Company for the year 1926 showed a decreased homicide rate as compared with 1923, 1924 and 1925 but "a slightly upward tendency" for the whole period 1911-1926 apart from slight annual fluctuations. See Metropolitan Life Insurance Company, *Statistical Bull.*, VII, no. 12, 1.

of the United States was sixteen times that of England and Wales.[1] The single city of Chicago had for several years a longer list of killings than all England; other great cities averaged about as badly. The highest death toll in proportion to population was in such states as Florida, Louisiana, Tennessee, Mississippi and Georgia, and may in part be explained by the large Negro population; but even orderly Massachusetts had a dozen times the homicide rate of Scotland in 1923. Hot-tempered Italy had only half the American murder rate; sedate Switzerland one thirty-sixth. Nor is it possible to lay the blame wholly on the pioneer and protest that in a "new country" like the United States frontier tradition prompts a ready resort to self-help and pistol law. Canada and Australia, too, were pioneer countries, but in proportion to population they had about one murder to the American five.

The typical American slayer was also a robber. In spite of the publicity given by the yellow press to crimes of passion, there is no reason to suppose that jealousy and malice were any commoner in the United States than in other countries. The real problem was the professional bandit who killed with the sole motive of overcoming resistance or of removing a witness to his theft. Indeed, the American robbery record was relatively much worse than the American homicide record. Burglary-insurance rates in American cities were from fifteen to twenty times as high as in England,[2] and foreign writers often commented on the shock it gave them to see money moved through the city streets in armored cars as though passing through a hostile army. "Every day," said an American criminologist,

[1] N. Y. Times, Nov. 28, 1925. For a detailed comparison of American and European conditions, very little flattering to American vanity, see R. B. Fosdick, American Police Systems (N. Y., 1920).

[2] Fosdick, American Police Systems, 17.

the observer can see an armored car draw up in front of a bank in the financial district. An armed guard jumps off, places his hand on a large pistol in a holster strapped to his side, and stations himself at the bank entrance; another man steps out of the car and, with his hand on a pistol, takes his post at the rear of the car; while a third man with his hand on his pistol steps out with the bag of money or other valuables and hurries into the bank. It is not merely in New York that this is to be seen, but in all our large cities.[1]

Year by year, New York, Chicago, St. Louis, Detroit and even smaller cities showed each a greater number of reported robberies than all Great Britain. William B. Joyce, chairman of the National Surety Company, estimated the annual amount stolen in the United States by burglars and robbers at two hundred and fifty million dollars, and the grand total loss from theft, fraud, forgery, swindling and other financial misdeeds at three billion dollars. Unlike most crimes, robbery seemed to be on the increase [2] and was certainly bolder and more contemptuous of the palsied arm of the law. Jewelry stores, banks and restaurants were held up even in broad daylight, the automobile affording a safe and sure escape.

There were fashions in crime. George W. Kirchwey, an eminent criminologist from New York, thought that general criminality was decreasing, but that there had been a small rise in homicides and a greater increase in robberies. It was "this new style banditry that has created the illusion of a general crime wave. . . . The high-power motor car . . . has also given us the ban-

---

[1] Lawrence Veiller, "The Rising Tide of Crime," *World's Work*, LI (1925), 134.

[2] Premiums paid on account of burglary insurance amounted in 1914 to $1,377,000, and in 1924 to $26,513,000; and losses increased in the same period from $508,000 to $11,812,000. F. L. Hoffman, "The Increase in Murder," Am. Acad. of Polit. and Social Sci., *Annals*, CXXV, no. 214, 21.

dit, with his automatic gun and his easy get-away in place of the old-time footpad. Prohibition, with however much of good to its credit, has incidentally endowed us with the hip pocket flask and the machine gun warfare of rival gangs of bootleg brigands." [1] Most robberies were committed at the revolver's point, about three fourths of all murders being due to this weapon.[2] Machine guns were sometimes employed, there being in most states practically no restriction on the private manufacture and sale of even the deadliest weapons.

Deliberate, as distinguished from incidental, assassinations were most commonly the work of professional gunmen equipped with automobiles and shotguns. The usual procedure was to mark the intended victim's movements and have a car with closed window blinds cross his path at the determined moment. The gunman, sitting at ease in the car with the muzzle of his sawed-off shotgun resting on the window ledge, would suddenly fire point-blank at his target and then drive his automobile into the swirl of metropolitan traffic. He was generally a stranger to the neighborhood, to his victim, and even to his employer, and thus trebly hard to trace. "New York may send to Chicago or Detroit, both recognized centers of the murder industry, for experienced men to 'bump off' an enemy in New York, and this city may extend a similar courtesy when Chicago or Detroit has an assassination on hand." [3] Usually a new motor car was stolen and every provision made for the get-away.[4]

Perhaps the most novel and characteristic develop-

[1] G. W. Kirchwey, "What Makes Criminals," *Current History*, XXVII (1927), 316-317.
[2] Marcus Kavanagh, *The Criminal and His Allies* (Indianapolis, 1928), 350-351. 450,000 revolvers were sold in the single year 1921.
[3] R. L. Duffus, "The Gunman Has an Intercity Murder Trade," *N. Y. Times*, July 8, 1928.
[4] In 1926 there were over 12,000 automobiles stolen in Chicago alone. Kavanagh, *The Criminal and His Allies*, 350.

ment in American crime during the period was "the
racket game." This was a form of commercial black-
mail under threat of violence. Under Mayor William H.
Thompson's rather lax administration it was estimated
that there were fifty major and one hundred and fifty
minor rackets in Chicago.[1] The racketeer, to take one
illustration, would establish a garage-owners' association
and all garage owners would be invited to join at a fixed
fee. If an owner ventured to refuse, the gang, known
jocularly as the "educational committee," would force
their way into the garage, "indulge in an orgy of glass
smashing and rubber slicing and leave the owner to
settle with his patrons. After this, if he had any money
left, and any judgment, the owner, even though not a
crook himself, would always come across." Similar rackets were worked in the fish business, trucking, the dairies,
the window-cleaning business, the laundries, the building trades, and many other small retail trades, even certain branches of the professions. Nor was racketeering
confined to Chicago, though it seems to have flourished
there with exceptional impunity. A Kansas City grand
jury investigated in 1928 a series of bombings, extending over three previous years, designed to frighten independent, or nonunion, builders, painters, teamsters,
cleaners and dyers out of business.[2]

Whether the postwar "crime wave" meant a real increase in lawlessness or merely a shift to newer forms of
it, the public was much disturbed. Crime commissions
were founded in many states. "At the present time," declared an authority on the subject, "they may be said to
be epidemic in the United States. . . . They differ
from such bodies as the American Prison Association,

[1] O. P. White, "Looting the Loop," *Collier's*, LXXXI, 10 (May 12,
1928). See also on racketeering John Gunther, "The High Cost of Hood-
lums," *Harper's Mag.*, CLIX (1929), 529-540.
[2] *N. Y. Times*, Nov. 4, 1928.

the National Probation Association, the American Institute of Criminal Law and Criminology in being expressions of what may be called the 'amateur spirit' in the field of criminology." [1] Lawyers and business men were their chief backers. Perhaps the most scientific of all the new bodies was the National Crime Commission, organized in 1925 as a fact-finding body. The surveys and studies of the crime situation, though they led to different recommendations, disclosed an appalling degree of incompetence in both police and courts. The careful survey made by the Missouri Association for Criminal Justice, to take an instance typical rather than exceptional, showed that for each hundred felonies there were only seven arrests and less than five indictments.[2] And the New York State Crime Commission disclosed that of more than twenty-five thousand prosecutions for felonies in 1925 less than twenty per cent resulted in any punishment.[3]

There was leakage of justice at every point. The criminal might evade arrest owing to the inefficiency of the police, or escape while on bail, or have his case postponed by ingenious legal expedients until the most important witnesses could no longer be found; he might have an appeal taken on some purely technical point and judgment reversed,[4] or be freed on the plea of some newly invented type of insanity, to which plea the courts gave the most amazing latitude, or, if convicted and sent to prison, use political influence to secure a speedy re-

[1] C. E. Gehlke, "Crime," *Am. Journ. of Sociology*, XXXIV, 164.
[2] Kirchwey, "What Makes Criminals," 318.
[3] John Knight, "Difficulties in Enforcing Criminal Law," *Current History*, XXVII (1927), 325. In 1929 President Hoover appointed a commission to study the whole problem of law enforcement.
[4] Kavanagh, *The Criminal and His Allies*, gives in chap. xiii more than fifty cases, from all parts of the Union, where judgment was reversed on such grounds as words omitted or misspelled in the indictment or similar purely formal errors.

lease on parole or full pardon. Governor Cole Blease of South Carolina (1911-1915) granted fifteen hundred pardons and paroles when in office,[1] and a similar record was made in Texas by Mrs. James E. Ferguson, the first woman governor of that state. In pure despair at obtaining justice from the courts, some men protected their property by private watchmen, or vigilance committees, or "horse-thief associations," or the Ku Klux Klan. More commonly they offered rewards "dead or alive." The Milwaukee clearing-house banks placed a full-page advertisement in the *Milwaukee Sentinel* for September 23, 1925, offering twenty-five hundred dollars to any officer "who shall hereafter lawfully kill any person in the act of robbing or attempting to rob this bank" provided the killing took place while resisting the robbery or effecting the arrest of the robbers.[2] The police were inclined also to shoot bandits at sight rather than risk court acquittals, and in the street battles between bandits and police the former seem to have suffered the heavier mortality.[3]

There was a tendency to stiffen the laws themselves and to improve court procedure. As a reaction against the lenience of the criminal law, New York's new code (the Baumes law, 1926) made the fourth felony punishable by a mandatory life sentence. Many other states followed this example, and there was no little stir in Michigan when it was discovered that under the literal interpretation of the law a person four times found guilty of making or selling unlawful liquor would be forced to spend the rest of his life within prison walls. The issue of capital punishment was widely debated

[1] W. J. Robertson, *The Advancing South* (N. Y., 1927), 195.
[2] Reprinted in *World's Work*, LI (1926), 502.
[3] Lin Bonner, "Killing Killers," *Liberty*, V, no. 3 (Jan. 21, 1928), gives some statistics on this point for 1926 and 1927.

and attempts made to reintroduce it where it had been abandoned.

One of the questions raised by inquiry into the cause and cure of the great American disease of lawlessness was whether the law was not attempting too much. As Rudyard Kipling had long since pointed out, the American seemed under a twofold compulsion, "to flout the law he makes" and again "to make the law he flouts." There was no diminution in the traditional cry, "pass a law about it," whenever a supposed evil was discovered. According to Silas H. Strawn, president of the American Bar Association, "It is not unlikely that even more than ten million laws and ordinances are theoretically in effect on our statute books and we are adding to the number at a rate of 200,000 new laws and ordinances a year." [1] Of course most of these laws and ordinances were merely special appropriations or the like,[2] but one investigator discovered that in a typical American town the police were expected to be familiar with and enforce thirty thousand state, federal or local enactments. The National Industrial Council announced that in 1925 state legislatures had considered over forty thousand bills and enacted over thirteen thousand of them into law.[3]

Perhaps the most serious result of this overburdening of the police and the courts with trivialities was that no serious pretense was made of enforcing a general system of law all the time. Instead, enforcement was divided into special periods—"raids" or "drives" against a par-

[1] W. S. Dutton, "You Look 'Em Over and You Obey Your Choice," *Am. Mag.*, CVI (1928), 52. See also L. M. Hussey, "Twenty-Four Hours of a Lawbreaker," *Harper's Mag.*, CLX (1930), 436-439.

[2] In Kansas one legislature passed 347 laws, but of these the great majority were appropriations, or rules for managing state institutions, or taxing, bonding and salary regulations. Only six were inhibitory on the ordinary citizen, and all of these were amendments of existing laws. J. S. Dean, "The Meaning of 'Democracy,' " *North Am. Rev.*, CCXXVI (1928), 177.

[3] *N. Y. Times*, Nov. 30, 1925.

ticular abuse, such as gambling, prostitution, the sale of intoxicants, or the violation of Sunday-closing laws. The papers would give due notice that on or after a particular date the police had determined to close up establishments which had been open in violation of law, with apparently no blush at the implied confession that the law had hitherto been ignored. In a similar spirit, the police would announce a "dead-line" around the financial district of a great city and treat with particular severity any outlaw found within it, as though confessing it were utopian to hope to repress robbery over a whole city's extent.

In one respect American criminal jurisprudence showed a real improvement. The prison system, still bad enough in many states, was greatly reformed. The efforts of such penologists as Thomas Mott Osborne, George W. Kirchwey, Frank Tannenbaum and others to substitute productive labor and healthful recreation for idleness met wide response, and the indeterminate sentence and the parole system—though both were greatly abused—at least placed a premium on good conduct during imprisonment.[1] Children's courts created a new technique in handling the offenses of the very young. As we shall see, several Southern states abolished the evil custom of leasing out convict labor to private employers. In the larger cities psychological clinics were established to discover the quirks of personality that made a man a wolf to his fellows.[2] Dr. L. Vernon Briggs of Boston fathered a law providing for psychiatric examination of persons indicted for capital offenses or repeated felonies. He de-

[1] H. E. Barnes, *The Repression of Crime* (N. Y., 1926), chap. v; T. M. Osborne, *Prisons and Common Sense* (Phila., 1924).

[2] S. S. Glueck, *Mental Disorder and the Criminal Law* (Boston, 1925), analyzes the existing legislation, legal practice and court decisions with respect to the question of irresponsibility in criminal cases because of alleged insanity.

clared to the National Conference on the Reduction of Crime, held in Washington in 1927, that "Before this law was passed the procedure employed in ascertaining the mental responsibility of persons accused of crime was almost inconceivably futile, cruel and wasteful. Hardly a day passed . . . without the spectacle in some one of our courts, of two or more physicians, possibly graduates of the same medical school and belonging to the same scientific and medical societies, pitted against each other, testifying to diametrically opposite opinions as to the mental conditions and responsibility of the person in question." [1]

A discussion of crimes of violence in the America of the period permits at least two cheerful postscripts. In spite of race riots and Ku Klux Klan activities there was a great decrease in the number of lynchings. [2] And the same statistical surveys that revealed a constant high level of homicides disclosed also a marked decline in suicides. The death rate from suicide, according to the life-insurance estimates, showed a decrease for all age groups for the whole period 1909-1924, especially at the younger ages. [3] Americans were learning to place a proper value on life—when it was their own!

[1] Watson Davis, "The Nation-Wide Campaign to Reduce Crime," *Current History*, XXVII (1927), 304. Colorado adopted a similar law in 1927. See also Malcolm Logan, "Demobilizing the Alienists," *North Am. Rev.*, CCXXVII (1929), 117-121.

[2] See later, chap. ix.

[3] Metropolitan Life Insurance Company, *Statistical Bull.*, VIII, no. 8, 1.

CHAPTER IV

THE EXPERIMENT OF PROHIBITION

OF all the social experiments made by the American people in the wake of the World War the most radical was the attempt to prohibit the production and sale of alcoholic drinks. But drastic as was the national law, it had behind it more than a century of agitation, controversy and local legislation.[1] So far from being merely a product of sudden impulse and war-fed emotion it was the final stage of a long process of restriction. By 1914 Maine, Kansas, North Dakota, Oklahoma, Georgia, Mississippi, North Carolina, Tennessee and West Virginia had adopted prohibition, and the autumn elections of that year added Virginia, Arizona, Colorado, Oregon and Washington. Together with territory in other states "dry" by local option, nearly half (forty-seven per cent) of the population and three fourths (seventy-four per cent) of the area of the United States had outlawed the saloon. In most parts of the country only the great cities and mill towns remained "wet"; the single city of Chicago had more saloons than all the states of the South.[2]

During the next four years the number of total prohibition states more than doubled.[3] Other restrictions,

[1] For the beginnings of the prohibitory movement, see C. R. Fish, *The Rise of the Common Man* (*A History of American Life*, VI), 260-268; and J. A. Krout, *The Origins of Prohibition* (N. Y., 1925).

[2] W. E. Lanphear, "Progress toward Ending the Saloon," *Independent*, LXXX, 349 (Dec. 7, 1914).

[3] Arkansas, Idaho, Iowa, South Carolina, Alabama (1915); Michigan, Montana, Nebraska, South Dakota (1916); Indiana, New Hampshire, New Mexico, Utah (1917); Wyoming, Florida, Ohio, Nevada,

due to the entrance of the United States into the war, still further limited the liquor traffic. One powerful argument was that it was unpatriotic to convert foodstuffs into distilled or fermented beverages at a moment when the nation was voluntarily rationing itself to send grain to Europe. In 1917 Congress restricted the use of foodstuffs in liquor manufacture and in 1918 prohibited altogether the war-time sale or manufacture of intoxicants.[1] The fact that some large brewers had been incautiously friendly to the German cause contributed to the prejudice against the trade.[2] Another influence of the war was the attempt to keep liquor away from the training camps and the shipping yards.

When national prohibition was at last established over two thirds of the American people already lived under local prohibitory laws, and the other third had submitted to drastic war-time regulation.[3] The return of peace brought no alleviation. Before the temporary war legislation could be repealed, the adoption of the Eighteenth Amendment to the Constitution put the whole traffic outside the pale of the law.

Constitutional prohibition was approved by the Senate and by the House of Representatives in 1917. The proposed Eighteenth Amendment forbade "the manufacture, sale or transportation of intoxicating liquors" for beverage purposes, gave to Congress and the states the concurrent power to enact enforcement laws, and con-

Texas (1918). The Webb-Kenyon act of 1913 had protected state-wide prohibition by prohibiting the shipment of liquor into states which forbade its sale.

[1] *U. S. Statutes at Large*, XL, pt. i, 282, 1046-1047. This was to go into effect July 1, 1919.

[2] See Justin Steuart, *Wayne Wheeler, Dry Boss* (N. Y., 1928), chap. vii.

[3] 68.3 per cent of the population and 95.4 per cent of the area of the nation were dry by state law or local regulation. See T. N. Carver, "The Greatest Social Experiment of Modern Times," F. H. Hooper, ed., *These Eventful Years* (N. Y., 1924), II, 584-585.

tained the unusual provision that the amendment would be inoperative unless ratified by the necessary number of states within seven years.[1] The legislatures of forty-six states acted favorably, only Connecticut and Rhode Island holding out to the end. In the legislatures of South Dakota, Idaho, Washington, Kansas and Wyoming the vote was unanimous. By January, 1919, when thirty-six states had approved the amendment, it became a part of the Constitution.

In accordance with its terms national prohibition went into effect a year later in January, 1920. Congress passed over President Wilson's veto the Volstead act (named after the Minnesota congressman to whom fell the duty of framing the enforcement statute), which defined as "intoxicating" liquor containing as much as one two-hundredth part of alcohol[2] and provided machinery for stringent enforcement. The sale of alcoholic liquor was still permitted for industrial, medicinal and sacramental purposes, and elaborate licensing restrictions proved necessary to insure that none of it was diverted to beverage purposes. A prohibition-enforcement unit, at first organized as part of the bureau of internal revenue under the treasury department, was established with the double duty of regulating the legitimate use of alcohol and of preventing violations of the law.[3]

[1] Ordinarily a constitutional amendment approved by Congress is before the country indefinitely and may be ratified by the legislatures at any subsequent time. Many people desired to limit the period of agitation for the prohibition amendment.

[2] U. S. Statutes at Large, XLI, pt. i, 305-323. The half-of-one-percent standard was older than the Volstead act, being the definition line, for revenue purposes, of the bureau of internal revenue for fermented liquor.

[3] No compensation was granted to saloon keepers for their loss of business. This was the rule in American laws as distinguished from British local-option laws. When the present writer questioned Wayne B. Wheeler, general counsel for the Anti-Saloon League, on this point, Mr. Wheeler explained that in England a license was considered as part of the property of the public-house keeper; in the United States as merely a permit to trade, granting legal "immunity from prosecution" for a limited term

Four factors, aside from the temporary influence of the war, seem to have been particularly effective in bringing about national prohibition. First, and most important, the spread of state prohibition had already made prohibition almost national, so that it was but a short step (though a daring one) from prohibition by state law to prohibition by federal authority. Next, there was the crystallizing conviction of the South that the race problem was made more grave by the liquor problem. Then the automobile, now becoming almost universal, was a factor. Finally, Congress and the legislatures were increasingly dominated by an energetic and resourceful "pressure group," the Anti-Saloon League.

The attitude of the South is unmistakable. Nearly the whole section was dry by state law before the federal amendment was proposed, and the Southern states, in spite of traditional state-rights scruples, were among the first to approve the Eighteenth Amendment and the staunchest in supporting it against later attack. In part, this may be explained by the predominantly rural character of the South, as the great cities were always the centers of opposition to prohibitory laws; in part, also, by the absence of European immigrant colonies to whom wine and beer were as much a matter of course as milk and water. But undoubtedly the major factor was the widespread conviction that to the Negro, as to the Indian, alcohol was a perilous incitement to crimes of violence.

It was not merely by chance that the age of machinery was also the age of prohibition. Railroad and factory managers found themselves forced to impose teetotalism

and under whatever restrictions the public authorities might impose. Perhaps there is a remote analogy in the fact that Great Britain granted, and the United States refused to grant, compensation to slave owners when slavery was abolished within their respective dominions.

on their employees to forfend accidents.[1] And the growing popularity of the automobile carried with it a well-grounded fear of the drunken driver; Henry Ford admitted that his cheap and popular cars were among the factors which banished the saloon. "Everything in the United States is keyed up to a new pace," he said. "The speed at which we run our motor cars, operate our intricate machinery, and generally live would be impossible with liquor. No, there is no chance of even modification."[2] In other words, having to choose between two luxuries, the intoxication of speed and the intoxication of drink, the majority preferred the former.

The final impetus needed to carry the Eighteenth Amendment was supplied by the Anti-Saloon League. Founded in 1893 and two years later given national scope, this League was only one of many "pressure groups" which used political means to obtain legislative ends but preferred to work through the existing political parties rather than form an independent one.[3] Their importance in American political life can hardly be overstated. It is not cynical to say that the two great political parties in the United States at this period, the Republican and Democratic, were organizations hunting for popular issues rather than organizations formed to make their issues popular. Until 1916 neither party had nationally committed itself to equal suffrage; until 1920,

---

[1] "Take the open hearth (steel process) as an illustration. When the loading of a furnace was carried on by wheelbarrow, a mistake made by the worker meant no real damage either to human life or property. With the mechanical loader how different the situation! A mistake may mean the death of several workers, a smashed furnace, a broken machine, and seriously interrupted production." Charles Reitell, "Men, Machinery and Alcoholic Drink," Am. Acad. of Polit. and Social Sci., *Annals*, CIX, 102-109.

[2] *N. Y. Times*, Aug. 18, 1928.

[3] For the best account of this aspect of the prohibition fight, see Peter Odegard, *Pressure Politics: The Story of the Anti-Saloon League* (N. Y., 1928).

and then only in the rather negative form of favoring "enforcement," neither party championed constitutional prohibition. The restriction of immigration, the grant of farm relief, the eight-hour day on the railroads, and nearly all other important public acts of the time were policies brought forward by special nonpartisan groups and adopted by the great parties only after they had proved their popularity.[1] Such diverse organizations as the Farmers' Nonpartisan League, the American Federation of Labor, the Chambers of Commerce, the League of Women Voters, the American Legion, the League of Nations Non-Partisan Association and the war-time organizations for pacifism, patriotism or preparedness, exerted considerable pressure on the state and national party machines. Each represented a block of voters, sensitive to certain issues that affected their interests or ideals, whose support would be valuable in a close election. Third parties, on the contrary, were rarely of importance, not even the Prohibition party which had campaigned continuously for a generation and, strangely enough, continued to put forth a national ticket each four years even after prohibition had become the law of the land.

The politics of the Anti-Saloon League differed from that of other temperance and prohibition societies in being severely practical and realistic. As early as 1914 it was generally admitted that "there are no shrewder politicians in America than the veteran leaders of the Anti-

[1] In 1923 Wayne B. Wheeler claimed that "To pressure groups we owe nearly all important legislation of the past century. Among other results of pressure group methods may be cited the common public school system, commission managerial government of cities, woman's suffrage, the rural delivery of mail, postal savings, parcel post, child labor restrictions, railroad regulations, federal income tax, popular election of senators, the initiative and referendum, immigration control, the Federal Reserve banking system, and the national prohibition of the beverage liquor traffic." Steuart, *Wayne Wheeler, Dry Boss*, 211. See also A. M. Schlesinger, *New Viewpoints in American History* (N. Y., 1922), 281.

Saloon League." [1] Their very name was an ingenious political device, for many Americans who were by no means prohibitionist had a fastidious repugnance for the social and political life which gathered round the corner saloon. The League tied itself to no party, threw its strength against any "wet" candidate, whether Republican or Democratic, and was even willing to support a candidate who drank but would vote for prohibition against a teetotaler who opposed prohibition. It welcomed converts, "brands from the burning," and hostile politicians who had changed their votes because of the demonstrated power of the League. Very cleverly Mr. Wheeler, the general counsel of the League, would publish the list of congressional candidates who had the League's indorsement and challenge the antiprohibitionist organizations (for "pressure politics" existed on both sides of the issue) to do likewise. Then the League would concentrate on the defeat of the "wet list" unless the individuals on it would repudiate the indorsement of the antiprohibitionists—as they frequently did. The same realism was extended to measures as to men. The Anti-Saloon League often threw its influence against extreme proposals likely to divide the ranks of the drys or offered in bad faith by the opposition. Of course, even the shrewdest manipulation of the League's voting strength would have been futile if the votes had not been so numerous that the politicians dared not disregard them. Without an enormous credit of popular support to draw on, including the rural districts of the South and West, the women's vote and the evangelical churches, the League could never have proved to the old

---

[1] "The League has always laid stress upon concrete results rather than merely upon ideals. It has thought it wise to take a half loaf where it could not get a whole one—a crumb, even, if there was no more to be had." F. C. Lockwood, "The Militant Anti-Saloon League," *Independent*, LXXVIII, 524 (June 22, 1914).

parties that it could "deliver the goods." Opponents of
the League usually met defeat by underestimating this
background of public sentiment.[1]

Unlike many prohibitionists, the Anti-Saloon League
did not declare a holiday with the enactment of the
Eighteenth Amendment and the Volstead law. General
Counsel Wayne B. Wheeler declared, "I haven't been
fighting for any prohibition amendment. I've been fighting for prohibition."[2] The League was more than ever
in politics now, with the aim of securing adequate enforcement laws and appropriations and the appointment
of officials agreeable to its views. This task was a much
greater one than the mere securing of the prohibition
amendment. To a large section of the American people
a law was a public New Year's resolution to be enacted
in a glow of moral enthusiasm, observed for a short
period, and then forgotten.[3] Anyone who had watched
whole families happily picnicking around a keep-off-
the-grass notice or riding in automobiles at forty miles
an hour past fifteen-miles-an-hour-speed-limit signs

[1] The growth of this sentiment in the old Yankee American stock,
especially in the West, is well described by Martha Bruère: "that trek that
brought one generation of steady ale and rum drinkers to the New England
coast . . . sent their children up to Vermont and New Hampshire and
the hard cider country; brought the next generation down again to western New York and Pennsylvania to an easier life, the beginning of temperance talk, 'Ten Nights in a Bar-room' as a refined entertainment in
the farm villages; sent their children on again into the Mississippi valley
to find food in such prodigal plenty as civilized man had never met before
and the growing sentiment that alcohol was the devil's servant; on again
to the Northwest—five generations from Europe to Oregon. . . . This
group has experimented with the liquor traffic by local option and state
control, by fines and blacklists, has come from dry to wet and back again,
and by the long, slow, costly method of trial and error found what is
right in the sight of its own eyes—prohibition." Martha B. Bruère,
Does Prohibition Work? (N. Y., 1927), 53-54.
[2] Steuart, *Wayne Wheeler, Dry Boss*, 168.
[3] Of course the liquor trade in license and local-option days had presented a similar enforcement problem. According to George S. Hobart,
2413 liquor dealers in the single state of New Jersey paid the federal tax
in 1915 without holding any state license. Am. Acad. of Polit. and
Social Sci., *Annals*, CIX, 86-87.

could hardly expect the thirsty minority to accept the new régime with Prussian docility. The saloons as such went out of business and stayed out; many of their former proprietors became restaurant keepers or ran soda fountains.[1] But a market remained for strong drink, and a new outlawed but sometimes prosperous trade sprang into existence to supply it.

The prohibition-enforcement unit employed nearly four thousand men during the first two years of the Harding administration. In less than two years (1921-1923) the federal government instituted 3500 civil and 65,760 criminal actions, winning 2314 of the former and 43,905 of the latter.[2] State enforcement was of little aid to the federal authorities. Some dry states rested on their oars, believing that what was now a national law had become a federal responsibility; and some of the wet states, notably New York, repealed their enforcement codes as a protest against there being any federal law at all.

The enormous prizes for the successful outlaw made it worth his while to bribe heavily the state and federal agents whose business it was to enforce the law. A legal authority, himself favorable to prohibition, admitted that

> Local enforcement is with very rare exceptions very insincere. . . . It is nothing unusual to find that the sheriff was himself a bootlegger or in quiet partnership with those who were. . . . Judges impose a light fine on some bootlegger brought before them for sentence and

[1] An investigation in Sioux Falls, South Dakota, showed that of twenty-two former saloon keepers and bartenders in that city, seventeen were still at work in other trades there: real-estate men, packing-house employees, a laborer, a waiter, an autioneer, a janitor, a baker, a summer-resort owner, a truck farmer, a butcher, a grocer, a salesman and a club secretary. Bruère, *Does Prohibition Work?*, 20.

[2] R. A. Haynes, *Prohibition Inside Out* (N. Y., 1923), 275.

then retire to their chambers to drink the liquor which
the same bootlegger has sold to them.[1]

In the federal prohibition unit nearly ten per cent of
those who served were dismissed for malfeasance in office.
Gradually, however, the worst offenders were rooted out
and stricter civil-service rules adopted regarding appointments. Yet excess of zeal by some prohibition
agents brought almost as much discredit on the law as
the dishonesty of others. Citizens whose houses were
searched without warrant or whose automobiles were
stopped by night on the suspicion of being rum runners complained that prohibition was taking from them
not one personal liberty but all.

The variety of ways in which the Volstead act might
be evaded or broken was enormous. To mention only
the more important channels, beverage alcohol reached
the consumer in the following ways: the redistillation
of industrial alcohol and its sale by professional "bootleggers"; the misuse of permits for making or using industrial alcohol; private manufacture—"homebrewing"
and the old-fashioned "moonshining"; the misuse of
druggists' prescriptions; smuggling from Canada, Mexico, the West Indies and Europe; smuggling from ships
stationed just outside the territorial waters of the United
States—the famous "rum row"; the use and sale of old
private stocks safely cellared before the dry law was
enacted; and the manufacture and sale of "near beer"
and other "temperance drinks" which secretly over-
stepped the legal half of one per cent of alcohol. By far
the most important of these methods, quantitatively,
was the redistillation of industrial alcohol to purify it of

[1] Albert Levitt, "Prohibition after Eight Years," *Current History,*
XXVIII (1928), 10-11. This article in particular and eight others in the
same symposium give the various current estimates as to the extent of
enforcement for the whole period 1920-1928.

denaturants. Expert authorities usually estimated that more than half of the consumer's alcohol drunk in the United States under prohibition was obtained through this channel.[1]

Amateur homebrewing attracted many at first because of its spice of adventure. In many of the larger cities shops openly sold copper stills together with yeast, hops and other accessories.[2] They dared not quite advertise the purposes for which these commodities—legal enough in themselves—were sold, but they could drop carefully veiled hints, even going so far as to depict in a street-car advertisement a procession of thirsty camels crossing a desert.[3] Where women used to exchange old family recipes for cakes and puddings, men now met in locker rooms at the country club or in "conference" in business offices to exchange recipes for homemade beer and whisky. There was also an expansion of the moonshine industry in the rural districts, originally an attempt to evade revenue laws.[4] Yet the homebrewer in the city and the moonshiner in his lonely cabin were but minor factors in the situation. Consumers preferred to trust the professional bootlegger who with unblushing effrontery represented his redistilled product as "genuine pre-war stuff"—a famous Scotch whisky or a fine French or Rhenish wine.

Though the proportion of genuine European stock

[1] Irving Fisher, *Prohibition at Its Worst* (N. Y., 1926), 42, 44.

[2] For an account of the homebrewing industry at its height, see J. T. Flynn, "Home, Sweet Home-Brew," *Collier's*, LXXXII, no. 9 (Sept. 1, 1928).

[3] The writer has seen this advertisement in Washington, D. C.; and in Detroit the shop sign, "Malt and Hops. Try Ours for Better Results." Though the desired "results" could not be legally stated every passer-by knew what was meant.

[4] A policeman in a Virginia city said, "White men used to get rich selling whisky to Negroes, but in these days the Negroes are getting rich selling whisky to white men." R. L. Hartt, "Prohibition as It Is," *World's Work*, XLIX (1925), 511-512.

available was very small, the liquor smuggled from abroad was in itself a considerable amount. An exact estimate is impossible, as lawbreakers do not keep statistics of their operations, but one can conclude much from the figures of shipment of spirituous liquors to countries neighboring the United States. From 1918 to 1922 Canada increased her British liquor imports almost sixfold; Mexico, eightfold; and the British West Indies not quite fivefold. Most remarkable of all was the increased importation of the Bahamas from less than one thousand proof gallons to almost three hundred and eighty-six thousand, and of Bermuda from less than one thousand to over forty-one thousand.[1] The British government, somewhat ashamed of the huge profits accruing to its subjects from violating the laws of a friendly state, permitted search and seizure in the case of smuggled liquor after 1924. The federal coast-guard service made many captures and cut heavily into the profits of "rum row." The whole traffic was a picturesque bit of twentieth-century lawlessness, reviving memories of the smugglers or "free-traders" of the eighteenth century who risked their lives to get a few bottles of brandy or yards of French lace across the English Channel in defiance of the revenue officers.

The Canadian border was a weak spot in the enforcement program. Close to such great urban centers as Detroit, with but a short stretch of water to mark the political frontier, smuggling presented a simpler problem than maintaining a rum fleet on the Atlantic fed by supplies from Europe. Slocum Sleeper, head of the river patrol at Detroit, stated in 1928 that his men had captured two million dollars' worth of liquor in twelve months besides a fleet of fifty or sixty speed boats and

[1] These tables were reprinted in *Annals* of the American Academy of Political and Social Science, CIX, 153.

numerous automobiles.[1] The partial abandonment of prohibition by several of the Canadian provinces created a base of supply for international bootlegging, and also an oasis for thirsty but law-abiding American tourists.[2] The smuggling was not confined to the liquor trade, as many profitable side lines suggested themselves, such as the smuggling of narcotics, of dutiable articles of luxury, and of immigrants in excess of the legal quota. Similar conditions existed along the Mexican frontier and parts of the Florida coast very accessible to the West Indies.

The automobile provided the smuggler with a new facility. Huge trucks, moving by night at high speed along the highways, conveyed millions of gallons of liquor into the United States. The hazards were always great, but the greater the risk the higher were the prices and profits on each delivery. Besides the risk of encountering the lawful authorities, the rum runner had to beware a new and lawless enemy, the "hijacker."[3] The hijacker was the pirate of the landward trails. He found his richest source of revenue in holding up rum runners because his victims, themselves outlaws, dared not call in the aid of the law. But bootleggers, not willing to submit to this imposition, often hired professional gunmen to fight or punish the hijackers—a fruitful source of the gang wars in Chicago and elsewhere.

The bootlegging industry became a thoroughly organized one. Professional experts in distilling were highly paid for instructing others in the art. Professional carriers (women retail smugglers) added twenty-

---

[1] J. B. Kennedy, "—And Mix with Fresh Water," *Collier's*, LXXXII, 9 (Oct. 27, 1928).

[2] Kennedy, "—And Mix with Fresh Water," 36. "Ontario's liquor commission has nearly 300,000 permits outstanding, about 55,000 of which have been issued in the 'temporary' class, presumably American."

[3] Said to be derived from the hailing cry of the holdup man, "Hi! Jack."

five cents a quart for their middleman services.[1] Bribery in many stages was a necessary part of the business and sometimes annulled the expected profit. Class distinctions crept in; there were "respectable" bootleggers who catered to the wealthy and occasionally sold real smuggled liquor, and disreputable thugs and moonshiners who dealt in redistilled denatured alcohol or cheap corn whisky from the mountains.[2]

With all the widespread defiance of the Volstead act, the strongest opponents of prohibition admitted a diminished consumption of liquor.[3] Just how much less is quite impossible to estimate. There were no direct figures of illicit sales, and such indirect information as is afforded by statistical estimates of drunkenness, hospital cases of alcoholism, and violation of the prohibition laws, is incomplete and often contradictory. Nor is it easy to interpret the facts when we have them. A sudden upward leap in arrests may mean either greater law violation or an increased rigor of law enforcement. An increase in hospital cases of acute alcoholic poisoning may mean either a growth in the quantity of liquor consumed or merely a decrease in its quality. In entering the blind jungle of propaganda and partisan statistics one must tread warily. The best antiprohibitionist estimates, such as that by Hugh F. Fox of the United States Brewers Association, placed the per-capita annual liquor consumption at about half as much in 1926 as in 1918, but

[1] Bruère, *Does Prohibition Work?*, 181.

[2] See the editorial, "For Better Bootleggers," *N. Y. Times*, Oct. 15, 1928.

[3] "It may be safely admitted by the opponent of prohibition that the consumption of drink now is not so great as before the adoption of the Eighteenth Amendment; though no one really knows what it amounts to." Senator William C. Bruce (Maryland), *Current History*, XXII (1925), 697. The printed debate, "Is Prohibition a Success?," in this number of *Current History* between Senator Bruce and Wayne B. Wheeler is a good summary of the experience of the first five years of prohibition as viewed by the wets and drys.

added the comment that, as most of the illicit liquor was stronger than the average lawful drink of preprohibition days, there might be an actual increase in the consumption of alcohol.[1] The drys, on the other hand, thought five or ten per cent of the former alcohol consumption a generous estimate.[2]

Such statistics on drunkenness as are on a sufficient scale to be useful seem to show two facts: a decrease in drunkenness for the whole period as compared with the years before prohibition, in spite of the worse liquor consumed and the stricter standards of the law; and an increase in drunkenness within the period from 1920 to 1923 and a fairly consistent level afterwards. The year 1920 was the soberest the United States ever had. Arrests from drunkenness in 514 cities and towns for the decade 1914-1924 show only 60 to a population of ten thousand in 1920 as compared with 169 in 1914, 126 in 1923, and 127 in 1924.[3] Deaths from alcoholism numbered almost five to the hundred thousand in 1914, only one in 1920, 3.2 in 1923, and 3.6 in 1925.[4] "It cannot be doubted," declared Dr. Matthias Nicoll, state health commissioner for New York,

> that this striking rise in the death rate since 1920 is due, in great part, to the establishment of a vast national and international machinery for the illicit manufacture, importation, and distribution of alcoholic beverages, a

[1] Levitt, "Prohibition after Eight Years," 15. It should be remembered that many states were already under prohibition by 1918.

[2] For an extended argument on this point, see Fisher, *Prohibition at Its Worst*, and for attacks on Professor Fisher's statistical estimates, see Clarence Darrow and Victor Yarros, *The Prohibition Mania* (N. Y., 1927).

[3] Herman Feldman, *Prohibition, Its Economic and Industrial Aspects* (N. Y., 1927), 367. The table for 626 towns and cities given by Professor Fisher, *Prohibition at Its Worst*, 43, shows the same fall to 1920, rise to 1923 and then plateau.

[4] Feldman, *Prohibition*, 397.

large percentage of which is unfit for beverage purposes, and more apt to bring about pathological conditions.[1]

Yet for the entire period 1920-1928 no year appears to have equaled the alcoholic death rate of the years before 1917.

Most sensational, though always exceptional, were the sudden deaths from wood-alcohol poisoning. To denature grain alcohol it was customary to add wood alcohol, a deadly poison which produces death or at least blindness in those who use it. Unscrupulous bootleggers sometimes failed to remove all this denaturant from their product. The sudden death in 1928 of thirty-four persons in New York City in four days revived bitter talk that the federal government was "murderer" and "poisoner" in denaturing industrial alcohol with poisonous agents, although the use of such denaturants antedated prohibition. Even more harmful, because more common, was the use of raw, crude alcohol distilled from corn mash or potatoes and mixed with coloring and flavoring agents, themselves often injurious enough.[2]

Prohibition was unequally received in different parts of the United States. Rural America was mainly dry. Though hard cider and moonshine whisky sometimes qualified rural temperance, in the main enforcement was an urban problem. But there were wet spots even in the dry areas: New Orleans and tourist Florida in the South; Reno and San Francisco in the Far West; the river towns of the Mississippi and Missouri valleys; the

[1] *Washington Post*, May 22, 1927.
[2] To quote a New York physician on these poisoning cases, "Instead of cut liquor, the working man who wants an alcoholic beverage is turning to raw alcohol. . . . This stuff is not poisonous in the ordinary sense of the term, but an ounce or two of it has an effect on the heart equal to that of a whole bottle of hard liquor that has been properly aged in wood." *N. Y. Times*, Oct. 8, 1928.

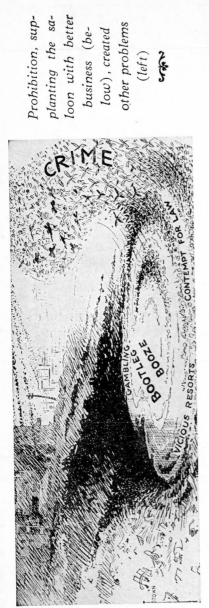

CRIME

GAMBLING

BOOTLEG BOOZE

CONTEMPT FOR LAW

VICIOUS RESORTS

Prohibition, supplanting the saloon with better business (below), created other problems (left)

Prohibition

Ohio mill towns. But along the Atlantic Seaboard, from Boston to Baltimore, the wet spots merged into a continuous belt, and here was the real focus of hostility to the Eighteenth Amendment. A map prepared in 1924 by Mrs. Mabel Willebrandt, assistant attorney-general, showed the degree of nonenforcement in different sections of the country to vary from five per cent in Kansas, Utah and Idaho to ninety-five per cent in New York City.[1]

This sectional alignment was reflected politically, although many districts of the South and West were drier in their votes than in their actual practice. Only from the Northeast were many congressional votes cast for modification of the existing laws. New York, Maryland, Nevada, Montana and Wisconsin repealed their state enforcement codes, thus placing a double burden on the overworked federal courts. New York, Illinois and Wisconsin (in 1926) carried state referenda in favor of modifying the Volstead act so as to permit the use of light liquors. The drys, believing that such advisory votes had no legal weight, concentrated their efforts on controlling Congress and pointed to the fact that the elections of 1920, 1922, 1924, 1926 and 1928 all returned large dry majorities in both houses. The party platforms of 1920, 1924 and 1928 indorsed strict enforcement, but the Democratic national convention of 1924 brought into the open a prolonged factional conflict between the prohibitionist forces, headed by William G. McAdoo, and the modificationists, who desired the nomination of Governor Alfred E. Smith of New York. In 1928 Governor Smith received the nomination and made his campaign to a great extent on the issue of restoring state home rule in the regulation of the

[1] *Collier's*, LXXIII, 5 (Jan. 26, 1924); *Literary Digest*, LXXX, 17 (Feb. 23, 1924).

liquor traffic. Though he carried only eight states of the forty-eight, losing several Southern states which had not been Republican since the seventies, he won the normally Republican electoral votes of Massachusetts and Rhode Island, carried New York City by a plurality of over four hundred thousand, captured Boston, Cleveland, St. Louis and San Francisco, and ran well in Chicago, Philadelphia, Detroit and a number of other urban centers.[1]

There were class lines as well as sectional lines on prohibition. Four social types were particularly numerous among the violators of the law. Of one little need be said—the "old soaks" who had a long-established alcoholic habit. They were not numerous and even the prohibitionists had taken for granted that, like the drug addicts, they would somehow or other get a supply. Also discounted in advance were certain foreign elements who had never experienced the old American fight against the saloon and could not understand why a normal part of their daily diet had suddenly been tabooed by law. An exception may be noted in the case of the Scandinavians of the Northwest. Like the old American stock they were accustomed to whisky and other very hard liquors and knew their danger; hence both Norway and Minnesota had engaged in prohibitionist agitation. But the beer-drinking German and the wine-drinking Latin resented the whole prohibitionist régime as an invasion of their personal liberty. A third type of malcontent was the natural rebel, the "Bohemian," the self-assertive collegian just old enough to feel social restrictions as intolerable. He alone began drinking with prohibition and because of it, obtaining more thrill from the thought that he was breaking a law than from the

[1] For the presidential election of 1928, see *American Year Book for 1928*, 1-6, 28-32.

drink itself. To these three classes there must be joined a fourth, the fashionable wealthy who had inherited the tradition that "a gentleman always serves wine at his table." This class and its sons were responsible for the most conspicuous violations of the law; they made disobedience "respectable" in their set; to them prohibition was a middle-class fad.[1]

Since one effect of prohibition was to increase the price of liquor from four to twenty times to the ultimate consumer, prohibition made much more change in the habits of the poor than of the rich. Many of the wealthy had well-stocked cellars before prohibition came,[2] and when the supply at last ran low the bootleggers found new customers. The sale of silver hip flasks for use at country-club dances and other convenient occasions became a widespread custom. There was a curious and almost comical inversion of class relations. Instead of Lady Bountiful visiting the slums to redeem the drunkard, the slums were now shocked at the conduct of the gilded youth. A janitor's wife in New York asserted, "It's not our people that are drinking so much. It's the rich bums that come from outside. . . . It used to be some lively down here before prohibition, but that was our own people and you could say to them, 'Jim, you go along home to Maggie 'till you get sobered up.' But these rich bums, you don't know where to tell 'em to go." [3] After studying conditions in Massachusetts, Dr. Richard C. Cabot of Harvard declared: "The rich may, for all we know, be as foolish as ever, but beyond any question the poor are better off. Drunkenness in

[1] Certain self-made millionaires like Henry Ford and Thomas A. Edison were dry in both habit and opinion; they did not have this background of aristocratic laxity.

[2] Hence the saying: "The rich are of two classes: those who still have a little and those who have a little—still!"

[3] Bruère, *Does Prohibition Work?*, 286-287.

women of the poorer classes has signally decreased; children under seventeen are much better off." [1]

Very much in the public mind was the alleged increase of drinking in the colleges; but careful surveys did not seem to bear out this common impression. [2] Certainly drinking continued, especially on occasions of special celebration such as a football victory or a class triumph. There were bootleggers near almost every campus and some fraternities patronized them regularly, but the habitual Saturday-night spree had vanished as an institution. Both college heads and college editors agreed that many a student drinker broke the law just because it was a law "on the same principle that his smaller brother takes the pie in his mother's pantry." The Eastern institutions were the wettest, or at any rate the frankest about their wetness. As late as 1928, one hundred and ten Princeton freshmen admitted that they drank. [3] A typical moderate statement of conditions under prohibition was that "the consensus of opinion of several informed groups is that about half of the student body at Harvard today is bone dry. Prior to prohibition not more than one-quarter of it could have been so rated. The increase in temperance, however, is attributed more to the expense and difficulty of obtaining liquor than to any abstinence on moral grounds." [4]

The liquor trade has always been associated with the darkest chapters in American politics, and this continued

[1] *Literary Digest,* LXXV, 8 (Oct. 28, 1922).

[2] See the opinions expressed by over two hundred college and university heads in *Literary Digest* for July 10, 1926, the opinions of student editors in the issue of July 17, and the comments of the public press in the issue of August 14.

[3] *Daily Princetonian* questionnaire, reported in *N. Y. Times,* Oct. 21, 1928. The college polls in 1930 showed a much larger percentage of drinking.

[4] Charles Selden, "Fashions in College Morals," *Ladies' Home Journ.,* XLII (1925), 6.

to be true when the trade became outlawed under prohibition. Honest officials, such as Governor Gifford Pin-
chot of Pennsylvania and Mayor William E. Dever of
Chicago, found their efforts to enforce the law blocked
by corruption in the courts and among the police, and
earned unpopularity besides. Investigations made in
Philadelphia by the grand jury in 1928 revealed that
the iron régime imposed by Brigadier General Smedley
D. Butler as director of public safety (1924-1925) had
only a temporary effect, being followed by a more intensive organization of the bootlegging industry and a
higher scale of bribery. Fifteen police officers were dismissed at one time on charges of corruption involving
unexplained bank deposits of more than eight hundred
thousand dollars.[1] "Gifts" from bootleggers to the police chiefs were of most liberal dimensions. "Because
the industry stood outside the law it had to have an
inner law and an inner government of its own. It had
a chief arbiter before whom disputes were taken. It had
attorneys who practiced in its own 'courts' as well as
handling such legal business as it had with the outer
world." It even had its own police, who protected its
convoys against hijackers and all other meddlesome persons, including officers of the law determined to do their
duty.[2] Similar though less elaborate systems existed in
Chicago under the "wide-open" administration of
Mayor William H. Thompson, and in other large cities.
Most discouraging of all was the widespread popular
indifference to the alliance of the illicit liquor traffic

---

[1] *N. Y. Times*, Nov. 8, 1928. For conditions in Philadelphia at their
worst, see also W. G. Shepherd, "The Price of Liquor," *Collier's*,
LXXXII, 8 (Dec. 1, 1928).

[2] R. L. Duffus, "Philadelphia Bares a Bootleg Kingdom," *N. Y. Times*,
Sept. 9, 1928. Federal estimates for the whole period from 1920 to April,
1929, showed 190 persons killed in the United States in the enforcement
of the prohibition laws: 135 law resisters and 55 prohibition agents.
N. Y. Times, April 6, 1929.

with underworld politics. The fact that the adoption of prohibition by an overwhelming vote "should be followed so soon by a virtual nullification of that policy by important sections of the population signifies something much deeper than administrative inefficiency and failure. . . . The trouble is with the people more than with their government." [1]

At least one charge against prohibition can be dismissed as disproved. Opponents of the policy declared that, if men could not obtain sound, well-made, fermented and distilled drinks, their unsatisfied craving would lead them on to experiment with narcotics, such as opium, morphine, cocaine and heroin. But the report of Doctors Lawrence Kolb and A. G. Du Mez for the United States public health service in 1924 showed that, so far from increasing since prohibition, the average annual consumption of opium in the United States was less than half as great in the period 1920-1923 as in the previous decade and had been steadily declining since its peak, about 1900. The number of drug addicts had fallen from a quarter of a million at the opening of the century to about one hundred and fifty thousand. [2]

In many respects, however, prohibition undoubtedly had a great effect on the dietetic habits of the nation. Strangely enough, at first glance, "near beer" (beer containing no more than the lawful maximum of alcohol) proved a financial failure, only seven per cent as much being sold in 1926 as of "real" beer in 1914. [3] The chief causes for this failure seem to have been the

---

[1] *The Prohibition Situation*, published by the Federal Council of Churches of Christ in America (N. Y., 1925), 78. This pamphlet is a useful summary of the situation, attaining a high degree of impartiality.

[2] "The Prevalence and Trend of Drug Addiction in the United States and the Factors Influencing It," U. S. Public Health Service, *Public Health Reports*, XXXIX, 1179-1203 (May 23, 1924).

[3] Feldman, *Prohibition*, 66-67.

competition with stronger illicit beverages,[1] and the failure of the brewers to realize that the Volstead law had come to stay and their consequent neglect of what was to them merely a temporary side line to their industry. Grape juice, tea and coffee, also, seem to have been less affected than one might expect.[2] But the sale of milk for the home increased by one half from 1917 to 1924 and an official of a milk-dealers' association estimated that a good third of this gain was due to prohibition.[3] Citrous drinks, ice-cream and candy sales made enormous advances; ice-cream consumption alone increased by fifty-five per cent from 1916 to 1925. The National Confectioners' Association ranked the industries benefiting from prohibition in the following order: (1) savings banks; (2) soft drinks; (3) moving pictures; (4) theaters; (5) candy.[4] In total sum, more than eleven billion bottles of nonalcoholic beverages were consumed in the United States each year.[5] Of course prohibition was only one factor in this development; for intensive advertising helped the soda-fountain trade, and the popular health magazines encouraged a more generous use of milk and fruit-juice beverages.

Food habits, too, were changing. The old-time saloon met three human wants: the specific craving for alcohol, the more general craving for something to satisfy the between-meal appetite, and the desire for a convenient hang-out where a man might gossip with his neighbor. Only by violating the law could the drug stores meet the first need, but the other two lay directly in its province. Sugar is an alcohol substitute as a quick fuel, and while ices might lack "kick," they were tasty and

[1] As the saying went, "The man who called that near-beer was a poor judge of distance!"
[2] Feldman, *Prohibition*, 80, 82-84.
[3] Feldman, *Prohibition*, 75, 77.   [4] Feldman, *Prohibition*, 89, 92.
[5] *Yearbook of Agriculture for 1927*, 324.

cooling. And a so-called "drug" store, which sold everything from stamps and ice cream to books and hot-water
bottles, and which remained open on Sunday when other
stores were closed, made a convenient social center. Moreover, the soda-bar was soon supplemented by the cheap
lunch, specializing in salads and sweets. Numerous con-
fectionery shops that did not even pretend to be drug
stores also broadened into quick-lunch restaurants. Said
one experienced hotel man, "Nibbles are taking the place
of bites. Salads and sandwiches are displacing steaks.
While good old-fashioned restaurants close their doors,
coffee shops, lunch rooms, and sandwich bars open at
the rate of several thousand a year." And he added,
"Whether or not one believes in the Eighteenth Amendment, we who deal in foods know that there is not
only less heavy drinking, but that it has resulted in
lighter eating." [1]

The more general social and economic effects of prohibition are hard to estimate. Certainly there was an
enormous reduction in pauperism and a great increase
in savings-bank deposits and other workingmen's investments.[2] But many factors had coöperated to elevate the
standard of living in the United States in the decade
following the war. Professor Irving Fisher's estimate
that prohibition had added six billion dollars a year to
the national income [3] may be sound or not; neither he
nor his critics were able so to isolate the effect of the
prohibition law from other causes of prosperity as to
make out a conclusive case. It would be safer to leave

[1] Feldman, Prohibition, 99. Of course other possible causes suggest
themselves, such as the aftereffect of war restrictions, health teaching, the
desire to reduce weight, and the greater number of women whose duties
forced them to lunch "downtown" instead of at home.

See later, chap. vi, on general economic trends.

[3] Fisher, Prohibition at Its Worst, chap. xi. His estimate is based
on the transfer of labor from the liquor industry to other forms of
production, and on the presumed increased efficiency of sober workmen.

the question on a qualitative basis and say merely that there was, in most parts of the country, some reduction of drunkenness and therefore a decrease in the poverty and inefficiency which it caused. Questionnaires sent to the members of the National Council of Social Work [1] and to the National Federation of Settlements [2] supported the conclusion of the latter that "There is less drinking; family life has improved—in some places in a quite remarkable degree; children are better fed and clothed and family ties have been strengthened; neighborhood disorder has been much reduced." In a word, the abolition of the corner saloon contributed its share to the elimination of the slum from American life. Whether or not this gain offset the new tasks and perplexities of enforcement was a question which a decade of prohibition still left to the future.

[1] Federal Council of Churches, *Prohibition Situation*, 14-16.
[2] Federal Council of Churches, *Prohibition Situation*, 38.

CHAPTER V

THE AMERICAN WOMAN WINS
EQUALITY

COUNT HERMANN KEYSERLING, one of the many distinguished European philosophers, authors and men of affairs who visited the United States after the World War, found as the most noteworthy of transatlantic marvels the complete and assured ascendancy of the American woman. In America, he wrote,

> all *men* are supposed to be equal. But women as a class are candidly accepted as superior beings. Thus America is today an aristocratic country of a peculiar type. It is a two-caste country, the higher caste being formed by the women as such. And this caste rules exactly in the way higher castes have always ruled. . . . Her inspiration and influence stand behind all American educators, as it stands behind all American prohibitionists. Her influence accounts for the infinity of laws and rules. She directs the whole cultural tradition. She also dictates in the field of moral conduct. Who wants to study the real meaning and purport of a caste system, should today not visit India, but America.[1]

Of course there was exaggeration here. The good count came from the country of Schopenhauer and brought with him not only the traditions of central Europe but, as a lifelong student of Oriental cultures, many of the views of eastern Asia as well. At almost any period of American history the position of women

[1] Hermann Keyserling, "Caste in America," *Forum*, LXXX (1928), 106.

would have seemed strange to him.[1] But his words are not too wide of the mark to call attention to the rapid advance of the feminist movement in the United States during and after the war. The most obvious change was the adoption of woman suffrage as the universal law of the nation. But the complete acceptance of the American woman in political life was only one phase of a general movement towards sex equality, older than the war and broader than America. The same generation that saw woman suffrage granted in the United States saw it granted also in most of the nations of northern Europe along with many other legal rights and privileges. Not in the field of politics, but in economic status and social prestige, did the American woman occupy her unique position. American feminism meant freedom from custom and tradition more than from positive legal restriction. Many European nations, for example, had enacted divorce laws as liberal as those of most American states, but in none of them (with the possible exception of Soviet Russia) were divorces so frequently obtained by discontented wives. European schools and colleges had been generally opened to women, but only in the United States did women look upon a college education as a natural right. Nowhere else in the world could a respectable unmarried girl spend her time and money with so little adult supervision. Nowhere else did the middle-class housewife have so wide a margin of leisure for amusement, self-development, or public work as her fancy might dictate.

Though the entrance of women into industry began long before the war, it was undoubtedly accelerated by it.[2] The census of 1920, coming conveniently just when

[1] For example, see C. R. Fish, *The Rise of the Common Man* (*A History of American Life*, VI), 269; and Allan Nevins, *The Emergence of Modern America* (same ser., VIII), 377-378.

[2] See chap. ii for woman's contribution to the work of war time.

the temporary labor displacements of war time had been mainly eliminated, showed eight and a half million women and girls over ten years of age engaged in gainful occupations, an advance of more than half a million since 1910.[1] This was not in itself a notable increase, indeed it did not quite keep pace with the growth in the general population; but the decreases were in occupations long open to women, such as farm work and domestic service, while in practically all "masculine" occupations the number of female workers greatly increased both in number and in proportion. There was a marked decline in the number of women employed as farm hands, laundresses, tailors, music teachers, midwives, charwomen, general servants and cooks, and a corresponding gain in the number of women chauffeurs, cigar makers, bankers, police and probation officers, social workers, lawyers, college professors, elevator "boys," clerks, typists, bookkeepers and barbers.[2] Almost one woman in four "gainfully employed" was married and presumably running a home as well as an outside job.[3]

For various sorts of routine clerical work employers definitely preferred women; men tended therefore to drift into other occupations rather than face the competition of the cheap and competent woman worker. There were, for example, eleven women stenographers and typists to every man so engaged. The capture of the elementary schools by the schoolma'am had made the old-fashioned schoolmaster an almost extinct type. No doubt the men had a real grievance in the fact that wages were kept down by the hiring of women to do

[1] *U. S. Fourteenth Census* (1920), IV, 34. The census bureau believes that the 1910 figures were "an overenumeration," especially for women farm laborers. Same vol., 23-24. If this be true, the increase in the number of women gainfully employed was much greater than the face of the returns would indicate.

[2] *U. S. Fourteenth Census*, IV, 34-43.

[3] *U. S. Fourteenth Census*, IV, 693.

the same work at cheaper rates,[1] but their grievance was rather against the employers who would not pay "men's wages" than against the women who frequently needed their jobs as badly as the men they displaced. Fortunately the rapid expansion of American industry made it usually possible for any adaptable man to find some occupation not yet unduly cheapened by feminine competition. Probably the worst effect of woman's invasion of industry was not the economic but the psychological; more men, perhaps, left such occupations as teaching and stenography from the feeling that their task was "no work for a man" than because of lowered incomes. One occupation after another had thus taken on a purely feminine color. A traveler from Europe shortly before the United States entered the war commented on how unnatural it seemed to him to see men running elevators and doing other work that European women had taken over when their men went to the trenches. In many trades this temporary effect of the war was merely an acceleration of the general tendency in industry.

There was a sharp schism in the feminist movement over the question as to whether women should or should not seek special protection for their health and welfare while engaged in industrial pursuits. Most reformers argued that the entire nation had a vested interest in the health of the mothers of the race and should therefore maintain by law wholesome standards for women workers. By 1922 forty-three states had limited by law the

[1] "The report for thirty-three industries in the State of Illinois showed that the average weekly wages for women during the month of May, 1924, was $17.15. In the cotton industry throughout the country the statistics showed that in 1922 the female employees received a wage ranging from about $12 to $19 a week. In the report of the women wage earners employed in the five and ten cent stores of New York State (1921) it is shown that of the total group of full-time women workers exactly one-half received less than $13.49 a week." B. P. Chass, "American Women Who Are Earning Wages," *Current History* (1925), 256.

hours of labor for women, thirteen states had enacted minimum-wage laws and sixteen states had forbidden night work in certain occupations.[1] But what appealed to most feminists as legal protection seemed to the more doctrinaire type, represented by the National Woman's party, as legal restriction. These advocated an "equal-rights amendment" to the federal Constitution which would sweep away all the legal disabilities of women, even those designed to safeguard them from competitive pressure in the ranks of industry.[2] Both political parties were urged in 1928 to indorse the equal-rights amendment, but both cautiously refused to commit themselves.

The institution of the home was affected in a hundred ways by the growing custom of American women to pursue a trade before matrimony and sometimes along with it. In some respects the influence was wholly constructive. No longer was marriage the inevitable way of getting a living. This set a higher standard for husbands than in the days when "old maid" (a term fast disappearing from use) might mean penury as well as loneliness. On the other hand, a conflict frequently arose between the man's desire to support his wife according to the old American tradition and the woman's desire to have "a career." The business girl gave up much in abandoning a job where all her earnings were her own to manage a household whose necessary expenses might leave little margin for the small luxuries to which she was accustomed. If she kept at her former work after marriage the double burden of home work and office work might easily prove too much for her health, or one of her tasks must be scamped. Nearly every popular magazine printed articles and stories innumerable around the

[1] Chass, "American Women Who Are Earning Wages," 254-255.
[2] Edna Kenton, "The Ladies' Next Step," *Harper's Mag.*, CLII (1926), 366-374.

problem, "marriage, a career, or both?" An interesting evidence of the interpenetration of man's world and woman's was the theme of Dorothy Canfield's novel, *The Home Maker,* which depicted a woman who had failed as a mother but made a success in commerce, while her husband, kept at home by an accident, found in educating his children the success which he had missed as a man of business.[1]

Other conditions of the time besides the commercial employment of women bore hard against the home as an economic unit. Domestic help had become almost unobtainable. Household servants, both men and women, numbered about one to the hundred of the whole population. Women cooks decreased in ten years from 333,-436 to 268,618.[2] The reduced immigration from Europe, the traditional recruiting ground of American domestic service, was certainly a major cause of this condition, but another reason was the opening of new and more attractive occupations for women. The cook might be wiled away from the stove not only by a wealthier neighbor, but equally by the chance of a more independent industrial job. Every mistress in employing servants felt the competition of the entire world of business.[3]

To a considerable extent the cook and the housemaid could be and were replaced by mechanical aids. In the decade following the war there was an increase "of over 100,000 in the employés for attending to (not manufacturing) electric refrigerators, oil heaters, and similar household appliances which so vividly typify the liberation of 'Mrs. Workman.' "[4] To get an accurate

[1] Dorothy Canfield (Fisher), *The Home Maker* (N. Y., 1924).
[2] *U. S. Fourteenth Census* (1920), IV, 43.
[3] For a discussion of the problem, see Ethel M. Smith, "America's Domestic Servant Shortage," *Current History,* XXVI (1927), 213-218.
[4] Julius Klein, "Servicing Our 260 American Wage," *Mag. of Business,* LIV (1928), 37.

idea of the transformation of the household economics we must reënforce personal impressions by statistics. Thus, "from the beginning of 1913 to the end of 1927 the number of customers for electric light and power increased 465 per cent. In 1912 only sixteen per cent of the population lived in electric-lighted dwellings, but sixty-three per cent had electric lights in 1927." [1] It is easy to visualize the meaning of such a change: the extension of daily time for work and play, the encroachment on the hours formerly devoted to slumber, the brightening of homes, the individualization of reading and study and the partial dispersion of the former "family group" about the parlor lamp or hearth fire, the adjustment of household temperature by electric heaters, fans and refrigerators. By 1926 about sixteen million homes had been wired for lighting and of these eighty per cent had electric irons, thirty-seven per cent vacuum cleaners, and more than twenty-five per cent had clothes washers, fans or toasters. [2]

The costly but cleanly and convenient oil heater began to displace the coal furnace. In 1926 the twenty-four leading makers of oil-heating apparatus installed in American homes 73,000 heaters; in 1927, about 100,000. The grand total in use in American homes by 1928 was not less than 550,000, to make no mention of some 220,000 installed in hotels, stores, theaters and other public buildings. [3] Where local costs permitted, gas heating was often substituted for coal and oil alike, though usually it was too expensive to be used for the family heating plant, however freely it might be employed in the kitchen or laundry. Many improvements were introduced into the domestic furnace for those who

[1] *Commerce Yearbook for 1928*, I, 275.
[2] *Commerce Yearbook for 1926*, I, 270.
[3] C. T. Crowell, "Is Coal Committing Suicide?," *Outlook*, CXLVIII, 417 (March 14, 1928).

still relied on coal, such as the "iron fireman" which automatically pushed into the flames as much coal as might be needed to maintain the desired temperature.[1] The traditional ice box, itself a rare luxury in all other countries, was being rapidly supplanted by the domestic refrigeration plant. The census would have done well to cease listing the American housewife as of "no occupation" and to have called her by her real name, "household engineer."

Yet the servant problem, in spite of the partial solution offered by modern science, compelled certain simplifications in domestic economy. The traditional nineteenth-century home, which survived in many parts of the United States down to the World War, required an amount of labor that would seem appalling to the latter-day urban American housewife. There were kerosene lamps to be filled and trimmed; coal scuttles to be emptied; huge expanses of rugs and carpets to clean; mountains of curtains, table cloths, doilies, napkins and other fabrics to require attention; cupboards of preserves to be put up for winter use; an annual earthquake of spring cleaning; and a huge Sunday dinner, requiring hours of preparation and a whole cookbook full of recipes. The visitor to an American home, especially a city home, in the postwar period would have found a very different picture. Instead of the roomy kitchen there would have been a kitchenette with dumbwaiter, sink, and gas or electric range. Small, brightly burnished aluminum pots and pans had replaced the morose array of ironware. The ice box or refrigerator served the purpose of the cool cellar, eliminating one story of the house. Little attempt was made to keep large supplies of food

[1] Of course the farmhouse had fewer such conveniences than the city or suburban home. For the distribution of home conveniences in the country, see later, chap. vii.

in the home. The delicatessen store around the corner was the accepted substitute for the pickle shelves in the cupboard; the commercial bakery had eliminated bread-making day, and ice cream was bought from the confectioner instead of being made by boy power in the freezer.

In the living rooms the same tendency towards compactness, convenience and simplicity prevailed, influenced no doubt by new artistic ideals as well as by labor shortage. The comfortable old American homes had come to seem "stuffy" and "cluttered." In place of the Victorian ideal of a homely coziness the new time emphasized an austere simplicity. The carpet gave way to the small rug on a polished hardwood floor, or to some new floor covering of the linoleum type which could be cleaned with water and soapsuds. Sofas, draperies, family portraits and miscellaneous paintings were used more sparingly, and wall paper was often abandoned. The parlor tended to disappear as an institution, if not as a room, for no longer was a special room reserved for curio cabinets, albums, the family piano and the Sunday afternoon. The whole house was put to use all the time; all rooms were "living rooms."

Upstairs, unless it were a single-floor apartment, were the bedrooms and the principal bathroom (the houses of the well-to-do had usually several bathrooms and toilets). With its white porcelain tub, its shining tiles, and its spotless cleanliness, the bathroom might have been mistaken by a traveler from the past for a hospital room, just as he might have mistaken the kitchen for a chemical laboratory. Ponderous wooden bedsteads with nine-foot headboards gave place to neat pairs of small single beds. Space as well as time had to be spared, for the cost of building operated as powerfully as the lack of domestic service to reduce the dimensions of the average home. Our imaginary Victorian visitor would have found fault with the low ceilings, the small dining room with its round table, and the paucity of bedrooms. Very often the unexpected friend or relative would be "put up" at the hotel instead of being taken into the home. There was hardly room for hospitality in the older meaning of the word.

Period furniture, especially of the eighteenth-century English styles, had come in during the preceding period, but some interior decorators now carried the trend towards simplicity to an extreme. The so-called "modernist" furniture, largely influenced by postwar experiments in France and Germany, was a severe scheme of straight lines, almost a "cubist" note in decoration. A bedroom mirror became a mere sheet of reflecting glass gripped by naked metal supports. Wall lines ran from floor to ceiling, unbroken by baseboards or molding. But this extremity of the fashion was, for the most part, followed only by the very wealthy who could afford to redecorate each time the mode changed. The middle-class home accepted the style of fewer and simpler lines, but refused to eliminate the curve.

The war struck a serious blow at domesticity by restricting the labor available for house building. A crisis in housing naturally resulted and, before new construction after the war could overtake the demand, rentals soared to unheard-of figures. New York City apartments that for many years had cost forty or fifty dollars a month increased suddenly to one or even two hundred, and the state legislature was forced to adopt emergency laws to prevent the eviction of thousands of tenants who could not meet the new rentals.[1] The decrease in

---

[1] "The most radical revision of that relation [landlord and tenant] ever attempted in this country." "Moving Day," Survey, XLV, 54 (Oct. 9, 1920). This editorial summarizes the rental laws.

building from 1913 to 1920—a temporary factor; the great increase in wages in the building trades—a probably permanent factor; the congestion of population in rapidly growing cities—all combined to enhance housing costs. In some places people with moderate incomes had to give up their dream of owning an independent home, or even a good-sized apartment, and content themselves with a three-rooms-and-a-bath suite, meantime storing half their goods in some warehouse. Landlords often subdivided apartments, making two families live where one lived before.

In most parts of the country the separate home still remained the standard type, and in rural districts there were almost as many dwellings as families, though there was a slight increase in the number of rented and mortgaged homes. But in a few places, notably New York City, the usual proportion of separate houses to apartments was reversed. On Manhattan Island there were about seven families to each roof, and the few private homes which relieved the monotony of ten-flat apartment houses were counterbalanced by the huge apartment hotels in which hundreds of families lived in great blocks of steel and stone. Manhattan was, however, in this, as in most matters, an extreme case. But the same trend could be noted almost everywhere, different only in degree. From 1920 onwards the bureau-of-labor-statistics collected figures on building permits and in each year except one (1924) the proportion of urban families housed in single-family dwellings decreased and the proportion of those lodged in multifamily apartments increased.[1] In 1928, for the first time, the permits issued for apartment houses showed a larger estimated expenditure than those issued for single-family houses. Average building costs for all types of dwellings ranged from

[1] *U. S. Daily* (Wash.), May 7, 1929.

*This typical
Fifth Avenue
Mansion gave
place to this
typical apart-
ment hotel.*

two or three thousand dollars per family in St. Louis,
New Orleans and Dallas, to more than seven thousand
in Manhattan Borough. Single-family dwellings varied
from $2671 in Dallas to more than nine thousand in
Providence, Rhode Island, and Newark, New Jersey.[1]
These averages included, of course, workingmen's homes.
Middle-class suburban houses cost usually from ten to
twenty thousand dollars to build, an amount equal to
four or five years' income of the typical owner, an un-
wontedly heavy item in the home budget.

Various solutions of the housing problem were ventured. Some feminist leaders, such as Charlotte Perkins
Gilman, advocated coöperative housing, and the transfer of cooking, cleaning and other industrial processes
of the "home plant" to central units for a whole block
of dwellings. New methods of construction made their
contribution. Sometimes houses were made in standardized parts, advertised through mail-order catalogues, and
assembled according to pattern. The increased use of
concrete saved wood and lessened fire risk. For many
Americans the automobile became a second home, and
the sole family residence for weeks or months of a family camping trip.

In every direction the economic functions of the
home had been reduced. Restaurant, delicatessen and
hotel invaded the sphere of the kitchen; the cannery cut
down the pantry shelves; the steam laundry proved a
formidable competitor to the hired washerwoman; the
public school, kindergarten, nursery school and public
playground assumed part of the care of supervising children. Such things, however, mattered little. When social
theorists spoke with dread of the coming "breakdown
of the American home," they were thinking of the family group rather than of the household "plant"; for

[1] *U. S. Daily,* Nov. 7 and Nov. 9, 1928.

so long as parents and children formed a congenial circle, the family would remain the fundamental human institution though its last economic function disappear. But if the family itself were breaking up, as some pessimists proclaimed, it mattered little where or how the homeless drifters found a place to sleep or eat.

The most common argument of those who believed that the traditional monogamous family was disappearing in America was, of course, the very high divorce rate, by far the highest rate for any part of Christendom where statistics were carefully kept. Moreover, this high ratio was not stationary but increasing, and very rapidly. From 1914 to 1928 the annual ratio of divorces to marriages rose from about one to ten to one to six. The increase was too steady over a long period of time to be attributed to the war, for though the war marriages of 1917 and 1918 may have been rash, apparently many civilian marriages were equally so.

The divorce rate varied greatly from state to state, but the American people were so migratory that this difference corresponded almost exactly with the differences in the local statute law of marriage and divorce, and not with the different social traditions of the states.[1] New York had one of the lowest divorce rates in the nation and yet no one supposed that domesticity was stronger among the apartment hotels of Manhattan than among the rural villages of Oregon where there were (in the 1920's) about two divorces to each five weddings. Nevada offered the extreme example. If one were to believe unanalyzed statistics, nearly every Nevada marriage ended in divorce, and in Reno, the chief city, people contrived to get divorced faster than they got married. As a matter of fact, Reno was simply a "Gretna

[1] E. R. Groves and W. F. Ogburn, *American Marriage and Family Relationships* (N. Y., 1928), chap. xxii.

Green" of divorce hunters, as Indiana had been in earlier days and South Dakota a little later.[1] The laws of Nevada did not differ greatly from those of other Western states with respect to the causes of divorce, but the necessary period of residence within the state was only six months (reduced in March, 1927, to three months) instead of the usual year or more.

The higher social ranks, by which is meant those who could easily afford foreign residence, made Paris divorces fashionable. Life in metropolitan Paris was gayer than in a small place like Reno and the law was almost equally complaisant. Also, a trip abroad for a divorce was an easy way to escape—or, if one preferred, to enhance —the publicity of the affair. Contrary to common belief, the curious incompatibility-of-temperament clause which appeared in the divorce laws of a few states was not frequently required. The great majority of divorces were for the standard causes of desertion, cruelty and adultery, but in the interpretation of these terms much laxity was employed. Desertion often meant a collusive arrangement whereby both parties had agreed to separate long enough to make divorce possible; cruelty was interpreted to cover "mental anguish" caused by any misconduct whatever of the party against whom complaint was laid; adultery was often a staged affair to satisfy the technicalities of law. The blunt truth is, that almost any American man or woman who was tired of the marriage relation could have it dissolved at the cost of a little time and trouble. About two thirds of all divorces were obtained at the instance of the wife, and this ratio was constant over many years. The freedom to depart at will from the legal ties of matrimony was therefore chiefly a woman's privilege.

[1] Nevins, *The Emergence of Modern America*, 216; A. M. Schlesinger, *The Rise of the City* (*A History of American Life*, X), chap v.

Little wonder, then, that a sober sociologist declared: "Our United States family . . . is monogamic in form with an apparent tendency toward term marriage and what is coming to be called the 'companionate.'" [1] "Term marriage" existed wherever a divorce was taken for granted if the venture did not turn out happily. If it were entered upon with no expectation of children the term marriage became the "companionate," a phrase first generally popularized by Judge Benjamin B. Lindsey, whose service in the Denver juvenile court had convinced him that conventional marriage laws were being increasingly disregarded by the oncoming generation.[2] Professor William F. Ogburn of the University of Chicago declared that the American family at least in "its extreme urban form has lost nearly all of its functions." [3] He noted seven ties that had held together the family of the past: economic, religious, protective, educational, recreational, social status and affectional. The first six of these had been greatly attenuated or snapped altogether by changes in industrial methods and social customs; only affection remained to hold the home together, and where it was absent divorce was apt to be the solution.

There was, however, no general trend in the United States toward increased celibacy; the marriage rate, in contrast to the rising divorce rate, was fairly constant. The very fact that the knot could be so easily undone perhaps encouraged marriage. Nor was there any general increase in the age at which marriage was contracted except, to some extent, among professional men, col-

[1] J. M. Gillette, "Family Life," *American Year Book for 1925*, 665.
[2] B. B. Lindsey and Wainwright Evans, *The Companionate Marriage* (N. Y., 1927). See also the same authors' *The Revolt of Modern Youth* (N. Y., 1925).
[3] W. F. Ogburn, "Divorce: A Menace that Grows," *N. Y. Times*, Dec. 18, 1927.

lege graduates and business employees working for salaries too small to support a family. In these classes matrimony was frequently postponed till the thirties, though
sometimes a solution to the economic problem was found
by an early marriage and the postponement of mother-
hood until the joint savings of husband and wife would
permit the proper care of children. For the nation as a
whole the most common age of marriage for a man was
about twenty-five; for a woman, about twenty-two.

Indeed, more moralists were concerned over rash
adolescent marriages than over the middle-aged bache-
lors and bachelor maids. They pointed out that it was
those who wed in haste who repented at leisure and
that by far the greater number of divorces occurred
among those who had gone to their wedding in a holiday mood, as on a lark or spree. More than a dozen
states adopted laws requiring an interval, usually of five
days, between the granting of a license or the filing of an
application therefor and the celebration of the wedding.
New York, Wisconsin and many other states adopted
so-called eugenic laws (more accurately, health laws)
requiring certain tests of physical fitness for marriage.[1]
But state lines were so easily crossed that the chief effect
of local restrictions on matrimony was to increase the
license fees of the state next door. Thus the coming into
effect in July, 1927, of a California statute requiring
three days' notice for matrimony, immediately increased
the number of marriages performed under the laxer laws
of Arizona and Nevada.[2]

The decrease of immigration by the European war
and by restrictive legislation was a factor in retarding the
rate of growth of the American population, but "even

[1] See the *World Almanac for 1930*, 283-285, for a summary of the
marriage and divorce laws of the states.
[2] *N. Y. Times*, Dec. 17, 1928.

had immigration continued at a record rate," said the expert analysts of the census, "the percentage of the national population increase still would have been lower than that shown by any previous census of the United States." [1] The United States shared with almost all countries of Western civilization in an accelerating fall of the birth rate. The native white stock of the nation was still enlarging at the rate of eleven or twelve per cent to a decade,[2] but this increase was made possible only by a decline in the death rate. If the birth rate of the 1920's had been combined with the mortality rate of 1910, the natural increase would have diminished to 3.6 per thousand per annum, and had it been combined with the mortality rate of the beginning of the century there would have been virtually no increase at all.[3]

But actual failure to keep up the existing population was confined to a small class. Unfortunately this class included many of the otherwise most successful elements in the nation—well-to-do and educated business and professional men and women. Celibacy, late marriage and birth control were all alike widespread in this group, as the late President Roosevelt had noted.[4] It was not "race suicide" that he really had had in mind, but the "class suicide" of the upper and middle classes. Although national mailing laws prohibited such public discussion of methods of birth restriction as was common in many European countries, there is no other way to explain the coincidence of a fairly high marriage rate with a decreasing proportion of births than to assume that, never-

[1] W. S. Rossiter, *Increase of Population in the United States, 1910-1920* (*Census Monographs*, I, 1922), 28.

[2] Rossiter, *Increase of Population*, 101.

[3] L. I. Dublin, *Health and Wealth* (N. Y., 1928), 219.

[4] H. U. Faulkner, *The Quest for Social Justice* (*A History of American Life*, XI), chap. ii.

theless, these methods were widely known and practised in the United States.

The small family had, apparently, come to stay. The passing of the open frontier, the growth of the great cities with their cramped housing conditions, the closing of the door to fecund immigrant races, the higher standards of comfort and the growing cost of education, all tended to make a family of two or three children the national standard. At first glance the smaller family seems even more important than mechanical invention and simplified housekeeping in setting feminine energies free for work outside the home. But one qualification must be made. If care for children in the home was less extensive than formerly, it was also more intensive.[1] At no previous period were children tended with such watchful care of their health, diet, habits and abilities. Never before were magazines of professional parenthood so widely sold or parent-teacher associations so generally attended. Even where the family had but one child, he often received as many hours of attention as had been distributed among the dozen brothers and sisters of his grandfather.

The effects of the changing standards in home and family life may be illustrated by what happened in a typical Middle Western city of forty thousand population.[2] In Middletown almost nine tenths of the high-school girls declared their intention of "going to work" after graduation, and more than a fourth of all commercially employed women were married.[3] Children

[1] See Faulkner, *The Quest for Social Justice*, chap. vi.
[2] R. S. Lynd and Helen M. Lynd, *Middletown* (N. Y., 1929). The community in question, an Indiana town thinly disguised under the name of Middletown, was studied by a corps of investigators after the manner of social anthropology. Its typical character was perhaps vitiated by its homogeneity: Negroes and foreign-born were relatively few. The field work was conducted in 1924-1925.
[3] Lynds, *Middletown*, 16-17.

were more independent of the family circle; fifty-five per cent of the boys and forty-four per cent of the girls spent less than four evenings a week at home.[1] Parents on the other hand greatly increased their range of solicitude for their children's welfare, typical statements being: "I accommodate my entire life to my little girl. She takes three music lessons a week and I practice with her forty minutes a day. I help her with her school work and go to dancing school with her," and "Everyone asks us how we've been able to bring our children up so well. I certainly have a harder job than my mother did; everything today tends to weaken the parents' influence. But we do it by spending time with our children."[2] The home was rapidly ceasing to be a unit of economic production, from five to seven loaves of bread out of every ten—according to the season of the year—were bought from the bakery and, in the well-to-do homes, most laundry was done outside the house, although the "advent of individually owned electric washing machines and electric irons has . . . slowed up the trend of laundry work—following baking, canning, sewing, and other items of household activity—out of the home to large-scale commercial agencies. . . ."[3]

Whether moral standards in the United States were improving or degenerating (and this, of course, was the crucial question for the survival of the home) was widely but most inconclusively debated. The issuance in a given year of one divorce decree to each six or seven marriage licenses was alarming if one considered it a symptom of growing marital unrest. But it might merely mean that unions were now formally dissolved by law

[1] Lynds, *Middletown*, 135.   [2] Lynds, *Middletown*, 146-147.
[3] Lynds, *Middletown*, 155, 174. Curiously enough, the authors regard this particular countercurrent as reactionary and retrogressive (175, 498), as though science has less "right" to bring industries back into the home than to take them out!

which in times past had been covertly dissolved by extra-legal relationships. The number of illegitimate births remained fairly low,[1] but this encouraging fact may be partly discounted by the wider use of contraceptive methods. The National Federation of Settlements, after a very wide and impartial investigation, came to the conclusion that commercial prostitution was much diminished. "Report after report says that disorderly houses are gone and there is practically no solicitation on the streets." [2] In nearly all cities the regulated or tolerated "red-light district" had disappeared, dispersed, or hidden itself from casual view. This great improvement might be explained by many causes. The committee of the National Federation of Settlements laid stress on the effect of prohibition. The increase of industrial wages certainly must have made "Mrs. Warren's profession" less attractive to working girls. Reform campaigns and welfare work among the poor cleansed many a sinister street.

But there was another side to the story. While commercial prostitution was disappearing, there was much talk of clandestine love matches, unsanctioned by law, among young people of the most "respectable" circles. Here, unfortunately, one must leave solid statistical ground for general impressions, and these seemed to differ according to the personal bias of each witness. There seemed to be no direct proof that sexual immorality was more common, but the opportunities for it were certainly greater. The game of personal caresses, or "petting," was not essentially different from the old-fashioned "spooning," but an automobile fifty miles from

[1] "The fact that out of a hundred white children ninety-six or ninety-seven are born in wedlock indicates that our society has attained a fair degree of success in the control of the sex relation." E. A. Ross, *What Is America?* (N. Y., 1919), 41.

[2] Martha B. Bruère, *Does Prohibition Work?* (N. Y., 1927), 301.

town or an unchaperoned road-house dance may have been a more dangerous place to play the game than a domestic parlor or veranda. Some conservative colleges forbade their students the use of automobiles as much to safeguard their morals as to protect their limbs. The necessary spice of intoxication which could no longer be obtained at a saloon might be carried on the hip in a silver flask. Girls were certainly less restrained by conventions and inhibitions from doing whatever boys of the same social set might do. Often their time and latch-keys were their own. Engagements were lightly entered into and usually considered in no way binding.[1] There was an evil cult of "the thrill," whose motto was "I'll try anything once" and which reduced the problem of happiness to the accumulation of the greatest possible number of "new sensations." Of course the natural result was to make the young "sheik" and his "sheba" bored and cynical at twenty when they should have been still full of absurd young enthusiasms.

Most of what alarmists said of changes in morals, however, should be translated into changes of manners. Even if one grants that shifts in social fashion do not go very deep into the bedrock of moral character, one must admit that these changes were swift enough after 1914 to alarm the elderly and sedate. Consider the question of clothing. Women's fashions have always fluctuated—the waistline moving up and down anywhere between neck and knee; skirts ballooning out till they covered much of the ballroom floor, or again tucked in till they shackled movement, as in the "hobble skirt" so

[1] We had nearly said that there were no statistics on twentieth-century lovemaking, but that would have done injustice to the tabulating epoch. "Marriage and Love Affairs," by G. V. Hamilton and Kenneth Macgowan, *Harper's Mag.*, CLVII (1928), 277-287, solemnly tabulates, with the proper graphs, the 1358 love affairs of two hundred young married persons of the educated classes; about seven cases of love apiece. It is a pity that we have no comparable figures for earlier generations.

briefly popular about 1911 or 1912; hats towering like mountains or spreading out like pancakes. But usually the new styles came by degrees, so that people could get used to them; they "evolved" like the British constitution. But during and after the war a real sartorial revolution took place. The skirt, in the old sense of the word, disappeared altogether to be replaced by a sort of tunic or kilt barely reaching the knee. Conservative eyes were shocked by this, although the change was in the direction of common sense and, had it taken a century instead of five or six years to complete, would have provoked little comment. Skirts were already "short," ankle-length, in 1914, but the "very short" skirt, knee-length, hardly became general before 1920 and required about three years more to become the accepted mode for all sections, ages and classes. In 1929 clothing interests, impelled by Paris, made a desperate effort to restore the long skirt at least for evening wear and formal occasions. But many American women refused, for the first time in history, to obey the Parisian dictators of fashion.

With the shortening of the skirt went many other changes. Hampering petticoats were discarded, the corset was abandoned as a needless impediment to free movement, silk or "rayon" stockings became practically universal even among the poor and for a time were often rolled at the knee, sleeves shortened or vanished, and the whole costume became a sheer and simple structure, too light to be the slightest burden. H. G. Wells, writing in war time, declared that his heroine "at fourteen already saw long skirts ahead of her, and hated them as a man might hate a swamp that he must presently cross knee-deep." [1] But by the time Joan would have been old enough for the long skirts there were none for her to wear. These simplifications of costume started with the

[1] H. G. Wells, *Joan and Peter* (N. Y., 1918), 293.

wealthier classes but were almost immediately copied everywhere. A survey in Milwaukee of more than thirteen hundred working girls showed that less than seventy wore corsets.[1] The commercial effect of these changes of style was profound. Factories which specialized in petticoats, corsets or cotton stockings had to change their trade or go bankrupt, but the sale of silk and rayon hose more than doubled in four years, and the sale of bathing suits tripled in two.[2]

During the sartorial revolution men proved to be, as usual, the conservative sex, making but minor changes in costume. A man who was well dressed for Roosevelt's inauguration would have provoked but little comment at Hoover's. What few alterations were made were usually in the direction of greater comfort. The soft hat replaced the derby for almost every occasion, warm weather permitted light tropical suitings, and softer shirts and collars passed muster for business wear in the daytime. But men still wore coat and collar in summer when women were comfortable in scanty one-piece frocks (unless they followed the fashion of summer furs). "Today our American women are in better physical condition than our men," declared Dr. Ephraim Mulford, president of the Medical Society of New Jersey. "And while there are many reasons, we might credit one to the fact that women do not wear too many clothes, especially in the summer. Their garments, light in weight and light in color, permit the ultraviolet ray of the sun to give its full benefit. Men, in their dark clothes which completely cover them from neck to ankle are denied this energy."[3] The tailors and textile fac-

[1] "The Passing Corset," *Collier's*, LXXXII, 50 (July 21, 1928).
[2] Percival White, "Figuring Us Out," *North Am. Rev.*, CCXXVII (1929), 69.
[3] *N. Y. Times*, Nov. 11, 1928.

tories even had a certain revenge on the male sex for their losses on the skimpier female raiment. Small boys often wore long trousers, and at adolescence they adopted trousers not only long but wide—huge, baggy affairs that moved hardly a step to each two steps of their owner but were raised above criticism by the name of "Oxford." In swimming, both men and women wore the simplest possible one-piece suits, the woman's suit often having less coverage than the man's. On hot summer days many girls went stockingless everywhere.

When the public had scarcely recovered from the shock of the disappearing skirt, it received another. The girls began to cut their hair. The barber shop was the last refuge of masculinity in America, the only spot which had not become "coeducational." The saloon was gone; the polls were now open to women; swimming tanks were crowded with fair mermaids; the very prize ring had its lady guests, and nearly all men's clubs had their ladies' night. But in the barber shop the unshorn male could lean back at his ease in the great chair, unashamed in his suspenders, while the barber stuffed his mouth with lather and gave him the latest gossip of politics and baseball. This last trench was now taken. A fashion started for hair fitting compactly around the head and fluffed or banged over the ears; long tresses were out of style; hence occasional visits to the barber shop. Persons over thirty viewed the fad with some misgivings, but presently began to try cautious experiments in the same direction. The flapper grew bolder. The "boyish bob" appeared, and ears emerged once again from their retirement. Soon there was no difference between a man's hair cut and a woman's, unless the man were an artist or musician and wore his hair long as a professional asset. One Chicago barber shop had to advertise, "Men's custom ALSO welcomed!" The double prophecy made more than four hundred years ago [1] had come true at last:

> Lo! yet before ye must do more, if ye will go with me,
> As cut your hair up by your ear, your kirtle by the knee.

The universalizing of the bob simplified the hat problem. Large, broad and unstably balanced hats were out of the question, as the hatpin found no anchorage. All the new hats took the form of a close-fitting, simple bonnet which a wind would not carry away. Birds and flowers on headgear largely disappeared, and the vanishing of the hatpin ended a major menace in crowded cars.

A third phase of the revolution in fashions, even more disturbing to the traditional than short skirts or short hair, was the freer use of cosmetics. In a way, this was a move in the opposite direction, as it represented a tendency not towards "naturalness" and freedom but towards artificiality and sophistication. If it be considered progress since the times of Victoria, when ladies got along with a little face cream and white powder, it might equally be considered a reversion to the days of Pompadour. Bright orange rouge and lipsticks advertised as "kissproof" were used by young ladies of the most unquestionable respectability. The fashionable "sun tan" was sometimes acquired at the drug store as well as on the beach. Like the other changes in fashion the cosmetic urge was democratic in the sense that it stopped at no class barrier. "Progress toward democracy," wrote a journalist,

> has made amazing strides in this matter of personal decoration. Formerly it was the ladies of the court who used it most; today it is the serious concern and dearest pastime of all three estates. It was the spread of the use

[1] *The Nut Brown Mayde* (spelling modernized).

of furs, to take but one example, to all classes (and also to all seasons) which inspired the just description of woman as America's greatest fur-bearing animal. And nowadays no one can tell, either by the quantitative or the qualitative test, whether a given person lives on Riverside Drive or on East Fourth Street.[1]

The business of the manufacturers of cosmetics and perfumes increased from less than $17,000,000 in 1914 to $141,488,000 by 1925, over eightfold in one decade.[2] The Foucaults (French perfumers) estimated that seventy-one per cent of the women of the United States over eighteen years of age used perfume; ninety per cent, face powder; seventy-three per cent, toilet water; fifty-five per cent, rouge.[3] "Beauty shoppes" blossomed on nearly every street of the shopping districts, their proprietors sometimes seeking to professionalize their status with the word "beauticians." Seven thousand kinds of cosmetics were on the market in 1927, a large majority of them being face creams.[4] Fortunes were made in mud baths, labeled "beauty clay," in patent hair removers, in magic lotions to make the eyelashes long and sweeping, in soaps that claimed to nourish the skin, in hair dyes that "restored the natural color," in patent nostrums for "reducing," and in all the other half-fraudulent traps of the advertisers for the beauty seeker.

One manufacturer of dentifrice based a clever advertising campaign on the vogue of the feminine cigarette, with such headlines as "Why are Men so Unreasonable about Women Smoking?" and "Can a Girl Smoke and Still be Lovely?" arguing that since women

[1] Devere Allen, "Personal Decoration," *The World Tomorrow*, VIII (1925), 77.

[2] White, "Figuring Us Out," 69.

[3] C. J. McGuirk, "A Subtle Something," *Sat. Eve. Post*, CXCIX, 72 (Dec. 4, 1926).

[4] Rose Feld, "The Cosmetic Urge," *Collier's*, LXXIX, 22 (March 12, 1927).

were determined to smoke they should keep their teeth stainless by the daily use of tooth paste. Cigarette advertisers took a similar ingenious advantage of the craze for the "boyish form"—*e.g.*, "And now, women may enjoy a companionable smoke with their husbands and brothers—at the same time slenderizing in a sensible manner. . . . Reach for a *Lucky* instead of a sweet." Thus one fad supported another. Earlier advertisers, not so bold, had usually depicted pretty girls not themselves indulging in a cigarette but in the company of young men so engaged, perhaps pleading, "Blow some my way!" The number of cigarettes sold in the period 1911-1915 averaged less than fifteen billion annually; for the period 1921-1925 sales averaged well over sixty-five billion,[1] and in 1928 reached one hundred billion.[2] As during the same period there was no greater sale of cigars and a much smaller sale of chewing tobacco, the increased vogue of the cigarette did not mean an increased tobacco hunger. Rather it meant the entrance of the American girl into the ranks of the smokers. A cigarette had about it a slim, feminine daintiness; it could be gracefully twirled and dandled like a fan between dances when a cigar or pipe would have been ridiculous. The war, too, had its effect. Y.M.C.A. secretaries who had spent years warning young men of the peril of the demon nicotine had perforce to hand out cigarettes by the thousand to the soldiers in France. Army life also convinced men who were sensitive about their masculinity that cigarettes and wrist watches were as suitable for "he-men" as the Pittsburgh stogie or the pocket Ingersoll. As for chewing tobacco—the nightmare of the European traveler since the days of Dickens

[1] Dept. of Commerce, *Statistical Abstract of the United States for 1925,* tables 757-759.
[2] *U. S. Daily,* March 23, 1929.

—it had been very largely replaced by the increased use of chewing gum, perhaps another victory for feminism.

Thus the flapper of the 1920's stepped onto the stage of history, breezy, slangy and informal in manner; slim and boyish in form; covered with silk and fur that clung to her as close as onion skin; with carmined cheeks and lips, plucked eyebrows and close-fitting helmet of hair; gay, plucky and confident. No wonder the house rang with applause; no wonder also that faint hisses sounded from the remoter boxes and galleries. But she cared little for approval or disapproval and went about her "act," whether it were a Marathon dancing contest, driving an automobile at seventy miles an hour, a Channel swim, a political campaign or a social-service settlement. Eventually she married her dancing partner, that absurdly serious young man with plastered hair, baby-smooth chin and enormous Oxford bags, and then they settled down in a four-room-kitchenette apartment to raise two children, another "younger generation" to thrust them back stage among the "old fogies."

The Nineteenth Amendment which extended the political franchise to American women, already emancipated in everything save politics, followed about half a year after the Eighteenth, prohibiting the sale of alcoholic liquors. The twin amendments—twin victories for feminism some would say—had much in common. Both prohibition and woman suffrage had roots deep in American history and represented a final triumph obtained after almost a century of continuous agitation. Both were attempted in many places on a state-wide scale before they forced their way to the front as national issues. Both were first mooted by Puritan reformers in the Northeastern states, then actually carried into effect by their radical sons who had moved to the Western plains and mountains, and opposed almost to the last ditch by their conservative grandsons who had stayed in the East. But in at least one respect there was contrast. However prolonged and bitter the opposition to woman suffrage, once the amendment was carried the issue disappeared from politics, whereas prohibition remained a bone of contention as much after its victory as before.

By 1914 equal suffrage existed in Wyoming, Colorado, Utah, Idaho, Washington, California, Oregon, Arizona and Kansas, and during the year Nevada and Montana were added to the number. Many other states had a limited woman suffrage, often for school elections only. Neither of the great parties had either indorsed or opposed the movement, except locally, but the Progressives in 1912 and many other third parties at various times had made equal suffrage a plank in their platforms. Though all the major victories had been confined to a single section of the country, politicians everywhere felt the pressure of the growing movement. It was ably captained, and one of the chief arguments for admitting women into politics was that they were showing themselves adepts at the game even before enfranchisement. Carrie Chapman Catt, Anna Howard Shaw, Alice Stone Blackwell and their lieutenants aroused much admiration, almost envy, among professional politicians, even those who were their opponents.

After 1916 the states rapidly fell into line. Already (1913) Illinois had adopted a curious compromise by which women could vote for all offices except those governed by the franchise stipulation in the state constitution; thus they could vote for presidential electors but not for Congress or most state officers.[1] Many other states followed with similar "presidential-suffrage" laws, and Arkansas permitted women to vote in party

[1] "The Suffrage Conquest of Illinois," *Literary Digest*, XLVI, 1409-1410 (June 28, 1913).

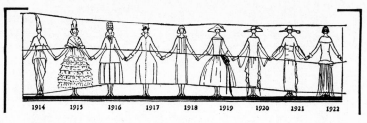

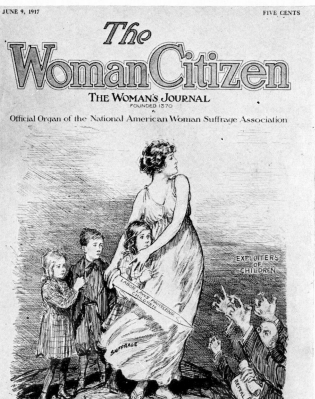

JUNE 9, 1917   FIVE CENTS

The WomanCitizen
THE WOMAN'S JOURNAL
FOUNDED 1870

Official Organ of the National American Woman Suffrage Association

They Shall Not Pass

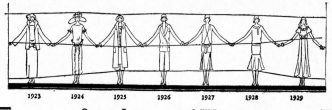

Some Interests of Women

primaries which were there, as in most parts of the South, the really important elections. New York capitulated in 1917, the first Eastern seaboard state to grant complete equality.[1] Nowhere else had the fight been so completely organized and well munitioned. Most of the suffrage, and equally the antisuffrage, associations had New York offices, and for several years the city had been accustomed to the sight of marching armies of suffrage paraders, each larger than the last and viewed by a more sympathetic crowd. The cries of "Go home and wash the dishes!" which greeted the first paraders were replaced by a continuous ripple of applause up and down Fifth Avenue. In 1918 Michigan, South Dakota and Oklahoma joined the caravan of equal-suffrage states, and interest shifted from the state campaigns to the prospect of a national amendment.

The so-called Susan B. Anthony amendment forbade the restriction of the franchise on the ground of sex. In June, 1919, it started from Congress on a tour of the state legislatures, and by the following spring had been accepted in thirty-five states and rejected by ten, all in the Southeast, Tennessee, Connecticut and Vermont were still doubtful, the national election was rapidly approaching, and neither party wished to appear as an obstacle in the way of the necessary thirty-sixth ratification. The governors of Connecticut and Vermont refusing to call the legislatures into special session to consider the amendment, the honor fell to Tennessee. A frantic effort by Tennessee antisuffragists to reverse the action of the legislature came just too late; in August, 1920, the amendment had been declared part of the Constitution.

Two features of the equal-suffrage campaign in the

[1] "Suffragists Take New York," *Literary Digest*, LV, 14-15 (Nov. 17, 1917) ; *American Year Book for 1917*, 180-181.

United States are of special interest. One, already alluded to, was the small part played by the parties in securing the amendment. The other was the almost complete absence of "militancy." In England a fairly large radical wing of the suffrage movement had tried to badger the government of the day into action by such means as breaking windows, interrupting public meetings, destroying mail boxes, and other "nuisance tactics." Nothing so extreme occurred in the United States, the nearest approach to it perhaps being the picketing of the White House with banners denouncing President Wilson (himself already a convert to the cause) for not putting more pressure on Congress to hasten the enactment of the proposed amendment.[1] Even this very mild form of militancy was frowned upon by the majority of American suffragists, who used no method except political organization and open discussion. Their speedy success seems to have been due in part to the skill of their political managers, in part to the chivalric tradition in American life which made it difficult to refuse any really sustained demand by women, in part to the rivalry of political parties to seize a popular issue before it was too late, and in part as a tribute to the indispensable services of American women during the World War.

With the ballot in hand most American women found their political ambition contented. Down to 1928 fewer women sought office than in some countries of northern Europe. After Jeannette Rankin of Montana started the fashion (1917-1919) there was usually at least one congresswoman. Two women served as governors, but in both cases the office was in some sense a legacy, Mrs. Miriam A. Ferguson being the wife of a former governor of Texas, and Mrs. Nellie Tayloe Ross the widow of a former governor of Wyoming. After the elections of

[1] Doris Stevens, *Jailed for Freedom* (N. Y., 1920), pts. ii-iii.

1928 the National League of Women Voters announced that there would be one hundred and forty-five women serving in thirty-eight of the forty-eight state legislatures, twelve of them serving for a fourth term.[1] All political parties gave to women positions of honor— though not always of much influence—on national and state committees. From the best obtainable estimates it appears that about thirty-five women out of every possible hundred voted at important elections.[2]

As the ballot was everywhere secret, one can only guess at the manner in which the woman's vote influenced American politics, but it is at least significant that those states which had lived longest under equal suffrage were usually very advanced in welfare legislation, and especially laws to protect the rights of women and children. On other issues there seems no evidence the women in the mass differed from men. Of all important groupings among voters, by place of residence, wealth, occupation, race, nationality, religion and sex, the last named made the least difference in the way the votes were cast.[3]

[1] N. Y. Times, Dec. 31, 1928.
[2] See H. L. Keenleyside, "The American Political Revolution of 1924," Current History, XXI (1925), 838.
[3] "Ten Years of Woman Suffrage," Literary Digest, CV, 11 (April 26, 1930).

CHAPTER VI

The Ways of Prosperity

DURING the decade of reconstruction which followed the World War the world watched with peculiar interest two experiments on the grand scale in economic revolution. One was a conscious, deliberate and political movement to shift industry from a capitalistic to a communistic basis, a movement accompanied by much violence and many spectacular incidents, the Bolshevist revolution in Russia. The other revolution had little to do with politics, embodied no particular theory, brought forth no striking events or incidents, and yet it altered the daily life of the average American citizen almost as profoundly as the revolution of 1917 altered the daily life of the Russian peasant. "The economic changes now occurring in the United States," said a keen contemporary observer, "are significant in their relation to the whole history of Western Civilization—as significant perhaps as the Industrial Revolution in England at the close of the eighteenth century." [1] They are, however, less easy to define because they did not arise out of a doctrine, such as Marxian communism in Russia, or out of any one outstanding invention, such as the steam engine in the English Industrial Revolution. The effect, the new American standard of living, was apparent to the whole world, but the causes were endlessly debated.

Western Europe, which had witnessed the Russian experiment with a mixture of interest and misgiving,

[1] T. N. Carver, *The Present Economic Revolution in the United States* (Boston, 1925), foreword.

turned a similarly speculative gaze across the Atlantic. Numerous books appeared in England, France and Germany, especially in Germany, on the new industrial structure of the United States, praising its achievements, condemning its materialism, but always seeking its secret.[1] Upon what meat had Cæsar fed that he should grow so great? Was the secret "big business" with its economies and standardizations; or efficiency with its studies of lost motion and duplication of effort; or greater trust in machinery, the Ford tractor, the typewriter, the telephone; or a generous wage which turned the laborer into a profitable customer? Or was it merely the rapid exploitation of virgin natural resources and profiteering at the expense of war-stricken Europe?

Certainly the change in American economic life in the postwar decade was something more than a mere increase of the national wealth. That increase was evident enough, but its scale was exaggerated by the inflation of prices which multiplied dollars faster than real values and by the relative impoverishment of Europe resulting from the World War. Even the United States of 1914 would have been envied by the Europe of 1918-1928. But quite aside from absolute or relative gains in wealth there were interesting developments in the way in which wealth was produced and distributed. Some of these were concerned with such matters as the transfor-

[1] Among the very numerous studies of American economic life by foreign observers the following may be mentioned as typical: J. E. Barker, *America's Secret; the Causes of Her Economic Success* (London, 1927); A. Demangeon, *America and the Race for World Dominion* (N. Y., 1921); Kurt Hassert, *Die Vereinigten Staaten von Amerika als Politische und Wirtschaftliche Weltmacht* (Tübingen, 1922); Julius Hirsch, *Das Amerikanische Wirtschaftswunder* (Berlin, 1926); Hermann Levy, *Die Vereinigten Staaten von Amerika als Wirtschaftsmacht* (Leipzig, 1923). See review by H. D. Hill, "European Books on America," *Sat. Rev. of Literature*, V, 1002 (May 11, 1929). For an able summary, see E. F. Gay's "Introduction" to Committee on Recent Economic Changes, *Recent Economic Changes* (N. Y., 1929), I, 1-12.

mation of the home into a unit of household engineering, with mechanical aids in place of servant labor; the treatment of farming as a speculative commercial enterprise to be handled by industrial methods rather than by peasant traditions; the ubiquitous automobile; the high-pressure salesmanship of modern advertising; and the multiform applications of science to profit and pleasure.[1] This chapter will deal more particularly with the tendencies in the world of "business." Our attention will be directed to such things as the accumulation and distribution of wealth and the upward trend of wages; the reduction of manufacturing costs by standardized and uniform methods and products; the increase in the power and wealth of corporations and the wider distribution of ownership in these enterprises; the multiplication of chain stores; the great extension of consumers' credits, as by the installment system; and the organization of business men for civic purposes. In some of these respects the new era merely brought a more rapid progress along roads already indicated prior to 1914; in others there was a positive change of direction.

In 1922 the census bureau estimated the wealth of the United States at a little over three hundred and twenty billion dollars, an increase of about seventy-two per cent over the figures for 1912. An estimate for 1925 indicated a further increase to three hundred and fifty-five billion dollars.[2] Allowance must be made for a depreciating dollar and a growing population, but even so it is evident that the nation had absorbed the costs of the war and its worst economic aftereffects by 1922 and from that point onward made positive progress in per-capita wealth. Of course, the census figures were only an approximation because, even supposing that the census

[1] See chaps. v, vii, viii, xiii and xiv respectively.
[2] National Industrial Conference Board, *Bull.*, no. 5 (1927), 34.

made no error of fact, economists are not agreed as to what assets can be reckoned as national wealth. The federal trade commission, using the figures of the 1922 census but including also roads, streets, highways and the site values of railways and public-service corporations, placed the total for 1922 as high as three hundred and fifty-three billion dollars.[1] On either basis the per-capita wealth averaged in the neighborhood of three thousand dollars.

Income rather than capital measures prosperity. In 1914 the per-capita national income was $339; in 1920, $703; in 1926, $671. If correction be made for the changing value of money, the "real" income of 1914 was $336; of 1920, $344; of 1926, $396.[2] The increase in real income per person *gainfully occupied* between 1914 and 1926 was 28.7 per cent.[3] Had it been possible without injury to the productive process to divide equally the nation's assets in the 1920's, each American family of five might reckon on an estate of about fifteen thousand dollars and an annual income of about three thousand dollars. Few nations make as careful a survey of their national wealth as the United States, but from such data as can be gathered it appears that the cash value of the nation as it stood—lands, mines, railroads, factories, livestock, manufactured articles and all the rest—was just a trifle less than that of the whole of Europe and perhaps as much as two fifths of the entire wealth of the world.[4]

A comparison of the wealth census of 1922 with that

[1] Federal Trade Commission, *National Wealth and Income* (69 Cong., 1 sess., *Senate Doc.*, no. 126, 1926). The latest study is M. A. Copeland, "The National Income and Its Distribution," *Recent Economic Changes*, II, 756-839.

[2] Natl. Indus. Conf. Board, *Bull.*, no. 5, 36.

[3] Natl. Indus. Conf. Board, *Bull.*, no. 5, 40.

[4] Using the estimate of the world's aggregate wealth given by Stuart Chase in the *N. Y. Times*, Aug. 22, 1926.

of 1912 shows also which items of the national Domesday Book were responsible for the progress of the whole and which forms of wealth were stationary or retrogressive. Real estate, the largest single item, accounted for about one hundred and seventy-six billion dollars, an increase of more than three fifths. No wonder Sinclair Lewis selected *Babbitt*, the "realtor," as the typical American to pillory in his novel. The real-estate booms in the vacation states of Florida and California, as well as in the fertile farm lands of Iowa, and the rising site values in the growing cities readily explain this increase. The money value of manufactured products, over twenty-eight billion dollars, had approximately doubled. The value of manufacturing machinery, tools and implements advanced from six to nearly sixteen billions. The value of furniture, clothing and other articles of personal use and consumption made a threefold gain. Motor vehicles appeared as a separate item, with a value of over four billion five hundred million dollars.

On the other hand, the money value of farm products increased but slightly in the decade—really a loss in actual buying power for the farmer—and the value of livestock decreased. The railroads and most other public utilities showed very slight advance. A small but significant item in the total was a three-fifths increase in the amount of gold and silver coin and bullion, an interesting evidence of the change of the United States from debtor to creditor among the nations.[1] In these figures we see reflected a stationary phase in railroad building, a relative decline in agriculture, a vast expansion of industry, a rapid growth of motor traction, and a greatly

[1] "At the beginning of the World War we owed $4,500,000,000 abroad whereas now we are creditors to the extent of about $16,000,000,-000." J. W. O'Leary, president of the Chamber of Commerce of the United States, "Twenty-Five Years of American Prosperity," *Current History*, XXIII (1926), 699.

increased social surplus for the comforts and luxuries of life.

Perhaps a better way of measuring the real wealth of a nation than the fluctuating standard of the dollar, even with correction for price levels, is its total labor power, the work of man, beast and machine being taken together. The primary horse power employed in manufacture in 1914 was a little over twenty-two million or 3.2 units per wage-earner; in 1925 it was nearly thirty-six million or 4.3 units apiece.[1] But we must break the period into two rather contrasting divisions, war-time and postwar, for there was little increase in the use of power from 1914 to 1919 and no increase in production per worker either in factories or on the railways.[2] The dislocation of labor due to the war must probably be blamed for this; millions of workmen and thousands of factories were engaged in unfamiliar tasks. From 1919 onward the productivity of labor sharply increased. From 1919 to 1925 the number of workers engaged in agriculture, manufactures and railway transport actually fell off, and the number of miners did not grow, thus creating a new problem of unemployment lessened somewhat by the closed door to immigration and increased activity in occupations such as the building trades. But with no enlargement in employed personnel there was a vast enlargement in output. The output per individual worker from 1919 to 1925 increased by fifteen per cent in transportation, by eighteen per cent in agriculture, by thirty-three per cent in mining and by forty per cent in manufacturing.[3] In part, this amazing result was due to the increased utilization of power from coal, oil and waterfalls in place of human effort, but in part also to

[1] *Commerce Yearbook for 1928*, I, 266.
[2] *Commerce Yearbook for 1928*, I, 18, 266.
[3] *Commerce Yearbook for 1928*, I, 19.

those miscellaneous improvements in industrial organization which are lumped together under the catchword "efficiency."

The power-wealth of the United States placed that nation not at the head of the class but in a class by itself. The combined production of all sources of power, measured in terms of thermal units as a common denominator for coal, oil, gas and falling water, was nearly half the world's total: two fifths of the world's coal, seven tenths of the petroleum, one third of the water power.[1] The per-capita consumption of energy in 1923 (as distinguished from production) was estimated at thrice that of France, thirteen times that of Japan and ninety times that of British India. Thomas T. Read, formerly of the United States bureau of mines, prepared an estimate of the comparative output of work per person in each of several leading countries.[2] It affords a pretty fair measurement of the real labor power available in different countries and shows that, for practical purposes, China was not four times as populous as the United States; on the contrary the United States had more than seven times the labor power of China. Or to put it another way, America was a vast slaveholding aristocracy in which the average citizen, potentially if not actually, held the equivalent of thirty slaves, inanimate, mechanical slaves like the cheap and docile robots of Karel Capek's popular drama, "R.U.R." In this sense, the American workman was less a "wage slave" than a slave driver, whose task

---

[1] *Commerce Yearbook for 1928*, I, 266-267.

[2] Taking China as the unit, the output of work per person in various countries was: British India, 1.25; Russia, 2.5; Italy, 2.75; Japan, 3.5; France, 8.25; Germany, 12; Great Britain, 18; Canada, 20; U. S. A., 30. T. T. Read, "The American Secret," *Atlantic Mo.*, CXXXIX (1927), 289-294. Of course, such comparative figures afford no measure of general civilization and are a little unfair to nations like France and Italy which were predominantly agricultural, for obviously a factory needs larger power plants than a farm.

was not pulling and hauling with his own muscles but guiding, directing and checking the work of the machines. Of course it may still be debated which was the harder task.

The fact that the United States was wealthy did not in itself demonstrate prosperity, for averages can be unduly raised by a few large fortunes. Was it true that while the rich grew richer the poor grew poorer? Or had Uncle Sam—in the phrase used by the Progressives of 1912—begun to "pass prosperity around"? Certainly the rich were growing richer. A bankers' estimate of 1926 placed the number of millionaires in the country at eleven thousand as compared with four thousand five hundred in 1914.[1] But were the poor getting poorer, either absolutely or relatively? That is a harder question to answer, but every indication points to the negative. A study made of more than forty-three thousand estates probated in thirteen states over a decade led to the conclusion that "although the tabulations suggest wide variations in the wealth of individuals and a rather high degree of concentration, a comparison of the estates probated in 1912 with those probated in 1923 indicates that this concentration was greater at the beginning of the period covered by the commission's study than at the end." [2] A study of the income-tax returns seems to confirm this impression that the increase of wealth among the very wealthy has not at any time tended to reduce incomes at any other point in the scale.[3]

[1] American Bankers' Assoc., *Journ.*, XIX (1926), 179.
[2] Federal Trade Commission, *National Wealth and Income*, 3.
[3] The thorough investigation of the distribution of income by the National Bureau of Economic Research, *Income in the United States* (2 vols., N. Y., 1921-1922), came to the conclusion (I, 147) that the most prosperous one per cent of income-receivers had nearly 14 per cent of the social income; the most prosperous five per cent, 26 per cent; the most prosperous ten per cent, 35 per cent; the most prosperous one-fifth, 47 per cent.

For the workers in the organized trades we have statistical evidence of prosperity in the comparison of wage scales and price changes. Combining the two index numbers of union rates of wages and the cost of living, the increase in the purchasing power of wages in 1927 was about one and a half times that of 1913.[1] In other words the buying power of an hour of skilled labor was one half greater in 1927. For labor in general, including the unskilled and unorganized, the improvement was probably nearly thirty per cent. Though nominal wages rose more rapidly from 1914 to 1921 than later, the cost of living in some cases rose even more rapidly, so the "real" improvement in the lot of the workingman, like the "real" increase in the general wealth of the nation, belonged to the years 1921-1928 and especially the latter half of that period. Farm wages, save for a brief war-prosperity increase in 1918-1920, did not share in the gains of labor as a whole, and the lumbermen and tobacco workers were almost equally unfortunate.[2] If we distinguish "social wages," that is, a proportionate share in the enlarged output of industry, from both money wages and "real" or buying-power wages, we can summarize the average wage movement from 1914 to 1927 in all branches of manufacturing as an increase from $580 to $1301 per year in money, of thirty-five per cent in buying power, and fourteen per cent in "social wages."[3] The average British wage in the 1920's was about half the American, and rates in continental Europe in very few cases rose as high as the British. But this difference in standard was old. More significant was the fact that, while American wages rose well above the increased cost of living, the European workingman but

[1] E. T. Devine, "American Labor's Improved Status since 1914," *Current History*, XXVIII (1928), 807.
[2] Devine, "American Labor's Improved Status," 807-808.
[3] Devine, "American Labor's Improved Status," 809.

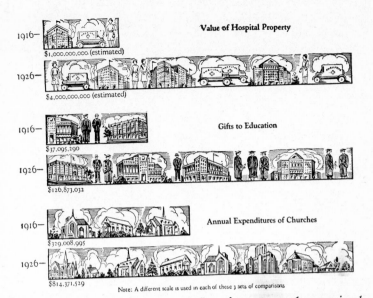

Value of Hospital Property

1916—
$1,000,000,000 (estimated)

1926—
$4,000,000,000 (estimated)

Gifts to Education

1916—
$37,095,290

1926—
$126,873,032

Annual Expenditures of Churches

1916—
$329,008,995

1926—
$814,371,529

Note: A different scale is used in each of these 3 sets of comparisons

While the economic surplus of America constantly sustained philanthropy,

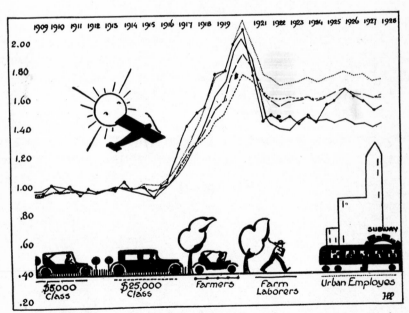

2.00
1.80
1.60
1.40
1.20
1.00
.80
.60
.40
.20

1909 1910 1911 1912 1913 1914 1915 1916 1917 1918 1919   1921 1922 1923 1924 1925 1926 1927 1928

$5,000 Class $25,000 Class   Farmers   Farm Laborers   Urban Employes

SUBWAY

HP

Prices made increased demands upon the dollars in the hands of various classes.

Spending the Dollar

little more than held his own within the prewar period.[1]

More interesting to most of us than the average wages of large classes is the picture of what they meant to the single home. Consider the case of a typical workingman in an American industrial town in 1924.[2] He was at the head of a family of five. In the course of a year he spent $548 for food, $237 for clothes, $186 for rent, $74 for fuel and light, $73 for furnishings and supplies about the house and $306 for all other expenses, besides saving about $79 for a possible rainy day in the future. Of course wages and prices varied much from town to town. New York may be selected to represent the large cities with their high rentals. A typical Brooklyn office worker ("white-collar man") would pay out each average week ten dollars to the landlord, fifteen to the grocer, butcher and milkman, five to the clothing stores and nine to all his other creditors.[3] His neighbor, a factory worker in the Borough of Queens, paid about seven and a third dollars to the landlord, over fourteen to the grocer, five for the clothing of himself, his wife and the three children and split eight dollars into sundries. Apart from a higher rent due to the supposed social necessity of living in a "respectable section of the town," and the need for a neat business suit in place of overalls, the office clerk and the factory hand had an almost identical standard of living.

[1] Julius Klein, director of the bureau of foreign and domestic commerce, estimated the increase in money wage in the United States for the period 1914 to 1927 at 160 per cent, and the British for the same period at 80 per cent, the cost of living in the two nations having gone up in the meantime by 45 and 42 per cent respectively. Julius Klein, "Servicing Our 260 American Wage," *Mag. of Business*, LIV (1928), 35.

[2] Data taken from "Cost of Living in the United States," U. S. Bur. of Labor Statistics, *Bull.*, no. 357. The survey included 92 industrial towns and cities.

[3] J. C. Laue, "Cost of Living Shown for a New York Family," *N. Y. Times*, Feb. 13, 1927.

An even more concrete picture of the times appeared in the answer to the following question: "What all is necessary to the trousseau of a bride marrying a man of moderate means? He is a bricklayer and we expect to have a five-room modern house." [1] The lady who answered such social queries in the newspaper stipulated in her reply, among other things: six linen bed sheets and pillowcases, summer and winter blankets, from six to twelve bath towels and as many smooth towels, three or four ordinary tablecloths and as many more "for occasions," eight pairs of stockings (in three shades) and "eight pairs of gloves to match," two hats, four pairs of shoes, a raincoat and several dresses, "one of them elaborate enough to do for the evening." It would be interesting to compare this list with the clothes and linens of a bricklayer's bride in any previous generation.

The hours of labor were reduced at the same time that wages were being raised. The six-day week and eight-hour day became thoroughly established as institutions, as part of the "American standard of living." Prior to 1914 an average factory week for mills on full time was about fifty-five hours; after the war it varied from forty-eight to fifty. The working week in mines and railways was about as in the factories, for the building trades a little less. From 1916 onward the eight-hour day constituted legal "full time" on the railroads. In 1923 the United States Steel Corporation, an old stronghold of the twelve-hour day, shifted to the eight-hour basis, enlarged its working force by over seventeen thousand men to meet the labor shortage thus created, raised wages and still showed an increased profit, thus refuting the fears once expressed by Chairman E. H. Gary of the corporation that the iron and steel industry could not afford to make the change.

[1] *Washington Post*, July 26, 1928.

With the marked improvement in labor conditions went a diminished antagonism between capital and labor. To be sure, in the months of reconstruction immediately after the war, what with rapidly changing prices and some radical agitators who mistook the Russian conflagration for a world-wide dawn, strikes were numerous, extensive and sometimes violent.[1] But in the years of "normalcy" that followed they greatly decreased. The American trade unions followed in the main a most enlightened policy of encouraging rather than restricting production. As President Samuel Gompers of the American Federation of Labor said in 1917, "The labor movement of the past thirty years . . . has changed that mode of thinking and that mode of procedure among the working people, so that instead of reducing output or opposing the introduction of machinery and new tools of labor we encourage them." And his successor in office, William Green, declared, "We are coöperating with the managements in the elimination of waste because the working man suffers most of all as a result of waste. We are also coöperating with the managements in the elimination of duplication of effort, and we are not opposing the introduction of improved machinery." [2] This was the subject of much favorable comment by foreign observers. A report by Colonel F. Vernon Willey and Mr. Guy Locock, as visiting representatives of the Federation of British Industries,[3] testified:

> In view of the shrinkage in the stream of immigration, and therefore more particularly of the pool of skilled labor, it is becoming more and more important for labor-saving devices to be used to the greatest pos-

[1] See earlier, chap. iii.
[2] J. E. Barker, *America's Secret* (London, 1927), 104-105.
[3] F. V. Willey and Guy Locock, "America's Economic Supremacy," *Current History*, XXIII (1926), 504.

sible extent. To this labor offers no opposition, and the result is a constantly increasing efficiency of production . . . and a comparative freedom from the restrictions on output which hamper us in England.

Such testimony was almost universal.

The trade unions did not cover so great a proportion of the world of labor in the United States as in Great Britain or some continental European nations.[1] The American Federation of Labor appears to have been at its strongest in 1920, with about four million members. Shortly afterwards, due probably to the depression of 1921, about a fourth of these ceased to pay their dues. Even with the restoration of prosperity the Federation did not rise again to more than three and a third millions. The next largest labor group, the railway brotherhoods of engineers, firemen, trainmen and conductors, mustered about four hundred and fifty thousand. The Industrial Workers of the World in quiet times had hardly thirty-five thousand active members though a particular strike might swell their numbers for a few weeks or months. The Amalgamated Clothing Workers with about one hundred and sixty thousand members represented a degree of radicalism somewhat between the revolutionary I.W.W. and the evolutionary American Federation. Some of the largest coal fields were nonunion and several great cities like Detroit boasted of being "open-shop towns."

Though the American labor unions were not coextensive with American industrialism, they represented the most skilled and best paid trades and held key positions in nearly every industry. The American Federation alone had one hundred and seven craft unions within its ranks in 1928. Some of these were strongly represented

[1] Leo Wolman, "Labor," *Recent Economic Changes*, II, 479-481.

by branches across the Canadian border. Their prosperity was clearly evidenced by the establishment of a series of labor banks. The first of these in the United States was established in Washington, D. C., in 1920. Six months later the Brotherhood of Locomotive Engineers opened one in Cleveland. Within five years scores had been founded.[1] Not all were successful, and the Federation resolved to discontinue authorizing new banks until the experiment had a chance to prove its value. Several unions interested themselves in establishing schools for immigrants and "colleges" for training labor organizers. In 1921 a Workers' Education Bureau of America was founded to stimulate this movement. It hardly realized the high hopes built on it and became "deflated into a prosaic auxiliary of the American Federation of Labor." [2]

Child labor continued to be a feature of American industry. The census of 1920 showed a decline in ten years from nearly two million to but little over one million for children from ten to fifteen years of age "gainfully employed." [3] After 1920 there seems to have been an increased employment of children, and in June, 1924, the National Child Labor Committee estimated that two million boys and girls under fifteen were at work.[4] The majority were farm laborers, usually under the care of their own parents. The beet fields, cranberry bogs and other seasonal branches of agriculture had their gangs of child workers, however, and the canneries found them useful. Thousands were also employed in textile mills, especially in the Southern states. Two attempts, in 1916

[1] Carver, *Present Economic Revolution*, 113.
[2] D. J. Saposs, "Labor," *Am. Journ. of Sociology*, XXXIV, 81-82.
[3] Some believe this to be an underestimate since the census of 1920 was taken in the winter when fewer children are employed on farms, while the census of 1910 was taken in the spring.
[4] B. P. Chass, "American Children in Bondage," *Current History*, XXI (1925), 855.

and 1919, to regulate child labor by barring from interstate commerce goods produced contrary to federal law
were declared unconstitutional by the Supreme Court,[1]
and a proposed Twentieth Amendment in 1924, which
would specifically grant to Congress power to legislate
concerning the employment of persons under eighteen,
met with astonishing lack of public interest. Most state
legislatures either failed to act or voted against it, and in
Massachusetts, where there was an excellent state law,
a popular referendum rejected the amendment by almost
three votes to one. Opinion is divided as to whether
apathy on this question was due to the belief that child
labor as it existed at the time was no great evil, or that,
being an evil, it could better be controlled by state legislation than by federal action. Certainly the defeat of the
Twentieth Amendment was a remarkable flare-up of the
old state-rights doctrine which had been so little in evidence when the Eighteenth and Nineteenth were enacted.

Unemployment was, like child labor, an industrial
problem which the "era of prosperity" left partly un-
solved. Aside from agriculture, the number of unemployed at different times varied, according to the best
estimates, from five to fifteen per cent of the whole body
of workers, amounting to over four million during the
temporary depression of 1921.[2]

Perhaps the fact which most tended to reconcile the
conflicting interests of capital and labor was their increasing identification. In many of the larger corporations the policy was adopted of placing shares of stock on
easy terms in the hands of their employees.[3] This did not
mean that the United States had become a land of eco-

[1] See R. G. Fuller, *Child Labor and the Constitution* (N. Y., 1923),
238-242.
[2] W. C. Mitchell, "A Review," *Recent Economic Changes*, II, 879.
[3] For an excellent discussion of employee ownership, see Carver, *Present
Economic Revolution*.

nomic equality, for the single share owned by John Doe Hunyak cannot be compared with the vast investments of the millionaire. But it did mean that the distinction between "owner" and "laborer" was of degree rather than of kind. The public at large also bought freely of small shares in big business, so that ownership became increasingly distributed. A study of corporations selling shares to their employees revealed from five to eighty-five per cent of the whole stock in the hands of employees, with an average for the larger companies of about twenty-two per cent.[1] In 1922 there were 14,400,000 stockholders in American corporations.[2] About 3,400,000 of these had been added in the three years following the entrance of the United States into the World War.[3] No doubt the intensive propaganda for the sale of liberty-loan bonds had increased the habit of investment among the general public.

More than a quarter of the employees of the United States Steel Corporation held stock, to a total value of over $100,000,000.[4] Standard Oil and its subsidiary companies had in 1925 over 300,000 shareholders, many of them employees.[5] The railroad and public-service companies showed the same tendency. There were about a million owners of railway bonds, and about twenty-eight per cent of all income-producing endowments of colleges and universities were in the form of railway bonds or stocks. As President C. H. Markham of the Illinois Central put it, "It is 'Main Street' and not 'Wall Street' that owns the railroads today." Public

[1] Carver, *Present Economic Revolution*, 99.
[2] Carver, *Present Economic Revolution*, 107.
[3] W. Z. Ripley, *Main Street and Wall Street* (Boston, 1927), 116.
[4] J. G. Frederick, "The Steel Corporation's 25-Year Record," *Current History*, XXIV (1926), 928.
[5] D. F. Houston, "Every Worker a Capitalist," *World's Work*, XLIX (1925), 274.

utilities, such as electric-light and power plants, gas works, and electric trolleys, counted over two million owners.[1]

Popular ownership was not, however, identical with popular control. As Professor W. Z. Ripley of Harvard pointed out, there was an increasing tendency to issue shares which did not carry voting privileges or even the right to acquire a share in new stock issues.[2] One artificial-silk concern gave voting rights to only two thousand out of a total of 600,000 shares; a well-known root-beer enterprise had 3872 "management shares," as against 180,000 nonvoting ones; a theatrical enterprise had 100,000 voting shares out of a total of 4,000,000. In 1925 the entire control of $1,500,000,000 of public investment in electric-light, power, gas and water companies resided in ten per cent of the capitalization.[3] The control of these public-service corporations was at once centralized and complex. Thus one concern which Professor Ripley described comprised, through interlocking agencies, eighteen gas, light and power companies, besides central heating, artificial ice, cold storage, street and interurban railways, etc., servicing a population of 1,725,000.

In all fairness to the corporations, it must be said that the average stockholder rarely dreamed of exercising his franchise when he had one, and preferred to use a proxy who would shoulder all the burden and responsibilty of checking up on the management. Many companies issued

[1] A typical instance was the Pacific Gas and Electric Company with 4128 stockholders in 1914 and 26,294 in 1923, or the Southern California Edison with 2000 holders in 1917 and 65,636 in 1923. One hundred and eighty-five companies reported to the National Electric Light Association 652,900 stockholders obtained through customer-ownership campaigns from 1914 through 1923. Hundreds of thousands of customers held some stake in either telephone or telegraph industries. Houston, "Every Worker a Capitalist," 275.

[2] Ripley, Main Street and Wall Street, 39, 87.

[3] Ripley, Main Street and Wall Street, 119, 123, 293.

a limited number of voting shares to those only who had the time and interest to follow closely the conduct of the business, and thus saved the bother of hunting up quorums and majorities of stock for the necessary formalities of the annual meeting. As one writer pertinently put it, to ask the average investor for his opinion on details of management was as useless as to "have handed him a page out of a Chinese almanac and asked him to vote whether it's February or August." [1] The great good of diffusing corporation ownership had to some extent been offset by the evil of divorcing ownership and management more widely than ever before in the history of American business. The small shareholder, whether voter or not, felt that his own prosperity was to some extent bound up with that of "Big Business" and Wall Street, hitherto vaguely regarded as his enemies. Perhaps this was one cause of the extreme political conservatism that marked the period from 1918 to 1928. [2]

Other evidences of prosperity besides the widespread purchase of industrial securities may be found in the growth of savings in bank accounts, insurance policies and building-and-loan associations. These were evidences all the more striking because in an age of high-pressure salesmanship thrift was not one of the popular

[1] Will Payne, "Owners and Voters," *Sat. Eve. Post,* CCI, 38 (Aug. 25, 1928). To quote further: "Probably the time is not a great way off when outside stockholders will own the greater part of the country's big business. Their voting power is only a second-line defense—something to fall back on after suffering a reverse at the front. The front must be left to the management."

[2] "Nothing," said one acute observer, "could conceivably have done nearly so much toward making of this a tightly conservative country as the widespread stock distribution that has occurred in recent years. . . . the Standard Oil Company no longer seems to the public mind merely Rockefeller, the steel companies are no longer only Morgan and Schwab, the New York Central Railroad is not now just the Vanderbilts." F. R. Kent, "Dividends *vs.* Radicalism," *World's Work,* LVI (1928), 503. See also the same author's *Political Behavior* (N. Y., 1928) for extended comment on the relation of stock distribution to the growing conservatism of the times.

virtues. In place of the three traditional virtues of the Industrious Apprentice, honesty, industry and thrift, current magazine fiction applauded the ability to carry through a bluff, to put up a huge "front" on small capital, to break out a new path, and snatch victory from defeat by daring assumptions of risk and defiance of orders—an economic romanticism superseding the economic classicism of Benjamin Franklin's day.[1] Yet in the spendthrift and speculative period from 1914 to 1925 the number of savings accounts increased nearly fourfold, from eleven to forty-three millions, and their sum from eight to twenty-three billions. About half of this was held in savings banks, which specialized in small accounts and were usually limited to them. By the end of 1926 more than 25,500,000 ordinary life-insurance policies and more than 76,000,000 industrial policies were in force in the United States, their total assets being $12,500,000,000.[2] In ten years building-and-loan policies increased in number from 3,103,935 to 8,554,-352 in 1924. Over eleven million families owned their own homes.

The combination of speculative spirit and prosperous industry, however, led to the investment of an undue proportion of the nation's savings in stocks of fluctuating value. Rash bidding raised stock values in 1928 and 1929 to artificial heights, and the inevitable collapse, in October of the latter year, wiped out "paper" values to a total estimated equal to the entire German war indemnity![3]

[1] "I told him I was the lady from the bank who had come to talk thrift to the workers. Immediately he raised an admonishing finger. 'Now, look ahere, lady, don't you come 'round here pullin' any of that Benjamin Franklin stuff on us. I know all about that guy. I've looked him up. He overdone it, he did.' " Experience related by Margaret Dodge in *Commerce, Finance and Industry*, May, 1926, 15.

[2] *Commerce Yearbook for 1928*, I, 653.

[3] S. S. Fontaine in *World Almanac for 1930*, 146.

Thrift in the sense of just not spending, as distinguished from investment, was indeed at a discount in all classes. The best proof of this was the great increase in consumer credits, the purchase of goods on so much down and so much a month. Before the war such installment purchases were usually for things permanent or very expensive: the house in which a man would spend his life or a diamond ring for the girl with whom he would spend it. But in the postwar period the habit of installment buying had spread to cover nearly every article subject to purchase. "You furnish the girl; we furnish the home," read the sky-line sign of the furniture factory. Automobile dealers attempted to keep their industry on a pay-at-once basis; but the installment system captured the automobile. Many Americans felt lost without some running account. Often the radio set, the phonograph, the piano player, the dinner jacket, the new curtains and the new car were worn out before the final payments were made.

By 1927 some fifteen per cent of all goods were sold on the installment plan, at retail prices about six billion dollars' worth, while at any given moment between two and three billions of outstanding debt could be accounted for by installment purchase.[1] Over eighty-five per cent of furniture, eighty per cent of phonographs, seventy-five per cent of washing machines, and the greater part of all vacuum cleaners, pianos, sewing machines, radios and electric refrigerators were bought in this way.[2] Most of the industries in which installment buying was the rule were new industries based on recent mechanical inventions. As home radios, refrigerators, electric washers and the like represented a considerable

[1] W. C. Plummer, "Social and Economic Consequences of Buying on the Instalment Plan," Am. Acad. of Polit. and Social Sci., *Annals*, CXXIX, supplement, 2.
[2] Plummer, "Social and Economic Consequences," 3.

investment, many a housewife would have hesitated at so much expense for a novel luxury but for the seductive argument of easy payments.

Whether the prevalence of the installment system was a cause of national prosperity or merely a symptom of national extravagance was much debated.[1] Its advocates represented it as an expansion of credit that had on the one hand made possible the building up of great industries and on the other enabled the consumer to acquire comforts and conveniences that otherwise he would never have ventured to buy.[2] "Enjoy while you pay," said the advertisers. Losses, at least during the prosperous period when the installment system was most rapidly extended, were very small. One large finance company, specializing in credit for retail automobile sales, lost less than one fifth of one per cent in eight years from failures to meet payments.[3] The reassuring increase in all forms of savings indicated, furthermore, that installment buying was not consuming all the weekly pay envelope but left plenty of margin for bank account and life-insurance policy. Some persons who had never been able to save first learned thrift by the paradoxical process of acquiring liabilities that *must* be met.

Opponents of the system said that all expansion of credit, however it might stimulate industry in good times, carried with it corresponding dangers and losses when times were hard. Even in the days of prosperity the increased purchase of luxuries often meant miserable little economies in the necessities. The National Grocers' Association complained that many customers with the

[1] The domestic-commerce division of the department of commerce published a *Reading List on Installment Buying and Selling* (Wash., revised to May, 1928).

[2] See E. R. A. Seligman, *The Economics of Installment Buying* (N. Y., 1927).

[3] Arthur Pound, "The Land of Dignified Credit," *Atlantic Mo.*, CXXXVII (1926), 259.

easy-payment habit proved unable to meet their bills at the corner grocery.[1] The National Association of Credit Men, representing thirty thousand merchants and manufacturers, declared that "the events of recent years clearly show that the stimulation of business by the unwise use of credits is merely a temporary measure and has a reaction in the serious disturbance of goods and prices."[2] Another objection was the increased ultimate cost to the consumer, for of course credit is not sold for nothing. A careful statistician estimated that "as a rule, it costs the buyer as much more to buy on the installment plan, as it would if he borrowed the money at an interest rate of from eleven to forty per cent and paid cash."[3] This extra cost meant less money to spend in other directions, and so robbed Peter the cash merchant even faster than it paid Paul the salesman on the installment plan.

Next to installment buying the most noteworthy tendency in American retail trade was the development of the chain store.[4] This was but one phase of the general drift towards standardization that marked the period. From the viewpoint of the consumer the important fact was not that the stores were under a central management —competitors in the trade had the worry of that—but that they gave a uniform service. After the war there was a greater increase of business in chain groceries, drug stores, candy shops and five-and-ten-cent stores than in any other class of retail trade. They held a doubly strategic position, combining the advantages of centralization (uniform management, wholesale purchase and the

[1] Pound, "The Land of Dignified Credit," 258.
[2] Hawthorne Daniel, "Living and Dying on Installments," *World's Work*, LI (1926), 331.
[3] Plummer, "Social and Economic Consequences," 30.
[4] The domestic-commerce division of the department of commerce prepared a *Chain Store Bibliography* (Wash., 1928) covering the books, reports, magazine articles and trade periodicals dealing with the question.

economies of combination) enjoyed by the city department stores with the advantages of decentralization hitherto enjoyed only by independent shops, a location in every neighborhood and consequent direct friendly contact with the consumer.

The chain-store movement first triumphed in the grocery field. The Great Atlantic and Pacific Tea Company, both pioneer and champion among its kind, opened 2200 new stores from 1914 to 1917 and had 5000 in all by 1922.[1] By 1928 it had 17,500 branches and did an annual business of $750,000,000.[2] The Kroger Grocery and Baking Company, the American Stores and the Safeway Stores were at that time the leading rivals. But the most interesting departure was the Piggly-Wiggly system devised and patented by Clarence Saunders of Memphis, Tennessee. The Piggly-Wiggly was a grocery-cafeteria, in which the customer entered by a turnstile, walked past the shelves, selected what he wanted from label and price tag, and paid the cashier on leaving. The clerks, like the waiters in self-help restaurants, had little to do except see that the shelves and counters were supplied. The appeal of the Piggly-Wiggly was partly psychological; many housewives, it developed, were flurried at too much attention by solicitous clerks and liked to make their selections at leisure. So keen was the competition of the chain groceries that more than five hundred independent grocers in the Far West organized the United Grocers, Incorporated, to protect their interests by collective buying and the pooling of good advice and suggestions on retail management.[3]

[1] W. S. Hayward, *Chain Stores* (N. Y., 1922), 332.
[2] Evans Clark, "Big Business Now Sweeps Retail Trade," *N. Y. Times*, July 8, 1928.
[3] "The Challenge of the Chains," an interview of the United Grocers in the *Mag. of Business*, LIV (1928), 28.

The five-and-ten-cent stores were usually part of chain systems. Although most of them ran over the ten-cent limit to small multiples up to twenty-five or fifty cents, they always were sufficiently true to their name to appeal to the bargain-hunting instinct. What was for a long time the tallest inhabited structure in the world, the Woolworth Building in New York, stood as a monument to quick turnover sales in nickels and dimes. The F. W. Woolworth Company, selling two hundred and seventy-two million dollars' worth of "notions" a year through nearly sixteen hundred branch stores, stood second in importance only to the Atlantic and Pacific Tea Company among all the chains.[1] The S. S. Kresge stores, the result of a Detroit merchant's efforts, established a more-than-hundred-million-dollar business and a twenty-three-million-dollar charitable foundation. Other outstanding examples of combination, such as the United Drug Company, the United Cigar Stores, the J. C. Penney department stores, the Childs restaurants and the Statler hotels, showed the wide applicability of the chain principle. Because of legal restrictions chain banking, so familiar to the traveler in Europe, did not develop in America, though there were strings of local banks more or less under the influence of certain large metropolitan institutions. The "Morris Plan banks" organized for small personal loans were exceptions to the rule.

The same desire for cheap goods, wholesale production and uniform quality which caused the rise of the chain store brought increased prosperity to a somewhat older American institution, the mail-order house. Such firms as Sears, Roebuck and Company and Montgomery, Ward in Chicago had long since extended their influence to every hamlet. The isolated station agent brought

[1] *N. Y. Times*, July 8, 1928.

within the sweep of American life by a fat mail-order catalogue was one of the truest of national types.[1] Its thousand pages of illustrated and animated detail were to his loneliness all that a library of the "world's best literature" would be to the hypothetical literary gentleman on a desert island. Even small business concerns found that the new facilities of the parcel post opened to them a most profitable channel of merchandising. One general store in Temple, Oklahoma, a town of nine hundred inhabitants—the case is mentioned because it is typical—made over a fourth of its mail-order sales beyond the hundred-mile limit.[2] But the independent local dealer generally felt the mail-order house an even deadlier enemy than the chain store, for it even more directly "took money out of the town." Often a politician did not dare buy beyond his city limits lest it be construed as a reflection on the local merchants. New slogans appeared on trolley car and bus signs, "Patronize your NABORHOOD druggist" and "NABORHOODS loyal to their stores have the best stores," boldly challenging at once the old-fashioned spelling and the new-fangled mercantile centralization.

One form of standardization, indeed, met with general approval from both big business and little and its benefits were passed on to the consumer in decrease of cost and increase of convenience. This was the reduction, effected by the so-called division of simplified practice within the federal department of commerce under the aggressive leadership of Herbert Hoover, in the sizes, types and varieties of manufactured articles. It was discovered that under the old régime of go-as-you-please

[1] Read the first chapter of S. H. Adams's novel *Success* (Boston, 1921).
[2] V. E. Pratt, *Selling by Mail* (N. Y., 1924), 394. "About 25 per cent of its business is done through the mails, and the annual volume of the store reaches as high as $1,500,000 . . . over 25 per cent of the sales are made beyond the hundred-mile limit."

competition different manufacturers had multiplied the variety of their products beyond all use and reason. Now, in goods for personal expression such as vases and dresses and books, too great a degree of uniformity is an evil, an evil for which Europeans have often reproached the United States. But nobody is sentimental about sewer pipe and coal shovels; nobody finds poetry in the subtle variations between one carpet tack and another. The task was to substitute order not for liberty but for a purely unintentional chaos.

Until 1922 there were sixty-six varieties of paving brick, although more than four fifths of all sales were of five kinds.[1] A brickmakers' conference at Washington in 1921-1922 recommended the elimination of fifty-five styles, the next year four more were dropped, and by 1926 only four styles remained in use; the producers had saved a million dollars annually and all the consumers seemed satisfied. Similarly, 428 sizes of tacks and nails were reduced to 181; 4460 varieties of spades and shovels to 384; 78 varieties of bed springs to two; 49 types of milk bottles to nine; and several thousand warehouse printed forms to fifteen.[2]

Conferences of producers and distributors of standard commodities, called together by the division of simplified practice, brought about an average reduction in varieties of seventy-three per cent in more than fifty lines of manufacture. All of these simplifications were voluntary as the department of commerce had no coercive power, and indeed many producers made experiments on their own account. One food manufacturer, for instance, cut his catalogued varieties by eighty-nine per cent, with the amazing result that he found he could cut his sales force by seventy-three per cent, his advertising costs by

[1] C. E. Russell, "The New Industrial Era," *Century*, CXII (1926), 4.
[2] See Department of Commerce, *Ann. Rep. for 1925*, 19-23.

seventy-eight per cent, his overhead by eighty per cent, and increase the volume of his sales sixfold! [1]

One feature of American business life which greatly impressed foreign observers was the extent to which everything was organized, not only within the factory but even among competitors. To cite once more from the report of visiting delegates of the Federation of British Industries: [2]

> When one examines the number of trade associations in the United States the total is amazing. It is estimated that there are seven thousand associations, Federal, State or municipal, dealing with trade matters. Undoubtedly there is a considerable amount of overlapping, a certain wastage of effort, but at the same time the leading trade associations, such as the Chamber of Commerce, the National Manufacturers' Association, the National Industrial Conference Board, the Merchants' Association, etc., are extremely efficiently organized and are performing valuable national work.

Some of these organizations, indeed, were civic or social rather than purely "business." For example, by 1928 the Rotary Club and its younger brother Kiwanis each counted more than a hundred thousand members, and the Lions' Club, founded in 1917, grew in a decade to over fifty thousand. Besides these national and international societies there were many local business clubs of similar type and purport. What among chambers of commerce, trade associations, civic-betterment clubs, local "booster" societies, church or charity "drives," fraternal orders and the like, the American business man often seemed to have time for anything and everything but his own special business. Charles Dickens must have

[1] Russell, "The New Industrial Era," 6.
[2] Willey and Locock, "America's Economic Supremacy," *Current History*, XXIII (1926), 504.

had him in prophetic mind when he said, through the medium of Marley's ghost, "The dealings of my trade were but a drop of water in the comprehensive ocean of my business!"

CHAPTER VII

THE CHANGING COUNTRYSIDE

AGRICULTURE in the United States occupied a paradoxical position of simultaneous progress and decline.[1] Never before in history had so considerable a majority of the American people dwelt in towns and cities. The profits of manufacture and trade overshadowed the incomes from the farm; tenancy and indebtedness somewhat increased, and in some parts of the country farms were abandoned to the chance comer or reborn as roadside inns and curio shops for the tourist trade.[2] Of the two great waves of prosperity which swept over the nation, the "war-prosperity" period of 1916-1919 and the "Coolidge-prosperity" period of 1924-1928, only the former brought riches to the farm, and the intermediate trough of depression injured farming more severely than other economic interests.

Yet this same period marked the greatest advances in agricultural efficiency. With fewer acres and a declining farm population production actually increased. Indeed, overproduction was often blamed as the chief cause for the low prices of farm products after the war. Motor traction and electric power on the farm increasingly made agriculture a form of applied engineering. And the farmer himself, in spite of the handicap of high costs and a poor market, was usually able to indulge in comforts

---

[1] E. G. Nourse, "Agriculture," Committee on Recent Economic Changes, *Recent Economic Changes* (N. Y., 1929), II, 547-602, is an excellent summary of the postwar agricultural situation.

[2] When, as one moralist put it, "many an abandoned farmhouse became an 'abandoned' roadhouse."

which had previously formed no part of rural life. The automobile, the telephone and the radio ended the traditional rural isolation, and the new machinery in both barn and kitchen lessened the burden of physical labor. Edwin Markham's "Man with the Hoe" had become a small capitalist with a power plant.

The new tendencies but further emphasized the characteristics of American agriculture as contrasted with the rural traditions of the Old World. In Europe, and still more in Asia, agriculture was a thing apart from the mechanized and sharply competitive life of the factory towns—it connoted tradition, provincialism, attachment to hereditary acres. It was generally organized after one of two systems, either a landlord's great estate worked by tenant farmers or a small patch of freehold owned and worked by a peasant proprietor. The American farmer corresponded to neither the English tenant nor the French peasant. As a rule he owned his land, though it might be subject to mortgage; there was hardly anything corresponding to a European landlord's estate since the downfall of the slave-plantation system in the Civil War.[1] But his farm was no peasant's plot; it was sometimes as large as a landlord's domain, though worked by machinery rather than by "hands," and land was usually so abundant that the crop yield was at once low per acre and high per laborer as compared with European standards.

Nor had the American much sentimental attachment to the land he tilled. The blood of restless frontiersmen was still in his veins. He grew easily impatient at hard times and would sell his holding and move to newer fields, or abandon farming altogether for some more

[1] A shadow of the old plantation system survived among Negro "share-tenants" in the cotton belt. See C. O. Brannen, *Relation of Land Tenure to Plantation Organization with Developments since 1920* (U. S. Dept. of Agriculture, *Bull.*, no. 1269).

profitable occupation. Farming was to him a business like any other. "Farming," said a shrewd commentator, "is an unscientific term, becoming obsolete. We speak instead of the wheat industry, of the cattle industry, of the dairy industry, of overhead, fixed charges, net income, quantity production, and turnover." [1]

Only in the states of the Atlantic Seaboard, and decreasingly even there, did son and grandson succeed as a matter of course to the ancestral farm. The typical Western farmer would sell out in Illinois to move to Iowa, sell in Iowa and move to Saskatchewan over the Canadian line, and retire at sixty to live on a fruit orchard in California. One of his sons would be studying in a Kansas agricultural college, another son would be a bank cashier or drygoods clerk in Chicago, and his daughter would be typing the letters of a Florida realestate salesman.

The agricultural conditions of the United States, characterized by large units of land management, freehold ownership, much use of machinery and power, costly and uncertain hired labor, frequent sales and migrations, though different from those of Europe, could to some extent be paralleled in western Canada and Australia. The chief economic defect of the system was that it put a premium on exploitation rather than conservation. Very often the farmer, treating his land as a temporary speculation rather than as a permanent home, would crop the land to exhaustion, cut off all the timber, and make a profit on current sales at the expense of permanent values. An example of this was the one-crop system which prevailed in the cotton belt until the combined effect of the boll weevil and the blockade of German ports by the British fleet in the early stages of the

[1] Garet Garrett, "A Fifty Year Crisis in Agriculture," *Sat. Eve. Post*, CXCVI, 4 (April 19, 1924).

World War, temporarily reducing cotton exports, forced farmers to diversify their crops. The European peasant, with his plodding, painstaking methods, often picked up a living on land which American owners had abandoned as worthless, as in some parts of New England; while in California the American farmer demanded an immigration wall high enough to bar all Oriental labor. Very often the American concentrated on his "cash crop," all for export, and imported his own fruit and vegetables in tin cans from the nearest big city. The psychology of American agriculture was identical with that of American business, with energy, initiative and willingness to experiment as its outstanding virtues, wastefulness and carelessness as its defects.

The industrialization of agriculture continued unchecked through years of prosperity and years of depression. When devastated Europe and the American armies overseas demanded increased crop production the farmer, whose own boys were often away in training camps, found the machine a necessary ally in expanding his acreage. When hard times followed the war and hired men drifted to the towns the farmer again turned to the machine to offset the labor shortage. The problem of production was easily solved at all times, thanks to the gifts of science; what was not solved was the problem of marketing. In most industries supply is easily adjusted to demand. In a few favored industries (such as the making of automobiles) the demand seemed to expand almost indefinitely with the supply. But the demand for foodstuffs is relatively constant, growing slowly with the population, whereas the supply is at the mercy of wind and sun, rain and snow, bird and insect, and other factors beyond human calculation. The market in the new age was a world market, thanks to cold storage and the steamship, and prices in Nebraska were determined by competitive conditions in New Zealand, Russia and the Argentine.[1] Least of all producers could the farmer control the price of his product. In this natural disadvantage of agriculture lies the explanation of our paradox, that the unexampled progress in farming did not mean exceptional prosperity for the farmer.

Work animals continued to furnish more power for farm work than oil, steam or electricity, but this superiority decreased year by year. Mechanical horse power, including stationary engines, electric power plants, steam and gasoline tractors and motor trucks, increased five times as rapidly as animal horse power diminished. The horse vanished from the scene faster than the mule. In 1914 there were over 20,000,000 horses on American farms, but from 1920 onward the number decreased to less than 15,000,000 in 1928.[2] But the 4,449,000 mules of 1914 increased to 5,740,000 in 1926 and had fallen only to 5,566,000 two years later. The war seems to have won for the horse a short reprieve and for the mule a somewhat longer one. The number of tractors in use on farms increased from 80,000 in 1918 to 853,-000 in 1929.[3]

The use of power machinery on farms had some tendency to increase their average size and to diminish their number. In the Great Plains region, especially in the Dakotas, the tractor was employed on more farms than elsewhere because the level ground, the great size of the farms (often more than six hundred acres apiece), and the prevalence of a single crop to each farm, rendered wholesale methods peculiarly applicable. The frontier of corn and wheat production was pushed farther west in the semiarid belt, while at the same time the acreage devoted to grain was reduced in many of the older states,

[1] Nourse, "Agriculture," 551-553.　　[3] Nourse, "Agriculture," 559.
[2] Nourse, "Agriculture," 558.

which suffered from the competition of the farmer-en-
gineers of the prairie. A new sectional differentiation
began. Where the country was adapted to large-scale
agriculture the land tended to concentrate in larger and
larger units so as best to take advantage of the tractor
and the "combine" (combined harvester-thresher).[1]
Where these wholesale methods could not be so well
employed there was an opposite tendency, to abandon
the growing of wheat, corn, cotton and other staple
crops for more diversified and specialized farming: fruit
culture, nut-tree raising, truck farming, bee culture,
flower gardening and the like.

The electrification of the farm was still something of
a novelty. In 1925 only two hundred and twenty-five
thousand farms, less than four per cent of the total number, were connected with electrical central stations.[2]
"The electric light and power companies," declared
Owen D. Young, chairman of the General Electric Company, "must now have their agricultural departments,
just as they have their industrial departments. . . ."
Though he admitted that, for the present, electric power
could rarely be supplied in practical form for some of
the heavy work about the farm such as tractors and
threshing machines, he saw an immediate future for it
in such chores as pumping, grinding feed, cutting silage,
milking, churning and housework.[3]

The results of this increased farming efficiency, the
benefits of which reached the consumer (or perhaps the

[1] The combine was one of the newest of important farm machines.
In 1927 it had been in use for only a decade, and only experimentally
till the last two or three years of the period. It was estimated by the
department of agriculture to reduce the labor required for harvesting and
threshing 400 acres of grain from 120 days of man labor to 30 days.
Nourse, "Agriculture," 561-565.

[2] Arthur Williams, *Power on the Farm* (published by the Acad. of
Polit. Sci., N. Y., 1927), is a useful brief discussion of the possibilities
and probable cost of universal farm electrification.

[3] *N. Y. Times*, July 5, 1925.

merchant) even if they did not sufficiently profit the farmer himself, were expressed by the department of agriculture in the striking statement that from 1919 to 1924, the postwar reconstruction period, crop production increased by an average of five per cent while thirteen million acres of crop land went out of cultivation.[1] Each farm worker produced on the average fifteen per cent more. The reduction in acreage was mainly due to hard times and low prices after the collapse of the artificial prosperity of the war. But there were other causes. The substitution of the automobile and the tractor diminished the land required to provide feed for horses. Improved methods of cultivation and the diversification of crops enabled the farmer to maintain his output while curtailing his cultivation. Less land was used because less land was needed.

Even more striking than the shrinkage in farm land, though evident over a much longer period, was the decline in the farm population. The magnetic attraction of the cities had long been evident, and the census of 1920 marked the point when for the first time the urban population of the United States outnumbered the rural.[2] The temporary demand for munition workers from 1915 to 1918 drew many to town, a term of military service uprooted others. During the years 1910-1920 the center of population remained almost stationary in the midst of Indiana, moving westward by a shorter distance than for any previous decade, and this in spite of the exceptionally rapid growth of California and the Farther West generally. For the first time the Eastern

[1] *Yearbook of Agriculture for 1927*, 8-9. This was the first time in national history that the area devoted to agriculture decreased.

[2] The census figures somewhat exaggerated the drift to the cities because the normal growth of population in a small village will often pull it across the demarcation line of twenty-five hundred inhabitants, and thus people who were "rural" may become "urban" without the trouble of leaving their homes.

states were outgaining the Mississippi-Missouri basin. Three mainly rural states—Vermont of the hill farms, Mississippi of the cotton plantations and Nevada of the ranches—actually decreased in population. Other agricultural states made slight increases, but mainly through the growth of towns and cities. The purely rural population was almost everywhere stationary or decreasing, except in the Far West where public irrigation works opened new farm lands.

Within the urban group the tendency was quite as much to build up small towns and cities as the great commercial centers. Manhattan Island, the heart of New York, actually decreased in population from 1910 to 1920, to the profit of outlying boroughs, such as the Bronx, or suburban villages within commuting distance. The same forces which were building the cities at the expense of the countryside were building the suburbs at the expense of "downtown." The cheap automobile, especially, spread out the residential districts of the cities like an expanding fan. But small towners and suburbanites are not usually active farmers, though they count many retired farmers in their number. If we take not "rural" but "farm" population the relative increase of industrial America at the expense of agriculture becomes clearer. The farm population in 1910 was placed at 32,-076,960; in 1920, 31,624,269; in 1925, 28,981,668; in 1927, 27,853,000.[1] The relative decrease of farm population for the census period (1910-1920) was greatest in the New England states and measured mainly the drawing power of the neighboring industrial towns, but for the five years following the heaviest farm losses occurred among the Negro farmers of the South.

[1] The figure for 1910 was an estimate based on the census, and for 1927 an estimate in a noncensus year; the figures for 1920 and 1925 are actual enumerations. See *Yearbook of Agriculture for 1927*, 1168. The possible error is believed to be insignificant.

A study of rural depopulation in New York state showed very forcibly the attraction of city wages, especially for men and women who had no ties of property to hold them in the country. It was found that the order of frequency with which men left the farms was: (1) hired men, (2) farmers' sons, (3) share tenants, (4) cash tenants, (5) owners.[1] In three districts studied three men out of ten and two fifths of the women brought up on farms were engaged in other occupations.[2] Another survey, covering several states, inquired as to the motives of migration from country to town. The chief reason, affecting considerably more than a third of the ex-farmers who sought the city, was the hope of making a better living outside of agriculture. Next in importance was old age or physical disability to carry on the hard manual labor demanded even by the modern mechanized farm. A large number thought that they owed their children better schooling than the country afforded, and about two in a hundred turned their farms over to sons or sons-in-law to give them a start in life. Only about one in forty went to the city because he had saved up enough to live on without labor and wished to spend his surplus for the comforts of city life.[3]

In the days of Napoleon, it is said, English farmers used to pray for a long war and good prices. Without accusing the American farmer, who was above all a humanitarian and even a pacifist, of such a prayer, the fact remains that the European conflict both before and after

[1] E. C. Young, *The Movement of Farm Population* (Cornell Univ. Experiment Station, *Bull.*, no. 426), 88.

[2] Young, *Movement of Farm Population*, 16, 21.

[3] The same survey questioned a group from forty-five states who had left town or city for the farm. Most of them were pleased with the change they had made, but it was significant that the great majority, almost seven out of eight, had either been brought up on farms or had lived in the country before. *Yearbook of Agriculture for 1927*, 514-515. 2745 individuals answered the first questionnaire (movement from country to city) and 1167 the second (movement from city to country).

the intervention of the United States brought a temporary prosperity to American agriculture. This is not to say that in the long run the war was beneficial to the farmer. On the contrary, the land boom, the fever of speculation, the planting of excess acreage to meet the extraordinary demands, the inflation of the currency, the increase of taxation, and all the other results of the abnormal economic conditions of war time turned to liabilities during the years of deflation and depression that followed. Fewer farmers would have been ruined in 1921 if they had never entertained the golden dreams of 1916-1919. Owing to the extraordinary demands of the war period the acreage of crop land in 1919 was more than nine years ahead of what had been the previous rate of expansion relative to the increase of population.[1] What was normal production of grain and hogs, just as what was normal production of shells and ships, in war time, became overproduction soon after peace was declared.

The grain market was particularly sensitive to war conditions and the grain states were those most affected by the war-time expansion and the postwar depression. During the three crop years of 1917, 1918 and 1919 the relative purchasing power of wheat as compared with the average of all other commodities was higher than it had ever been before, and relatively higher than for other farm products.[2] The artificial support of government regulation was gradually withdrawn, leaving the grain grower at the mercy of the law of supply and demand. The United States food administration terminated its work in June, 1919, and the federal grain corporation ceased to operate as a purchasing organization in

[1] U. S. Bureau of Agricultural Economics, *Changes in the Utilization of Land in the United States, 1919-24* (Wash., 1926), 4.
[2] F. M. Surface, *The Stabilization of the Price of Wheat during the War* (U. S. Grain Corporation, Wash., 1925), 25.

May, 1920. The blow, though delayed, was not averted by the expedients used to uphold prices after the armistice. Working together to feed the hungry in central Europe, the American Relief Association and the grain corporation managed to market several hundred million dollars' worth of flour, pork and dairy products after the war.[1] Wheat and pork in particular benefited from this reprieve. But philanthropy could not fill so wide a place in the market as a world war.

An index of this war-time prosperity was the rapid rise in land values prior to 1920 in the grain states.[2] The money value of the average American farm by the census of that year was over twelve thousand dollars, nearly twice what it had been by the previous census. But in some of the Western states farm prices were much higher. In Iowa an average farm was worth almost forty thousand dollars. Iowa was indeed the center of the land boom based on grain speculation, just as in the next decade Florida became the seat of a land boom based partly on tropical-fruit prospects but mainly on the tourist industry.[3] In Iowa farm land averaged nearly $200 an acre over the whole state,[4] as compared with $82 ten years earlier. The neighboring states of Illinois and Indiana in the corn belt were second only to Iowa. The spring-wheat belt, farther from the industrial centers, had a lower level of land values but showed proportionate progress. Minnesota's lands had increased from $36 to $91 an acre; South Dakota's from $34 to $64.

[1] Surface, *Stabilization of the Price of Wheat*, 17. Herbert Hoover's chief aim in overruling European objectors and opening up the former enemy countries of Germany and Austria to American food before the final conclusion of peace was humanitarian, to diminish the aftereffects of the Allied blockade on the civilian population. But much incidental benefit went to the American farmer.

[2] Nourse, "Agriculture," 587.   [3] See later, chap. viii.

[4] If buildings are included, the average value was $227 an acre.

Parallel to the progress of the corn and wheat states was the rapid development of the agricultural areas of the mountain states and the Pacific Slope, based in large part on irrigation enterprises. In each of the Western states of California, Colorado, Idaho, Montana, Utah and Wyoming more than a million acres had been reclaimed by irrigation, and Oregon closely approached that figure. California farm lands had a higher value than those of any state outside the corn belt. Many optimists spoke of settling all the returned soldiers who did not already have good jobs on lands redeemed by irrigation in the arid West or by draining in the swampy South. They did not foresee that within a few months the census of 1920 would offer statistical proof of an overexpanded agriculture and that a cry would go up from millions of distressed farmers for a curtailment of crops.

Fundamentally the agricultural depression of 1920-1921 was but a part of the general business slump. Credit had been stretched too far; deflation inevitably followed; the European market was disappointing because of the impoverishment the war had caused; retrenchment all around seemed inevitable. But the farmer had good reasons for believing that he was harder hit than his fellow sufferers in trade and manufacture. Generally speaking, agricultural prices fell sooner, faster and farther than the goods which the farmer had to buy, and recovered value more slowly. In other words the "farmer's dollar" went below par.[1]

[1] On one estimate the buying power per unit of farm product, taking the average of the prewar years 1910-1914 as par, stood at 107 in 1918, 105 in 1919, sank to 85 in 1920 and to 69 in 1921, and was only 85 in 1926. Report by Business Men's Commission on Agriculture, *The Condition of Agriculture in the United States and Measures for Its Improvement* (Chamber of Commerce, Wash., 1927), 45. Again, it was figured that in the 1910-1914 period the average farmer earned 72 per cent and the farm laborer 53 per cent of the average earnings of men in

The high land values that had once been such an asset became an added handicap. A corn-belt farmer who had bought his holding at the boom prices of the war and armistice period, perhaps borrowing heavily to do so, found a very costly white elephant on his hands. At the crest of the wave of prosperity American farmers were carrying a mortgage debt of more than four billion dollars, besides a great deal of unsecured or otherwise secured personal indebtedness. These mortgages were often assumed not to meet a pressing need but as a calculated business investment in the hope that the land purchased with the borrowed money would yield more than the six-per-cent interest demanded by the lender; so they signified prosperity rather than want. But now the banks, chary of making new loans and themselves hard pressed to find paying investments in a time of falling prices, had to be very exacting in demanding payment from their debtors. In the period 1920-1925 more than two thirds of all bank failures took place in ten agricultural states of the South and West.[1] The number of farm bankruptcies increased, the proportion of failures averaging nine times as much for the three years ending in 1926 as for the prewar decade. But the greatest number of farm bankruptcies took place two or three years after the big slump because the farmers, not wishing to abandon their homes at the first bad year, took their losses, hung on to their holdings, and stretched their credit until they could neither borrow again nor repay what they owed. Farms still solvent staggered under a burden of debt. The ratio of indebtedness to

other occupations, whereas for the period 1920-1925 the farmer earned only 44 per cent and his hired man 42 per cent of the average urbanite's earnings (p. 56). This estimate allowed five per cent interest to the farmer on the value of his investment as a property owner, and stated the *remainder* of his income as "wages" of labor and management.

[1] *Yearbook of Agriculture for 1927,* 110-114, discusses the whole question of farm failures.

farm values increased from twenty-nine per cent in 1920 to nearly forty-two per cent in 1925.[1] Continued high freight rates and local taxes also handicapped the farmer. From 1913 to 1922 the burden of direct taxes on farm property had grown from $315,000,000 to $861,000,000.[2] And the farmer, whose wealth is frozen into land and buildings visible to all, was least able of any taxpayer to escape a property tax.

Yet another handicap of agriculture was the wide gap between the price to the producer and that to the consumer. Many middlemen and carriers handled agricultural products and profit was distributed among many hands. We laugh at the legendary farm boy who sold a load of apples in town and bought a bushel of them in a grocery store with the money he got, but Senator Arthur Capper told of a farmer paying more for a pair of calfskin shoes than he got for the live calf, skin and all; and, again, of the Texan who sold cabbage for six dollars a ton which brought two hundred dollars a ton in the Mid-Western cities.[3]

We can picture the Western farmer of the early 1920's as bewildered and resentful at the sudden shift in his fortunes. Hard times are doubly hard when they follow close on a period of prosperity. He had counted on another good year or two to see his girl through college, or buy a new tractor, or clear off his mortgage. He had been accustomed to high taxes, high prices and a good market. The high taxes remained, for the farmer could not do without good roads and did not wish to have the schools closed to his children. The prices of his grain fell by half, touching lower levels than in any year since

[1] *Condition of Agriculture*, 62. Farm tenancy also increased. It remained still true, however, that a majority of American farmers were owners rather than tenants.

[2] *Condition of Agriculture*, 79.

[3] Arthur Capper, *The Agricultural Bloc* (N. Y., 1922), 52, 81.

1896. The price of what he bought, "store goods" from the town, fell also, but more slowly. He had to cut the wages of his hired man from almost a hundred dollars a month (without board) to about sixty. Very often he was left without help to run the farm as agricultural laborers began their trek townwards. Many of his neighbors lost their farms or abandoned the unequal struggle and went to town themselves, feeling fortunate to get fifty cents on the dollar when they sold their land. The radical politicians told him that the hard times were due to the iniquitous policy of the federal reserve banks in calling in loans at the behest of Eastern capitalists. Conservative politicians talked vaguely of "natural economic laws" and advised patient waiting for a return of good times under a Republican administration. Economists spoke of the perils of overproduction, but this was locking the stable door after the horse had been stolen for the crops had been planted in the expectation of good times. The farmer hardly knew what to believe, but he hoped that some solution might be found if his class would stand together and demand "favorable legislation" of some sort.

The American farmer has always had his own brand of radicalism, which bears little relation to the radicalism of the big towns. It is a native growth and has a long American ancestry: the Grangers, the cheap-money "greenback" movement, the Populists, the Bryan Democrats of 1896, the insurgents and Progressives of the Roosevelt era, the Nonpartisan League during the World War, the Farmer-Labor party of 1920, the agricultural bloc in Congress, the La Follette Progressives of 1924, the Lowden Republicans of 1928. The farmer is a capitalist in a small way and has an individualistic tradition. But he is often a distressed capitalist, and anxious to use the powers of state and nation to relieve hard times.

Unlike the Socialist he does not desire government ownership of the land; he prefers to run a farm as freeholder to holding it as tenant of the commonwealth. But government regulation is a different matter. The remedy sought differs with the nature of the emergency; sometimes it has been cheaper money, paper or silver standing in legal parity with gold, sometimes easier credits and guaranteed bank deposits, sometimes reduction of freight rates by legislation, sometimes a lower tariff on farm machinery and a higher tariff against Canadian farm products. The means to his end may differ also—an economic union like the Grange or the later coöperative societies, or a third party like the Populist, or a group within the dominant political party of the region.

The Farmers' Nonpartisan League antedated the depression of 1920. Originally it was an outgrowth of the quite peculiar conditions of North Dakota, a spring-wheat state and more of a one-crop community than any other north of the cotton belt. It had a considerable foreign population, largely Scandinavian, who were unattached to the Anglo-Saxon two-party tradition and combined the energy and initiative of the Norseman with the recent immigrant's resentment at any injustice by the native-born, the suspicious fear—equally characteristic of New York's East Side Jew—that "the capitalists may be putting something over on us." Though the Germans and Scandinavians of the rural Northwest had, on the whole, melted into American life more easily than any other immigrant strain, even here minor instances of snobbishness on the part of the older American element caused occasional hostility that expressed itself in political radicalism. This slight degree of racial (or, more accurately, national) friction was no doubt much intensified by the extensive patrioteering of the war period.

But the fundamental grievances of North Dakota were economic, and affected equally the Yankee farmer whose ancestors came over in the *Mayflower* and the Norwegian farmer who himself came over in the steerage of a transatlantic liner. North Dakota, practically one vast wheat field, sent her products to the world through the flour mills. The economic rulers of the state were the millers, and they were not even native rulers, for most of the North Dakota wheat went to the neighboring state of Minnesota.[1] The farmers complained especially that the millers paid good prices only for the highest quality of firm, hard wheat, taking other grades at a much lower rate, and then mixing the grains together without distinction when they got them. Senator P. J. McCumber, an orthodox Republican, estimated that farmers in the wheat states lost about seventy million dollars a year by false grading.[2] Twice the voters of North Dakota had approved the erection of state grain elevators (in 1912 and 1914) and twice their demand was set aside by the legislature. The crisis came in February, 1915, when a delegation of farmers demanding legislation were contemptuously ignored. According to one account an angry representative told them to "go home and slop the hogs."[3]

The hour found its man. Arthur C. Townley had

[1] "The principal grievances in North Dakota were the exactions of the middlemen and the control of the grain and stock market by the Board of Trade and the Chambers of Commerce of the cities of St. Paul, Minneapolis and Duluth." Andrew Bruce, *The Non-Partisan League* (N. Y., 1921), 34. See also H. E. Gaston, *The Nonpartisan League* (N. Y., 1920), chap. iii.

[2] C. E. Russell, *The Story of the Nonpartisan League* (N. Y., 1920), 63.

[3] Russell, *Story of Nonpartisan League*, 107. Gaston, *Nonpartisan League*, 43-44, also carries this story, but admits that the exact words used have been questioned. Russell and Gaston are strongly pro-League, while Bruce, *Non-Partisan League*, is very hostile. A. S. Tostlebe, *The Bank of North Dakota* (N. Y., 1924), is fairly impartial, but covers a more limited field.

just the qualities needed to crystallize the farmers' in-
surgency into a definite movement and to place himself
at its head. Townley was a farmer of a restless, experimental turn of mind, who at the moment seemed to be
something of a failure in life. He had started flax raising
in western North Dakota and all men praised him as a
pioneer in scientific farming; then the price of flax broke,
the farm failed, and Townley was ruined. He carried
with him a sense of personal injustice which made him
a natural spokesman of the grievances of his class. For a
time he drifted into the ranks of Marxian socialism and
became a party organizer. But he resented his associates'
stodginess and lack of imagination, their reluctance to
experiment with new methods of agitation. He longed
to try out his ideas without the impediment of party
discipline and economic dogmas.[1]

The crisis of 1915 gave him his opportunity. He
promptly started a Farmers' Nonpartisan League on the
basis of "an idea, a Ford, and sixteen dollars." The Ford
was for canvassing the enormous spaces of Wheatland.
The idea was a farmers' party which would "bore from
within" and capture through the primaries the Republican and Democratic machines, especially the former. The
legislators chosen by the League would be pledged to
put agricultural interests above partisanship and would
be obedient to the instructions of the League caucus. To
finance the League every supporter was expected to become a member and every member a dues-paying con-
tributor. The program was simple and practical; every
item in it was already desired by the majority of the
North Dakota farmers: (1) state-owned and operated
elevators, mills and packing plants; (2) state hail insurance; (3) exemption of farm improvements from
taxation; (4) fair grading of grain; and (5) rural

[1] Gaston, *Nonpartisan League*, chap. vi.

credits at easy rates. Though the doctrinaire theories of socialism were wisely let alone by the Leaguers, many energetic young Socialists joined the movement and thus gave a little color to the most familiar charge of its enemies that it was simply disguised socialism adapted to a rural constituency.

The League won its first great victory in 1916 when it captured the lower house of the legislature, and would have captured the state senate but for its hold-over members whose terms had not yet expired. Lynn Frazier, a farmer who had never occupied himself actively with politics, was placed in the governor's chair. Many of the new legislators were naturally inexperienced in the forms of parliamentary procedure, and, as the more clever and unscrupulous of their opponents were always laying lawyer's traps for them in the form of harmless-looking amendments and substitute motions, they relied almost wholly for directions on caucus meetings and the advice of legislative experts thoughtfully furnished by Townley.[1]

As the courts held that many of the League proposals were unconstitutional, House Bill 44 was introduced, a constitutional reform (really a substitute constitution) permitting the state to engage "in any occupation or business for public purposes." Because of senate opposition it was not until the legislative session of 1919 that the greater part of the League program was made law. An industrial commission was created, consisting of the governor, the attorney-general and the commissioners of agriculture and labor, with power to govern the Bank of North Dakota and to supervise the operation of public grain warehouses and flour mills. The legislature approved also a home-building association, a graduated income tax, state hail insurance, the exemption of farm

[1] Gaston, *Nonpartisan League*, 134.

Have you placed a Sentimental Value on your Horses out of proportion to the work they are able to perform?

Mechanization, as advised by this advertisement, brought profits to the farm,

But Governor Frazier, visiting North Dakota farmers, could still point out many an injustice.

On the Farms

improvements from taxation and the fixing of assessment rates, the eight-hour day for women, workmen's compensation against sickness or accident, a bonus to returned war veterans, the designation of an official newspaper in each county for public printing and the regulation of railroad rates.[1]

In 1917 the Nonpartisan League prefixed National to its name and began a vigorous drive for members outside of North Dakota. By 1920 the National Nonpartisan League claimed two hundred and thirty thousand members. Minnesota had fifty-four thousand, North Dakota fifty thousand and there were smaller contingents in South Dakota, Montana, Wisconsin, Colorado, Idaho, Washington, Nebraska, Iowa, Kansas, Oklahoma and Texas.[2] But east of the Mississippi it had very little influence, and its real political importance was practically limited to the Northwestern wheat states. The entrance of the United States into the war handicapped it by giving its opponents a chance to raise the cry of disloyalty. The Nonpartisan League, to be sure, had not followed the example of the Socialist party and declared flatly against the war, but its speakers concentrated their efforts on demanding heavy taxes on the rich ("conscription of wealth"), a high price for grain and other foodstuffs regulated by the government in war time, and a definite statement of war aims. They were sometimes open to the charge of having no concern in the war except as it touched the local interests and factional politics of their immediate neighborhood. Their opponents were in some degree guilty of the same narrowness, for they took advantage of war conditions to break up League meetings and arrest its organizers.[3] Townley

[1] Gaston, *Nonpartisan League*, chap. xxi.

[2] Bruce, *Non-Partisan League*, 8.

[3] Gaston, *Nonpartisan League*, chap. xvii, gives many instances of war time prosecutions and persecutions

himself was prosecuted in Minnesota for discouraging enlistment.

The postwar depression in the wheat country proved fatal to the League's supremacy. Its banking experiments could not weather the hard times. The chief error of the Bank of North Dakota seems not to have been its state character, but the fact that it was directly administered by politicians and run on a political rather than a sound financial basis. There had been marked favoritism in the selection of the Scandinavian-American Bank of Fargo for deposits, and personal loans had been made in a haphazard and reckless fashion.[1] There was a confusion of functions in its financial policy, as a reserve bank and as a mortgage-loan bank, and the natural desire to gratify the farmers had led to many unwise decisions.

The Farmer-Labor party was not directly an outgrowth of the National Nonpartisan League although it drew most of its support from the same section and the same discontents. It was an attempt to create a vigorous radical third party in the political doldrums of 1920, but it failed to receive a generous support from either the trade unions or the embattled farmers.[2] Its chief victory was in Minnesota, where the discontented wheat farmers made the party their own and captured two senatorships, for Henrik Shipstead (1922) and Magnus Johnson (1923). Elsewhere, however, the farmers preferred the tactics of the Nonpartisan League, the capture of hostile Troy by remaining inside the wooden horse of Republicanism or Democracy. There were many agrarian radicals in Congress between 1920 and 1928,

[1] Tostlebe, *Bank of North Dakota*, 107, 189.

[2] Its national ticket polled only about a quarter of a million votes, of which 77,000 were cast in the single state of Washington. *World Almanac for 1925*, 864.

but with few exceptions they wore the old party labels. The attempt of the veteran radical Robert M. La Follette, senator from Wisconsin, to organize a Progressive third party in 1924 failed as completely as the Farmer-Labor movement four years earlier, though it won a larger popular following and the electoral vote of Wisconsin by taking in the Socialists and the La Follette faction of the Republicans.

Agrarian senators and representatives, whether Republican, Democratic or Farmer-Labor, discovered that they had sufficient interest in common to form a definite group in Congress, acting together to protect agriculture. The Congress of 1921 met in the darkest period of agricultural depression. Senators W. S. Kenyon of Iowa and Arthur Capper of Kansas, both Republicans in good and regular party standing, exerted themselves to organize a farm bloc independent of party lines.[1] Thanks very largely to the political pressure exerted by this group a number of laws to meet the agricultural crisis were enacted. The war finance corporation was revived in 1921 to finance exports, coöperative associations were encouraged to enter interstate commerce (1922), the federal land banks were given greater power to make loans on mortgages and agricultural credit was extended to include as security livestock and farm products on the way to market, speculation in grain and meat was discouraged, an emergency tariff (May, 1921) erected a wall against foreign competition in foodstuffs, and the very high rates of the Fordney-McCumber tariff of 1922 confirmed the protective policy. Many publicists attacked the farm bloc, not so much for its actual policies, which were for the most part acceptable to the party managers, as because it introduced or, rather, avowed what was claimed to be a new principle in American

[1] See Capper, *Agricultural Bloc.*

politics, the priority of sectional economic interests over party allegiance.

The most ambitious part of the legislative program supported by the farm bloc and the various farmers' associations which stood behind it was embodied in the McNary-Haugen bill, twice introduced in slightly different forms but blocked on both occasions by the outspoken opposition of President Coolidge. The veto of the measure in its final form, on the very eve of the national party conventions in 1928, interjected a new issue into the campaign. The bill provided for the marketing of surplus crops under the supervision of a specially created federal board, with power to levy an "equalization fee" on the production, processing or distribution of a commodity in order to reimburse the producers if the surplus must be marketed at a loss. President Coolidge objected that the equalization fee was probably unconstitutional, certainly difficult to administer, and pernicious in that it encouraged an unprofitable overproduction which in the long run would not benefit agriculture.[1] In 1929, however, Congress established a federal farm board to supervise the loaning of money to coöperative associations, and Alexander Legge, president of the International Harvester Company, was appointed chairman.

Many American farmers learned the lesson of coöperation in economics as well as in politics and, on the whole, with greater profit.[2] By the end of 1925 the department of agriculture had listed 10,803 coöperative associations with an estimated membership of 2,700,000

[1] William MacDonald, "The Close of the Seventieth Congress," *Current History*, XXVIII (1928), 664-665.

[2] The best comprehensive account is R. B. Forrester, *Report upon Large Scale Coöperative Marketing in the United States* (London, 1925), made for the British ministry of agriculture and fisheries. An excellent summary account, of later date, is included in M. T. Copeland, "Marketing," *Recent Economic Changes*, I, 374-389.

(1,800,000 individuals, for many farmers belonged to more than one organization) transacting $2,400,000,-000 worth of business in a single year. Nearly three fourths of these marketing and purchasing organizations were in the twelve North Central states. Thirty-one out of every hundred handled grain, twenty dairy products, sixteen livestock, and eleven fruit and vegetables. Although the most rapid growth of the coöperative associations was from 1914 to 1920—their number practically doubling in that brief period—even more significant was the tendency after 1920 to consolidate them into larger units. Instead of buying through the local associations the farmers began to purchase through large-scale organizations which handled supplies by the trainload. One such association covered New England; a single purchasing agency supplied the Minnesota creameries, another the citrus fruit growers of California, another the apple growers of Oregon.[1] During war time there had also been a considerable development of interest in general protective bodies, standing as watchdogs over agrarian interests, such as the Farmers' National Council, the Farm Bureau Federation, the American Cotton Association, the Wheat Growers' Association and the United Farmers of America.

Agricultural values did not, like industrial values, regain all the ground lost in the postwar depression, but there was a partial recovery. Agricultural prices became fairly stable after 1924 and in some parts of the country land values rose again.[2] This was notably true of New England, New Jersey, Florida and California. The cases of Florida and California explain themselves: their land boom rested on special climatic conditions.

[1] *Yearbook of Agriculture for 1927*, 195-196.
[2] E. H. Wiecking, *The Farm Real Estate Situation* (Dept. of Agriculture, *Circular*, no. 377, Wash., 1927).

The bettered conditions in New England, New Jersey and a few parts of New York reflected the fact that dairy and poultry products commanded relatively high prices with the greater growth of cities, these providing "an ever-widening market for milk, poultry products, and vegetables, while the higher freight rates have afforded slightly increased protection against the competition of Western products." [1] It is significant that agrarian radicalism only showed itself acutely in trans-Mississippi politics.

Some new specializations helped many farmers back to prosperity. On the Pacific Coast the cultivation of fruit and nut trees and bee culture took on a new importance. A single irrigated district in the state of Washington sold seven hundred and fifty thousand pounds of honey and one hundred thousand pounds of beeswax a year. [2] In Maine, at the opposite edge of the continent, land hitherto scorned as worthless supplied the filling for millions of blueberry pies. "Blueberry land rose in value to $1,000 an acre, and produced more fruit than the great canneries recently established in Maine could handle with their present equipment." [3] Fur farming proved an interesting trade and a profitable one, for the United States led the world in fur manufacture and fur consumption. Skunk furs netted trappers of the United States more than three million dollars a year, and fox ranches were established in a dozen states. [4] Of much greater importance was the more commonplace introduction of diversified crops, especially garden vegetables, in the wheat and cotton belts in consequence of the fall in grain prices and the ravages of the boll weevil. One

[1] U. S. Bureau of Agricultural Economics, *Changes in the Utilization of Land*, 31.
[2] Floyd Parsons, *Everybody's Business* (N. Y., 1923), 57.
[3] Parsons, *Everybody's Business*, 38.
[4] Parsons, *Everybody's Business*, 41-42.

Southern town erected a memorial to the boll weevil to honor its services in compelling an abandonment of the single-crop system.[1]

The boll weevil was not the only insect foe which forced the American farmer to change his policies of land management. The Mexican bean beetle, a humble intruder when first appearing in Alabama in 1920, moved north at an average rate of one hundred and fifty miles each year and by 1927 had spread from Georgia to Ontario.[2] The European corn borer spread ruin in ever widening radius from the neighborhood of Lake Erie. When it had destroyed almost the whole crop in southeastern Ontario, invaded about half of Ohio and Michigan, and begun to encroach into Indiana, the sixty-ninth Congress appropriated the unprecedented war fund of ten millions to fight it.[3] The chief method used was the burning of all debris, and farmers were indemnified for the extra labor involved in the clean-up campaigns. In many places the roads were watched and passing automobilists challenged to show that they were carrying no corn into the still uninfested area. Many farmers shifted to other crops, especially sugar-beet cultivation, because of their loss in corn.

Surveys of rural-life conditions show a higher standard of living in spite of the hard times.[4] The multiplica-

[1] The inscription at the base of a memorial fountain in Enterprise, Alabama, read: "In Profound Appreciation of the Boll Weevil and What It Has Done as the Herald of Prosperity. This Monument is Erected By the Citizens of Enterprise, Coffee County, Alazama." The farmers turned from their blighted cotton crop to raise corn, sugar cane, cattle, hogs, peanuts, hay and sweet potatoes. The peanut crop alone brought in as much money as cotton did formerly. *Guide to Nature*, XVI (1924), 184.

[2] *Yearbook of Agriculture for 1927*, 460.

[3] *Yearbook of Agriculture for 1927*, 202.

[4] In the period 1919-1928 detailed studies were made by the U. S. department of agriculture, in coöperation with the state colleges of agriculture, covering the annual family consumption and expenditures of 5000 farm families situated in fifteen states. See Dept. of Agriculture, *Bulls.*, nos. 1214, 1382, 1466.

tion and usual cheapening of such luxuries as the automobile, telephone service, phonograph, radio, central heating, plumbing fixtures and the like transformed the farmhouse radically. By 1925 over two fifths of the homes in the country had telephones to link them with the world.[1] There were nearly a million rural radio sets, and ninety broadcasting stations lent their facilities for half an hour daily to the department of agriculture. A survey of more than four hundred homes showed that one in four had been repainted within five years, and that three out of four had all the floors finished or covered with carpets or linoleum.[2] The sagging window shutter, the peeling paint, the scuffed and splintered softwood floors of a previous generation, were almost as rare as the floorless log cabins of Lincoln's day. Almost two farmhouses in five had furnaces; one in ten, running hot water; fifteen per cent, modern bathrooms; three fourths, sinks with drains in the kitchen. Of course, even this record showed some inferiority to the conveniences enjoyed by the housewife in the city, and this was still more apparent with respect to methods of illumination. About nine per cent used electric lighting, twenty per cent gas, acetylene or gasoline, and most of the rest the traditional kerosene lamp.

One interesting survey of Edgar County, Illinois, made by a business firm in the course of studying the consumer market, gives us a vivid picture of the more prosperous type of farm community in the upper Mississippi basin.[3] Two thirds of the homes had phonographs and half had radios; "the aerial is already more familiar than the windmill." Only fifteen per cent of the farm-

[1] E. R. Eastman, *These Changing Times* (N. Y., 1927), 29. This book is a somewhat optimistic account of the newer agriculture.

[2] Eastman, *These Changing Times*, 197-199.

[3] A. D. Albert, "Where the Prairie Money Goes," *Scribner's Mo.*, LXXXII (1927), 476-480.

houses, however, had better lighting than that afforded by the kerosene lamp. The farmhouse, too, was little changed. "They know when a telephone call is for them by the number of rings. They keep old fashioned parlors. They have 'jay' calendars on the walls and do without refrigerators." They stood the dishes on the kitchen table, for half the farmers' wives had no cupboards; writing materials went on the sideboard for lack of a desk, "a vivid machine-rug and a huge rocking-chair" were "the high points of decoration in the best room," but they had beautified the front lawns and planted circular flower beds around the house. Goods were increasingly purchased by the installment system on the recommendation of mail-order catalogues. Money circulated rapidly, "an annual income of less than $15,-000,000 becomes more than $66,000,000 in bank clearings." [1]

One of the most important crops of the nation was still handled very unscientifically; in fact, "mined" instead of "cropped," as conservationists put it. This was timber. The United States had an excellent forest service, but it was compelled to wage war on two fronts: against the greedy and shortsighted exploiters who wished to reap all possible quick profits by turning every tree into lumber within a single generation, and against the motoring picnickers whose smoldering luncheon ashes caused forest fires innumerable. For each seven feet of lumber taken from the forests one foot was lost by fire.[2] There were other heavy losses in wasteful methods of logging and sawing. The rate of cutting was about four times the rate of growth, and at least seven tenths of the nation's woodland had already disappeared.

[1] Albert, "Where the Prairie Money Goes," 479.
[2] S. S. Sheip, "The Menace of a Treeless America," *Current History,* XXIV (1926), 198.

Much of this cutting had been necessary to clear the way for agriculture and the pioneer's ax is perhaps the best symbol of American progress; but what excuse could be made for the stump deserts of northern Michigan where stood neither grain nor tree? A rebel doubt sometimes arose, not only with respect to waste but even what was called "use," whether the acres of fine trees cut down to make a single Sunday edition of a yellow journal, two thirds advertisement and the rest scandals and comic strips, did not represent almost as great a loss as a forest fire.

It is not easy to summarize all these diverse tendencies in American agriculture. The average standard of living in rural districts seems to have been a little better in 1928 than in 1914, though not better than in 1919. Industrialism had conquered tradition; only the transformation of the farm into a food factory, with factory methods and factory mechanisms (though still with individual ownership) enabled the farmer to gain ground in the face of falling prices. Permanent equality with the city worker and an end to the migration from the farms seemed little likely to come until the growing urban population raised the demand and hence the price for foodstuffs to a profitable level. At all events, the farmer held the last card, if not the first, for he controlled the most truly indispensable of commodities and all men were more dependent on his exertions than he on any other man's.

CHAPTER VIII

THE SAGA OF THE MOTOR CAR

IF any one feature of American life was uniquely characteristic of the nation and the age it was the ubiquity of the automobile. In 1896 there were but four gasoline cars in the United States, the Duryea, the Ford, the Haynes and the imported Benz.[1] By 1914 more than half a million passenger cars were sold each year; twelve years later about four million, besides nearly half a million trucks.[2] In 1928 over twenty-four million cars, old and new, were in use,[3] and more Americans had automobiles than telephones. The industry employed directly 375,000 workmen in the construction factories and used either directly or indirectly the services of 3,700,000 persons, counting factory workers, makers of accessories or supplies, salesmen, chauffeurs, garage attendants and the like. It was America's largest industry as measured by the money value of its product, outranking even the packing industry and the steel manufacture.[4]

In the postwar years the day of "one family—one auto" had almost arrived, and the general European impression that "in the United States everyone drives an

[1] H. L. Barber, *Story of the Automobile* (Chicago, 1927), 74.
[2] For statistics of production, see *Facts and Figures of the Automobile Industry,* issued annually by the National Automobile Chamber of Commerce, N. Y.; also such historical surveys as R. C. Epstein, *The Automobile Industry* (Chicago, 1928). The contrast between the humble beginnings and the mighty growth of the industry is well brought out in the series of articles by Chris Batchelder, *Nation's Business,* XV (1927), no. 10, 20-22, and no. 13, 40-42.
[3] *N. Y. Times,* April 12, 1929.
[4] Epstein, *Automobile Industry,* 4, 6.

automobile" was at least more nearly correct than most foreign impressions of American wealth. For the continental United States there was almost one automobile to each five persons, and in some Western states the proportion was one to each three or four. Ownership was no longer a class distinction in 1928 as it had been in 1914 and still was in all European countries.[1] The decreasingly small minority who did not yet own cars was composed mainly of elderly or timid folk or dwellers in the city apartment houses who preferred the safety of the trolley car or the professional skill of the taxicab chauffeur.

The effect of the rise of the automobile industry on American business as a whole would be hard to overestimate. By 1928 the automobile accounted for more than four fifths of the rubber used in the United States. It had made this nation the world's chief rubber market, and created the great industry of plantation rubber in the East Indies, Dutch and British. The automotive industry consumed also half the plate glass, eight per cent of the copper, eleven per cent of the iron and steel, sixty-five per cent of all leather upholstery, and more than seven billion gallons of gasoline annually.[2]

Not the automobile itself but its universality was the real American contribution. Europe had had imagination enough to envisage the automobile but not enough to picture it becoming almost as cheap as a bicycle, as commonplace as a donkey, and as necessary as the four

[1] In 1926 Canada and New Zealand, with one passenger car to about ten persons, came nearest the record of the United States. Great Britain and Ireland had 43, France 44, Germany 196, Italy 325, Russia over 7000, and China over 21,000 persons to each automobile. *Facts and Figures of the Automobile Industry for 1927*, 44. In 1927 nine tenths of all passenger cars and four fifths of all busses and trucks were of American manufacture.

[2] E. G. Fuller, "The Automobile Industry in Michigan," *Mich. History Mag.*, XII (1928), 281.

walls of a house. Many factors favored its growth in the United States, apart from the characteristic American bent for quantity production and a wide market. Most raw materials of manufacture were to be found within the country and usually in abundance. Methods of organization and salesmanship for making and pushing new commodities were more highly developed than anywhere else. The consumer was eager, having an Athenian fondness for whatever was novel in doctrine or in invention. The general prosperity enabled many to buy even in the early days of the industry, and increasingly so as prices went down with more wholesale production. The Yankee tradition for tinkering with machinery, already well practised on bicycles, farm machinery and domestic appliances, encouraged even novices to dispense with a chauffeur. The huge size of the Western farms, the distance between farm and market town, the remoteness of the cities from each other, and the national habit of travel, all placed a premium on rapid locomotion. Europe, excepting always impoverished and backward Russia, was at once more crowded and less migratory.

While the automobile as a machine is the culmination of decades of invention, the automobile as a social force is as definitely associated with one man as the steam engine with Watt or the electric light with Edison.[1] Other young inventors in the experimental 1890's had tinkered with motors, but only Henry Ford had had the vision of the automobile as an engine of democracy rather than as a hall mark of aristocracy. His career was the story of the popular automobile at popular prices. The Ford factories were far more novel, interesting and important than the Ford itself. His famous Model T,

[1] H. U. Faulkner, *The Quest for Social Justice* (*A History of American Life*, XI), chap. viii.

a convenient little car painted in sober black like a Venetian gondola, was for a long time his sole product and it sold more widely in its day than all other automobiles combined. The butt of a thousand jokes, in which affection was blended with amusement, the "flivver," the "tin lizzie," became the family pet of the nation.

On May 26, 1927, Henry Ford and his son Edsel Ford drove the fifteen-millionth automobile which had come from his factories. As soon as they reached Dearborn old Number One was brought from the museum, a two-cylinder veteran of 1903. It proved to be still in good driving condition, so short was the space that separated the beginning of the automobile from its universal prevalence. But even Model T eventually joined the pageant of history. In 1927 Ford shut down for several months, thus reducing the aggregate automobile output in America by almost a quarter as compared with 1926. There had been no sign of a satiated market, but competition was keener and Ford had a new idea and it must be tried! Of course the experiment was costly, a conservative estimate was fifteen million dollars spent to January 1, 1928, in the preparations for launching the new car.[1] As usual, the car itself was far less novel than the improvements in the methods of production. In some respects the new Ford more greatly resembled rival automobiles than did the old Model T; the great individualist had partly capitulated to current standards of car form and equipment. But the machinery for production was improved beyond recognition. The company boasted that raw iron ore at the docks at eight Monday morning could be marketed as a complete Ford car on Wednesday noon, allowing fifteen hours for shipment.[2]

[1] Waldemar Kaempffert, "The Dramatic Story behind Ford's New Car," N. Y. Times, Dec. 18, 1927.
[2] Fuller, "Automobile Industry in Michigan," 288.

Fords

Certainly up to the end of the twenties the American idea of mass production had never been carried further than in the Ford factories. Many European industrialists from Britain to Russia, but especially perhaps in Germany, made a painstaking study of the Ford methods as literally a "god from the machine" to cure underproduction and all the poverty which it causes. Mr. Ford himself had no doubts on the matter, for in numberless newspaper interviews he expatiated with a certain modest vanity on the reign of universal prosperity that would be sure to follow the adoption of his policies by industry at large, including agriculture.[1] These policies might be summarized as: (1) centralized management; (2) control of raw materials by the manufacturer; (3) tools and machinery made to order, and with a view to maximum output without much regard to initial cost; (4) subdivision and specialization of labor to the greatest possible extent; (5) motion study and efficient shop arrangement; (6) high wages and short hours but no tolerance of shop rules or trade-union demands that might curtail production; and (7) abolition of all traditions, custom, office ritual and red tape that might limit output. Each of these concepts deserves a word of comment.

Centralization of control in the Ford factories was almost absolute. The Ford Company enjoyed the same advantage as France under Napoleon or Prussia under Frederick. There could be no question of conflicting jurisdictions; one man's will wove every strand of policy into a common fabric. His chief fellow stockholder was

---

[1] There were few magazines of general circulation which did not have one or more articles on the Ford factories after 1914, when his sudden increase of wages first attracted universal attention to his industrial methods. Probably the fullest summary of his ideas is in his autobiography, *My Life and Work* (Garden City, 1922), written in collaboration with Samuel Crowther.

his own like-minded son. Rivals within his company withdrew, in some cases to found automobile companies of their own (as, for example, the Dodges). Managers who opposed his policies had to conform or resign. His enemies termed him an autocrat and even his admirers had to admit that he was a "benevolent despot." [1]

Centralization of management was backed up by centralization of production. Needing iron ore, Ford bought iron mines and built blast furnaces and steel mills. Needing wood, he acquired forest properties. Needing steel parts, he bought and dismantled one hundred and ninety-nine freighters from the shipping board at a cost of $1,697,470. Needing rolling stock for hauling materials, he took over the decrepit Detroit, Toledo and Ironton Railway and put it on a profitable basis. The tools used in his shops were for the most part made in his shops; the rest were custom-ordered according to his specifications. He operated meat and grocery markets in Detroit, mainly for the use of his own employees but open also to the public, a step which nearly created a panic among retail merchants. [2] He even branched out into aviation, turning his attention to the possibility of a cheap and practical airplane.

The Ford ideas of factory management were the subject of endless comment and not a little criticism. The plant had room for many experts and specialists in machine and tool designing, but the majority of the employed were unskilled and set to the most routine tasks imaginable, tasks that required neither strength (since the machines themselves did all the "blacksmithing") nor skill. Ford dealt frankly with this question of soul-deadening monotony, saying that while he himself could

[1] Waldemar Kaempffert, "The Mussolini of Highland Park," *N. Y. Times*, Jan. 8, 1928.
[2] *Chicago Daily Tribune*, March 29, 1927.

never endure a life of routine he had many workmen, good, industrious men, who were unhappy at anything else.[1] Other critics complained that the speed of operation was too great, that even with short hours there was a nervous strain that meant short lives. Again Ford replied that he timed his machines by experiment to find the best speed at which work could be done without loss of efficiency.

Certainly there was something almost uncanny in the endless process of a Ford plant. Efficiency experts so arranged the order of operations that no workman need stir from his place or stoop to pick up anything. On principle, no human labor was used for any operation that a machine could perform, and no skill was employed where deft, routine motion would do as well. The workman did become a part of the machine, an adjustable bit of mechanism to connect one operation with the next while the river of motor or chassis parts flowed by at unvarying speed. It became the Paradise of the motion-study expert, and perhaps the Purgatory of the artist soul, but beyond question it was the cheapest way of making automobiles!

Ford's labor policy was equally criticized and commended. It reflected alike the highly individualistic philosophy and the humane temper of the man himself. He disclaimed, with perhaps unnecessary indignation, any reproach of being a philanthropist and mixing business with charity. "Efficiency" was his sole motto. But his conception of efficiency included the prevention of human waste as well as of other kinds. Everyone who wanted work must be given a fair chance in the factory.

[1] "Probably the most monotonous task in the whole factory is one in which a man picks up a gear with a steel hook, shakes it in a vat of oil, then turns it into a basket. . . . Yet the man on that job has been doing it for eight solid years . . . and he stubbornly resists every attempt to force him into a better job!" Ford, *My Life and Work*, 106.

If he made good he could stay, and Ford would stand by him in fair weather or in foul, as he stood by his German workmen during the World War when many criticized the retention of men of "enemy alien" birth at a moment when the Ford plants were working for the war needs of the government. During a period of slackness in industry good workmen should be retained even at the employer's cost. There must be safe machinery, high wages, short hours, good housing. But factory discipline might not be questioned. Trade unions should be ignored—they did not harmonize with enlightened despotism. In the Ford coal fields, near the border of West Virginia and Kentucky, the average daily wage in 1928 was seven dollars a day as compared with an average of $4.40 for rival companies, but the "open shop" prevailed.[1] Detroit was an open-shop town.

In January, 1914, the Ford factories adopted the eight-hour maximum working day and the five-dollar minimum wage. Such an announcement would have created little stir after the war, with the shorter working day the rule and wage scales trebled to meet the enhanced cost of living, but in 1914 it placed Ford operatives in a class by themselves. Liberal bonuses were added for workmen of good conduct, especially those with families to support. Unfortunately the definition of "good conduct" involved an investigation of the home life of employees, which was sometimes resented as paternalistic interference. This bonus-on-conduct system was later modified, but the general principle still prevailed of dividing the profits of the Ford industries with the employees. One interesting phase of the labor policy was the abolition of any sharp distinction between "bench" jobs and "desk" jobs. Very few executives had titles and very often superfluous clerical employees were

[1] Evans Clark in the *N. Y. Times*, April 15, 1928.

forced to transfer to the shops. Administration never long remained in a rut—the restless owner of the business was too apt to come around and shake up the whole organization. Ford mentioned as one reason for his success the fact that he wasted no time in "conferences."

In direct philanthropy Ford gave less than most multimillionaires. He did not give as lavishly to universities as Rockefeller, to libraries as Carnegie, or to museums as Morgan. Yet he was popular with millions of the very people who looked on Rockefeller, Carnegie and Morgan as the diabolic trinity of Capitalism. Until he put a stop to the talk by indorsing President Coolidge's administration, there was a strong popular movement to boom him for the Democratic presidential nomination, a compliment which would have been offered to no other man of comparable wealth. The newspapers found him better "copy" than any other private citizen, and not just for a week or so, as might be the case with an athletic hero, but year in and year out. This great popularity rested in part on the Ford policy of reducing costs to the consumer and raising wages to the worker out of his own profits, instead of letting wealth accumulate and then distributing it as charity; but in part it must be explained by the pleasant personality of Henry Ford himself.

In a manufacturing plant Ford was an exceptional man, a genius for organization. But anywhere else he was merely a very agreeable and expansive Middle Westerner. He had the democratic geniality and "folksiness" which Michigan and her neighbor states ranked as the chief of human virtues. He was interested in colonial furniture, in old American folk music and in birds. His camping parties with Edison and John Burroughs were his pleasantest recreation. In politics he proved the reverse of a superman, but his blunders were a product of ignorance and good will, the nemesis of a very competent cobbler who was too American to stick to his last. As we have seen, he associated his name disastrously with the peace ship that was to put an end to the war, and he ran for senator on the Democratic ticket in the most Republican of states. He confessed his complete ignorance of history, and then demonstrated it by letting the *Dearborn Independent,* his own organ, enter on a campaign against an imaginary "international Jewish conspiracy." [1] It says much for the public impression of Ford's basic good will and candor that no succession of blunders in fields not his own could permanently injure the real respect which the American nation paid him.

Not the Ford car alone but the automotive industry as a whole tended toward standardization during the boom period of the war and the decade following. Cars differed in little save magnificence of accessories and number of cylinders—plebeian fours, middle-class sixes and aristocratic eights and twelves. [2] In mechanism they were rather more alike than typewriters. The gasoline type prevailed almost to the exclusion of the steam and the electric. It was cheap, convenient and adaptable to rough roads and hilly country. The very increase in the sale of gasoline cars promoted still more rapid purchase, not only because the imitative American likes to follow his neighbor's example, but because the multiplication

[1] See later, chap. xi. His amusing blunder on the witness stand, when suing the *Chicago Tribune* for libel, has often been quoted: "Benedict Arnold? Why, he was a writer." But his own explanation was commonplace enough, and did not even endanger the reputation of Arnold Bennett. Ford thought that the attorney was asking about a man named Arnold who used to write articles for the Ford Company. S. T. Bushnell, *Truth about Henry Ford* (Chicago, 1922), 142.

[2] In 1917 only one car in five was of the six-cylinder type; by 1926 two in every five. Epstein, *Automobile Industry,* 122.

of service stations along the main roads made travel safe and easy.

To drive a car had once been an adventure because if the "gas" did give out the unhappy occupant would have to walk a mile or so to the nearest telephone and summon relief, or beg alms of fuel from an infrequent fellow motorist. But in and near the cities, or along any of the great transcontinental highways, or even on the more modest state and county roads, it would not have been easy in the middle 1920's to break down far from a supply station. Here and there the short-sighted tradition of exploiting the stranger still prevailed. Usually this took one of two forms: either the erection of "speed traps," where a slight excess over the local speed limit, often ridiculously low,[1] would bring an extortionate fine to the local justice, or a road left deliberately muddy so that horses might be lent for hire to embogged motorists. But when the word went around that a particular road was beset with speed traps and mudholes motorists simply went another way.

Both the Ford methods of mass production and the standardization of type favored a steady decrease of cost to the consumer. The average sales price for all passenger cars dropped from its peak of $2123 in 1907 to $820 in 1916.[2] The rapid fall in the value of money during and immediately after the World War obscured the real decline in cost. At almost any time after the war five or six hundred dollars would buy a new car of the

[1] Even in the 1920's old signs on bridges warned all vehicles not to exceed five, three, or even two miles per hour. Few automobiles could be driven so slowly and even the most conscientious drivers disregarded the signposts. Only the very conscientious regularly observed the customary ten-to-fifteen-mile-an-hour limit for towns or the thirty-five of the open highway. The police who were not running speed traps customarily allowed a "reasonable" surplus over the legal limit before making an arrest.

[2] Barber, Story of the Automobile, 174.

cheaper type, and a thousand would purchase one of the better grade. Moreover, the purchaser received more for his money than earlier. Most automobile firms strove to introduce each year some improvement over the car of the year before. Some of these changes were merely for the sake of a new fashion, but almost always there was some added advantage or value as well. When the Ford became "dressy" in 1927 to meet the competition of the more colorful cheap cars, it was evident that mere cheapness, convenience and a good engine were no longer all that the clerk or farmer expected. The spread of luxury was shown in the increased proportion of closed cars: twenty-eight per cent of the production in 1922; seventy-four per cent in 1926, and the tendency continued.[1] On the other hand hardly one car in a hundred was a "sport model" specialized for speed. The cheap car still ruled the market, but the buyer insisted on better value every year.

Ford's nearest rival for the general market was a company with many strings to its bow, the General Motors Corporation, first established in 1908. William C. Durant, who fathered this combine, abandoned the once profitable manufacture of buggies for the newer field. But instead of becoming more and more concentrated under a single management and confined to a single type, the General Motors came to take in more than seventy thousand stockholders with very decentralized management under Alfred Sloan as "easy boss," and to develop different types of car for every need. At one time the General Motors produced the Chevrolet, the Pontiac, the Oldsmobile, the Oakland, the Buick, the LaSalle and the Cadillac passenger cars, besides making trucks, taxicabs and, last but not least, the Frigidaire domestic re-

[1] W. F. Sturm, "The Motor Outlook for 1927," *Liberty*, IV, 93 (May 7, 1927).

frigerators.[1] The Chevrolet at popular prices rose to about a million customers and had much to do in compelling the manufacture of a newer type of Ford. Third in the industry was the combine of the Chrysler with the Dodge, consummated in 1928. The Ford, the General Motors and the Chrysler-Dodge companies controlled in that year about four fifths of the whole industry, a very high degree of trustification for an industry that rests on no natural monopoly. Yet the motor trust, if one may use the word in a popular and inexact sense, did not share the unpopularity of the oil, steel and meat-packing combines or of the railways and mines. The public felt that in automobiles, at any rate, consolidation meant better values and lower prices for the consumer.

As a supplement to the private car and a rival to the steam railroad and electric trolley, the motor bus became of increasing importance. In 1926 some seventy thousand auto busses were in use. More than half of these operated as common carriers, but about twenty-seven thousand were used to take children to and from school. During the period 1916-1926 about twenty-five hundred miles of electric railway track were abandoned, and bus service substituted for four fifths of the lost mileage.[2] Not all the discontinued trackage can be laid directly to bus competition, however, as in many cases the electric railway went out of use some time before the motor-bus line filled its place. The competition of the passenger automobile sufficed to drive out of use many small-town or suburban electric lines. The steam rail-

[1] J. T. Flynn, "Riders of the Whirlwind," *Collier's*, LXXXIII, 8 ff. (Jan. 19, 1929), tells the story of William C. Durant, the Fisher brothers and the General Motors Corporation.

[2] E. F. Loomis, in National Automobile Chamber of Commerce, *Pamphlet*, no. 217 (N. Y., 1926), lists all the places in the United States where the bus replaced the electric railway.

roads, too, suffered a loss from bus competition estimated at anywhere from a tenth to a quarter of their passenger revenues; in a few cases the sale of local tickets had dropped one half by 1925.[1]

At first, in fact down to about 1926, motor busses engaged almost exclusively in short-haul operations within the limits of a hundred-mile radius and usually within the limits of a single state. The average trip was about thirty miles. But in 1926-1928 a few companies began to operate a through passenger service, divided of course into several stages marked by the large cities, almost across the continent. One series of lines linked up Detroit with the Pacific Coast. The advantages to the passenger were obvious. The motor bus was not smoky, nor did it proceed through the city slums and railroad yards; it could offer clean air and an interesting landscape. It could exploit a thinly settled route where there was some traffic but not enough to justify the cost of laying track. The railroads bitterly complained that the automobile represented "unfair competition" since it did not have to meet all the conditions and restrictions laid down by law for railway companies or in the charters of the street-car companies.

Many of the wiser carriers did not content themselves with bemoaning the competition of the gasoline auto, but determined to enlist the new force in their own service. Early in 1928 steam railroads, either directly or through subsidiaries, operated more than a thousand motor coaches over some ten thousand miles.[2] A magazine journalist gives a typical instance of a stumbling-block turned into a stepping-stone. One Western street-railway company, hard pressed by free-lance "jitney"

[1] C. S. Duncan, *Motor Bus and Truck Operation* (pamphlet, Wash, n.d.), 14.
[2] W. J. Cunningham, "Transportation," Committee on Recent Economic Changes, *Recent Economic Changes* (N. Y., 1929), I, 273.

cabs, installed ten motor coaches to parallel its electric line until competition was killed off, and then planned to discard the busses. But in this particular case,

> the railway company's plan worked in an unexpected way. . . . No sooner was the service established than all the jitney operators on the line were compelled to quit. The public appreciated the difference between uniformed chauffeurs, clean cars, dependable time tables, and proper organization, and the kind of service furnished by the irresponsible jitneys. Incidentally the traffic on the electric cars did not decrease, but instead slightly increased, while patronage on the motor line jumped by leaps and bounds.[1]

The company abandoned the idea of discarding its most profitable asset.

What the motor bus was to the railway passenger car the motor truck was to the freight train, at once a useful auxiliary and a dangerous rival. By 1928 more than three million motor trucks were in use in the United States. These fell into three general classes: the common carrier, the contract carrier and the owner-operator. The common carrier operated between fixed points on a regular schedule, like a freight train; the contract carrier hauled for anyone on terms and conditions agreed between shipper and truckman; the larger manufacturing companies ran their own fleets of trucks. The contract-carrier class was by far the largest, replacing to a great extent the old-fashioned drayman and his team of Percherons. In the period 1914-1928 the number of horses reported on American farms decreased by nearly a quarter, but the number employed in the city streets by more than half. One or two curious survivals remained: for example, milk wagons were still for the

[1] F. W. Parsons, *Everybody's Business* (N. Y., 1923), 215.

most part horse-driven. The reason was simple: a milk wagon must stop at nearly every door, and a horse knows enough when signaled to move ahead while the motor car remains passive until its driver climbs aboard and goes through some rather complicated mechanical operations. The only real advantage of the horse over the motor was in such situations as this that require "horse sense."

Obviously the main advantage of auto trucking over railroad freighting was in the short haul, within a thirty-mile radius. But it was not possible to fix any definite limit to the possible utility of the truck in special cases. A man living in New York who must move his household goods to Philadelphia or even to Washington might prefer to pay slightly more per mile and save the bother and cost of elaborate packing and crating and the risk of breakage from rough handling at the freight terminals. For certain classes of spoilable food the truck was particularly useful. Two million boxes of Hood River apples were annually shipped by truck to the railway terminals; and the poultry district around Petaluma, California, changed from railroad to motor truck for its fragile annual export of four hundred and fifty million eggs.[1]

The farmer probably profited more than anyone else from motor traction. The passenger automobile, though rarely more expensive than the Ford, ended his rural isolation and enabled his wife to visit town at will. The truck carried his perishable fruit and vegetables to market, and in 1926 seven per cent of the farmers operated their own trucks, while many others used the common carriers or contract truckers.[2] The tractor made an even greater difference in the farmer's life than car or

[1] Parsons, *Everybody's Business*, 213, 245.
[2] Epstein, *Automobile Industry*, 9.

truck. Henry Ford was prouder of his Fordson tractor than of his Ford car, described it as a "versatile power plant," and boasted that it had not only plowed, harrowed, cultivated and reaped, but also threshed, run gristmills, sawmills and the like, pulled stumps, cleared away snow, hauled with tires on the roads and with sledge runners on the ice, and been used in ninety-five lines of service, including the supply of power to get out an edition of the *Dearborn Independent* during a coal famine! [1]

The automobile brought with it two serious highway problems: the repair of roadways and the safety of automobilists and pedestrians on the streets. American highways in the 1920's carried about three times the volume of goods carried by all the railways. [2] Roads wide enough and strong enough for horse and wagon were soon torn to pieces by the hammering wheels of motor trucks. The cost of repairs and improvements, along with increased school expenses, was the main reason for the heavy burden of local taxation. The federal bureau of public roads estimated that the total expenditure for rural-road maintenance amounted to more than one billion dollars a year, while the cities spent about a third as much on their own streets. [3] Federal aid extended highway construction at an average rate of about ten thousand miles a year. [4] The through highways, designed primarily for motor traffic, were surfaced with asphalt or concrete. During the period 1914-1926 the mileage of artificially surfaced highway increased from 257,291 to 521,915; [5] about one sixth of all roads were surfaced. In many states the chief issues of state politics were: how much should

[1] Ford, *My Life and Work*, 201-204.
[2] Parsons, *Everybody's Business*, 227.
[3] *Commerce Yearbook for 1926*, I, 323-324.
[4] A. F. Macdonald, *Federal Aid* (N. Y., 1928), chap. v.
[5] Dept. of Agriculture, *Bull.*, no. 1279.

be spent on new highways, where they should be located, and what share of their cost automobile owners should pay, in gasoline tax or otherwise. Sometimes road appropriations were little short of collective bribery, a governor or highway commissioner urging special facilities for "loyal" rural districts. A politician, such as Governor Small of Illinois, sufficiently "liberal" on the roads issue had much tolerance from an electorate who lived on wheels.

But it was not enough to construct highways; they had to be made safe for the new democracy of motordom. During eight years (1919-1927) over 137,000 persons were killed and 3,500,000 injured in automobile accidents—a heavier toll of deaths and wounds than suffered by the American armies in the World War. The number of accidents grew year by year, but this was not a sign of increased recklessness or a proof that safety-first campaigns had altogether failed. The increase seems to have been due solely to the multiplication of cars on the road, for there was an actual decline in the proportion of fatal accidents to the number of automobiles in use.[1] Perhaps the wonder is, considering the national vice of recklessness and the ownership of high-powered motors by many persons with no mechanical aptitude, that the death toll was not ten times as great. Much popular indignation was roused by the so-called "hit-and-run" drivers who left their victims on the road while they hurried ahead to cowardly security. As about a fourth of the motor victims were children, the schools in most parts of the country introduced safety drills on the proper method of crossing the roads. An increasing number of states required prospective drivers

[1] In 1917 there were 178 fatalities to each 100,000 cars; in 1922, 112; in 1926, only 95. *Facts and Figures of the Automobile Industry for 1927*, 58.

to pass examinations demonstrating their skill in operating a car.

The democracy of the road created by the cheap automobile made the American people more than ever a migratory folk. An ever restless people, whose grandsires were immigrants and whose fathers were pioneers, who had almost abandoned the very idea of an ancestral homestead and were accustomed to change their jobs and their homes a dozen times in the course of a single career, would naturally welcome the new opportunity for independent travel provided by Henry Ford and his fellow manufacturers. In the day of the buggy and the bicycle five or six miles from town was a good distance for a picnic, and a two weeks' vacation camping trip was usually spent at the nearest sea beach or mountain resort. But the automobile opened up a hundred miles for the most impromptu picnic, and the whole United States for a serious vacation.

The demand for accommodations en route created the supply. Not only were service stations, road houses, inns and curio shops set up along the speedways to meet the needs of the car, the man at the wheel and the wife on the back seat, but well-appointed camping grounds were established wherever tourist traffic was heavy. This made the "tin-can tourist" independent of hotels. Many vacationists instead of making the automobile a mere equivalent of the railway, a means to get to the summer resort, kept on the road during their entire trip. When night came the car would be transformed into a tent by a little spread of portable canvas or, if the party were large enough to need more elaborate housing, tents might be set up on the camping ground or the shelter of a wooden roof rented for a nominal sum from the tourist-camp owner. In the winter of 1925 Florida had one hundred and seventy-eight certified tourist camps with accommodation for six hundred thousand persons. Sixty per cent of the Florida transients came in automobiles; and about two out of every five visitors to southern California.[1] The lower proportion in the latter case is, of course, explained by the fact that many preferred to save time by taking a railroad trip over the Rocky Mountains.

Pleasure-resort owners, local chambers of commerce and railroad companies serving particular regions saw the advantage of exploiting the growing tourist industry. This involved a certain rivalry: Europe as a whole against America; one state or section against another. The virtual cessation of European travel from 1914 till 1920 by pleasure seekers gave a great impetus to the movement to "See America First." The reader who was detached from all local patriotism or local interests might read with a certain cynical smile how many parts of the country claimed in their advertising to be "*The* Playground of America." Every state had some places attractive to tourists, and these "talking points" were played up with the most skilled salesmanship.

Four types of appeal were principally stressed: historic associations, scenic beauty, opportunities for sport, and climate. The greatest of these was climate. "Icicles or Roses. . . . Which do *your* children see at the window-pane?" pertinently inquired a leading booster association, Californians Incorporated, of the frost-bound East and Middle West. In the summer months the most urgent appeals came from those northern climes "where you have to sleep under blankets every night," to quote the stereotyped phrase of a thousand circulars. But the

[1] R. L. Duffus, "Putting Wheels under the Old Homestead," *Independent*, CXVI, 183-184 (Feb. 13, 1926). He estimated that the majority of winter motorists were retired farmers or business men with incomes ranging from $2000 to $5000 a year; in a word, the typical American middle class.

argument from climate did not always work in the obvious way. Taking a leaf from the recent history of Switzerland, the mountain resorts of New England and various parts of Canada began to sell the idea of winter sports where unbroken ice made them really possible.[1]

New England, which had long suffered from the competition of Western farms [2] and more recently of Southern cotton mills, was fortunately able to combine the appeal of history with that of climate and scenery in developing the tourist industry. The motorist along Cape Cod and around Plymouth was greeted every few miles with billboards advertising not commodities but historic events. A huge pen pointed to a huger open book on which was written, in letters so bold that he who rode might read, the chief event that had taken place in the village the traveler was approaching. In Virginia every battlefield of the Civil War bore a memorial tablet on the highway. Legends were as useful as history. Longfellow's *Hiawatha* proved to be worth millions to the upper peninsula of Michigan ("Hiawathaland," as the advertisers called it), and was scarcely less profitable to Minnesota where Minnehaha was conventionally supposed to have dwelt. The sentimental revival of American antiquities had its comic side in the multiplication of "Lover's Leap," "Ye Olde Inne" and houses where Washington slept; its sordid side too in the sale of pseudoantique furniture. But on the whole it was one of the most amiable aspects of the strong

[1] "We are greatly indebted to the recent fashion of wintering in the country because it is possible the fashion may awaken dwellers in the country of rigorous winters to the desirability of their place of residence and to its winter charm, scarcely inferior to that of summer. The mass of mankind, largely untouched by intrinsic beauty, may be led to see beauty when it becomes a fad to do so." Wallace Nutting, *Massachusetts Beautiful* (Framingham, Mass, 1923), 85.

[2] Especially before 1920. After the great fall in grain prices the relative advantage of the West had much decreased.

nationalist feeling of the time. The motor tourist must be credited with a large share in bringing again to the consciousness of America the romance of her history, the beauty of her scenery and the inspiration of her literature.

More important than the seasonal migration of the casual tourist was the permanent settlement of health and pleasure seekers in the land of sunshine. Until very recently work and not play had been the determining cause of the more important movements of population in the United States. If men went to Wyoming it was not for mountain scenery and cloudless skies but to raise cattle. If they went to California it was not so much to enjoy an eternal summer as to dig for gold or to plant fruit trees. If they went to Florida it was not for the leisure and warmth of the tropics but because oranges grew best where there was no frost. For many years, to be sure, some invalids had sought a new climate on the advice of a physician; Colorado, California and Arizona drew a trickle of immigration from this source. Others of the small leisure class sought seasonal recreation, playing golf at Asheville, North Carolina, fishing for tarpon in Florida, or hunting in the Maine woods and the Adirondacks. But migration by the million, not to make a living but to enjoy life under sunnier skies, was a phenomenon peculiar to the period after 1914, and was made possible only by the wave of prosperity which enabled large classes to turn from business to recreation and thus establish recreation as a profitable business.

The Farther West and the Lower South profited most by the rapid expansion of the tourist industry. The clean, dry air of Colorado and Arizona was more than ever sought by sufferers from lung trouble. The national parks, much developed under the wise direction of Secretary F. K. Lane of the interior department (1913-1920), offered a score of pleasure grounds to the tourist, and the automobile made them all accessible. "Dude wrangling," the popular cowboy name for the entertainment of visitors to the ranches, in many cases turned out to be more profitable than the herding of sheep and cattle.[1]

But the richest growth of tourism lay beyond the Rockies, in California. The census of 1910 ranked California twelfth in population, less than New Jersey; that of 1920 placed her eighth, ahead of Missouri and not far behind Michigan. Only Arizona and Montana showed a more rapid proportionate increase for the decade, and the absolute increase was almost as great as that of New York state. When Congress failed to reapportion seats after the census of 1920, California was reckoned the greatest loser of any state by that injustice. Of course California attracted settlers by her fruit farms and growing industries as well as by her bid for tourists, and still possessed great mineral wealth. But the metallic gold which attracted the forty-niners, and even the liquid gold of the oil wells, were overshadowed in commercial importance by the golden sunshine which welcomed the pleasure seeker.

Los Angeles, the metropolis of southern California, was, it is true, as famous for its motion-picture industry as for its tourist trade. But both owed their importance mainly to the climate. If the skies of California had been dull and cloudy there never would have been a city of movie actors in Hollywood, Los Angeles's best-known suburb. Moreover, the moving-picture industry offered yet another attraction to the tourist, who delighted to see his favorites in person and who not infre-

[1] See Mary Roberts Rinehart, "Dude West," *Ladies' Home Journ.,* XLVI (1929), 14 ff.

quently cherished the hope that his own latent talent might be discovered by discerning directors.

Los Angeles in 1910 was a city of 319,000, quite overshadowed by her northern rival San Francisco. The census of 1920 indicated a startling leap to 576,000, placing her about 70,000 ahead of San Francisco and making her the largest city lying between St. Louis and the Pacific Ocean. Official estimates after 1920 indicated an unslackening growth, attaining by 1926 some 1,300,000 inhabitants.[1] Building progressed at a rate of about $150,000,000 a year, and $15,000,000 was invested in transforming an open roadstead into a good harbor. As the community was both new and wealthy its houses and those of its suburbs were very attractive modern examples of architecture, usually following, in a general way, the old Spanish style introduced into California by the earliest white settlers and well suited to a warm, dry climate much like that of Spain. One of the most notable structures was the Hollywood Bowl, a concrete stadium where forty thousand people might gather to hear summer evening concerts under the stars.

Simultaneous with the Los Angeles boom was a similar one in Florida. The two regions being much alike, their rivalry was keener. Both Florida and California are rich in history and romance, dating back to the days of Spanish occupation.[2] Both have an almost winterless climate, attractive alike to fruit growers and to tourists. Both were, in a sense, almost "frontier" states, for although they had long been settled their great expansion of wealth and population had been very recent and very rapid. Both attracted colonies of the wealthy, and both passed through flurries of real-estate speculation almost

[1] *World Almanac for 1928*, 313. The growth was in part due to enlargement of her city limits.

[2] See H. I. Priestley, *The Coming of the White Man* (*A History of American Life*, I), 71-82, 200-207.

without parallel. Each had a skeleton in the closet—California taunted Florida with her Atlantic hurricanes, and Florida retorted with allusions to earthquakes.

Florida is the paradox of these United States. St. Augustine is the oldest city in the nation. Spaniards under Ponce de Leon had sought in Florida the waters of eternal youth a century before the English colonized Virginia or Massachusetts. Yet it was not until the twentieth century that Florida stepped into the limelight as a state capable of great economic development. There were in truth two Floridas. The northern part of the state belonged socially, politically and economically to the Lower South, the "cotton kingdom." It had a large Negro population who worked as plantation slaves until the Civil War, when Florida, like her neighbors, joined the Confederacy, endured the war and suffered reconstruction. Citrus fruits, garden vegetables such as potatoes and celery, corn, peanuts, sugar cane, tobacco, livestock, turpentine and phosphate rock were the chief economic assets of the state. Industry and commerce were little developed, and education was rather backward. This elder Florida, growing gradually in prosperity, remained the politically dominant half of the state. But its supremacy was increasingly threatened by the development of modern or tourist Florida farther south.

Southern Florida lay almost empty till within the twentieth century. Midway on the western coast stood Tampa, marking the southward limit of development. The east coast had many scattered settlements, but south of Jacksonville they were very small, Miami, one of the most important, having in 1910 only fifty-four hundred inhabitants. Between the coast towns of the southern half of the peninsula was a flat, swampy plain culminating in the marshes of the Everglades, a land of alligators, malaria and wild Seminole Indians, as forbidding to settlers as the alkali deserts of eastern Nevada, and thought to be forever incapable of profitable development.

The main factor that kept back southern Florida was difficulty of access. To be sure, the chief advantage that Florida had over California was geographical. As an Eastern state, near to the great centers of population, she could draw many tourists who would not take the time to cross the continent. But until Florida had good highways and good railroads she could take no advantage of her location. Bad roads or none are a more significant form of distance than mere miles.

Much of the ground for future prosperity in Florida was prepared when Henry M. Flagler undertook to build a through railway down the Eastern Coast. The Florida East Coast Railway not only linked the villages of the Atlantic shore and enabled them to grow into towns and cities, but even extended across the keys or islets to the port of Key West, the line across the keys being completed in 1912. In 1925 the railway began to double-track its line north of Miami. In the meantime the Seaboard Air Line began to penetrate southern Florida from the north, and Henry B. Plant built a line in the west, aiming to develop the Gulf of Mexico shore as Flagler had the Eastern Coast. The Atlantic Coast Line took over and developed Plant's undertaking, and several connections were completed between the Florida lines and the great railway systems of the East and the Middle West.

However unwittingly, Henry Ford must be ranked with Henry Flagler and Henry Plant as one of the builders of southern Florida. The white coral sand of the coast made excellent speedways, and the laws were indulgent to fast driving. Along the new roads came automobiles by the tens of thousands. Some were the touring cars of wealthy men who preferred the freedom of the open road to the confinement of even the most luxurious Pullman car, but the majority were the humble flivvers of men who could not have afforded a Florida vacation if Ford and his fellows had not democratized the automobile. Sometimes the car represented the entire capital of the immigrant, except a little cash in hand with which to buy a lot in Florida.

For several winters the influx of winter tourists was more than equal to the entire permanent population of the state, and they spent during the season from six hundred million to one billion dollars.[1] That many settled permanently is shown by the growth of the population from 752,000 in 1910 to 968,000 in 1920, and an estimated 1,263,000 in 1925, when the boom was at its height. Palm Beach was one of the first resorts in lower Florida to be developed, and even before the World War readers of the pictorial sections of the Sunday papers were accustomed to pictures of the sons and daughters of the very wealthy in bathing costume at Palm Beach in winter, very like the pictures of the same individuals at Newport or Bar Harbor in summer. But it was only after the war, when growing prosperity and assured peace permitted the realization of many a postponed wish, that the envious readers of these papers sought to taste for themselves the attractions of the American tropics.

Miami, still farther south than Palm Beach, became the focus of the new migration. Not much more than a village before the war, even the census of 1920 granted it less than thirty thousand inhabitants as compared with more than fifty thousand for Tampa in the west and over ninety thousand for Jacksonville in the conservative north. From 1920 to 1926 Miami expanded with

[1] Florida Trust Co., *Business Survey of Florida* (Miami, 1926), 62.

the ominous acceleration of a snowball rolling down a mountainside. In the latter year a special count placed its population at more than one hundred and thirty thousand. Where the crowds came, other crowds followed for that very reason. Many who cared little about climate for themselves hoped that they could reap a fortune in real estate by selling that commodity to others. Soon real-estate values soared far above what could be justified on the basis of existing agriculture, or even tourist traffic, and represented nothing more substantial than the hope of the speculator to sell at a still higher price before the boom broke. Real-estate agents and advertisers found it an earthly paradise. Local newspapers broke two world records. The *Miami Daily News*, owned by James M. Cox of Ohio, former Democratic candidate for president, printed in 1925 a special edition of 504 pages, the largest newspaper issue ever printed. The *Miami Herald* in the same year broke the world's record for total volume of advertising (mainly real-estate) carried in a single year.[1]

Many fortunes were made and many lost in the land boom of 1925. Something like a quarter of a billion dollars changed hands in real-estate sales that year, but many transactions were on credit. The best business lots sold at from one to five thousand dollars a front foot. In one case a man sold a lot for $40,000 which had been given him fifteen years before free of charge on condition that he build a garage on it.[2] In another case a purchaser paid $35,000 for a lot which he himself had sold for $2500 two years earlier. But of course many who sold either too soon or not soon enough suffered for the gambler's risk they had taken. After 1925 speculation

[1] F. P. Stockbridge and J. H. Perry, *Florida in the Making* (N. Y., 1926), 195.
[2] For many such instances, see Felix Isman, "Florida's Land Boom," *Sat. Eve. Post*, CXCVIII, 14-15 (Aug. 22, 1925).

became less acute, prices sagged and the feverish phase of the boom was over.

Other winter resorts shared in but slightly less degree the prosperity of Miami. Palm Beach, West Palm Beach, Hollywood (not its namesake in California), Coral Gables and other East Coast resorts were built up, rebuilt, and expanded until they almost formed a single continuous city along the Atlantic. As in California the Spanish architecture, traditional to the land, was tastefully adapted to the modern hotel and cottage. Tampa, the chief city of the western shore, claimed a population rivaling that of Miami. In 1924 D. P. Davis dredged and pumped from the half-submerged marshes of Tampa Bay an island, which within a few months was covered with hotels, cottages, country clubs and amusement parks.[1]

In September, 1926, a hurricane from the Atlantic struck directly across Miami and southern Florida.[2] Hundreds of houses and business buildings were wrecked, and the Red Cross rushed in aid to rescue the homeless. The town of Moore Haven suffered the most as the overflow from Lake Okechobee practically drowned out the community. But rebuilding started at once at Miami and every preparation was made for another busy season. The northern part of the state had suffered little, and the south recovered as rapidly as did Chicago and San Francisco after their great fires.[3] The only permanent harm done to the state was nature's tactless demonstration

[1] The intercity rivalry was an old one. When Flagler received an invitation to attend the opening of the Tampa Bay Hotel he telegraphed to Plant, "Where is Tampa?" Plant wired back, "Follow the crowd!" Stockbridge and Perry, *Florida in the Making*, 190.

[2] For a full account of the disaster, see J. H. Reese, *Florida's Great Hurricane* (Miami, 1926). A similar storm wrecked some Florida towns in 1928.

[3] See Allan Nevins, *The Emergence of Modern America* (*A History of American Life*, VIII), 84-85, for the Chicago fire.

that even the most amiable climate may have its eccentricities.

In order to encourage the investment of capital and attract the patronage of business men on a holiday and induce them to make Florida their permanent home, the laws were made peculiarly favorable to wealth. In 1924, by a constitutional amendment ratified by popular referendum, it was made illegal to levy any state inheritance or income tax on any citizen or resident of the state. At the time forty-six of the forty-eight states had inheritance taxes and eleven had income taxes (to make no mention of federal income and inheritance taxes which, of course, remained effective in Florida as everywhere else). Eulogists of Florida boasted that this "progessive" legislation placed Florida in the lead of all other states, though certain other states, such as Wisconsin, had usually termed "progressive" the opposite policy of laying heavy burdens on great fortunes for the public weal. Other features of Florida legislation, such as laws making easy the establishment of corporations and permitting counties and municipalities to levy taxes for publicity purposes, showed a similar desire to put no political obstacle in the way of economic expansion.[1]

Behind the tourist came the farmer. Southern Florida, with tropic warmth and often rich soil (when once drained), proved an important factor in the American fruit market. The great enterprise of draining the Everglades has been compared by many writers with Holland's project of draining the Zuyder Zee. The northern and central parts of the state also greatly improved the yield of their farm lands. Great progress, too, was made in educational lines. But the development of Florida in agriculture, industry and general public welfare can be paralleled in the contemporary development of other

[1] Stockbridge and Perry, *Florida in the Making*, 155-157, 169.

Southern states. Where Florida remained unique was in the swift discovery and exploitation of her natural heritage of sunshine and sea.

Foreign travel, too, became a growing habit of the well-to-do American. In 1927 tourists from the United States spent in foreign lands about $770,000,000 as compared with $175,000,000 when Taft was president.[1] For the year 1925 the French estimated that there were 220,000 Americans visiting France and spending in that one country $226,160,000.[2] The richest two per cent, vaguely termed "millionaires," spent $5000 or more to a trip; the next most prosperous eighteen per cent averaged $1760 each; eight per cent, traveling for business, not pleasure, $1500; forty-four per cent, "middle-class" tourists, $850; and the remaining twenty-eight per cent, including employees on short vacations, students earning their way, and others who had to study economy, $425. Here again the automobile played its part. Most in the first two classes took their cars with them to Europe, and nearly all the rest economized time and effort in sightseeing by using *chars-à-banc,* or hired cars, to reach Shakespeare's birthplace or the battlefields of France. Herbert Hoover declared in 1928 that "our tourist expenditure alone in Europe since the war would enable them to take care of the entire amount" of their annual debt payments to the United States.[3]

The automobile conditioned American life in its every aspect. As we have seen, it greatly complicated

[1] "The best estimates indicated an annual expenditure by our tourists during 1909-1910 of about $175,000,000 a year. In 1927 the figure was $770,000,000." Julius Klein, "Servicing Our 260 American Wage," *Mag. of Business,* LIV (1928), 87.

[2] *Je Sais Tout,* no. 272 (1928), 306.

[3] *Washington Post,* Oct. 16, 1928. See also Hiram Motherwell, "The American Tourist Makes History," *Harper's Mag.,* CLX (1929), 70-76, for discussion of the effect of tourism on the intercontinental financial balance.

the crime problem by giving every criminal who had three hours' warning a circle with a hundred-mile radius in which to conceal himself from the police. It gave fresh urgency to the liquor problem by turning the simple drunkard into the more sinister figure of the drunken driver. It multiplied national parks and playgrounds and made tourism a leading industry. It placed mortgages on homes when the automobile was a luxury, and took them off farms when the motor truck became a necessity. It enabled the farmer to use the services of the town physician and send his children to a consolidated town school. It took this farmer, too, straight by the neighboring hamlet to trade in the city twenty or thirty miles away, causing the country store to languish and the mail-order houses to worry. The latter, to meet these new conditions, straightway set up chain department stores in the smaller cities to recover their losses.

The motor car replaced the parlor and porch as the courting ground of the new generation. It made the American people more than ever a nation of mechanicians and, according to some hostile witnesses (such as Sinclair Lewis), swallowed up all other topics of male conversation from religion to politics. It gave a new aspect to feminism by making the flapper a gay and gallant *chauffeuse*. It freed the nation from provincialism, though at the heavy cost of increasing standardization of manners. It necessitated wider units of rural and suburban administration and, according to one high authority, did "more in two decades to revolutionize the areas of local government than all the events of history since the battle of Hastings."[1] It opened a new age of the nomads. In a word, it is the main subject not of this chapter only but of the volume as a whole.

[1] T. H. Reed, *The Vanishing Township* (Univ. of Michigan, *Official Publs.*, XXIX, no. 43), 17.

CHAPTER IX

The South in Black and White

THE fact that during these years sectional differences were less clearly defined than in any earlier period was due only in part to the integrating effect of the war. Even more potent, because more constant, was the influence of industrialism. Land is local; capital is cosmopolitan. The Yankee farmer and the Georgia planter in an agricultural age differed as the factory operative of Boston cannot differ from his fellow workman of Atlanta. Men still spoke of "the West," but they could no longer draw its boundary on the map, for Michigan and Illinois were now as industrialized as Connecticut. The automobile, as we have seen, transplanted large numbers of the agricultural Middle West to urban and suburban Los Angeles, and brought a colony of wealthy business men from the Northeast to southernmost Florida. The growing habit of travel mitigated provincial differences, and the standardization of goods made all parts of the country more and more alike in dress and manner of life. In the main this leveling process, at least on its economic side, was a leveling upwards, tending to bring to all sections the standards of the most prosperous communities; but it robbed the United States of much picturesque local variety and subjected it to the reproach of being a land of interchangeable citizens whose minds were as alike as the money they used.

Of all the sections of the nation the South was the most persistent in maintaining its collective individuality. The process of standardization was at work here as elsewhere, perhaps more than elsewhere, but the original differences were greater. For over a century, ever since the cotton plantation became the norm of economic life, the South had felt a consciousness of kind wider than the state and narrower than the nation, a regionalism comparable perhaps to that of Catalonia in Spain or Scotland in Great Britain.[1] In each decade since 1865 journalists had repeated the discovery of a "New South," and doubtless each time they were right, for the growth of industrial wealth and educational opportunity had been fairly continuous. The period after 1914 did not change the direction, but it certainly accelerated its momentum. The war played a part by merging sectional with national effort; the boll weevil, as we have seen, diminished the relative importance of cotton. At the same time the textile factories of the piedmont multiplied, the oil wells of Oklahoma and Texas brought a new influx of capital, tourist travel and winter golf became important, the Negro population tended townward and northward as the munition factories enticed them from the plantations, illiteracy became rare, and new forces were astir in politics.

Yet with all these changes the South still differed collectively from other parts of the Union in several important particulars. As a section it continued to be distinguished by large numbers of the Negro, the relative absence of the recent European immigrant, its still mainly agricultural economy, the great influence of the Protestant clergy, its emphasis on kinship, its reluctance to embark on radical social or economic reforms, and its jealous conservation of the older American traditions. The political support which the South gave generally to the prohibition amendment may seem out of harmony

[1] See C. R. Fish, *The Rise of the Common Man* (*A History of American Life*, VI), 281 ff.

with its essential character, but this particular reform stood in a special position, enlisting the active support of the clergy and appealing to the dread of the effects of drunkenness upon the Negro population.

The race situation was certainly one distinguishing mark of the Southern tradition. "It is a land with a unity despite its diversity," wrote Professor Ulrich B. Phillips in 1928, "with a people having common joys and common sorrows, and, above all, as to the white folk a people with a common resolve indomitably maintained—that it shall be and remain a white man's country." [1] Because of the adaptation of race to climate over so many centuries it may be questioned whether the majority of Negroes in America will ever consent to live in the states with cold winters. Nevertheless, during these years, the race problem showed signs of becoming less sectional and more national. From 1915 to 1928 about one million two hundred thousand Negroes moved from South to North, although many made but a temporary stay. [2] The census of 1920, though covering but the first phase of this northward migration, showed a proportionate decrease of colored population to the whole in almost all sections of the South, and in a few cases this decline was absolute as well as relative. From 1910 to 1920 Michigan's Negro population increased from seventeen to sixty thousand, while during the same period Mississippi showed a loss of more than seventy-four thousand.

The townward movement of the race was even more striking than the northward trek, as it affected all sections of the country. The Northern cities made by far

[1] U. B. Phillips, "The Central Theme of Southern History," *Am. Hist. Rev.*, XXXIV, 31.

[2] C. S. Johnson, "The Changing Economic Status of the Negro," Am. Acad. of Polit. and Social Sci., *Annals*, CXL, 131; C. H. Wesley, *Negro Labor in the United States, 1850-1925* (N. Y., 1927), 291-298.

the most rapid and striking gains, but it is worth noting that Southern cities also attracted Negroes from the farms. Nearly 235,000 moved from country to city in the census decade in the South Atlantic states, and in the South Central states, east of the Mississippi, "although each state lost Negro population, this loss was wholly rural, for the urban Negro population in the entire division increased over 62,000, or 12 per cent." [1] This townward movement was accompanied by a lesser rate of increase for the Negro population as a whole. In some cities, where climatic or sanitary conditions were unfavorable, deaths actually exceeded births. Professor Walter F. Willcox of Cornell, analyzing the census returns of 1920, predicted a steady decrease in the proportion of Negro population to the white in the United States. "It also seems reasonable to anticipate that the Negroes, who at the census of 1790 were over 19 per cent, or nearly one-fifth, of the population of the country and are now one-tenth, are likely by the end of the century to be not more than one-twentieth." [2] The white South, relieved of its former fear of being overwhelmed by an alien race, came to view the whole problem more calmly.

The northward movement of the Negro was not to be explained wholly by any single cause. [3] One of the most important factors was the location of the great munition centers in the Northeastern states. The shutting off of European immigration by the war at the very time when cheap labor was most in demand caused manufacturers to look towards Dixie. The Negro field hand might be unaccustomed to factory labor, but he was physically strong, docile by temperament, inexpensive, and hitherto

[1] W. S. Rossiter, *Increase of Population in the United States, 1910-1920* (Census Monographs, I, 1922), 127.
[2] Rossiter, *Increase of Population*, 132.
[3] Wesley, *Negro Labor*, 291-293.

remote from Socialist and trade-union agitation. After the war stricter immigration laws and the revival of general industry following a period of depression brought a new demand for labor in 1923, and in the first three months of that year a single Pittsburgh concern imported colored workmen at the rate of a thousand a month.[1] Alarmed at the activity of these recruiters, the white South discouraged labor agents by fines, levied on various pretexts, and by counterpropaganda. In December, 1923, a Mississippi planter went to Chicago scattering handbills urging Negroes to return to the South and sent out a wagon plastered with signs describing the charms of the cotton fields.[2] The expansion of industry coincided with a decline of cotton planting in districts ravaged by the boll weevil. Said one Southern planter, "It was a billion-dollar bug that got behind the Southern Negro and chased him across Mason and Dixon's line." [3]

Certain long-standing grievances of the Southern Negro made him more willing to listen to the labor agents. These were of three kinds: unequal treatment before the law, mob terrorism and social discrimination. Legal discrimination, to be sure, did not always operate to the disadvantage of the colored man, as, following an old tradition, Southern white men often viewed with indulgence disorders among the Negroes which they would not have tolerated among their own kind. But in Georgia and certain other states the county and police officials were compensated by a fee for their services, which meant they were paid so much a head for every man they arrested. The effect was to render these officials overzealous in rounding up Negroes for gambling,

[1] R. L. Hartt, "When the Negro Comes North," *World's Work*, XLVIII (1924), 84.
[2] Hartt, "When the Negro Comes North," 86.
[3] Hartt, "When the Negro Comes North," 84.

drinking and other petty infractions of the law. As punishment for such offenses Negroes were usually sentenced to work on the county roads.[1] When more serious offenses were brought to book, especially offenses against the whites, the sentences imposed were often disproportionately heavy.[2]

Purely political discriminations seem to have weighed less than these judicial partialities. The issue of the franchise was not very widely agitated during this period; the Fifteenth Amendment remained in the Constitution, which seemed to satisfy Northern sentiment, and it was quietly disregarded throughout the black belt, which seemed to meet the desires of the white South. The federal courts disallowed the "grandfather" test when the issue was raised, and declared unconstitutional the Texas "white-primary" law of 1924 which drew a racial line in party primary elections.[3] But literacy tests, ability to "interpret" the state constitution, the payment of a poll tax and other similar devices, long in use and in form not discriminatory, were tolerated however unequally they might be administered. On the other hand, in the North where Negro suffrage was a reality the colored vote, thanks to the great migration, became far more influential than ever before, especially in such urban centers as Chicago which elected a Negro congressman in 1928.

Other grievances that seem to have counted with many Negroes were local acts of mob violence—it is significant that many emigrants came from the particular localities where such outrages had taken place—inferior

[1] See H. H. Donald's careful study, "The Negro Migration of 1916-1918," Journ. of Negro History, VI (1921), 415-416.

[2] For statistical evidence on this point, see J. T. Sellin, "The Negro Criminal," Am. Acad. of Polit. and Social Sci., Annals, CXL, 52-64.

[3] Myers v. Anderson, 238 U. S. 368; Nixon v. Herndon, 273 U. S. 536; J. W. Johnson and H. J. Seligmann, "Legal Aspects of the Negro Problem," Am. Acad. of Polit. and Social Sci., Annals, CXL, 91-92.

school accommodations, injustice in sharing farm profits between tenant and landlord or between borrower and creditor, discrimination on common carriers, the denial of courtesy titles (such as mister, doctor, etc.) to educated Negroes, and the lack of opportunity for employment in certain "white" trades. Such incidents as the murder of eleven Negroes on a Georgia plantation to keep indebted peons in subjection had wide repercussions.[1] Several Southern white editors, while asserting that the Negro ought to remain south of Mason and Dixon's line both for his own good and for that of his section, pointed out that he could not be expected to do so unless he met better treatment. Thus in South Carolina the *Columbia State* declared on December 2, 1916, "If the Southern people would have the Negroes remain they must treat the Negroes justly," and the *Memphis Commercial Appeal* in Tennessee urged on October 15 of the same year, "The South needs every able-bodied Negro that is now south of the line, and every Negro who remains south of the line will in the end do better than he will do in the North."[2]

On the other hand, while the South valued the Negro's services more as he threatened to leave the section, many Northern newspapers expressed much apprehension as the race problem appeared in their midst. White laborers resented the competition of the cheap and docile black workingmen and out of this resentment grew serious riots. In East St. Louis, Illinois, where Negro strike breakers had been imported by the meat packers in 1916, the trade unions in vain protested to the city authorities against their coming. In July, 1917, a disastrous riot took place on a scale quite as large as

[1] "Peonage and Murder," *Independent,* CV, 407 (April 16, 1921).
[2] Cited from E. J. Scott, *Negro Migration during the War* (N. Y., 1920), 154, 155, which gives many other newspaper comments to the same effect.

any that had ever occurred farther south. Over a hundred Negroes were killed or wounded, five thousand were made homeless, and hundreds of thousands of dollars' worth of property destroyed.[1] Similar but lesser riots took place in factory towns in Pennsylvania and New Jersey in the same year, and in Chicago, Omaha and Washington, D. C., in 1919. Thus unhappy proof was given of the truth of the old contention of the white South that race violence was national and not sectional and that if the Negro moved northward race riots would follow in his wake.

By a curious anomaly, in spite of the prevalence of race riots in the hectic postwar days and the revival of the Ku Klux Klan,[2] the old American custom of lynch law fell into almost complete disuse. In the first four months of 1928 there was not a single recorded lynching, a record without parallel since exact statistics on the subject began to be kept. For the decade 1914-1923 inclusive the average number was fifty-seven annually, a much better record than that of previous years but still discreditably high. Though the proposed Dyer anti-lynching bill, which would have given the federal courts jurisdiction in cases of mob violence, failed of action in the Senate after passing the House of Representatives in 1922, it stirred the local authorities to vindicate state rights by greater zeal in law enforcement. There were only sixteen lynchings in 1924 as compared with thirty-three in the previous year, seventeen in 1925, thirty in 1926, sixteen in 1927, eleven in 1928 and ten in 1929.[3] It became the exception instead of the rule for a mob to meet with no effective opposition from the constituted

[1] Donald, "The Negro Migration," 438-439.

[2] See later, chap. xi.

[3] These statistics are mainly from the record kept by the Tuskegee Institute. The annual figures vary slightly according to their source but not enough to make an appreciable difference.

authorities. A notable instance of civic courage was the personal rescue of a Negro from a mob at Murray, Kentucky, in 1917, by the governor of the state, A. O. Stanley.[1] Noteworthy also was the denunciation of lynching by a committee of white women associated with the Commission on Interracial Coöperation in Louisiana: "We hold that no circumstances can ever justify such violent disregard for law and that in no instance is it an exhibition of chivalric consideration and honor of womanhood." [2] Similar resolutions were passed in many other states.[3]

The Negro reacted in various ways to his unfavorable position in the United States. Some became ashamed of their race and tried to tone down its characteristics as much as possible, and fortunes were made in hair-straightening devices, the reverse process to the white girl's "wave." Others, in increasing numbers, became race conscious and took pride in their African blood. These race-conscious Afro-Americans were, however, divided in policy. Those who followed the tradition of Booker T. Washington, whose work at Tuskegee was ably continued by Robert R. Moton, sought first of all a solid economic position for the race, as educated, trained, property-owning farmers and artisans, for whom the whites would feel a respect which would eventually bring with it political reënfranchisement. To

[1] Thomas Randolph, "The Governor and the Mob," *Independent*, LXXXIX, 347-348 (Feb. 26, 1917).

[2] J. W. Johnson, "The Practice of Lynching," *Century*, CXV (1927), 68.

[3] In the period 1914-1928, as in previous periods, only from a fifth to a fourth of all lynchings were for rape or attempted rape. The usual accusation was murder. One interesting phenomenon of the period was that in all years the number of white persons lynched was small, and in three or four years none. During the nineteenth century the lynchings of white persons were but little less numerous than the lynchings of Negroes. So the passing of frontier conditions, as well as improvement in racial relationships, helps explain the remarkable decline of what many criminologists have termed "*the* American crime."

more fiery and impatient spirits this program seemed too slow, and as a result there had arisen in the early years of the century a second type of racial leader, typified by W. E. B. Du Bois, editor of the *Crisis*, and associated with the National Association for the Advancement of Colored People, who demanded the immediate grant of equal civil and political rights.[1] After the war and the return of Negro regiments from France (where racial discriminations do not follow the American tradition) much was heard of the "New Negro" who would no longer, cap in hand, submit to injustice, but "when the mob moves, meet it with bricks and clubs and guns."[2] One tiny, picturesque group did indeed carry Negro nationalism far beyond the simple demand of Du Bois for equal rights in America. These were the followers of Marcus Garvey, president of the newly formed Universal Negro Improvement Association, who dreamed of nothing less than the reconquest of Africa as a black man's republic—a sort of African Zionism. "The hour has come," he declared, "when the whole continent of Africa shall be reclaimed and redeemed as the home of the black peoples." He projected a "Black Star Line" of steamers for transporting the American Negro back to his ancestral homeland, there to erect a racial empire under the banner of black, red and green to the strains of

> Ethiopia, thou land of our fathers,
> Thou land where the gods loved to be,
> As storm cloud at night sudden gathers
> Our armies come rushing to thee!

[1] See H. U. Faulkner, *The Quest for Social Justice* (*A History of American Life*, XI), chap. i. For an expression of the radical viewpoint, see especially W. E. B. Du Bois, *Darkwater* (N. Y., 1920); for the conservative view, prevalent at Tuskegee, see R. R. Moton, *What the Negro Thinks* (N. Y., 1929).

[2] R. L. Hartt, "The New Negro," *Independent*, CV, 76 (Jan. 15, 1921).

Garvey was later prosecuted and imprisoned for swindling, and nothing came of his enterprise, too vast and vague for a world of solid realities, but at least his movement was a sign that to many Negroes their race had become a pride rather than a humiliation.[1]

On the whole, the economic situation of the American Negro improved during and after the World War. Though due in part to the competitive bidding of field and factory for his services, the improvement came even more from the spread of education which qualified him for better positions. From 1917 to 1927 the number of institutions for the higher education of the Negro more than doubled, and enrollment in them increased more than sixfold.[2] A larger proportion of the race also attended Northern and Western institutions open to all races. The number employed by the federal government rose from 22,540 in 1910 to 51,882 in 1928.[3] More Negro high schools were built in the South from 1918 to 1928 than in the entire past.[4] In spite of the boll weevil and a bad credit situation, the majority of those who stuck to the farm found themselves better off. William S. Scarborough, former president of Wilberforce University, testified in 1925: "The Virginia Negro farmers may be said to belong to a thrifty group. Virtually all are members of a church and of one or another of the many fraternal societies. . . . Most of the Negroes have automobiles and many own victrolas."[5]

[1] For Garveyism, see T. H. Talley, "Marcus Garvey—The Negro Moses?" and "Garvey's Empire of Ethiopia," *World's Work*, XLI (1920-1921), 153-166, 264-270; and R. L. Hartt, "The Negro Moses," *Independent*, CV, 205 (Feb. 26, 1921).

[2] *U. S. Daily* (Wash.), Sept. 15, 1928.

[3] *U. S. Daily*, Sept. 14, 1928.

[4] N. C. Newbold, "Common Schools for Negroes in the South," Am. Acad. of Polit. and Social Sci., *Annals*, CXL, 213-214.

[5] W. S. Scarborough, "The Negro Farmer in the South," *Current History*, XXI (1925), 569.

262 THE GREAT CRUSADE AND AFTER

Probably the most successful, certainly the most famous, of the colored urban communities was the Harlem district in New York City. By 1928 the Negro population of New York City was estimated at 250,000, of whom 170,000 lived in Harlem.[1] Not all came from the Southern states, for the West Indies contributed perhaps 40,000. Many races and nationalities in Manhattan's cosmopolitan flux were swept aside by the oncoming tide. Steadily the colored merchants and shopkeepers drove the whites out of business. "A Negro millinery shop offers 'a variety of styles in the latest Parisian shapes created by expert Negro designers.' A Negro apothecary advertises, 'Why not go to our own drugstores? They employ all colored men.' "[2] There was a thriving trade in black doll babies, advertised "Why should a Negro child play with a white doll?"[3] Here one saw the crude beginnings of race pride and race culture; the Garveyite movement was largely fostered in Harlem. The colored artist was also taking himself more seriously; he had long been a favorite in the lighter arts, vaudeville and minstrel-show song and dance, but the dramatic power of such actors as Charles Gilpin and Paul Robeson, the musical art of Roland Hayes, the famous tenor, and the poetry of Countee Cullen rivaled the art of the European races in their own chosen fields.[4]

The general economic progress of the South was even more rapid than that of most parts of the North and West, and this quite apart from such local booms as the oil fields of Oklahoma or the winter-vacation colony of tropic Florida. If we take the section as a whole in its

[1] *N. Y. Times*, Dec. 10, 1928. Estimate by the New York Urban League.

[2] R. L. Hartt, "I'd Like to Show You Harlem," *Independent*, CV, 335 (April 2, 1921).

[3] Hartt, "I'd Like to Show You Harlem," 357.

[4] E. F. Frazier, "The American Negro's New Leaders," *Current History*, XXVIII (1928), 56-59.

broadest sense,[1] the population of the South increased by about a quarter from 1910 to 1927; and the aggregate value of its property doubled from 1912 to 1925.[2] Cotton spinning shifted increasingly near to the region of cotton planting. In 1910 about a third of the active looms and spindles of the nation were in the South; in 1927 approximately one half.[3] Seven barrels of petroleum were produced in the South in 1927 to each barrel in 1910. Coal production in the same period more than doubled. The rate of increase in the use of electricity for the decade 1913-1923 was over 212 per cent, while the increase for the remainder of the country was less than 148 per cent.[4] The increasing utilization of water power in manufactures was, indeed, a major explanation of the industrial expansion of the Southern highlands. Alabama, Tennessee, and especially North Carolina showed the most marked effects of the new sectional industrial revolution; states possessing little water power, such as Louisiana and Mississippi, showed far less alteration.[5]

The cotton mills of the piedmont reached out their tentacles and increasingly swept into urban life the most isolated rural communities in America, the Southern highlanders, where the purest English stock in the nation had stagnated for generations on rocky hillside farms in poverty and ignorance. Lowlanders also of the poor-white class came to the factories. The Negro did not come, or came only as an outdoor laborer for odd jobs

[1] That is, including the border states of Kentucky, Maryland, Missouri, Oklahoma, West Virginia and the District of Columbia as well as the eleven ex-Confederate states.

[2] *Blue Book of Southern Progress for 1928* (published by the *Manufacturers' Record*), 202-204.

[3] *Blue Book of Southern Progress for 1928*, 203-204.

[4] T. W. Martin, "Hydro-Electric Development in the South," *The South's Development* (Balt., 1924), 241.

[5] For a discussion of the Muscle Shoals development, see chap. iii.

of carpentry and the like. The actual textile operatives were almost exclusively of the white race; as in earlier years, many of them were women and children.[1] The issue of child labor thus raised was much debated. Advocates of national action contended that Southern laws as to age of employment, hours of labor and working conditions were below the standard of other sections. Opponents pointed out that Southern mill owners did so much welfare work among their employees that their health, education and social opportunities were better secured than if they had remained on the farm, and that many had passed through the mill door to a future of wealth and community leadership.

Curious indeed were the contrasts presented by the advance of the textile industry in the South. A people possessing a strong individualistic tradition were brought under a paternalism almost feudal in character, for in some mill villages the manufacturer owned or controlled all the land, the homes, the shops and the places of recreation. City ways were quickly copied by the younger generation, while their elders held to mountain customs. As a recent student has pointed out, the mill village "is the link between poverty and prosperity; it is the meeting place of old and new. Granny wears a sunbonnet and came to the mill in a farm wagon, the young-'uns wear georgette and silk hose and own a Ford car. . . ."[2] Similar transitions to the industrial epoch might be observed in northern Alabama where the

[1] Marjorie A. Potwin, *Cotton Mill People of the Piedmont* (N. Y., 1927), 58. This careful and interesting study, mainly of South Carolina mills, stresses the philanthropic work of the mill owners, is favorable to the expansion of industry, and conservative on the child-labor question. Frank Tannenbaum, *Darker Phases of the South* (N. Y., 1924), chap. ii, "The South Buries its Anglo-Saxons," points out the drawbacks of mill life under the benevolent feudalism of the manufacturers. In 1929 serious labor riots took place at Gastonia and Marion, North Carolina.

[2] Potwin, *Cotton Mill People of the Piedmont*, 64.

A new cooperation of white men and black marked the period.

North Carolina turned her mud roads into boulevards.

heap power, cheap labor and cheap material brought industry into the upland South.

More Like the North

Birmingham iron district was rapidly becoming another Pittsburgh.

North Carolina was perhaps the outstanding example of rapid economic progress in the South. In the days of the great plantations North Carolina was rather over-shadowed by the importance of her immediate neighbors, Virginia and South Carolina. Much of her territory was too rugged for the most profitable forms of agriculture, her mineral wealth was not outstanding, her manufactures unimportant. An industrial revival which began early in the new century did not begin to bear full fruit until after the war. The state's manufactures, valued at $216,000,000 in 1910, rose to more than a billion in 1927.[1] In the same period the cotton mills more than doubled their capacity; and the tobacco crop increased over threefold in quantity and about ninefold in value. Owing to agricultural schools and such excellent rural journals as Clarence Poe's *Progressive Farmer*, the quality of farming improved almost beyond recognition.[2] Expenditures on highways increased from $5,000,000 a year in 1914 to $47,000,000 in 1926.[3]

But the greatest triumphs of North Carolina were in the field of education. North Carolina carried into modern times a staggering burden of illiteracy, but from 1910 to 1920 the rate fell from eighteen and a half to thirteen per cent. Public-school expenditures increased tenfold from 1910 to 1926. Several other Southern states were equally successful in developing elementary education, but perhaps no other made such progress in higher education. Aside from some small colleges, like Wake Forest which made an excellent record under

[1] *Blue Book of Southern Progress for 1928,* 214.
[2] "It is a common saying in the South that you can tell by a man's farm whether he is a reader of the Progressive Farmer." Edwin Mims, *The Advancing South* (Garden City, 1926), 67.
[3] *Blue Book of Southern Progress for 1928,* 214.

President W. L. Poteat, this activity centered in two large institutions, the State University at Chapel Hill and Duke University (formerly Trinity College), heavily endowed by the millionaire tobacco merchant James B. Duke.[1] The University of North Carolina was nicknamed in academic circles the "Wisconsin of the South," and the phrase was a compliment to both institutions. The wholesome rivalry between the State University and Duke caused both to strengthen their faculties and equipment. Durham, the seat of Duke University, was also much commended for its racial tolerance. Said Booker T. Washington, "Of all the Southern cities I have visited I found here the sanest attitude of the white people toward the black." In no other city of similar size did he find "so many prosperous carpenters, brickmasons, blacksmiths, wheelwrights, cotton mill operatives, and tobacco factory workers" of his own race.[2]

Virginia had a notable agricultural development, with a great extension of agricultural education and the building of a network of fine highways in place of the muddy roads which had discouraged motorists in the past. Much of this improvement came under the administration of Harry Flood Byrd, elected governor in 1926, brother of the even more famous aviator and explorer of both poles, Richard E. Byrd. In less than two years of Byrd's administration a quarter of a billion dollars was invested in the industrial development of the state, mainly by capitalists from the North.[3]

In greater or less degree the economic and educational advance of North Carolina and Virginia could be paralleled in the development of the Gulf states, even apart

[1] For Duke's earlier career, see Allan Nevins, *The Emergence of Modern America* (*A History of American Life*, VIII), 5.
[2] Mims, *The Advancing South*, 273.
[3] R. V. Oulahan in the *N. Y. Times*, Oct. 21, 1928.

from the exceptional case of Florida. There were, however, heavy arrears of the past to make good. As Horace M. Bond put it in a sympathetic article in the *Nation,* "The Southern states are now spending as much money for education as many Northern states, if we take basic taxable wealth as a criterion of effort." But, he added, "considering the double burden of poverty and excess ratio of children, it is just as unfair to expect Mississippi to maintain a system of education equal to that of California as it would have been in the time of Horace Mann to expect a district in rural Massachusetts to maintain a school . . . equal in efficiency to that supported by a tax on the property of the [wealthiest] district in Boston." [1] Many Southerners continued to complain that to make a real career—as Woodrow Wilson and Walter Hines Page did—the Southerner must leave his section and that "We measure our professional folk by the extent to which they hold degrees from Northern and Western universities, albeit often complaining of the bad influence of those universities upon us." [2] But the justification for such complaints lay mainly in the past, though the fact that they were freely voiced, that a spirit of self-criticism was abroad in the South, was the best of omens for the future.

The political change in the South was even more dramatic, though probably of less real importance, than its economic and intellectual evolution. The fact that a president of Southern birth, with a cabinet half Southern in personnel and a Congress led in both branches by Southern Democrats as chairmen of important committees, held power during the World War did much to restore the self-confidence of a section which had counted

[1] H. M. Bond, "What Lies behind Lynching," *Nation,* CXXVIII, 371 (March 27, 1929).
[2] H. W. Odum, *Southern Pioneers in Social Interpretation* (Chapel Hill, N. C., 1925), 11.

for little in national or international affairs since 1860. As one loyal North Carolinian wrote, "it seemed almost a miracle to see that aged taunt of the Republicans— 'The Democrats will put the South in the saddle'— turned into a proud fact at the most crucial moment of modern history." [1] The disastrous rout of the Democratic party at the polls in 1920, 1924 and 1928 did not undo the growing political influence of the section. On the contrary, the Republicans saw an opportunity for winning the South from its Democratic allegiance and more than ever courted its support.

The growing industrialization of the South tended to modify its attitude towards the one fairly consistent test of American party allegiance, the tariff. "Today one sees the Solid South crumbling a bit in its attitude toward the tariff . . . ," wrote one observer. "Cotton mills that rival or exceed those of New England; iron factories, comparable in many ways to those of Pennsylvania; phosphate mines, and petroleum wells, not to mention Louisiana's acre after acre of sugar cane, not only are not averse to protection, but are actually seen clamoring for it!" [2] Other factors, such as the immigration of many Northern voters, especially to southern Florida, the lessening stress of the race question, the equal disregard of both parties when in office for the principle of state rights, divisions of opinion on the Wilsonian foreign policy, the gradual fading of historic antagonisms and the prevalent prosperity, gave the Republicans many victories in the border states and even won ex-Confederate Tennessee in 1920. But in general the Solid South remained unmelted until 1928.

In that year the Democratic party strained the loyalty of the South to the breaking point by the nomination

[1] P. M. Wilson, *Southern Exposure* (Chapel Hill, N. C., 1927), 188.
[2] W. J. Robertson, *The Changing South* (N. Y., 1927), 269.

of Alfred E. Smith, governor of New York, a man of unquestionable ability but bearing the fourfold handicap of being a Northerner, an official of Tammany Hall, an enemy of prohibition and a Roman Catholic. Not even the nomination for vice-president of Senator J. T. Robinson of Arkansas—the first nomination of an actual Southern resident on a major national ticket since the Civil War—quieted the resentment of the section. The result was that all of the border states, together with Tennessee, Virginia, North Carolina, Florida and Texas among the old Confederate states, went for Herbert Hoover and against Governor Smith, that Alabama was saved by a narrow margin, and a heavy Republican vote was cast in Arkansas and Georgia.[1] Only Mississippi, Louisiana and South Carolina had anything like normal Democratic majorities. The same election placed in the Democratic column Massachusetts and Rhode Island. Though perhaps with other candidates some of these overturns would not have taken place, the fact that they could happen under any circumstances proved that American politics, North and South alike, was no longer the mere by-product of sectional tradition that it had been since 1856.

[1] *World Almanac for 1929*, 895.

CHAPTER X

THE BUSINESS OF SPORT

NEXT to the sport of business the American enjoyed most the business of sport. Politics, religion, education, the fine arts and other human activities had to compete for third prize at best. "Not far from one quarter of the entire national income of America is expended for play and recreation broadly interpreted," wrote Stuart Chase in 1928. "Perhaps half that sum is expended in forms of play new since the coming of the industrial revolution, and requiring more or less complicated machinery for their enjoyment." [1] All forms of amusement required increased outlay, from the two hundred million dollars a year spent on sporting goods [2] to the manufacture of twenty million dolls a year for American children. [3]

The high tide of prosperity after 1914 popularized recreation far beyond anything known in any earlier period and made the provision of pleasure the most comprehensive of national industries. Other influences helped in the same direction. There was, for example, the invention of new toys with which the nation could play. Obviously the rapid and almost simultaneous development of the automobile, the moving picture, the phonograph and the radio opened pleasant ways of killing time quite impossible to any previous generation. [4] De-

[1] Stuart Chase, "Play," C. A. Beard, ed., *Whither Mankind* (N. Y., 1928), 338. The whole article is valuable in giving evidence of the magnitude, standardization and mechanization of American amusements.

[2] W. S. Hiatt, "Billions—Just for Fun," *Collier's*, LXXIV, 31 (Oct. 25, 1924).

[3] *Science News-Letter*, Feb. 12, 1927.

[4] See chaps. viii and xiv for the automobile, the radio, the movie and other contributions of science to recreation.

mand may create supply, but supply may also nourish demand. Without these new pleasures many might have been content to put in more time at work, not being sufficiently attracted by the older forms of recreation. Perhaps, too, the continued growth of the great cities with their confining indoor life caused increasing numbers to seek outdoor play to meet the physical needs once satisfied by outdoor labor.

Nor should we forget the skill of the merchandisers of sports in hawking their wares. The same arts of publicity which made bathtubs, face creams and vacuum cleaners universal were employed to sell sporting goods, and the same press-agenting which helped make the reputation of a grand-opera star or a politician was also at the service of a pugilist. Millions went to see "Babe" Ruth play baseball, "Red" Grange play football, or Jack Dempsey fight in the ring, because they had learned to know these stars in the columns of the press. The sense of proportion thus created was amusingly illustrated in July, 1928, when the debarment of the tennis champion W. T. Tilden from the amateur ranks drove from the front pages a presidential campaign, the assassination of the Mexican president-elect, the mysterious death of a Belgian millionaire, and the search for lost aviators in the Arctic. Charges of bribe-taking by the White Sox professional baseball team a few years earlier created wider popular excitement than charges of bribe-taking by members of the cabinet.

The pleasure-loving American, however, did not form a leisure class in the European sense. He carried into sport the same grim seriousness that had served him so well in trade, and the desire to excel was as cruelly competitive in sport as in commerce. This brought to the United States many trophies and world championships, but the spirit of play was lost. There was a technical distinction between amateur and professional athletics in the United States, insisted on with such pedantic precision that a player could be disqualified as an amateur for writing articles on his own sport or coaching a schoolboy for money in another game; but there was little psychological distinction. Both amateur and professional had the essentially professional attitude which takes training seriously, admires technical form, and would make almost any sacrifice for victory. "Does handling ice," wrote one earnest young athlete to the sports writer Handley Cross, "develop the arms for weight throwing?" "We told him that it did. We did not add that, even more important, weight throwing develops the arms for handling ice. What was the use?" To that boy, as to many thousands of his elders, play was neither recreation from work nor preparation for it, but work itself, and of the most exacting and important type.

Football and baseball were close rivals for leadership in the business of sport. Football remained essentially a college game in spite of the attempt to make it a popular professional sport by inducing athletes on graduation from college to enter the commercial teams. Baseball, on the contrary, was the unquestioned leader among professional games. Though amateurs joyfully played it everywhere, from six-year-olds on the vacant lots up to the university teams, not all these amateur contests together awoke a tithe of the interest aroused by the games of the National and American leagues, the leading professional organizations. In 1913 the world baseball series had an attendance of one hundred and fifty thousand and receipts of $325,980; in 1923, the attendance was three hundred thousand and the receipts more than a million dollars.[1] A single game in the 1928 series at-

[1] Hiatt, "Billions—Just for Fun," 19.

tracted over sixty thousand spectators and reaped a harvest of more than $224,000.[1]

The world series—justly named, for in baseball the United States was virtually the world—was the last week's culmination of a whole summer of intense rivalry. Although the baseball teams in no sense really represented the cities after which they were named, so hearty was the American capacity for make-believe that a contest between two financial organizations whose players were assembled from all over the nation became a strife in which the pride of the cities was directly involved, and feeling was as intense as at any college football game, though it no longer found frequent expression in assaults on the umpire who gave a decision against the "home team." From mid-spring to mid-autumn, even encroaching on the season sacred to football, the baseball teams battled around the country, the newspapers carefully recording their percentages, until one team emerged clearly at the head of its league, and then came for one brief week the struggle of the giants. When Washington, D. C., first won world honors in baseball in 1924, the city held such a jubilee as would have done credit to the close of a great war or the inauguration of a president. George ("Babe") Ruth of the New York Yankees, by hitting the ball for fifty-nine home runs in 1921 and for sixty in 1927, made himself one of the best-known individuals in the United States.

Football, with altered rules to encourage open play—running, throwing and kicking—won a greater following than ever before. Though the most important of the new rules had become established before 1910, the possibilities of the more open game were not fully developed until the years following the World War, which had temporarily deflected interest even from football. But

[1] *N. Y. Times*, Oct. 5, 1928.

from 1919 to 1928 football reigned supreme in college life. Thirty years earlier only a few schools and colleges played the game, and most of these without expert coaching, so that Walter Camp could make up his list of "All-American" football stars by selecting the best men from Harvard, Princeton and Yale. For a thousand players in the whole nation then, there were two hundred thousand playing in 1926, and from six to ten thousand professional coaches and trainers to keep them fit.[1] Any school which chose to spend the money could have expert coaching, and Harvard and Yale were sometimes outranked in gridiron efficiency by a score of other schools. No college could longer claim national ascendancy; the old dynasties of the East had given place to a turbulent democracy of sport. A very small college, like Centre in Kentucky, would blaze as a star of the first magnitude for a single year or two and then sink back to obscurity. The only permanent advantage of the larger colleges was their superior reservoir of man power for reserves. Games were no longer of team against team but of squad against squad, and the larger institutions had at least two competent substitutes for every man on the field.

One of the differences between the old game and the new was that the older football interested chiefly the students and the alumni; the new game, more spectacular, attracted also the general public. Although the football season, except in California, lasted only from late September to Thanksgiving, thirty million spectators in 1927 paid some fifty million dollars in gate receipts.[2] To accommodate these enormous crowds huge stadiums of steel and concrete were built, seating about eighty thou-

[1] Grantland Rice, "The Real All-America," *Collier's*, LXXVIII, 16 (Nov. 20, 1926).
[2] *New International Year Book for 1927*, 302.

sand at Yale and California, and seventy thousand or more at Illinois, Ohio State, Michigan and several others. For the greater part of the year these enormous "lunar craters," as Coach A. A. Stagg of Chicago aptly called them, stood empty, but on the day of a great game they were filled to overflowing with the largest crowds that ever witnessed athletic sports since the fall of Rome. Many went to enjoy the pageantry of the affair as much as the game itself—the gay colors in the stands, the organized cheering under specially drilled cheer leaders, the military parade of the college band, the tense atmosphere of suspense when seventy thousand clamorous voices were hushed as a pigskin hesitated in mid-air above the wooden crossbar. The games played by the West Point and Annapolis teams were always popular, whether they were weak or strong, because the drills, the songs, the uniforms and the "stunts" of the army and navy boys were particularly picturesque.

The complaints against the new football as voiced, for example, by a committee of the American Association of University Professors were not so much, as formerly, against brutality or dishonesty, though neither had become wholly extinct, but rather against the danger of transforming an amateur sport into a commercial amusement business run by coaches and alumni for the benefit of the general sporting public.[1] Not even the huge gate receipts reconciled everyone to spending hundreds of thousands of dollars on football equipment, stadiums, uniforms, coaching and travel, at a time when many departments of the university were starved of funds for teaching and research. It should in fairness be said, however, that a large part of the profits of football

---

[1] See *Literary Digest*, LXXXIX, 31 (May 15, 1926). See also Carnegie Foundation for the Advancement of Teaching, *Bull.*, 23 (1929), a critical survey of collegiate athletics.

were used to make up deficits in general athletic equipment or to support less profitable "minor sports." Gambling was common, and the attitude of alumni and townsfolk often thoroughly unsportsmanlike.

But the public was impatient with these faint misgivings. A typical editorial in the news-stand periodical *Liberty* retorted to the hostile report of the professors that the whole trouble was faculty jealousy of the superior abilities and earning power of coaches and ex-players: "The problem is not the elimination or restriction of football, but how long it will be before red-blooded colleges demand the elimination or the restriction of those afflicted with this inferiority complex." [1] Sometimes alumni were impatient of the increased standards of scholarship when they threatened to interfere with the superior claims of football. "When high class athletes with a passable and qualifying school record are turned aside as unfit," complained one alumnus, "it is just as foolish as it would be to turn aside high class scholars who had only a passable record in physical training." [2] It was often noted that alumni were more concerned over the prospects of a football team than the students themselves, perhaps because they had gone to college in a day when campus interests were more concentrated. "When I was in college," said President Ernest Hopkins of Dartmouth, "a man would have been considered white-livered . . . who was not present at every football game. Now, except for some great dramatic spectacle during the season, undergraduates will be found upon the golf links, the trout streams and the Outing Club trails, and in canoes on the river on the fall afternoons of the most important games." [3]

[1] *Liberty*, III (July 17, 1926).
[2] *Columbia Alumni News*, XX, 16 (Jan. 11, 1929).
[3] J. R. Tunis, "The Great God Football," *Harper's Mag.*, CLVII (1928), 751.

The football game between two university teams, played in a gigantic stadium, had become America's favorite spectacle.

Next to a world-series baseball game or a football match between two great universities, a prize fight drew the largest crowds. After a period of eclipse, the well-staged and decorous contests in a twentieth-century arena more than recaptured the fashionable note of a hundred years earlier when English gentry, nobility and even royalty (as represented by the crown prince who was later George IV) attended bare-knuckle fights and themselves studied the art of self-defense under expert boxers.

In 1926 a world's championship boxing contest took place in Philadelphia as part of the entertainment of the sesquicentennial exposition. The attendance was estimated at one hundred and twenty-five thousand, not including the millions who listened to the thud of the boxing gloves over the radio. The public paid $1,895,000 for admission, of which Jack Dempsey, who was that day uncrowned as king of the pugilistic world, drew $700,000. Thus was celebrated the hundred and fiftieth year of American independence! Other heavyweight contests were almost as plutocratic. Spectators paid $1,626,000 to see Jack Dempsey defeat the gallant French challenger Georges Carpentier in 1921. Two years later he defeated the Argentine giant Firpo before a crowd which had paid more than a million to see him do it. But the record athletic event was Dempsey's return match against Gene Tunney, the new world champion, in 1927, a contest with gate receipts of more than $2,650,000. So rapid was the development of pugilism from a sport into an industry that nineteen fights between 1918 and the end of 1924 yielded more than $100,000 each, as compared with only four such costly contests for all previous history.[1]

[1] William Cunningham, "No Wonder They Want to Fight," *Collier's,* LXXIV, 14 (Sept. 18, 1924).

Successful pugilists were often able to augment their prize-ring income by going into vaudeville or the moving pictures, or by writing—perhaps with a reporter's assistance—sport comment for the newspapers. Under such circumstances the champion was not apt to waste his precious fisticuffs on barroom brawls. Years often elapsed between his battles, the diplomatic preliminaries whereof might occupy several months. Most states permitted professional pugilism under certain legal restrictions, and in about a third of the states salaried state officials supervised boxing contests. At the better and larger fights the crowds were usually quiet and well behaved, the press was largely represented, distinguished literary lights wrote up the fights from their own point of view at generous space rates, ladies were welcomed, and a radio hook-up brought the whole nation to the ring side. Twenty or thirty years before pugilism had been an outlawed sport, banned by the authorities and shunned by the respectable. This transformation was due largely to the promoting activities of George ("Tex") Rickard.

Tex Rickard had lived a varied and colorful life for many years before he was able to carry into effect his life's ambition of making pugilism a society sport. He had tramped the snows of Alaska and the Yukon, hunting gold in mines, gambling halls and saloons. He tried his fortune in the alkali deserts of Nevada. There he had staged prize fights with some success, but not on the scale of his later operations. For a time he raised cattle in South America. Soon after his return to the United States he discovered Jack Dempsey, who had not only the ability to win the heavyweight championship but also (and more important from Rickard's viewpoint) the personality to attract a paying public. At Toledo in 1919 Dempsey defeated Jess Willard, a heavy Kansas

giant who had taken the honors from the Negro champion Jack Johnson four years earlier. Dempsey was disliked at first for his failure to enlist in the World War,
but the fickle crowd which at first went to see him defeated later made him their favorite because he so per-
fectly embodied their ideal of a human fighting machine,
scowling, ruthless, aggressive. With the genius of a
Barnum in master showmanship Rickard capitalized his
find.[1] From the moment when he staged "the battle of
the century" between Dempsey and Carpentier the fortunes of both Rickard and Dempsey were made.

The man who defeated Dempsey in 1926 should have
been even more the idol of the crowd. Gene Tunney had
fought in the war as a marine; he was handsome, genial,
with the manners of a gentleman and interest enough
in letters to talk to a class of Yale students on Shakespeare. Moreover, he was the best boxer in the heavyweight division. But the "fans" never took to Tunney
because he did not fit their abstract Platonic ideal of what
a pugilist should be. They labeled him a "highbrow"
and made no effort to detain him when he voluntarily
left the ring to enjoy the higher levels of society. Tunney's retirement, Dempsey's defeat, and the death of
Rickard the supersalesman left pugilism in 1929 divested
of the chief attractions of its golden decade.

The worst feature of the new pugilism was that dishonesty was so rife that, even when an honest fighter
was defeated, his disappointed backers were likely to
claim that he had been paid to surrender the victory
by gamblers on the other side. Wrestling, professional
track meets, horse racing in its many forms, shared with
boxing the reproach of being "fixed" by gamblers too

[1] The story of Rickard's clever exploitation of the business of pugilism
has been often told, perhaps best by H. W. Clune, "Palookas and Pluto-
crats," *North Am. Rev.*, CCXXVII (1929), 49-55.

frequently for the spectator to feel that he was watching a real contest. Hence the popularity of amateur tennis, golf, football and track, which were usually conducted with a sincere desire to win. Honesty was, perhaps, the only real moral superiority which amateur athletics could claim over professional, and this superiority lasted only so long as gambling could be kept to a relatively unimportant place. There was real commercial advantage in not making sport too commercial.

Golf, tennis and polo had been the traditional sports of the wealthy amateur. Polo, because of the cost of good ponies, continued to remain a rich man's game, but golf and tennis greatly widened their appeal. By 1928 golf represented an investment of more than two billion dollars, and employed over three thousand professional instructors, a hundred thousand workers to keep the courses in condition, and half a million caddies.[1] Private courses were often very expensive, but as early as 1924 eighty-nine cities had established municipal golf courses.[2] No other sport suited so well the average American business man. The increasing popularity of tennis was shown by the attempts to professionalize this most amateur of sports. Suzanne Lenglen, a highly temperamental Frenchwoman who had at various times held the championship of her sex, entered the professional game and her example was followed by other stars to the exaggerated horror of many amateurs.

Of other sports, basketball, ice hockey and swimming developed most rapidly. As earlier, basketball was the favorite indoor sport of schools and colleges; hockey, once so largely Canadian, became thoroughly naturalized in the United States, and winter sports generally, such

[1] Grantland Rice, "The National Rash," Collier's, LXXXII, 10 (Oct. 20, 1928).

[2] R. L. Duffus, "The Age of Play," Independent, CXIII, 540 (Dec. 20, 1924).

as ski jumping, skating and ice boating, increased in popularity. Swimming enjoyed a double stimulus, from the indoor tanks now provided in most schools and from the growing popularity of the seashore. When Gertrude Ederle and Mrs. Clemington Corson swam the English Channel in 1926, a feat which but few men had ever accomplished, they were hailed as treble victors, vindicating alike the country which they represented, the physical prowess of their sex, and the interests of their chosen sport. The one-piece bathing suit transformed American women from "bathers" into "swimmers." Wide popular interest was aroused, and deftly commercialized, by the "bathing-beauty" contests, the winner enjoying the title of Miss America and a week or so of concentrated publicity.

Interest in track and field sports was increased by the Olympic Games, international contests in conscious imitation of the intercity contests of ancient Hellas. The World War interrupted the games from 1912 to 1920, but thenceforward they took place at each four-year interval. The well-trained Americans held championships in most forms of running, leaping and weight throwing, but were compelled to yield honors in the very long runs, requiring patient endurance rather than dash, to the more stolid English, Canadians, Finns and Scandinavians. Indeed, in the Marathon long-distance race of 1928 at Amsterdam, the winner was a native of French North Africa, who was followed in order of time by a Chilean, a Finn, a Japanese and an American.

Of less strenuous amusements dancing was the chief. There was nothing new about dancing, of course, but never before had this ancient and natural amusement been forced through such rapid changes. Even before the war the tango and the turkey trot had enlivened the scene and brought with them an imitative swarm of hops, wriggles, squirms, glides and gallops named after all the animals in the menagerie. After the war dancing tended to become a mere shuffle in a confined space, "dancing on a dime" with a partner all evening long. This culminated in a climax of folly—the "dance-marathon" in which heroic imbeciles entered an endurance contest, keeping their feet in slow motion for several days and nights. Then the pace quickened; instead of the close hug and slow glide the dancers indulged in the violent acrobatics of the "Charleston" and the "black bottom" to the imminent peril of neighboring shins. To learn all the intricacies of the hundred new fashions in dancing steps the youth of the nation attended dancing academies by the thousand.

More and more young peoples' parties abandoned other amusements and made dancing the entire evening program. Few hostesses dared give parties without providing for dances; churches used the dance to attract and hold the new generation; schools taught folk dances to little children. The finer art of the dance, as exemplified on the stage by Russian artists, won attentive crowds. Henry Ford interested himself in reviving the almost lost art of the old "square dances" of the pioneer days of the republic. "There are thirty million people who dance in the United States, daily, weekly, or frequently," said a statistician in 1924. "A billion dollars for dancing by rich and poor would be a modest bill." [1] To the music of the phonograph, the radio and the jazz band all the nation paid homage to Saint Vitus.

Jazz music spread with the new dances and each urged the other to fresh triumphs. There have been many attempts to define jazz, but one of the men who did most to give it such artistic expression as it could attain, Paul Whiteman, was obliged to confess, "What is jazz?

[1] Hiatt, "Billions—Just for Fun," 31.

Is it art, a disease, a manner, or a dance? Has it any musical value? After twelve years of jazz I don't know." [1] His account of its origin, in the same article, was more revealing.

> Jazz is the folk music of the machine age. There was every reason why this music sprang into being about 1915. . . . In this country especially the rhythm of machinery, the over rapid expansion of a great country endowed with tremendous natural energies and wealth have brought about a pace and scale of living unparalleled in history. Is it any wonder that the popular music of this land should reflect these modes of living? Every other art reflects them.

Technically, jazz was an exaggeration of the tendencies implicit in the ragtime and pseudo-African melodies long popular on the American stage. Jazz combined the older syncopation with a superimposed accompanying rhythm, "and it is this subsidiary, *one, two, three* on top of the underlying tempo that makes shoulder muscles twitch, that bedevils hips, that provokes wiggles and twists on the dance floor, and causes blue noses to cry out that jazz is a great immoral influence." [2] To those accustomed to suave and melodious Viennese waltzes the new music seemed a mere chaos of ugliness, but Europe welcomed American ragtime and jazz as something exotic, original and interesting, if not wholly beautiful, and in the United States its rule was as wide as the art of the dance. Twenty typical radio stations, ten large and ten small, were "on the air" for an aggregate of 651 hours one week, and it was noticed that 448

[1] Paul Whiteman, "In Defense of Jazz," *N. Y. Times*, March 13, 1927.
[2] "The soprano saxophone has been blamed for the sins of the secondary rag. In fact, that silvery screecher merely releases impulses which the constant tickling of *one*, two, three upon one, two, three, four [the underlying rhythm] has brought clamoring to the surface." Don Knowlton, "The Anatomy of Jazz," *Harper's Mag.*, CLII (1926), 581.

hours of this total, over two thirds, were spent playing jazz.[1]

The fundamental melodies and rhythms of the popular music were borrowed largely from the classics without credit or apology. Jazz orchestrations were often original and ingenious, "as well balanced and as effective in rendition as those produced for our symphony orchestras."[2] The words, blasphemously termed the "lyrics," were usually more devoid of beauty, sincerity and meaning than the respectable songs of any other age or nation. Now and then an Irving Berlin would introduce a welcome touch of humor or pathos, but in the main they were mere sensuous sentimentality expressed in baby-talk jingles.

The rapid succession of new styles in dress, dancing and music was not more kaleidoscopic than the shift in minor parlor amusements. For a period of about two years mah-jong, an imported Chinese game played with decorated tiles like dominoes and involving calculations as intricate as an income-tax blank, threatened to wean the bridge enthusiasts from their loyalty and even to menace the smaller but equally fanatical sect of chess players. A few months passed, and mah-jong was but a fading memory. The cross-word puzzle had succeeded to its honors, a more complexly patterned development from the old acrostics.

Cross-word puzzles provided an interesting chapter in the history of the American publisher. Richard Simon and Lincoln Schuster, boys in their twenties, ambitiously tried to launch a publishing house of their own. Needing capital, they began as a humble side line, under another firm name, the first series of cross-word puzzle books. "We hired halls. We drafted by-laws and rules

[1] Charles Merz, "Tom-Tom," *Golden Book*, IX (1929), 60.
[2] Knowlton, "The Anatomy of Jazz," 584.

for amateur cross-word orgies. . . . We visited editors, urging them to put cross-word puzzles in the papers. . . . Soon we were selling thousands of copies a day and breaking into the best seller lists." [1] Of course, once the ball was so started it needed no more pushing, but gathered momentum on its own account. For three or four years after 1924 the Egyptian sun god, Ra; eel, "a snakelike fish"; the Oo bird of Hawaii; and the printers' measures "em" and "en," were among the most familiar words in the language, because so convenient to the architects of puzzles. Many of the by-products of the fad were valuable. It boomed the market for dictionaries and thesauri, widened the vocabulary, stimulated study of the recondite terms of science and the arts and, incidentally, earned enough money for the firm of Simon and Schuster to enable them to become the publishers of serious books.

The cross-word puzzle was but one of several such parlor hobbies. "One wonders if anything that has happened to us in America in the past generation is half as important as this latest tendency, this sudden need for intelligent play," declared an acute observer.

> The newspapers are full of games—words to guess, rimes to fill in, ingenious picture autographs to make, novels to identify. Clerks and plumbers and school teachers and school children go home elbow to elbow in the subway, muttering five-letter words that mean "commonplace," or trying to supply the laddergram links between Bride and Groom. [2]

But these excellent brain-teasing diversions were usually all too briefly popular. One of the chief amusements of

[1] Beatrice Barmby, "What It Means to be a Book Publisher at 29," *McClure's*, LIX (1927), 63.

[2] Kathleen Norris, "I Know a New Game," *Ladies' Home Journ.*, XLV (1928), 14.

the American was to change amusements. Yet some of them seemed likely to become a permanent legacy. The arts of the motion picture, the radio and the phonograph bade fair to be as enduring as the camera, the theater and the piano.

On the whole, the increased emphasis on recreation was a positive contribution to American life, though the American still needed instruction in the difficult art of enjoying leisure. As Dorothy Canfield told the students of the University of Kansas, American psychology had been framed in a pioneer age and adapted to the problem of meeting work, want and hardship. "Nobody forearmed us with forewarnings about the dangers from the *lack* of material hardships. . . . We had neither the tools nor the knowledge to deal with the wholly unexpected phenomenon . . . of evenings with nothing to do. . . ." [1] American play was still too strenuous for those who took part and too idle for those who looked on; too expensive for those who bought and too commercially profitable for those who sold; too dominated by fashion, imitation and advertisement. [2] The highest function of play, the personally creative, was mainly absent.

[1] Dorothy Canfield (Fisher), address before Kansas University in 1928, Univ. of Kansas, *Graduate Mag.*, XXVI, 8-9.

[2] A questionnaire investigation covering the period 1923-1926 showed that the most frequent form of amusement mentioned by children and young people of all ages was the newspaper, especially the comic section. Next in order, among eighteen-year-old boys, stood automobiling, moving pictures and "watching sports." Chase, "Play," 341.

CHAPTER XI

THE CULT OF NATIONALISM

THE outstanding spiritual phenomenon of the times was the remarkable intensification of nationalism. By one decision this generation closed the door to most European and all Asiatic labor. By another the American people placed themselves outside all international unions for world peace. But the same spirit showed itself in humbler forms as well—in a dramatic revival of nativism, in an aggressive watchfulness against unconventional political doctrines, in an exaltation of the virtues of the "Nordic" race, in an extraordinary revival of popular interest in American history and, in general, in a glorification of "one-hundred-per-cent Americanism." In large measure this efflorescence of nationalism was a product of the war. The epoch which witnessed the climax and collapse of Pan-Germanism and the rebirth of a dozen nationalities in central and eastern Europe was one of intense national feeling everywhere. In many countries, such as Fascist Italy and the states of the Balkans, the Danube and the Baltic, as well as among the insurgent students of China and Hindustan, the fever rose many degrees higher than in the United States.[1] Its evil side, so tragically illustrated in the Old World, was only feebly reflected in the New. And yet, relatively to the immediate past, the United States was keenly and intolerantly patriotic after 1914.

The direct influence of the war showed itself at first

---

[1] The best American study of nationalism in general written during this period is C. J. H. Hayes, *Essays on Nationalism* (N. Y., 1926).

in self-pleasing contrasts between war-torn Europe and peaceful, prosperous America, and later, as active propaganda was carried on by foreign governments among immigrant Americans, in a fear that the integrity of American citizenship was endangered by alien sympathies. Though in the actual test of battle most of the recent comers proved as loyal as the sons of the *Mayflower*, the years of hesitation which preceded the abandonment of neutrality were so marked by "hyphenism" and the echoes of Old World feuds as to awaken pardonable misgivings that a divided allegiance might appear in times of crisis.[1] Theodore Roosevelt spent his last energies in appealing for a united nation. He popularized the phrase, "one-hundred-per-cent Americanism," though in his mouth it meant a common allegiance by men of all races and not, as so often misused, the supremacy of a single racial type. But as the passions of war mounted the man of foreign accent became as much suspected as the man of foreign sympathies. To be sure, the popular feeling against the "Hun" quickly evaporated after the war, but it left behind it a residual dislike of aliens and "radicals" and a general suspicion of greedy and unscrupulous European diplomacy.

The controversy over the peace treaty, which the press in general represented as a victory of France and England over the United States, and that over the League of Nations, portrayed by the same papers as a trap set by Old World diplomats for American armies and dollars, heightened the distaste for international politics engendered by the war. Other influences as well helped to discredit President Wilson's foreign policy. Thus, many German Americans and pacifists could not forgive the war itself; Italian Americans disliked the president's

[1] See earlier, chaps. i, ii and iii, for the war of propaganda which preceded, accompanied and followed the war of arms.

opposition to Italian claims east of the Adriatic; some
Irish Americans, powerful in the president's own party,
feared lest the League might augment the power of the
British Empire. Certain leaders of liberal thought, represented by the *Nation* and the *New Republic*, who had
given a general, though hesitating, support to the Wilson administration, now broke with it on the ground
that the peace contained many injustices which might
provoke new wars. They were joined by men of exactly
opposite habit of thought who believed that the whole
idea of a League of Nations was a mirage of pacifism that
might lead the nation to neglect its military security.
Still others opposed the president because they disliked
him personally, or were his opponents in the game of
party politics, or disapproved of his rather high-handed
disregard of the opinion of the Senate.

But, when all is said, the chief opposition to the
Treaty of Versailles was simply dislike of playing world
politics. Faced with the question of ratification, the Senate expressed its hostility to the treaty by drawing up
lists of reservations, unacceptable to the president, which
aimed to restrict American participation in the League's
activities and to limit the jurisdiction of the League over
American foreign policy. The opposition centered its
fire particularly on Article Ten of the Covenant, guaranteeing against external aggression the territorial integrity and political independence of member nations.[1]
The rejection of the treaty in 1920 and the negotiation
of a separate peace with the enemy countries in the following year marked a complete reversal of the tendency
to identify the United States with the "concert of the
Powers" which began with President Roosevelt's first
administration. The United States declined a proffered

---

[1] J. H. Latané, *A History of American Foreign Policy* (Garden City,
1927), chap. xxvii.

mandate over Armenia, withdrew its forces from the guardianship of the Rhine, refused to conclude a proposed defensive alliance with Britain and France, and weighted down the proposal to join the Court of International Justice with reservations which brought on interminable discussion. The department of state, relieved of responsibility for the political stability of Europe, devoted its attention mainly to routine national business, such as the settlement of war debts with former associates in the World War [1] and the policing of disorderly Caribbean republics.

Some qualification must be made to the assertion that the United States pursued from 1920 to 1928 a policy of isolation from world politics. In a conference held in Washington (1921) the chief naval powers of the Pacific agreed to a limitation of capital battleships and promised to respect each other's insular dependencies within the Pacific area.[2] They agreed also to respect the integrity and existing commercial rights of China. The Coolidge administration sent frequent "observers" to European conferences and coöperated with the purely humanitarian and nonpolitical activities of the League of Nations. Private individuals did much more than the national government. Though the United States failed to join the World Court, Elihu Root assisted in its organization and John Bassett Moore and Charles Evans

[1] During the war and immediately afterward the United States had made loans, in part military and in part philanthropic, to many European nations. Poverty in Europe after the war made these debts, amounting to more than $10,000,000,000 in all, difficult to collect, and the debtor governments urged also that the American loans should be considered as contributions to the common cause. Compromise settlements were negotiated, reducing the rates of interest. H. G. Moulton, "The Interallied Debts: Their Origin and Present Status," *Current History*, XXX (1929), 367-374.

[2] For an excellent account of the work of the Washington Conference, see R. L. Buell, *The Washington Conference* (N. Y., 1922). Another naval conference was in progress in 1930.

Hughes served on its bench. Charles G. Dawes, later vice-president, Owen D. Young and other financial experts helped devise the plan eventually adopted for the payment of German reparations. An American committee, including General Tasker Bliss, Professor James T. Shotwell, David Hunter Miller and other prominent citizens, proposed methods of procedure in cases of international aggression which were later incorporated into the Geneva Protocol of the League of Nations and thence, indirectly, into the Locarno Pacts and similar regional agreements. Even the League itself—though still the *bête noire* of the politicians—employed many American citizens in its service.[1]

The deadlock between the Senate and foreign governments with reference to the terms of admission of the United States to the Court of International Justice, and the failure to arrive at an understanding with Great Britain for the limitation of cruisers and other minor war craft, led the Coolidge administration to seek for some new expression of pacific intentions. Frank B. Kellogg, secretary of state, combining a hint from the French statesman Aristide Briand with the desire expressed by Senator William E. Borah of Idaho for the "outlawry" of war, negotiated a series of treaties with

[1] One may mention, among many others, Raymond Fosdick, under-secretary general in the critical early days of the organization; George L. Beer, the historian, active in the regulation of mandates administration; Arthur Sweetser, of the League secretariat; Florence Wilson, librarian at Geneva; Manley O. Hudson, legal adviser to the international labor conference; Royal Meeker, chief of the scientific division of the International Labor Office; Jeremiah Smith, who reorganized the entire financial life of Hungary, refusing all payment for his services; Abram I. Elkus, commissioner to settle the Aaland Islands dispute between Finland and Sweden; and Norman Davis, chairman of the committee which established the rights of Lithuania in Memel. The charitable services of Americans connected with the American Relief Administration, the Near East Relief, the Red Cross, the Rockefeller Foundation (specializing on the world-wide fight against epidemic disease), the Y.M.C.A. and the missionary boards and colleges saved millions of lives in China, Russia, Turkey, the Balkans, Poland, Austria and other afflicted countries.

other Powers for "the renunciation of war as an instrument of national policy." In August, 1928, representatives of the Powers met at Paris to approve the antiwar pact. One notes, however, that the multilateral antiwar treaty did not commit the United States to any positive action to associate with other nations in the forcible maintenance of world peace. It was an expression of pacifism rather than of internationalism.[1]

The panic over Russian Bolshevism, needless though it was, served almost as much as the war itself to bring about an antialien sentiment.[2] The activity of so many East Europeans in radical labor agitation and the boast of the Russian revolutionists that their agents were active in all parts of the world undermining the foundations of capitalist society, caused many to see in every humble immigrant a potential spy or rebel. The civil war in Ireland, also, caused some Americans to hate England as an oppressor, and others to hate Ireland as a disturber, and both alike to deplore the injection of the feud between the Orange and the Green into American life. It is not surprising that European dictatorships, civil wars and class struggles made many Americans feel that their peaceful, wealthy and stable country stood on another and higher level than the rest of the world. So the eagle screamed again as loudly as in the days of Andrew Jackson. The *Chicago Tribune* flaunted in each day's issue the arrogant motto, "Our country, right or wrong," and the Hearst papers, perhaps to recover a reputation for patriotism somewhat damaged during the war, lost no opportunity to contrast the virtuous American with the sinister European and the quite demoniac Asiatic.

[1] See J. T. Shotwell, *War as an Instrument of National Policy* (N. Y., 1929); and D. H. Miller, *The Peace Pact of Paris* (N. Y., 1928).
[2] See earlier, chap. iii.

With the bulk of the press, however, the fault was rather ignorance than malice. Although the war had greatly increased the space given to international events, very few papers had foreign correspondents of their own.[1] Domestic affairs, except during the actual prosecution of the war, at all times held the spotlight. Nor did the trickle of daily news items from the Associated Press and similar agencies supply the lack of historical background in the editor's mind. For example, the separate representation of the British Dominions in the League of Nations Assembly, really an expression of the insurgent nationalism of those self-governing commonwealths, was everywhere presented by the press as a mere trick to secure extra votes for London. Disturbances in Mexico were represented as caused by intrigues from Moscow. A particularly persistent error was the tendency to lump Europe together as a unit in contrast to America and blame the whole continent for conditions characteristic of only the more backward nations. It must have been highly exasperating to a Swiss to find "Europeans" scolded as militaristic and imperialistic, or to a Norwegian to hear that Europe was a home of despots and dictators ruling over an oppressed and illiterate proletariat.

But if the postwar American was supercilious, the postwar European was in an even more dangerous mood. At least half the insults, and those the sharpest, were flung westward across the Atlantic. This was partly the bitterness of poverty, for many nations were poorer than they had been in 1913 and not one of them had quite attained the standard of living prevailing in the United States. There was now a new style in criticizing the Americans. In the days of Dickens and Matthew Arnold

[1] "Only seven of our newspapers maintain any considerable foreign service." Silas Bent, "International Window Smashing," *Harper's Mag.*, CLVII (1928), 428. This article gives several instances of antiforeign "scares" in the postwar period fomented by the American press.

the United States had been pictured to unfriendly eyes as a crude, backwoods encampment devoid of all civilized comforts. The accusation was still of materialism, but of a materialism triumphant in its own sphere and embodied in industrialism. Englishmen spoke of the United States much as a Hindu critic might have spoken of Victorian England at the height of her complacency and commercial power. "By 'modern civilization' I mean American civilization. . . . America leads the pack, and if we want to know whether the pack is heading for heaven or for hell, we shall be well advised to examine the direction taken by the leader," said one of the most savage critics.[1]

"Spiritually the country is a corpse, physically, a terrific machine. Materialism is the tyrant which rules from ocean to ocean, and its backwash is superstition and an effervescing froth of cranks." [2] Again, "As the present tendency to superficiality increases, as the vigour of the race is divided more exclusively between money getting and pleasure getting and all life is measured in terms of the pay envelope and the dance floor, that part of the American brain that should be devoted to the acquisition of knowledge, the appreciation of beauty and the exercise of wisdom will atrophy." [3] In a similar vein, though with milder temper, spoke the peripatetic German philosopher Count Keyserling, and the Hindu prophet Gandhi. Materialism was the modern devil, and the United States therefore the modern inferno.

Even more sympathetic foreign observers contrived to widen the Atlantic gulf of misunderstanding. Hilaire Belloc's *The Contrast* (1923) was not wholly hostile, but his assertion that the difference between the United

[1] C. E. M. Joad, *The Babbitt Warren* (N. Y., 1927), intro.
[2] Col. J. F. C. Fuller, *Atlantis* (London, 1926), 28.
[3] C. H. Bretherton, *Midas, or The United States and the Future* (N. Y., 1926), 87.

States and Europe was greater than that between any two European countries played all too easily into the bad American habit of treating Europe as a unit.[1] André Siegfried in somewhat similar fashion summed up America with a gentle sigh as a strange continent peopled by incomprehensible Puritans.[2] Rudyard Kipling, once the idol of the American reading public, sneered at the American war effort and compared the United States to the laborer who had come at the eleventh hour to the vineyard but demanded a full day's wages. Indeed, the two debates, "who won the war?" and "who will pay the war debts?" caused more international hostility than anything else. Insistence on collecting war debts caused Uncle Sam to be dubbed in certain foreign newspapers "Uncle Shylock."[3] On a few occasions American tourists were hissed and pelted in the streets of Paris. Such incidents, absurdly exaggerated by the press, crystallized into the common saying that "America is hated by every European country."

The effect was to drive the American back on his own pride. He felt that he had done his full share in the war, which was none of his making, and that he had been more than generous after the peace. The rapid transition from being called "soldier of humanity" and "savior of civilization" in 1918 to being called "Uncle Shylock" in 1921 made him feel that he had been wasting beneficence on ingrates. Henceforth he would keep his sons and his money at home. As for the sinfulness of material comfort, it was recalled that the fox who could not reach

[1] Compare also Bertrand Russell, "European countries (except Russia) differ far less from each other than all differ from the United States." Bertrand Russell, "Science," C. A. Beard, ed., *Whither Mankind* (N. Y., 1928), 72.

[2] André Siegfried, *America Comes of Age* (H. H. Hemming and Doris Hemming, trs., N. Y., 1927).

[3] See particularly J.-L. Chastenet, *L'Oncle Shylock, ou l'Imperialisme Américain à la Conquête du Monde* (Paris, 1927).

the grapes had found them to be sour. At any rate, none of the numerous lecturers on American materialism refused their fees.

A similar defensive reaction was called forth by the hostile and unsympathetic depiction of American life by Americans of native or foreign birth. No doubt H. L. Mencken, Sinclair Lewis and the thirty authors of *Civilization in the United States* [1] performed a useful service in puncturing national complacency, but their manner of doing it merely transformed complacency into irritation. Just as the average American refused to recognize himself in the European mirror as a calculating dollar-worshipper, so he refused to recognize himself in the Greenwich Village mirror as a gloomy, hypocritical Puritan incapable of humane culture. [2] Any competent psychologist could have told the critics that an indiscriminate assault upon a national sentiment makes the nationalist more set in his ways than ever. If his very virtues are derided as faults, he will erect his very faults into virtues. [3]

The fact that the outbreak of the war had temporarily turned aside the flood of immigration led to a reëxamination of the traditional national policy of encouraging all who were discontented with their lot to seek a better home in America. [4] Despite an increasing amount of restrictive legislation in recent years the gates at Ellis

[1] H. E. Stearns, ed., *Civilization in the United States, an Inquiry by Thirty Americans* (N. Y., 1922).

[2] See later, chap. xv.

[3] Agnes Repplier, "On a Certain Condescension in Americans," *Atlantic Mo.*, CXXXVII (1926), 577-584, is perhaps the best account of American assertions of superiority as regards Europe, and Struthers Burt, "Furor Britannicus," *Sat. Eve. Post*, CC, 6 ff. (Aug. 20, 1927), is a typical example of American resentment at similar European assertions of superiority to the United States.

[4] The number of immigrants in the fiscal year 1914 was more than 1,200,000; in the following year only 326,700, and it remained low until the close of the war.

Island still stood wide in 1914. The criminal, the contract laborer, the anarchist, the polygamist, the physically or mentally diseased, the pauper with no visible means of support, the Oriental coolie, were all debarred. But there was no fixed numerical barrier. Immigrants might come in whatever numbers economic conditions should determine. But as the sparsely populated parts of the country became more thickly settled and the alien competed with the native-born laborer in the great urban centers, the question became increasingly acute whether the future of America could be wisely intrusted to the children of the more recent comers in preference to the children of the men and women whose forefathers had long been here. The problem was rendered more urgent by the change in the national composition of the later arrivals, for in recent years hundreds of thousands of bread seekers from Sicily, Naples, the Slavic and Magyar parts of Austria-Hungary, and the Jewish Pale in Poland and western Russia had formed the bulk of the newcomers.[1] The annihilation of distance by means of transportation had brought the whole world to the doorstep of Uncle Sam.

The new immigration contained much that was valuable to American life, much that it had traditionally lacked.[2] It must be remembered that the earlier German and Irish arrivals had provoked nativist feeling. The southern Italians were, as a group, light-hearted, thrifty, temperate and hard working. The Polish Jew combined with his marked aptitude for commerce a thirst for learning and a zeal for social reform. The Slav and Magyar undertook the hardest and heaviest tasks of

[1] There were very few true Russians (Muscovites); most of the Russian-born were of non-Russian nationality, such as the Jews, Poles and Lithuanians.

[2] C. R. Fish, *The Rise of the Common Man* (*A History of American Life*, VI), 115.

mine and mill. Without these new additions to the working force of the nation the economic progress of the new century must have been slower and costlier. Many regarded the prospect with as little dismay as Dr. Abraham Flexner, scientist and educator, who declared, "Far from regarding the mixed composition of races in this country as unfortunate, I regard it as a distinct advantage of which not enough use has been made. Every one of the stocks represented in the American people has made to this country its own unique contribution in the establishment of the native culture." [1]

But there was another side to the question. Even granting the good qualities of the new immigrants, could they be assimilated to American life in such quantities and in such variety? A million aliens a year, settling in compact racial blocks in the slums of the great cities and rarely coming into touch with the real life of the nation, might in time reduce the United States to a mosaic of nationalities as unstable as Austria-Hungary. The immigrants from southern and eastern Europe rarely understood English on their first arrival and often could not read or write in any tongue. They were accustomed to a meager livelihood and could underbid alike native American labor and the immigrant from the more prosperous countries of northwestern Europe. The trade unions advocated laws restricting European and excluding Asiatic immigration. In this they were supported not only by the nativist prejudice which intolerant men always feel against a foreigner, but also by the more considered judgment of statesmen who believed that a temporary stimulus to industry would be too dearly bought if it impaired either the racial quality or the standards of living of the nation. As Dr. H. H. Laughlin expressed

[1] For newspaper comment, pro and con, on Dr. Flexner's statement, see *Literary Digest*, XCIX, 32 (Oct. 13, 1928).

it, "immigration is a long-time investment in family
stocks rather than a short-time investment in productive
labor." [1]

The first important attempt at restriction was to bar
the illiterate. The proposal was certainly not a new one,
for a literacy test had been vetoed by three presidents,
Cleveland, Taft and Wilson. It finally became law
in 1917 in spite of President Wilson's continued opposition, based mainly on the ground that literacy was a
test of opportunity and not of inherent ability. The
comprehensive act of 1917 summed up the existing laws
on immigration and added the important provision (section 3) that, with certain exceptions such as very near
relatives, "all aliens over sixteen years of age, physically
capable of reading, who cannot read the English language, or some other language or dialect" should
be denied admission. [2] Congress might have rested
content with this measure, which clearly favored
northwestern Europe as compared with the rest of
the continent, had not the close of the World War
and the general poverty which succeeded it in central and eastern Europe threatened an exceptionally high
tide of immigration. Facing this contingency Congress
determined to add to the existing restrictions a fixed
numerical quota for each nation.

The emergency law of 1921 limited the annual immigration from any transatlantic country to three per
cent of the number of its nationals resident in the United
States as determined by the census of 1910. [3] The new
plan met with so much popular favor that in 1924 a

[1] R. DeC. Ward, "Our New Immigration Policy," *Foreign Affairs*,
III (1924), 104. This article (99-111) is a good summary of the
restrictionist argument.
[2] *U. S. Statutes at Large*, XXXIX, pt. i, 874.
[3] *U. S. Statutes at Large*, XLII, pt. i, 540. On the quota laws, see R. L.
Garis, *Immigration Restriction* (N. Y., 1927), chaps. vi-viii.

more drastic measure reduced the quota from three to two per cent and based it on the census of 1890, choosing that date as the turning point when the old immigration from the British Isles, Germany and Scandinavia was beginning to be largely supplemented by the new immigration from southern and eastern Europe. It was further provided that after July 1, 1927, the annual quota of any nationality should be such proportionate share of one hundred and fifty thousand as inhabitants of that national origin bore in 1920 to the entire population of the United States. But the national-origins basis was not brought into effect until 1930 because of difficulties in making a satisfactory analysis of the very mixed blood of the American nation. Not everyone was subject to the quota restriction, as foreign-born wives and children of American citizens, travelers and students, Canadians, Mexicans and other natives of American countries were exempted. To prevent the tragedy of broken homes and disappointed hopes, American consular officers abroad were directed to see that intending immigrants obtained certificates before starting for the United States.

One difficult question involved in the law of 1924 was the exclusion of Japanese labor. As a highly civilized Great Power with a respectable army and navy Japan did not like to be classed with powerless China. But the Far Western states feared Japanese immigration quite as much as Chinese, regarding both as too alien in race ever to become merged into the general body of American citizenship. Since President Roosevelt's time a "gentleman's agreement" between the American and Japanese governments had prevented Japanese of the laborer class from coming to the United States. But in spite of the protests of Japan and the misgivings of President Coolidge Congress insisted on definitely barring Japanese immigration by law.[1] The dread of a new racial problem on the Pacific Coast prevailed over all diplomatic and political considerations, though the general immigration law would have admitted only 146 Japanese per year.

The new quota system of 1924 favored most the British Isles and Germany. Great Britain and Ireland together could send about 62,000 immigrants a year and Germany over 50,000; no other nation exceeded 10,000. This meant, among other results, that the late enemy was favored over all but one of America's recent associates in the war. Italy's great flood of immigration sank to a mere trickle of less than 4000 a year. All southern and eastern Europe together could scarcely muster 20,000. In but one respect did the non-Nordics win an advantage. Owing to the fact that American republics did not come within the restrictions of the quota, thousands of Mexicans crossed the border to meet a demand for cheap labor no longer supplied from Europe. Negroes also, as we have seen, moved north to take industrial positions that formerly would have gone to Italians or Slavs, but in the latter instance this was a matter of migration within the nation, not of immigration into it.

Apart from the decrease in immigration and the change in its national character there was a significant change in the occupations of the newcomers. For the period 1911-1914 three times as many unskilled laborers came to the country as skilled, while in 1925 and 1926 the two classes of immigrants were about equal in number. If allowance be made for emigration, the decrease in unskilled labor becomes even more evident.[2] The number of immigrant farmers increased both relatively and ab-

[1] Garis, *Immigration Restriction*, chap. x; R. L. Buell, "Japanese Immigration," World Peace Found., *Pamphlets*, VII (1924), nos. 5-6.
[2] *Monthly Labor Review*, XXIV (1927), nos. 2, 3.

solutely. The economic effects of the quota law were therefore much greater than the mere restrictions on number would indicate. Immigration practically ceased to be a factor affecting wages in the labor market.

Inevitably the law worked many individual hardships, surprisingly little latitude in its interpretation being allowed to the port officials. As an example, one might mention the case of Professor Peter M. Jack of the University of Michigan. Called from Scotland to occupy the chair of rhetoric, he was delayed for months on the technicality that he had not practised his profession for two years immediately before applying for admission. Even the rich and titled found it hard to pass the jealously guarded gate. The Countess of Cathcart discovered that a divorce case involving the charge of adultery was construed as "moral turpitude" within the meaning of the law. The Countess Karolyi of Hungary was barred from fear of Bolshevist propaganda, a charge which showed the color blindness of the authorities to the different shades of European socialism.

On the other hand, much was done to protect the admitted immigrant from mistreatment and exploitation. Many immigrants had become bad citizens through fraudulent notaries, banks, employment agencies and the like, often conducted by men of their own nationality who were in a position to take advantage of their confidence. To cope with such evils state agencies were established, notably the Massachusetts bureau of immigration founded in 1917 "to bring into sympathetic and mutually helpful relations the commonwealth and its residents of foreign origin, to protect immigrants from exploitation and abuse, to stimulate their acquisition and mastery of the English language, to develop their understanding of American government, institutions and ideals, and generally to promote their assimilation and naturalization." [1] Elaborate Americanization programs, greatly stimulated by the war, were undertaken by municipalities, employers, schools and welfare agencies of all sorts.

Unfortunately not all Americans were tactful Americanizers. During the war occurred such incidents, based on mutual misunderstanding, as the stoning of a Czech patriotic meeting by the local Loyalty Legion which ignored any fine distinction between a foreign language spoken by allies and one spoken by enemies. [2] In another instance an Armenian immigrant, almost pathetically ready to admire all things American, tells what happened when he gave his name to a grammar-school teacher.

> She looked at it for a moment and then turned to me and said, "Oh, give that up and change your name to Smith, Jones or a name like that and become Americanized. Give up everything you brought with you from the Old Country. You did not bring anything worth while anyway." I was shocked by her idea of Americanization and thought to myself: "The Turkish sword did not succeed in making me become a Turk, and now this hare-brained woman is trying to make an American out of me. I defy her to do it." After that I was more of an Armenian patriot than I had ever thought of being. [3]

Many of the foreign-born, like this Armenian, became increasingly sensitive and resentful in the face of forcible Americanization. The motion-picture industry

[1] *Mass. General Acts of 1917*, chap. cccxxi.

[2] E. H. Bierstadt, *Aspects of Americanization* (Cin., 1922), 97. The present writer witnessed a parallel instance when an Italian woman who had carried the flag of her homeland in a "parade of the Allies" was hooted at, her sidewalk critics shouting, "Why don't you carry an American flag?"

[3] B. K. Baghdigian, *Americanism in Americanization* (Kansas City, 1921), 17-18.

found it impossible to present a villain or a stock comic character of any nationality on the films without being deluged by complaints from compatriots who conceived their national sentiment insulted.[1] When Claude G. Bowers in his keynote speech at the Democratic national convention of 1928 accused the Republican administration of degrading the American farmer to the status of a Rumanian peasant, the American Rumanian Association sent a solemn note of protest, declaring, "The state of the Rumanian peasant is not so out-of-date as to justify a party taking it as an example of misery." [2]

The controversy over immigration aroused a keen interest in problems of population. This interest concentrated upon three momentous questions: Was America in danger of having too many people? Was she in danger of having too many inferior individuals? Was she in danger from the presence of inferior races? Books on all these themes multiplied and found an eager market. That these important scientific questions should have awakened so much popular interest was a tribute to the public intelligence, although unfortunately quite unqualified journalists and propagandists obtained as good an audience as the men of scientific training.

The first question, that of quantity, had been in the minds of educated men at least since the days of Malthus. Obviously a country could be too crowded for its economic good, like modern Sicily, or insufficiently peopled for proper development, like modern Alaska. As compared with most European countries the United States was still underpeopled, but the cheap land was almost gone, the cities crowded, the birth rate of the native stock falling, and the balance of exports shifting from food-

---

[1] Mary B. Mullett, "Queer Kicks about the Movies," *Am. Mag.*, CVI (1928), 44-45.
[2] *N. Y. Times*, June 28, 1928.

stuffs and raw materials to manufactured goods.[1] Careful students of the population question, such as Professor Edward M. East of Harvard, challenged the popular optimism which regarded America's capacity for numerical growth as practically unlimited.[2]

The second question, that of quality, was the problem of eugenics. As we have seen, the falling birth rate had affected chiefly the educated and thrifty classes who demanded much of life for their children. Fears were widely expressed that the recent marked progress in popular education and material well-being had done nothing to improve the real physical, mental and moral qualities of the individual; that the civilized man differed from the savage only in training and equipment. The eugenics record office, under the direction of Dr. C. B. Davenport, and the studies by Professor Lewis M. Terman and others on psychological tests in the schools and the army, furnished a wealth of material which was utilized in a crusade for eugenics by such popularizers of science as Albert E. Wiggam.[3]

But the third problem, that of race, bore most directly on the new nationalism, for it threw into contrast the pioneer American stock with other races seeking American opportunities. It was in this field, therefore, that science was most endangered by current political controversy. So widespread was the discussion of anthro-

---

[1] For the relative decline in the importance of agriculture, see chap. vii.

[2] E. M. East, *Mankind at the Crossroads* (N. Y., 1923). For a searching and hostile criticism of Malthusian statistics, see R. R. Kuczynski, "The World's Population," *Foreign Affairs*, VII (1928), 30-40. J. R. Smith in *The World's Food Resources* (N. Y., 1919) held out hopes that new sources of food supply would permit a growth of population far beyond the limits assigned by such biologists as E. M. East and Raymond Pearl.

[3] A. E. Wiggam, *The Fruit of the Family Tree* (Indianapolis, 1924). See also E. M. East, *Heredity and Human Affairs* (N. Y., 1927); L. F. Whitney and Ellsworth Huntington, *The Builders of America* (N. Y., 1927).

pological problems in the press that technical terms which had been before the war the monopoly of a few score research workers were now familiar in every cross-roads cracker-barrel debate. Popular talk on race in the United States had once been in terms of "white men" and "niggers," or, at a higher social level, discussed in terms of language groups: "Anglo-Saxon supremacy," "the Latin races" and the "Slavic peril." But magazine science replaced the talk of "wops," "kikes," "sheenies," "dagoes," "greasers" and "Dutchies," with disquisitions on "Nordics," "Alpines," "Mediterraneans," "cephalic index" and "atavism."

The favorite was the Nordic, the tall, long-headed, fair-haired, blue-eyed son of the Vikings. Most anthropologists seem agreed that, quite apart from present advantages of environment, the Nordics are an inherently energetic group with a high average of ability, perhaps because many of the lazy and stupid were eliminated by natural selection in the cold winters of the Baltic forests. So much might reasonably be conceded. But it is the fault of popular journalism to take more out of an idea than science puts into it. With such writers as Madison Grant and Lothrop Stoddard, the Nordic became almost the sole author of human progress, and America was warned that her future destiny depended on keeping the pure Nordic gold of her population from being debased by Alpine roundheads and swarthy Mediterraneans.[1] At a still lower level, what might be termed the Ku Klux Klan school of anthropology not only identified the old-stock American with the Nordic (in itself a very questionable piece of guesswork),[2] but assumed that the

[1] Madison Grant, The Passing of the Great Race (N. Y., 1916); Lothrop Stoddard, The Rising Tide of Color (N. Y., 1920); same author, Racial Realities in Europe (N. Y., 1924).
[2] Aleš Hrdlička, the anthropologist, found in an intensive study of the old American stock of pure colonial ancestry (Old Americans, Balt.,

Protestant religion, the English language, the institutions of democracy, and the moral qualities of truth, honor and respect for womanhood were all bound together in a magic and inseparable racial tie. Such notions had no standing whatever in the courts of science, but they are of importance to the historian because they were widely credited on Main Street.

The rise of the Ku Klux Klan was perhaps the clearest manifestation of the popular belief that Americanism was no longer—as it had been for Jefferson and Lincoln—a gospel to all the nations, but a national secret which could not be shared with those "not of the blood." [1] When the shadow of impending war hung over a yet neutral America, Colonel William J. Simmons, preacher, salesman and amateur organizer of fraternal societies, determined to revive the Reconstruction organization. On an autumn night in 1915 he led a band of associates, including three members of the original Ku Klux Klan, to the top of Stone Mountain, Georgia, for this purpose. At first the order was hardly more than a sentimental and patriotic reminiscence, an attempt to throw Southern tradition into the scale against alien influence at a moment of national crisis.[2] For four or five years it remained small and mainly sec-

---

1928) that the pioneer stock was a mixed one, tending to the tall Nordic stature and light eyes, but with a head form intermediate between Nordic length and Alpine breadth, and with a preponderance of brown rather than fair hair.

[1] "Americanism, to the Klansman, is a thing of the spirit, a purpose and a point of view, that can only come through instinctive racial understanding . . . . he believes also that few aliens can understand that spirit." Imperial Wizard H. W. Evans, "The Klan's Fight for Americanism," *North Am. Rev.*, CCXXIII (1926), 53.

[2] "Fired by war talk from across the seas, and visualizing our own entry into the fray, at some later time, the idea of '100 per cent Americanism' seized him. Nativism caught his fancy. Perhaps the German represented the arch-opponent to American nativism as he envisioned it, but all foreigners, more or less, must be foes." W. J. Robertson, *The Changing South* (N. Y., 1927), 245.

tional; probably it had no more than five thousand members. But in 1920, when Edward Clarke and Mrs. Elizabeth Tyler took over the financial management, it was put on a business basis and began a nation-wide membership campaign. The ten-dollar membership fee was divided: four dollars to the local Kleagle, one to the King Kleagle of the state, fifty cents to the Goblin of the district, and $4.50 to the headquarters of the Invisible Empire at Atlanta.[1] The boom was now of giant dimensions. By 1925 perhaps four or five million Americans had placed their names on the rolls of the organization.[2] In December, 1922, Hiram Wesley Evans, a Texas dentist, became the new Imperial Wizard and Emperor in succession to Simmons.

The Ku Klux Klan was essentially a protest of American nativism against the pressure from alien races, creeds and social ideals. Though there was no organic connection with the original Ku Klux Klan of the days of reconstruction following the Civil War [3]—its spiritual father was rather the Know Nothing party of the mid-century—the new organization copied, or rather adapted with slight variations, the robes, the mask, the ritual and the secret-society language of its titular predecessor. Its slogan was "native, white, Protestant" supremacy and it was directed quite as much against the Catholic, the Jew and the alien white immigrant as against the colored man.

The Klan, however, turned to other purposes as well. Indeed, the chief source of its strength seems to have been that it was all things to all men. In one state it would be chiefly a champion of the prohibition law

[1] Robertson, *The Changing South*, 250-251.
[2] Frank Bohn, "The Ku Klux Klan Interpreted," *Am. Journ. of Sociology*, XXX, 385.
[3] See Allan Nevins, *The Emergence of Modern America* (*A History of American Life*, VIII), 349-353.

against the bootlegger; in another a stern censor of morals, sending warning notes and even flogging expeditions to punish men and women who had violated the seventh commandment. Often it denounced internationalism and pacifism, demanding a strong navy and abstention from the wiles of the League of Nations and the World Court, or insisting on a more militantly patriotic tone in school histories.[1] Here and there it allied with the Fundamentalists and denounced evolution as "European infidelity." For brief periods in certain states the Klan was a political machine, concerned chiefly in bestowing local offices on its members and their friends. And, finally, to many Americans it was merely another secret society whose imposing ritual, with its Imperial Wizards, Kleagles, Klaverns, robes, signs and burning crosses in the night, afforded the same harmless pleasure that a Greek-letter fraternity brings to the college boy. In the processions of Klansmen who marched in solemn file through the streets of the national capital and many other great cities, there was a sprinkling of alarmed patriots, fanatics and political schemers, but the rank and file were just average Americans who would join any organization whatever that professed vaguely patriotic aims and promised a social good time.[2]

The anti-Romanist propaganda on which the Klan more and more concentrated [3] was the revamping of an old phobia which dates back to Bloody Queen Mary and the Book of Martyrs. It had been continued in Amer-

[1] "The textbooks have been so perverted that Americanism is falsified, distorted and betrayed." Evans, "The Klan's Fight for Americanism," 58.
[2] See J. M. Mecklin, *The Ku Klux Klan: a Study of the American Mind* (N. Y., 1924).
[3] "The Negro is not a menace to Americanism in the sense that the Jew or the Roman Catholic is a menace. He is not actually hostile to it. He is simply racially incapable of understanding, sharing in or contributing to Americanism." Imperial Wizard H. W. Evans, *The Klan of Tomorrow* (pamphlet, n.p., 1924).

ica by the strongly Protestant character of early American Christianity and had found new fuel to feed on in the vast expansion of Catholicism of more recent years. New York and other Eastern centers had long since fallen into the hands of clannish groups of immigrant politicians, usually Roman Catholic Irish or Italians. Many old-stock Americans were also alarmed by the rapid growth of Roman Catholic organizations, such as the Knights of Columbus, with over seven hundred thousand members in 1928, or puzzled by the legal complexities of dual allegiance to the pope in spiritual matters and to the nation in civil matters.[1] Finally, the refusal of many Catholics to enter the public schools and their support of a complete system of Catholic schools and colleges offended people who believed that the "little red schoolhouse," supported by public taxation, was the most potent agency in Americanizing the immigrant. Out of such miscellaneous material a nightmare was fashioned. One paper found in the honors paid to Columbus a "brazen defiance of the fact that America was not discovered by a Roman Catholic but by a Norseman who landed in Vinland nearly five hundred years before the Pope's agent raised the cross of Inquisition at San Salvador." The motion pictures, too, were revealed as a huge conspiracy. "Jews and Roman Catholics own 95 per cent of the big producing and distributing companies. . . . This accounts for so much papal propaganda being displayed before American audiences."[2] Rome also controlled, so Senator Heflin of Alabama asserted, most of the press![3]

In the years from 1920 to 1922, when the Klan had

[1] Note the debate between Charles C. Marshall and Alfred E. Smith on this subject, *Atlantic Mo.*, CXXXIX (1927), 540-549, 721-728.

[2] From an anonymous pamphlet, *The Foreign Language Press, America's Greatest Menace* (n.p., 1923), 20.

[3] Reported in the *Fellowship Forum*, June 2, 1928.

become a huge profit-making machine, slipping from the bewildered founder into the hands of practical men who "sold hate at ten dollars a packet," occurred the period of greatest violence.[1] Under the protection of the mask and the added protection of a secret membership list sinister elements entered the Klan and used it for their own purposes. Between October, 1920, and October, 1921, revelations by the *New York World* showed four killings, one mutilation, one branding with acid, forty-one floggings, twenty-seven tar-and-feather parties, five kidnapings and forty-three persons driven into exile.[2] Klansmen said, and no doubt with much truth, that the majority of these outrages were not by Klansmen at all but by private individuals assuming the robe and mask to disguise their identity; yet it was the existence of the robe and mask that made these crimes possible. In 1922 two mutilated corpses charged to the Klan were discovered in the swamps near Mer Rouge, Louisiana. Hardly less merciless were the factional fights within the Klan. In 1923 William S. Coburn, an opponent of Wizard Evans, was murdered by Philip Fox, an Evans adherent. By the new "Western Method" of recruiting the recommendation of a single Klansman would now admit a new member.[3] Little or no discrim-

---

[1] "By 1921 the Wizard [Colonel Simmons] resembled the hen which had hatched out a mixed brood of goslings and turkeys. . . . To go into a county of 25,000 inhabitants and organize a thousand healthy, sturdy, adventure-loving young men . . . to fire their hearts with the thought that their beloved country was in imminent danger of destruction; and then to expect them to be satiated by repeating the Klan ritual twice a month and waiting for election day, surely that was expecting to pluck figs from thistles." Bohn, "The Ku Klux Klan Interpreted," 397-398.

[2] Robertson, *The Changing South*, 253.

[3] W. G. Shepherd, "The Fiery Double Cross," *Collier's*, LXXXII, 8 (July 28, 1928). His series of articles: "How I Put Over the Klan" (an interview with Colonel Simmons), *Collier's*, LXXXII, no. 2; "Ku Klux Koin," LXXXII, no. 3; and "The Fiery Double Cross," together tell the story of the change in ownership of the Klan mainly from the standpoint of the Simmons faction.

ination was used in filling the ranks, and membership became a convenient refuge for criminals who wanted protection and politicians who wanted a ready-made "machine."

Politically the Klan became a power in the North as well as the South. It was a major issue in gubernatorial contests in Texas, Louisiana, Oklahoma, Maine, Kansas and Indiana. It made war on Judge Ben B. Lindsey, the nationally known reform judge of the juvenile court in Denver, Colorado.[1] It loaned its support to the agitation for doing away with Catholic parochial schools by requiring all children to attend the public schools.[2] In 1924 the fight in the Democratic national convention to have the Klan denounced by name in the party platform threatened a disruption of the party and contributed to its defeat. As a compromise the convention adopted a general affirmation of civil liberty and religious equality without specific mention of the Klan. The Klan fought in 1924 the nomination and in 1928 the election of Alfred E. Smith of New York as presidential candidate because of his religion. In general, the order was Democratic in the South and more frequently Republican in the North, though it often controlled factions in both parties.

The most amazing story in the political history of the Klan was that of the dictatorship of David Curtis Stephenson over the state of Indiana. Indiana was not a Southern state with bitter memories of Reconstruction to excuse a racial panic, nor an illiterate backwater where political apathy might permit an unrepresentative minority to seize power. On the contrary Indiana was a

[1] Norman Hapgood reproduces a denunciation of Judge Lindsey on Klan stationery in "The New Threat of the Ku Klux Klan," *Hearst's International*, XLIII (1923), 60.

[2] Oregon passed such a law, but it was disallowed by the courts. Michigan and several other states repeatedly rejected the proposal on referendum.

typical Mid-Western commonwealth, well balanced between agriculture and industry, active and alert in politics, served by excellent schools, distinguished for its literary output. A foreign and Catholic element existed, but in much smaller degree than in such states as New York or Massachusetts. Here, if anywhere, the old America was safe, and white, Protestant, Nordic, Gentile supremacy unendangered. Yet by the arts of salesmanship, the shrewd exploitation of rumor, Stephenson had thousands of honest villagers believing that the papal crown had been imposed as a watermark on the paper money issued by the government, that the pope planned within a decade to leave Italy and establish himself within the United States, and that every time a Catholic child was born an extra rifle was placed in the vaults of the local cathedral.[1]

Stephenson captured the Republican state machine, forced the two senators from the state to adopt a friendly attitude towards the Klan, and elected his candidate for governor, Ed Jackson. But he desired to be more than a boss: he wished to stand in the limelight as senator and perhaps some day as president. His vanity brought him to disaster. Thinking himself above the law, he kidnaped a girl, terrified her into suicide, and was sentenced to imprisonment for life. Governor Jackson was indicted for bribing ex-Governor Warren McCray, himself a convicted felon. Several members of the Indianapolis city government were indicted for bribery or election frauds. Judge Clarence Dearth, an active Klan agent, was impeached, though not convicted, on charges

[1] "The left-wing leaders even went so far as to move the Pope's new headquarters to Cincinnati, and some Klansmen exhibited pictures of the Jewish hospital as his headquarters until he could take over a section of the city suitable to his needs." On one occasion fifteen hundred persons met a train at North Manchester to repel the pope. The lone passenger who dismounted had to prove his innocence of the charge. Morton Harrison, "Gentlemen from Indiana," *Atlantic Mo.*, CXLI (1928), 679.

of oppression in office. The Klan was now in disgrace throughout the state and its honest, patriotic members left the Stephenson organization in horror when they found out how their credulity had been abused. By 1928 there were less than seven thousand active Klansmen in all Indiana.[1]

As late as 1927 an epidemic of floggings took place in Alabama under the protection of Klan politicians,[2] but on the whole the story of the Klan from 1923 to 1928 was one of political intrigue rather than of violence. Both, however, had done their work in making the Klan unpopular. In an effort to regain credit with the public and remove the reproaches which secrecy had cast upon its doings, Wizard Evans chose Washington's birthday, 1928, as the occasion to ordain that henceforth "no mask or visor shall be upon the helmet of the regalia of any Klansman." A new degree was created, the Knights of the Great Forest, and all Klansmen required to assume it. Thus terminated the subterranean days of the Ku Klux Klan. No longer a mysteriously threatening "invisible Empire," it was revealed as little more than an organization for propaganda against alien and Roman Catholic influences.

The campaign against the Jew in America was far less active than that against the Roman Catholic, although the two were yoked together in the formal denunciations of the Klan—truly a strange association in view of their centuries of opposition to each other. One of the dupes of the anti-Semitic propaganda was Henry Ford, the automobile manufacturer, by nature a kindly man and seemingly one of the last to cherish a racial or religious feud. Yet his newspaper, the *Dearborn Inde-*

---

[1] Harrison, "Gentlemen from Indiana," 684.
[2] R. A. Patton, "A Ku Klux Klan Reign of Terror," *Current History*, XXVIII (1928), 51-55.

pendent, became simultaneously spokesman for Mr. Ford and for reactionary Europeans who traced all the social ills of modern times to "international Jewish finance." On the basis of an alleged "protocol of the elders of Zion," repeatedly exposed by historians on both sides of the Atlantic, a Jewish conspiracy for the subjugation of the Gentile world was charged.[1] It is possible that some of Mr. Ford's personal experiences with Jewish bankers and business rivals may have affected his attitude in the matter, but his zeal in the cause was without question, though eventually, when faced with court action, he dropped the campaign.[2]

Chauvinism found another target in "unpatriotic" schoolbooks. The same type of unhistorical mind that could believe in the enthronement of the pope or the elders of Zion on the ruins of American liberty found it equally easy to believe in an Anglo-Saxon conspiracy for bringing back the United States into the British Empire. The elements in this conspiracy were the late Cecil Rhodes and his Oxford scholarships, the Sons of St. George, the English-Speaking Union, the Sulgrave Institute, the "multiform Carnegie institutions," the universities and the writers of textbooks dealing with the American Revolution.[3] Charles Grant Miller, vocal in

---

[1] Norman Hapgood, "Henry Ford's Jew Mania," *Hearst's International*, XLII (1922), 39.

[2] Still cruder myths found occasional circulation. When Mayor Gilbert Hawes of Massena, New York, suggested to a state trooper that the disappearance of a missing child might be due to a "ritual murder," the simple-minded corporal started an investigation among the Jewish priesthood. The Permanent Commission on Better Understanding between Christians and Jews in America, an organization of leading Protestants, Catholics and Hebrews, at once denounced the ritual-murder charge as an old libel, refuted century after century by "the best minds of all ages and creeds." The mayor apologized and the corporal was reprimanded. *N. Y. Times*, Oct. 6, 1928.

[3] Bessie L. Pierce, *Public Opinion and the Teaching of History in the United States* (N. Y., 1926), chap. vii, contains the best account of the war on the textbooks.

the Hearst papers which were always ready for a chance to "twist the lion's tail," was the chief spokesman of the protest against the Anglo-Saxon conspiracy, and he easily obtained the indorsement of veterans' organizations, patriotic-hereditary societies and some of the more irreconcilable racial groups.[1] The politicians began to be interested. Oregon and even liberal Wisconsin enacted a law forbidding the use in public schools of textbooks defaming or misrepresenting the heroes of the War of Independence or the War of 1812. Mayor John F. Hylan in New York and Mayor William H. Thompson of Chicago gravely conducted investigations of textbooks alleged to be overfriendly to the British cause in 1776. The spirit of these inquiries is indicated in the report of the committee to investigate school histories in New York in 1922, from which we learn that "strictly speaking the textbook writer is not a historian. . . . It is for the teacher to determine what material is needed. It is for the textbook writer to supply it. . . . Truth is no defense to the charge of impropriety." [2]

The opposite spirit of American historians was well expressed in a resolution adopted by the council of the American Historical Association: [3]

> In the opinion of this Association, the clearly implied charges that many of our leading scholars are engaged in treasonable propaganda and that tens of thousands of American school teachers and officials are so stupid or disloyal as to place treasonable text-books in the hands of children is inherently and obviously absurd. . . . Genuine and intelligent patriotism, no less than the requirement of honesty and sound scholarship, demand

[1] A. M. Schlesinger, "Points of View in Historical Writing," *Publishers' Wkly.*, CXIII (1928), 147, lists the supporting organizations.

[2] Pierce, *Public Opinion and the Teaching of History*, 312-316, gives the text of this report.

[3] Am. Assoc. of Univ. Professors, *Bull.*, XIV, no. 2, 134.

*Mayor William H. Thompson of Chicago and the
Ku Klux Klan thought that America could keep its
character only by rigorously excluding all foreign
influences.*

An initiation in the presence of the fiery cross and the flag.

that text-book writers and teachers should strive to present a truthful picture of past and present . . . criticism of history text-books should therefore be based not upon grounds of patriotism, but only upon grounds of faithfulness to fact.

The real charge against the historians was not that they were propagandists but that they refused to be.

It would, however, be a gross injustice to the American public of the period to say that they were interested only in the censorship of history. There was a more positive and pleasing side to the general interest in the national past. Single-volume texts on American history appeared annually, and were supplemented by studies in series such as *The Chronicles of America*,[1] *The Pageant of America* [2] and the *Dictionary of American Biography*.[3] Biography was especially popular. Certain authors made an effort, sometimes with more zeal than discretion, to "humanize" George Washington, so that he would be liked as a man instead of being revered as a marble statue. Abraham Lincoln, who never needed humanizing, was an even more popular subject—the records of the Library of Congress show about eight new books or booklets on Lincoln for each year of the period 1914-1928.[4] A corresponding cult for General Robert E. Lee as the central figure of the Epic of the South reached comparable proportions. Hamilton, Jefferson, Marshall and many lesser heroes, especially West-

[1] Allen Johnson, ed., fifty volumes, New Haven, 1918-1921.
[2] R. H. Gabriel, ed., fifteen volumes, New Haven. 1926-1929.
[3] Allen Johnson, ed., twenty volumes, N. Y., 1928-   , in progress.
[4] Including such important biographies as those by Albert J. Beveridge, N. W. Stephenson, William E. Barton and Carl Sandburg. England, too, awoke to the American Civil War period, and as a result of this interest we had Lord Charnwood's interpretation of Lincoln, John Drinkwater's historical plays on Lincoln and Lee, and Sir Frederick Maurice's military studies of the war. Stephen Vincent Benet's *John Brown's Body*, an epic of the Civil War, attained popularity with both public and critics. It was awarded the Pulitzer prize for American verse in 1929.

ern pioneers and unconventional figures in the social history of the country, were reportrayed for the new generation. "A glance over a bookshelf which holds some new American biographies that I have read in the past year or two," said a critic,

> shows George Washington and Billy the Kid, Thomas Jefferson and Wild Bill, Aaron Burr and Jesse James, William Lloyd Garrison and Brigham Young, Poe and P. T. Barnum, Carl Sandburg's Lincoln, Bill Nye, Andrew Jackson, Commodore Vanderbilt, John Paul Jones, Margaret Fuller, Benjamin Franklin, Henry Ward Beecher. What a hash! But they are all good biography. Not a plaster saint on the list. They are written scientifically, trying first of all to get at the truth about the man and set it forth.[1]

Some of the most successful motion-picture films likewise dealt with American history: the Oregon pioneer in "The Covered Wagon," the building of the Union Pacific in "The Iron Horse," an earlier generation of Gothamites in "When Old New York Was Young." There was a notable revival of interest in the "Paul Bunyan" legends of the north-woods lumber camps and similar American folklore. Colonial furniture became more than ever the fashion among the wealthy, and prices were paid for counterpanes and obsolete lamps that would have gone far to purchase a spinning machine or furnish a house with a complete installation of electric lights. State historical societies rescued from oblivion traditions of the pioneers. Historic homes, such as Thomas Jefferson's Monticello estate, were refurnished for public exhibition. Many excellent monuments—from the Lincoln Memorial in Washington, D. C., to the sculptures in honor of the Confederate

[1] Will Payne, "Where You From?," Sat. Eve. Post, CC, 167 (April 14, 1928).

army on Stone Mountain—commemorated heroic deeds of the past. A typical venture by America's most typical citizen was Henry Ford's restoration of the Wayside Inn of Longfellow's poem, and his "village of yesterday" which aimed to "assemble a complete series of every article used or made in America from the days of the first settlers." [1] Through the munificence of John D. Rockefeller, jr., work was begun to restore the old town of Williamsburg in Virginia to its colonial appearance.

If this chapter has been mainly a chronicle of the absurdities and extravagances of American nationalism, the fact should not be taken to imply that there were no compensating gains. One should reckon on the credit side the devotion of all classes and all sections of the country to a common cause in the World War, the extension of federal aid to education and welfare work, the increased civic pride which made many an ugly mill town a garden city. H. G. Wells in the years before the war criticized the American chiefly for his lack of any "sense of the state"—he was too individualistic, selfish, preoccupied with his private business, to think of the nation. No such charge was brought against the postwar American citizen, indifferent, perhaps, to party politics but immersed in a tangle of civic duties and welfare movements. Public spirit there was in abundance; only instruction was needed to harness it to useful tasks.

[1] Samuel Crowther, "Henry Ford's Village of Yesterday," *Ladies' Home Journ.*, XLV (1928), no. 9, 10. See also Henry A. Haigh, "Henry Ford's Typical Early American Village at Dearborn," *Mich. History Mag.*, XIII (1929), 506-543.

CHAPTER XII

AMERICA AT SCHOOL

THE outstanding achievement of the American school during the period from 1914 to 1928 was to make secondary education almost as universal as the previous hundred years had made primary education. In 1914 there were less than one and a half million high-school students in the United States; by 1926 nearly four million.[1] By 1927 approximately half of all children of high-school age were enrolled in either public or private schools.[2] Most of this expansion was at the taxpayer's expense, for private secondary schools and academies reported an enrollment of a bare quarter of a million, about one sixteenth of the whole.[3] "In every country," wrote Professor Edward A. Ross, "the national education has the outline of a lofty mountain, broad at the base and tapering upward into a peak. Now the peculiarity of American education is not breadth of base, for there are countries which are more successful than the United States in getting children into the public elementary schools. It is not height of peak, for American universities stand no higher than those of certain other countries. But it is *breadth of education in the middle range*—say from the seventh year of instruction to the twelfth—for nowhere else do so large a proportion of the children receive secondary education." [4]

[1] Bur. of Educ., *Bull. for 1927*, no. 21, 2.
[2] *Ibid.*, no. 33, 10.
[3] *Ibid.*, no. 31, gives statistics for private schools.
[4] E. A. Ross, *What Is America?* (N. Y., 1919), 63.

Higher education—the college, the university and the professional school—showed a proportionate increase comparable to that of the high school, but much less in absolute amount, for while secondary-school instruction reached half the population of its age group higher education reached only about one in eight. The federal bureau of education, comparing American statistics with European, estimated in 1928 that both secondary and higher education were offered to almost as many students in the United States as in all the world besides, although the elementary schools of the nation included less than three tenths of the world's pupils.[1] The expenditure on education in the United States aggregated about half the world's total, and was estimated in 1925-1926 at $2,744,000,000.[2] The total cost of the public primary and secondary schools doubled from 1913 to 1920 and doubled again from 1920 to 1926.[3] Only this latter increase was, however, a real gain, for the rapid rise in prices during the war kept more than even pace with the enlarged school appropriations, and, in terms of price levels, the schools were actually poorer in 1920 than they had been five years before.[4]

One of the gravest consequences of this price inflation was the heavy blow struck at the salaries of the teaching profession. These salaries, usually fixed by law, responded slowly to the upward rush of commercial prices and wages. In purchasing power the average teacher's earnings in 1920 were less than those of 1915 or even

[1] U. S. Daily (Wash.), May 5, 1928, 3.
[2] U. S. Daily, May 1, 1929.   [3] N. Y. Times, Dec. 8, 1928.
[4] G. S. Counts, "Education," Am. Journ. of Sociology, XXXIV, 185. Thus the evidence from expenditure on schools agrees with the evidence from so many other indices of prosperity that the real economic advance of the American people was entirely an affair of the middle and later 1920's, the war and reconstruction period being one of inflated prices but not of enhanced prosperity, except for a few fortunate individuals or classes.

1905.[1] As the teacher's pay slumped from the level of skilled to that of unskilled labor, teaching itself ran some danger of becoming an unskilled occupation, and might have done so, particularly in the case of new recruits to the profession, but for the gradual closing of the gap between teachers' income and costs of living. As late as 1924 it was asserted that only half the rural and village school teachers had even a high-school education.[2] Rural teachers usually earned from seven to eight hundred dollars;[3] in towns and cities pay tended to vary with the size of the municipality. The median salary in 1926-1927 for elementary-school teachers in small towns (under five thousand) was $1169; for high-school teachers, $1542. In the largest cities elementary teachers averaged two thousand dollars a year and high-school teachers twenty-five hundred.[4] Rural education remained, on the whole, distinctly inferior to urban, and only about a third as many country children went to high school as did city children.[5] In hardly any city was a grade-school teacher's pay equal to the minimum standard of living as proclaimed by trade unions and social reformers.[6]

One natural effect of the inadequate salaries was to drive family men almost entirely from the ranks of the grade schools. As late as 1915 one public-school teacher in five was a man, taking elementary and secondary grades together; in 1920, when the economic condition

[1] Bur. of Educ., *Bull. for 1927*, no. 13, 3.
[2] B. P. Chass, "America's Poorly Paid School Teachers," *Current History*, XXIV (1926), 68.
[3] Chass, "America's Poorly Paid School Teachers," 69.
[4] W. S. Deffenbaugh, "Recent Movements in City School Systems," Bur. of Educ., *Bull. for 1927*, no. 8, 11.
[5] *N. Y. Times*, Dec. 8, 1928.
[6] In general the highest salaries were in the great cities and on the Pacific Coast and the lowest in the cotton belt, but as this was true of wages and salaries generally it still left the teacher everywhere at a disadvantage by the standards of his own locality.

of the profession was particularly bad, less than one in seven; in 1925, about one in six.[1] Most of these men were city high-school teachers, administrative officers, or teachers of some specialty, such as manual training, in the grades. Nearly everyone seemed to deplore in theory the "feminization" of the schools; but the only practical remedy, raising salaries to what a family man in the professional classes expects, would at least have doubled the salary budget, and even the most generous taxpayers did not desire to pay such a price to restore the balance of the sexes. There was a marked tendency towards equalizing pay as between men and women in the same grade and also towards reducing the former difference between elementary and high-school salaries.

Apart from the difficulty of securing well-trained teachers at a longshoreman's wages, there was a most encouraging advance in educational standards. From 1915 to 1925—really from 1920 to 1925—the average number of days in the school session increased from 159 to 169 and the average attendance from 121 days to 136.[2] The number of one-room schools decreased by more than thirty-seven thousand from 1918 to 1926.[3] This decline meant school consolidation, and was made possible by lavish public expenditure, amounting sometimes to over twenty million dollars a year, for the transportation of children from their scattered homes to large graded schools. Illiteracy decreased from 7.7 per cent in 1910 to 6.1 per cent in 1920 according to the decennial census, and the Southern states, where illiteracy was most common, made the most rapid progress in reducing it. Though the foreign-born had the high illiteracy rate of thirteen per cent, so efficient were the school

[1] Bur. of Educ., *Bull. for 1927*, no. 13, 12.
[2] Bur. of Educ., *Bull for 1927*, no. 13, 3-4.
[3] Bur. of Educ., *Bull. for 1927*, no. 13, 2.

systems of the great cities where they congregated that the children of foreign parents had actually a lower illiteracy rate than white folk of native-born ancestry. As the oncoming generation was almost everywhere in school, such illiteracy as remained was largely among the older folk, a relic of past negligence.

There were many reasons for the enhanced cost of public education quite aside from the readjustment of salary schedules and the prolongation of the average period of schooling. Buildings and equipment were much more costly. The old-fashioned one-room "little red schoolhouse," now so rapidly disappearing, was a cheap affair that any competent carpenter could put up. The modern school, a splendid structure of brick or concrete in several stories, was often better designed than the average college building. School libraries and laboratories, auditoriums, gymnasiums, school theaters, swimming pools, playgrounds and athletic fields made the classroom the least costly part of the structure. The classroom itself, with its movable desks, wall blackboards, window boxes of flowers and reproductions of famous paintings on the walls, was not in the least like the plain little rooms of a previous generation. The almost tripled high-school membership, in particular, necessitated the erection of new buildings and, because they were new, they had all the advantage of the latest theory in school construction.

In order to keep the overcrowded school plant in efficient full-time use, many large cities adopted the "platoon system," sometimes called the "Gary system" after the Indiana city where it was first employed on a large scale. By this plan the pupils were divided into three groups, and while one group was using the classrooms another would be at work in the manual-training shops or on the playground or assembled in the audi-

This building was one of four abandoned

When this consolidated school was instituted.

The Passing of the Little Red Schoolhouse

torium.[1] William Wirt, who had fathered the scheme at Gary, was called by Mayor John Purroy Mitchel of New York City in 1914 to organize a similar system in the metropolis. The emphasis on manual training was disliked by some parents who wanted their children to rise in the world on the ladder of "book learning" and who listened sympathetically to the demagogic cry, "Rockefeller is stealing the schools," voiced by the Hearst press and other opponents of Mayor Mitchel.[2] Partly on the issue of opposition to the Gary system, John F. Hylan, the Tammany Hall candidate, defeated Mayor Mitchel in the election of 1917 and held office for eight years to the dismay of municipal reformers.[3] In 1927, 115 cities had 740 schools on the platoon system and in thirty-four of these cities all the schools were so organized.[4]

With the children themselves the new emphasis on vocational training was very popular. "Boys bring repair work from their own homes; they study auto mechanics by working on an old Ford car; they design, draft, and make patterns for lathes and drill presses, the actual casting being done by a Middletown foundry; they have designed and constructed a house, doing all the architectural, carpentry, wiring, metal work and

---

[1] See H. U. Faulkner, *The Quest for Social Justice* (*A History of American Life*, XI), chap. vi.

[2] The General Education Board, a Rockefeller philanthropic enterprise, was offering financial aid to popularize the system.

[3] There were other factors in the Tammany victory. Mayor Mitchel, though a Catholic, had made enemies by exposing the maladministration of some church charitable institutions which received public money; the Republican vote was split by an independent candidate, and the pacifists of all parties voted for Morris Hillquit, the Socialist, who polled an enormous vote, greater than that of any other Socialist candidate for any office in the history of the city. Hylan's second election was secured by his struggle with the private transportation companies on the five-cent-fare issue. Under Mayor Walker Tammany continued to rule New York for the remainder of the period.

[4] Deffenbaugh, "Recent Movements in City School Systems," 6.

painting." [1] Teachers of such special courses were usually better paid than those who taught the traditional academic branches. The necessary equipment of a kitchen in a "domestic-science" course for girls, or of a machine shop for boys, was much more expensive than the equipment necessary to teach Latin, mathematics or even elementary natural science. Hence the diversification of the school curriculum added greatly to the school budget. The addition of doctors, nurses and physical-education directors or paid athletic coaches to the teaching staff also added to the obligations of the school. There was constant pressure on school authorities, especially in the primary grades, to set aside certain hours for talks on fire prevention, the safe way to cross streets, the use of the toothbrush, the duty of keeping the street clean, kindness to animals, the virtues of milk and spinach as contrasted with the vices of pastry and sweetmeats, and many other worthy but too numerous causes. Traditional courses in European history and American civics tended to yield place to vaguer courses on "world history," "good citizenship," "social problems" and various adumbrations of sociology for the youthful mind.

Changes so many and so rapid naturally provoked a conservative reaction, especially when hard times and high taxes hit the agricultural Middle West where school expenditure had been very lavish. "In Minnesota, Iowa, the Dakotas, Nebraska, Missouri, Illinois and other neighboring states thousands of local school boards wiped out of existence their domestic science, manual training and physical education departments. 'Back to the three R's' became the battle cry." [2] The conservatives

[1] R. S. Lynd and Helen M. Lynd, *Middletown* (N. Y., 1929), 194-195.

[2] J. H. Butler, "Our Spendthrift Schools," *Current History*, XXVI (1927), 49.

contended that the enrichment of the curriculum merely distracted attention from the essentials and that graduates of the elementary and even of the high-school grades were less well equipped for business life than their parents had been. A partial answer to these contentions was supplied when one state superintendent gave examinations in spelling identical with those that had been in use several decades earlier and compared the new records with the old; he also arranged spelling bees between "stars" of the adult community and the children in his schools. Both tests were victories for the modern methods.[1] Some parts of the traditional curriculum stood out against the utilitarian spirit of the age with strange tenacity. Though Greek was rarely taught, Latin remained more prominent than any of the modern foreign languages in most high schools and its survival secured also as a consequence the survival of many courses of ancient history. In a typical Mid-Western city ten per cent of all student hours in the high schools were devoted to Latin, as against only two per cent to French and Spanish.[2] German had hardly recovered from the effects of the temporary boycott of war time.[3]

The rapid development of the junior high school and the spread of the junior-college idea broke up the traditional uniformity of the American public school. In 1914 most public-school systems included an eight-year elementary school and a four-year high school resting on top of it and not forming a separate educational approach like most European secondary schools. Children kept together till about the sixth year of schooling and then began dropping out as family need or inability to meet school requirements or the temptation of an offered

[1] Butler, "Our Spendthrift Schools," 51.
[2] Lynds, *Middletown*, 193. Only English, mathematics, history and vocational courses exceeded Latin.
[3] See earlier, chap. ii.

job might determine. By 1928 many cities had shifted to the "six-three-three" plan, six years in the elementary school, three in the junior high school and three in the senior high school. But there were many other combinations. "Six-year elementary schools stand alongside seven-year elementary schools. We have three-year and two-year junior high schools . . . 'regular' four-year high schools and senior high schools. . . . The traditional four-year college is matched by new collegiate units of two years, three years, and six years." [1]

Federal aid to education was greatly extended, though each state maintained a completely autonomous school system, and the prolonged agitation for a separate secretaryship of education in the national cabinet did not achieve its aim. But much was done by subsidies shared between national and local funds.[2] The Smith-Lever act of 1914 provided for extension work in agriculture by coöperation between the department of agriculture and the land-grant colleges, and the more comprehensive Smith-Hughes act of 1917 established a federal board for vocational education and granted appropriations to aid work already locally undertaken in commercial, industrial and domestic-science vocational work as well as in agriculture. Equal sums were contributed by the nation and by the states for the purpose. By 1926 federal aid in agriculture reached nearly one third of the rural high schools in the nation and in home economics over eight per cent of all high schools.[3] The bureau of education, the children's bureau and the departments of agriculture, labor and commerce proved useful sources of information to educators, business men and farmers.

The enormous expansion of secondary schools made

[1] H. W. Holmes, "Chaos or Cosmos in American Education," *Atlantic Mo.*, CXL (1927), 493.
[2] A. F. Macdonald, *Federal Aid* (N. Y., 1928), chap. vii.
[3] *U. S. Daily*, Jan. 24, 1929.

possible a similar, though less striking, expansion of colleges and universities. This increase was not at all regular. The war brought a temporary halt in 1917-1918, when many students of military age entered the army, but immediately afterward, in 1919 and 1920, the registration of most colleges and universities suddenly increased by half. Between 1922 and 1924 there was another upward leap, followed by a period of more normal growth. From 1910 to 1920 the enrollment in institutions of higher education (excluding preparatory departments) rose from 266,654 to 462,445; in 1926 it reached 767,263.[1] What would be the "saturation point"? Already collegiate attendance was about one eighth of the entire population between the ages of eighteen and twenty-one.[2] At least four or five times as large a proportion of American youth as of British, French or German were attending college. Of course this was a measure of quantity, not of quality, as no one would pretend that all of the 975 colleges, universities and professional schools listed by the bureau of education ranked in academic merit with Germany's modest score of historic universities.[3]

Though nearly every endowed institution increased its fees,[4] in many cases doubling the cost of tuition, this seemed to have no effect on registration. "Under present conditions," wrote Arthur J. Klein in 1927, "the costs are not the decisive factor in determining whether students shall or shall not attend college."[5] Higher educational standards had equally little visible effect, although

[1] Counting all departments, there were 822,895 students enrolled (509,732 men and 313,163 women). Bur. of Educ., *Bull.*, no. 40, 1, 3.

[2] One editor ventured the estimate that there would be no final halt until the ratio increased to one in five. *Boston Transcript*, Jan. 12, 1927.

[3] Bur. of Educ., *Bull. for 1927*, no. 40, 1.

[4] By an average of seventy per cent from 1919-1920 to 1926-1927. Am. Assoc. of Univ. Professors, *Bull.*, XV, no. 2, 144.

[5] A. J. Klein, "Higher Education," Bur. of Educ., *Bull.*, no. 34, 10.

entrance examinations were now supplemented in many cases by intelligence tests of the type made familiar by the army. The state universities were practically helpless under the flood, as they usually admitted directly from high school and it was the overflow from the high schools that was filling the colleges. The endowed colleges and universities often used a "quota" method in stemming immigration, not unlike the policy adopted by the nation itself at the same period. To apply too late for admission at such popular institutions as Yale, Princeton, Leland Stanford or Dartmouth was to be sent back to a waiting list. Particularly interesting was the Dartmouth plan of allowing a certain quota to each section of the country to insure against becoming a merely regional school.

One method of relieving overpressure on the four-year college was the establishment of junior colleges, offering no degree and giving only freshman and sophomore instruction. By 1927 one hundred and fifty-three junior colleges existed in thirty-one states.[1] For economy's sake such institutions were often housed with a large municipal high school, and their constant peril was that of sinking to be mere secondary continuation schools. On the other hand, they offered the advantage of a taste of higher education dissociated from the social perils of adolescence spent away from home. Complementary to the junior-college movement was the concentration of some of the larger universities, notably Johns Hopkins and Chicago, on the junior and senior years of college work with a view to the eventual dropping of all freshman and sophomore work. Alumni influence was thrown against the change, not only as a departure from tradition but because the undergraduate years supplied nearly all the material for intercollegiate athletics.

[1] Bur. of Educ., *Bull. for 1927*, no. 40, 3.

Professional schools, also besieged by numbers, tended increasingly to become postgraduate or, at all events, to require two or three years of undergraduate preparation for entrance. Thus, in New York state, until the fall of 1924 the only law schools requiring prelegal education were Columbia, Syracuse and Cornell. "In 1924 Fordham and New York University law schools fell in line by adopting a one-year rule. The following year the University of Buffalo and the Brooklyn law school did likewise, and last year (1926) the Albany law school and the New York law school took the first step." [1] Kansas in 1921, Illinois in 1923, and several other states, including Ohio, West Virginia, Montana and Wisconsin, required two years of college work, some before beginning the study, others before the practice of law. Medical and engineering training and the courses in education given by universities—as distinguished from the more elementary instruction in the normal schools—also became generally senior-college or graduate studies.

The so-called nonprofessional graduate schools, leading to the master's or doctor's degrees, provided essential professional training for ambitious teachers. More than ever before the best city high schools expected their new teachers to have a master's degree, and most of the colleges demanded the doctorate of their young instructors, or took them on the understanding that the degree would later be obtained. As the higher degrees became pedagogical necessities, the graduate schools became crowded with applicants who had little of the true spirit of research. A committee of the North Central Association issued in 1926 a significant word of warning: ". . . this crowding of the graduate schools has been so great as to

[1] Foster Ware, "Education of the Lawyer Comes to a Test," *N. Y. Times*, Feb. 27, 1927.

raise some question as to the quality of the work done
and the value of the degree. Certainly in some way the
young, ambitious teacher should be protected as far as
possible from spending his time and money in acquiring
a graduate degree which will not be regarded favorably
by his colleagues." [1] The value of graduate instruction
was discovered by the manufacturers as well as by the
high schools and colleges. In Wisconsin before the war
the majority of those who received the doctorate in
chemistry became teachers—from 1899 to 1919 only
eight persons with that degree had entered industry. On
the other hand, of one hundred and nine who received
the degree from 1919 to 1928, fifty-six were in industrial work. [2]

The first effect of America's entrance into the war
was to paralyze ordinary academic work while spurring
into furious activity the technical courses of a military
or semimilitary character. The American University at
Washington turned over practically its entire plant for
training camps and chemical research work. [3] Most other
institutions kept their grounds and buildings, but gave
the curriculum a war-time color. Courses were launched
in the chemistry of explosives, in radio and field telegraphy, in military engineering, ship construction,
aviation, food conservation, [4] nursing, practical gardening, in the history of the war and international politics.
Many students hurried away from the campus to enlist.
In the liberal-arts colleges the loss of enrollment was
about twenty per cent; in most of the professional

[1] Committee on Graduate Degrees, North Central Assoc., *North Central
Quar.*, I, no. 2, 216.
[2] Am. Assoc. of Univ. Professors, *Bull.*, XIV, 621.
[3] P. R. Kolbe, *The Colleges in Wartime and After* (N. Y., 1919),
124-125.
[4] "This is the most general of all college war courses." Kolbe, *Colleges
in Wartime*, 110.

schools it was still greater.[1] The teaching of German decreased in two years by about forty per cent.[2] In 1918 the government organized in most of the important colleges and universities units of a Students' Army Training Corps, designed to give technical instruction which would fit students to become either field officers or experts in special branches of service—such as the medical corps, engineering and chemical warfare—before the draft, now lowered to the age of eighteen, brought them into the ranks.

The temporary transformation of the American college into a sort of officers' training camp necessitated much difficult readjustment after the armistice. The purely military courses were abandoned, or lingered only as drill offered, usually on a voluntary basis, for the Reserve Officers' Training Corps. The faculty had to be reassembled from industrial plants, censorship offices, experimental munition laboratories, the Red Cross, the Y. M. C. A. and the advisory staff of the peace commission. The students, in the majority of cases, resumed their interrupted classes, bringing with them a horde of newcomers: wounded veterans seizing the chance at a college education which the nation allowed them, farmers' sons riding on the crest of the brief wave of agricultural prosperity, young business men converted by the war into a belief in the commercial value of college training, high-school boys whose college entrance had been temporarily delayed by war conditions. Lecture rooms that had been more than ample in 1916 offered scant standing room in 1919. Laboratory courses had to turn away students who could not be provided with desks. Quiz sections were offered to young graduate students with any sort of passable academic record.

[1] Kolbe, *Colleges in Wartime,* 127-131.
[2] Kolbe, *Colleges in Wartime,* 103-106.

The greatest, or at least most pressing, problems were all financial. Building costs had doubled and new construction had been patriotically postponed during the war. Nearly every institution in the country found itself in cramped, inadequate quarters and with insufficient funds on hand for the necessary new building. All kinds of equipment, from lawn mowers on the campus to the current newspapers in the library, and all kinds of service, from the janitor in the basement to the stenographer in the president's office, commanded a higher price. At the same time the increase in student enrollment necessitated new courses and a larger staff of instruction. The salary of the faculty had been virtually cut to half by the rise in the cost of living, and the universities shared the fear of the elementary and secondary schools of a "flight from the profession." Every endowed institution girded its loins for a campaign among its alumni for new gifts, using much the same methods of persuasive appeal found fruitful in the liberty-loan drives of the war. Every tax-supported institution besieged the legislatures for a more generous share in the public budget.[1]

The generosity of the response from private donors and taxpayers alike was remarkable. A British report at the end of the war showed that private benefactions to universities and colleges in the United States were over twenty times as great as in the United Kingdom.[2]

[1] Sometimes several institutions would join forces in a common publicity campaign, perhaps the most notable instance being the collective appeal by the presidents of the best known women's colleges, Barnard, Bryn Mawr, Mount Holyoke, Radcliffe, Smith, Vassar and Wellesley. "The Question of the Women's Colleges," *Atlantic Mo.*, CXL (1927), 577-584. For a criticism of incompetent financial management by the colleges, see W. B. Munro, "Are Our Colleges Playing Poor?," *Atlantic Mo.*, CXLII (1928), 433-440, and also the rejoinder by W. A. Neilson, "Women's Colleges Reply," *Atlantic Mo.*, CXLIII (1929), 111-115.

[2] J. E. Barker, *America's Secret* (London, 1927), 222. See also the comparisons in D. R. Fox, "The Economics of Higher Education in Great Britain," *Polit. Sci. Quar.*, XLIV, 1-15.

An American High School

Rockefeller and Carnegie found many imitators, and the wealth accumulated in tobacco, chocolate and cameras went as readily to educational purposes as the wealth formerly accumulated in oil or steel. Milton S. Hershey, the "chocolate king," donated in 1918 about sixty million dollars for the industrial education of orphan children. George Eastman, inventor of the Kodak, gave about fifty million to higher education, and made Rochester one of the richest institutions of the East. James B. Duke, tobacco manufacturer, expanded Trinity College, North Carolina, into Duke University and made it the wealthiest institution in the South.[1] At the beginning of 1929 the Rockefeller Foundation was merged with the Laura Spelman Rockefeller Memorial (founded in 1918) to form a new corporation with assets of more than a quarter of a billion dollars, "by far the greatest sum which has ever been concentrated in a single philanthropic endowment fund."[2] Many new funds, such as the Commonwealth Fund and the John Simon Guggenheim Memorial Foundation, gave opportunity for scientific research and travel. A score of universities and technological institutes raised their endowments beyond the ten-million mark. The state universities and agricultural colleges spent collectively in 1926-1927 over a hundred millions for maintenance and over twenty millions for new buildings.[3]

Yet with all this enlargement of funds the universities were much in the plight of Lewis Carroll's Alice in *Through the Looking Glass* who found that she had to run as fast as she could to stay in the same place. The expansion of numbers and the increase of costs absorbed the most munificent gifts and still left many serious in-

[1] *Literary Digest,* LXXXIII, 36 (Dec. 27, 1924).

[2] *N. Y. Times,* Jan. 4, 1929.

[3] J. C. Schmidtmann, "State Universities Add Billions to Nation's Wealth," *Current History,* XXVI (1927), 206.

336 THE GREAT CRUSADE AND AFTER

adequacies. For example, though the average salary of all ranks of instruction in three hundred and two liberal-arts colleges had risen from $1724 in 1914-1915 to $2958 in 1926-1927, yet the buying power of the latter was only about a hundred dollars more than the buying power of the former.[1] The increase of nearly thirty per cent from 1919-1920 to 1926-1927, however, was a real increase as it came at a time of falling prices and restored the losses of 1914-1920. In 1923 an investigation of the family budgets of half the married members of the University of California faculty (where salary scales were far above the national mean) showed that these families spent an average $900 for food, "a sum that passes everywhere just now as the cost of minimum food requirements for those living at a subsistence plus level," that "two-thirds of the husbands and one-half of the wives spent annually between $100 and $200 each for their personal wardrobes," and that "ten per cent of these wives of professional men spent nothing for help in their housework. Fifteen per cent paid $25 or less during the year. . . . No family with a total expenditure below $6000 had a full-time resident help." [2]

The need for rapid expansion of educational facilities affected the American teacher unfavorably in several ways. It dispersed over new courses and a larger staff the funds that might have been used to raise the salary of the existing faculty, it made some presidents and trustees timid of offending wealthy givers and thus endangered academic freedom, and it imposed on the uni-

[1] General Education Board statement, *N. Y. Times*, Dec. 29, 1928.
[2] Jessica B. Peixotto, "Family Budgets of University Faculty Members," *Science*, LXVIII, 497-501 (Nov. 23, 1928). See also *Getting and Spending at the Professional Standard of Living* (N. Y., 1927) by the same author; Yandell Henderson and M. R. Davie, eds., *Incomes and Living Costs of a University Faculty* (New Haven, 1928), and Rodney H. True, "The Economic Status of Scientific Men and Women," *Science*, LXX, 47-56 (July 19, 1929).

versity or college an autocratic political structure. Faculty control does very well under European conditions, where an anciently endowed institution has only routine administrative tasks and can devote its main energies to teaching and research. But where an institution is rapidly developing from a college of a few hundred to a university of ten thousand, where millions of dollars must be raised within three or four years, where a rigid classical curriculum is being rapidly broadened into an elective system which offers every imaginable course from aeronautics to cemetery planning, where the university is expected to serve a whole state with extension courses, correspondence work, loan libraries and agricultural demonstration stations, there is imperative need for an executive of the "captain-of-industry" type. Under such conditions the president becomes a general manager responsible to a board of regents or trustees as "directors," the deans are managers and division superintendents, the department heads are foremen, the rank and file of the teaching staff employees, the students are the raw material, and the alumni the manufactured product, bearing the "college stamp" and, too frequently, standardized on a single pattern.

Against this system many voices of protest were raised. J. McKeen Cattell, Thorstein Veblen, J. E. Kirkpatrick and many others of the "professoriat" advocated the establishment of a system of faculty control.[1] The American Association of University Professors kept vigilant watch for local violations of academic liberty and its reports are the most accurate source book for that subject. In the South the chief danger was the Fundamentalist attack on evolution which caused three states,

[1] J. M. Cattell, "Academic Slavery," *School and Society*, VI, 421-426 (Oct. 13, 1917) ; T. B. Veblen, *The Higher Learning in America* (N. Y., 1918) ; J. E. Kirkpatrick, *The American College and Its Rulers* (N. Y., 1926).

Tennessee, Mississippi and Arkansas, to forbid the teaching of man's animal ancestry in any tax-supported institution. In the North the attack shifted from the religious to the political and economic front, and internationalism, pacifism and all the shades of socialism were
the chief quarries of the heresy hunters.

The indefatigable crusader Upton Sinclair attempted
to show in *The Goose Step* (1923) that all the colleges
and universities in the United States were bound hand
and foot to capitalism. This thesis was at once exaggerated and inadequate—exaggerated because interference
by wealthy donors or trustees was the exception, not the
rule, and inadequate because such pressure was but one
of many enemies to academic freedom. Yet in the bag of
chaff were several grains of truth. The shadow of wealth
hoped for was a much greater danger than the substance
of wealth given, for the latter was usually given with
few conditions and spent without much deference to the
opinions of the donors. John E. Kirkpatrick was dismissed in 1926 from Olivet College in Michigan on
the avowed ground that his views on faculty control
were displeasing to wealthy friends of the institution,
though this degree of frankness was highly exceptional.[1]
One of the most thoroughly investigated cases of the
dismissal of an admittedly competent professor for his
economic views was that of Louis Levine (Lewis Lor-
win) at the University of Montana in 1919. At the re-
quest of the chancellor, he had prepared some studies of
taxation. The conclusions reached favored heavier taxation of the copper-mining interests and the chancellor,
fearing a political fight that would injure the university,
forbade the publication of Dr. Levine's findings and suspended him for insubordination when he refused to
acquiesce. Prompt agitation of the case resulted in Pro-

[1] *School and Society*, XXIII, 810 (June 26, 1926).

fessor Levine's reinstatement by the state board of education.[1] The fear of "capitalist" influence led the University of Wisconsin to refuse all further financial aid from private philanthropic foundations—perhaps an excessive scruple. It would be easy to match every such case as that of Professor Levine with a dozen where no principle at all was involved and dismissal came as the result of a purely local, personal or factional disagreement within the university. The real menace to the independence of the teacher was not capitalism, but insecurity of tenure and the absence of a deeply rooted tradition of free speech.

There was a strong tendency towards educational innovation and experiment, resulting partly from the dislocation of accustomed methods by the war and the increased student load, partly from the desire to break away somehow from the "education-factory" standardization with which the universities were threatened. Harvard University, as in all periods of American history, was one of the pioneers. Among the devices there tried were comprehensive final examinations for all seniors to test their mastery of an entire field of study, such as economics or literature; a large force of tutors to encourage independent reading outside the formal courses; and a period of term time without lectures to be entirely devoted to study and self-education. Perhaps the most discussed innovation, and one which met with considerable criticism from students, was the construction of dormitory units within the university, not unlike the individual "colleges" inside Oxford or Cambridge. Special independent work for honors, in which reading and consultation with the professor displaced in large part at-

[1] Am. Assoc. of Univ. Professors, *Bull.*, V, no. 5, 13-25. See also Am. Assoc. of Univ. Professors, *Bull.*, XV, no. 8, 578-591, for an instance of penalized radicalism at the University of Pittsburgh as late as 1929.

tendance at lectures or examinations in course, was found in many institutions, notably Columbia and Swarthmore. Independent work for honors was in part an approach to the English distinction between "pass" students who desired only a general cultural education and "honors" students with genuine scholarly interests and in part an attempt to break down the arbitrary slicing of the living unity of education into courses, "points" and "hours," which had given to American higher education so mechanical an aspect.[1]

On a small, what might almost be termed a laboratory, scale, some institutions dropped the lock step of courses altogether. President Hamilton Holt abolished the compulsory lecture system in Rollins College, Florida, and substituted conference work for the whole school. Alexander Meiklejohn, president of Amherst College from 1912 to 1924, worked out a plan which merged the work of several departments into one comprehensive study of classical civilization and, after the trustees of Amherst had terminated his presidency, disliking his radical innovations as well as his financial management, President Glenn Frank of Wisconsin called him in 1926 to carry through the experiment there.[2] Since Wisconsin was too large a university to remodel its entire curriculum on the new plan, a special experimental college was created within the university and housed in a special dormitory. Bennington College for Women, Ashland College (Michigan), and several other small

---

[1] A detailed account of the honors work offered by more than a hundred American universities and colleges was prepared by President Frank Aydelotte of Swarthmore, "Honors Courses in American Colleges and Universities," Natl. Research Council, *Bull.*, X, no. 52, 1-96, supplementing his first *Bull.*, VII, no. 40.

[2] Alexander Meiklejohn, *The Experimental College* (Univ. of Wis., *Bull.*, 1928), and *The First Year of the Experimental College* published by its "pioneer class" (Madison, 1928). See also R. M. Lovett, "Meiklejohn at Madison," *New Republic*, LV, 193-195 (July 11, 1928).

experimental groups for education by association and discussion rather than by formal instruction were significant new ventures at the end of the period. The summer lectures by distinguished European statesmen at Williamstown, Massachusetts, afforded a type of advanced study in the realities of international politics to professors as well as to students.

Former President Eliot of Harvard shortly before his death referred to Antioch College as "the most interesting and perhaps the most important experiment now going on in the whole range of American education."[1] A little college in Ohio, first directed by Horace Mann, Antioch was completely reorganized by President Arthur E. Morgan as an "in-and-out" combination of cultural college and industrial school. Students were encouraged to take five or six years to obtain the degree, but in the meantime they spent about half their time in actual industrial employment in neighboring cities. To hold down the job, two students would ordinarily go into partnership and alternate with each other between the college and the shop or factory.[2]

The most common complaint against the American college was neither the capitalistic conservatism of the trustees nor the pedagogical pedantry of the faculty, but the light-hearted carelessness of the students, who seemed apt, in the punning popular phrase, to interpret "college bred" as equivalent to a "four years' loaf." As a matter of fact, the attitude of the student body was, on the

[1] *Literary Digest*, LXXIX, 28 (Nov. 17, 1923).

[2] Minor reforms and innovations were widely adopted throughout the land; for example, orientation and survey courses, such as the "contemporary civilization" course at Columbia; "new-type" examinations, which could be more objectively graded; and the sectioning of classes on the basis of ability. Some critics charged that university presidents thought more of heralding some striking new project or method than of soberly building up a strong teaching force in the traditional departments. See, for instance, W. B. Munro, "Quack-doctoring the Colleges," *Harper's Mag.*, CLVII (1928), 478-482.

whole, better than that of the preceding generation. Not only did there seem to be less drunkenness,[1] but there was certainly less hazing and general riotousness. Standards of admission and graduation were almost everywhere more exacting than ever before—the heroes of George Fitch's delightful "Siwash" stories might well have been dismissed from a postwar college in their first semester. Athletic contests were, on the whole, cleaner and less brutal and, though much more costly, were probably not more absorbing.[2]

Yet there were undoubtedly some symptoms which might cause not unreasonable disquiet. Social life in coeducational institutions became yearly more feverishly intense. Dancing was a universal convention, and the formal balls, "proms" and "hops" became extremely expensive affairs. Campus organizations multiplied beyond all reason, some large universities containing several hundred clubs, associations and fraternities. What with campus politics, social activities and athletics, the average student was content to keep up with the required reading in his courses and not venture on any independent reading above the level of the magazine stand. Debating fell on evil days and, except in a few colleges like Bates, was scorned and neglected. The literary societies and magazines, which two or three generations before had been the chief relaxation from the steady grind of study, now usually languished in poverty or ceased altogether. The only types of publication that prospered were the daily or weekly news sheet, valued for information as to campus doings, and the monthly comic paper. Now and then would appear an "outlaw" paper, such as *Challenge* at Columbia in 1916 or G. D. Eaton's *Tempest* which ran a brief career at Michigan, as the expression of a small knot of discontented stu-

[1] See earlier, chap. iv.   [2] See earlier, chap. x.

dents, but such ventures rarely survived more than a year or two.

Aside from athletics, fraternity life and purely commercial journalism, the only important student activity in most colleges was dramatics. In the staging and acting of plays, and occasionally in their authorship, American students displayed remarkable aptitude. Literary societies gave revivals of Elizabethan plays; classical clubs revived the Greek drama; modern-language societies presented French, German and Spanish comedies, often in the original; dramatic associations boldly undertook Ibsen, Molnar, Capek or Shaw; and there was often, in addition, a huge comic opera with elaborate costumes and topical hits. In spite of the despotic reign of jazz, glee clubs, varsity bands and student orchestras were frequently capable of real music; and many students sketched admirably, the illustrations in the comic papers being as good as their jokes were feeble. Perhaps in the field of the drama and the fine arts, so greatly neglected by the "colleges of arts," the American student was beginning to find a field of intellectual self-expression.

The unspoken questions of many parents found voice in an article by I. M. Rubinow, "The Revolt of a Middle-Aged Father," who estimated the average annual cost of sending a student to college at fifteen hundred dollars a year to the parents, not to mention the social cost of supporting the institutions from philanthropy or taxation and the postponement of active business life for four critical years.[1] Even granting that students were not more idle or mischievous than formerly, their parents were paying more for their good times, and many more were paying. Could society endure the cost of burdening middle age so heavily for the pleasure of the younger generation? Various critics of the article con-

[1] *Atlantic Mo.*, CXXXIX (1927), 593-604.

curred in thinking that fifteen hundred dollars a year was an overestimate or, at all events, applicable only to the more expensive institutions. For the nation as a whole, eight hundred dollars a year seems closer to the average.[1] Moreover, much of the expense was shouldered by the students themselves. The bureau of education ascertained that nearly half of the men and almost a quarter of the women students earned all or part of their own expense while in residence.[2] Complete self-support was perhaps more rare than formerly, because only the exceptional student could carry a full schedule of classes and earn from six to twelve hundred dollars in leisure hours or during summer vacation.

One asset of the larger American universities was the considerable attendance of foreign students who flocked to the United States in even greater numbers than the Americans who had gone to German institutions a generation earlier. The Institute of International Education found in 1923-1924 nearly seven thousand foreign students in four hundred American institutions.[3] A very large proportion were Orientals. In a single institution within a brief period there was an Egyptian, a Chinese and a Japanese on the football squad, a Filipino captain of the swimming team, and an East Indian captain of the polo team.[4] European students often came to the United States on traveling fellowships. American postgraduate work was considered by many critics as superior to that in Europe, while the undergraduate work was often inferior.

[1] M. J. Moses, "The Cost of College," Good Housekeeping, LXXXV (1927), no. 5, 247-248, circularized six hundred college presidents on Mr. Rubinow's contentions and summarized their findings.

[2] This conclusion was based on data collected from 763 colleges and universities. U. S. Daily, Jan. 18, 1929.

[3] D. A. Robertson, ed., American Universities and Colleges (N. Y., 1928), 865.

[4] Robertson, American Universities and Colleges, 49.

CHAPTER XIII

JOURNALISM AND ADVERTISEMENT

IN the first rank of American educational agencies must be placed the news items in daily papers and periodicals and the advertising pages of both. These were true continuation schools which influenced the adult perhaps more profoundly than school textbooks did the child. One notes, it is true, a certain growing skepticism, a "sales resistance" to news page, editorial and advertisement alike, a tendency to say "You can't believe all you read in the papers," but, after all, even an incredulous generation must acquire information and ideas from some source, and journalism was by far the most convenient. From colonial times the American public, more than any other in the world, had been an omnivorous devourer of news, any sort of news about any part of the world, provided only that it were fresh and written so that it could be quickly read. The World War quickened this interest,[1] and the vast expansion of advertising in the subsequent business boom enabled the press to be more lavish with space than ever before. The domestic production of newsprint was not much greater in 1927 than in 1914, but imports from Canada were more than six times as great, and more than twice as much was consumed. The index price of newsprint tripled from 1913 to 1920, though it eventually became stable at about a seventy-per-cent increase over the former year. The bulk of newspaper and periodical advertising approximately doubled.[2]

[1] See earlier, chap. i.   [2] *Commerce Yearbook for 1928*, I, 553-566.

Several tendencies in the newspaper world were dominant after 1914: consolidation of ownership, an expansion in size and the addition of novel special features, and a standardization and syndication of material. In all these respects journalism merely followed the general trend of American business to consolidate into larger, more efficient and more impersonal units. The World War sadly clipped the wings of the war correspondent; at best he could add only a few descriptive touches to the official bulletins of the warring governments. The personality of the editor was merged in his paper, though this phenomenon was not new to American life. Only a few of the old type of personal journalists remained, and most of them lived in the small towns. No editor in New York, for instance, had the individual quality of William Allen White of the *Emporia Gazette*. Though journalism was a bigger business than ever, it was also more strictly a business than ever.

Except in the magazine field, this concentration was not of the European type, that is, concentration in a single city. New York newspapers did not dominate the United States as Parisian newspapers did France. They circulated widely outside the metropolis, especially in their (half-magazine) Sunday editions, but did not in any way displace the local papers of Chicago, Philadelphia, Boston or other large cities. The size of the nation and the reluctance of the American reader to wait a day or two, or even a few hours, for the latest news guaranteed a local group of papers to each considerable city. With periodicals, where timeliness of news was less important, New York was almost another London or Paris to the nation. Except for the Curtis publications in Philadelphia and certain magazines of scholarly appeal in Boston, few periodicals of national importance were printed elsewhere. True even in 1914, it was still truer in 1928. In the former year, for example, Springfield, Ohio, was the publishing center for the *American Magazine*, for *Farm and Fireside,* and for several other periodicals of very wide circulation; in the latter year both of these publications were dated from New York and some others had either gone to the metropolis or pushed farther west out of its immediate radius. But, in the main, concentration was economic rather than geographic, and took place in two ways: reduction in the number of competing papers in each city, and the development of chains of newspapers under a common ownership in several cities, an interesting parallel to the chain hotels and chain groceries which multiplied so rapidly at the same period.

There were nearly two thousand fewer publications in the United States in 1929 than in 1914.[1] This falling off did not imply a decrease in readers. The aggregate circulation of daily newspapers in the United States and Canada by 1929 reached over forty million, divided between evening and morning papers in the proportion of two to one, and Sunday papers sold over twenty-six million copies. The aggregate subscription lists for all types of newspaper and periodical, including the weekly and monthly magazines, increased by more than a quarter in the decade after 1914.[2] The weekly barely held its own in circulation and greatly decreased in number of publications; the semiweekly and triweekly, mostly rural or small-town types, tended towards extinction. The daily, on the other hand—the Sunday edition of the daily in particular—flourished. The greatest gain of all was that of the monthly magazines which grew from

[1] *American Newspaper Annual and Directory* (1914, 1929). The actual figures were 22,977 in 1914 and 21,057 in 1929. If Canada and Newfoundland be included the figures are 24,527 and 22,619 respectively.

[2] W. A. Dill, *Growth of Newspapers in the United States* (Lawrence, Kan., 1928), 29.

seventy-nine million subscribers in 1914 to one hundred and eleven million in 1925.

In the small towns consolidation meant that a single newspaper rather than several served the county seat and the country districts around it. The *New York World* estimated in 1928 that there were a thousand American cities in which the press was monopolized in the hands of a single paper or a group of papers with a single ownership.

> A generation ago nearly every considerable city had its Democratic and Republican organ. . . . The largest cities had four, six or eight newspapers, nearly all with decisive political convictions; and no school of thought lacked its expression. But today real discussion is being submerged. . . . A great and growing section of our population has no choice but to take a newspaper that is either colorlessly neutral or wholly one-sided.[1]

The new consolidated organ, having to please the whole community, was usually content to reprint syndicated editorials on national affairs and comment on local matters in a way to make the fewest possible enemies. To select one typical instance from a thousand, the Democratic *Laramie Boomerang* (Laramie, Wyoming), whose quaint name dates back to Bill Nye, was merged with its Republican rival, the *Laramie Republican,* and thus a party duel which had existed for more than a generation ended in a placid unity.

In the cities consolidation eliminated some of the historic mammoths of American journalism. New York City furnished the most striking series of mergers. From 1914 to 1924 New York was reduced from seventeen to eleven general newspapers (not counting suburban or foreign-language dailies). Frank A. Munsey, a rather

[1] *N. Y. World* (editorial), Aug. 26, 1928.

colorless capitalist of journalism, owned the *Telegram* and the *Sun*. In a few months' space he merged the *Mail* with the *Telegram*, extinguished the well-edited and liberal *Globe* in the rays of the *Sun*, and acquired the historic *Herald* and sold it to Mr. Ogden Reid of the *Tribune*. The *Evening Post*, a paper of high literary traditions, sold out to a Philadelphia company, and the Socialist *Call* became silent. In fifteen years Chicago lost five out of seven morning papers. Detroit cut its morning papers from three to one while growing fivefold in population.[1]

Chains of newspapers, already formed before the war, continued to grow and new ones made their appearance. The Hearst chain was perhaps the best known. In more than twenty cities William Randolph Hearst was represented by a personal organ to further his political and economic ideas and interests. Once purveying to the public a sort of urbanized Bryanism, the Hearst papers after 1914 became increasingly conservative, giving general support to the Coolidge administration and upholding the financial policy of the most conservative wing of the Republican party. In foreign affairs they advocated an aggressive attitude towards Mexico, where Hearst had important investments, abstention from the League of Nations, and a watchful suspicion of Japan and, until 1928, of the British Empire.

The Scripps-Howard group closely rivaled the Hearst papers in distribution across the face of the nation, differing chiefly in locating by preference in cities of moderate size. They were, on the whole, creditably independent and outspoken in their policy and did much to

[1] The facts as to these consolidations are excellently stated in two magazine articles that appeared on the same day: Will Irwin, "Newspapers and Canned Thought," *Collier's*, LXXIII, 13 ff. (June 21, 1924), and R. L. McCardell, "Our Newspapers Now—and Then," *Sat. Eve. Post*, CXCVI, 18 ff. (June 21, 1924).

clear up local abuses in several cities where they became established. There was also the Munsey chain, the group owned by James M. Cox of Ohio, Democratic presidential candidate in 1920, the Lee group, the Shaffer group and several others. From 1923 to 1927 the number of chains doubled and the number of newspapers which they controlled increased by half.[1] The chain newspapers enjoyed much the same advantages as chain enterprises in other industries: the ability to buy raw material (chiefly newsprint paper in this case) at quantity prices, the ability to furnish all their units with standardized features at a single cost, and the ability to maintain high-salaried managers.

The fundamental reason why a newspaper of moderate circulation could not prosper, especially in a large city, was the high cost of paper. Deforestation, the war, the rise of wages and the increase of demand for wood pulp had all contributed to this increase. Printers, typesetters and other employees who represented the mechanical side of journalism had doubled and trebled their wages, adding again to the overhead cost. The popular demand for attractive "features," and for sufficient reading matter to carry the necessary advertising without turning the paper into a mere department-store catalogue, compelled the newspapers to increase their bulk to three or four times what it had been before the war. The *Detroit News,* one of the most prosperous of all evening papers, apologized in 1928 for raising its daily price to three cents a copy on the ground that "the cost of the white paper alone on which it is printed is in excess of a million and a half dollars per year more than the total revenue from its circulation." [2] Such a maga-

---

[1] Silas Bent, "Adding One Newspaper to Another," *Century,* CXV (1927), 90.

[2] *Detroit News* announcement of April 2, 1928.

zine as the weekly *Saturday Evening Post,* often running to over two hundred pages in a single issue, gave the reader several times as much money value in sheer weight of paper as the nickel it demanded in exchange. Only copious advertising could meet the situation, and only very wide circulation could attract the advertising. The proportion of newspaper costs paid from subscriptions fell from four tenths to three tenths in the decade after 1914,[1] in spite of the fact that the "penny paper" had almost vanished, and newspapers of general circulation usually cost two, three or five cents a copy, and often ten cents on Sunday. Don C. Seitz of the *New York World* declared that he would not undertake to establish a regular daily in a large city for less than ten million dollars,[2] and Will Irwin, a veteran of both the old and the new journalism, declared that no metropolitan daily could prosper unless assured of a circulation of at least one hundred thousand.[3]

Of course, the reader got more for his money in this era of newspaper trusts, in news as well as in newsprint. "In 1900, fourteen pages was a good run for the *New York Times,*" wrote Charles Merz in 1926; "now four times fourteen pages is not unheard of in Saint Louis." When the Republican national convention met at Cleveland in 1924, one hundred and fifty news circuits handled fifty words a minute. "When Washington played Pittsburgh in the first game of the 1925 World Series a circuit of 46,500 miles was hooked into a single telegraphic system never behind the news two seconds. When Bryan and Darrow fought over John T. Scopes at Dayton, Tennessee, that small village was actually the shipping point for two million words of telegraphic

[1] Dill, *Growth of Newspapers in the United States,* 76.
[2] O. G. Villard, "The Disappearing Daily," *Forum,* LXXIX (1928), 275.
[3] Irwin, "Newspapers and Canned Thought," 13.

news within ten days." [1] All European journals, with the exception of the *London Times*, looked meager to the American reader accustomed to his acres of print and, without even that exception, they seemed needlessly dull and badly arranged. The technical improvements made possible by better presses, better means of photographic reproduction, and the great volume of advertising revenues to bear the cost, kept more than pace with the better means of gathering and conveying information afforded by huge news syndicates and press bureaus. Many new kinds of service to the public were added, such as radio broadcasting, initiated by the WWJ station of the *Detroit News*. Such feats as the transmission of the radio photograph of Einstein's pamphlet on new mathematical theory, published in the *New York Evening Post* in February, 1929, testify to the amazing technical progress and the even more amazing catholicity of interest of the American press.

The side shows threatened to swallow the main tent. In one hundred and ten daily newspapers in sixty-three cities in 1924, forty-five per cent of all the space was occupied by advertising, either of commercial goods or classified personal "want ads," a great increase over the one third so allotted twenty-five years before. Illustrations and special features encroached heavily on the news columns; general news, in fact, averaged only twenty-two per cent of the contents. Editorials were much subordinated, covering hardly more than two per cent of the space, and public opinion, as voiced by letters to the editor, amounted to but half of one per cent. News columns rather than editorials or letters made opinion.[2]

Newspapers had, indeed, become departmentalized to

[1] Charles Merz, "The American Press," *Century*, CXIII (1926), 104.
[2] *Editor and Publisher*, May 31, 1924. See also *Nation*, CXVIII, 725 (June 25, 1924), and for another survey *Literary Digest*, XCVIII, 30 (Aug. 4, 1928).

the last degree. The journal had to cater to all tastes; to omit even the most trivial column would offend some special group of subscribers. Among the expected features in an average city paper were: a sporting section, rivaling in length the whole news section; a real-estate section, sometimes (as in Florida or Detroit) the largest part of the paper; moving-picture announcements and programs; radio announcements and programs; medical advice by some popularizer of hygiene; a column of advice to investors, with answers to questions; two or three columns of advice to the "lovelorn" by Dorothy Dix, Beatrice Fairfax or other accredited experts on domestic relations; puzzles and all sorts of engaging brain-teasers; comic strips, cartoons and columns of jest. In the Sunday edition one might also find: two sections of rotogravure pictures; from eight to ten pages of colored comics; a collection of short stories, humorous or sentimental; syndicated essays and editorials of an inspirational sort, such as those by Frank Crane and Bruce Barton; a section or two for women's and children's interest; some pages of "wonders of science"; and, in the "yellow journals," a section of "society scandals" about the English aristocracy, the Hollywood colony of actresses, or some other fashionable group.

The amount of space devoted to sport, scandals and humor alarmed many critics.[1] Most newspapers deplored the emphasis on sensationalism, but to very few did any thought of personal responsibility occur. Former President Charles W. Eliot of Harvard, generally considered the leader of American education, died on August 22, 1926, and Rudolph Valentino, the moving-picture actor, the following day. Though many newspapers printed editorials solemnly deploring that so

[1] For example, Silas Bent, *Ballyhoo, the Voice of the Press* (N. Y., 1927).

much more interest was taken in the death of Valentino, the same papers in their news columns devoted a page to the actor for every column they gave to the educator. In the same way many a newspaper would condemn gambling on its editorial page and print the odds on the horse races on its sporting page, or write a sermon-editorial on the American ideal of the purity of the home while devoting a whole section of the same issue to realistic descriptions and illustrations of the most sordid divorce scandals. This inconsistency was too open to be called hypocrisy; it meant merely that the newspaper was a business enterprise devoted to selling what the market was believed to demand, not what the editor might sincerely wish the public to prefer. The *Christian Science Monitor* of Boston continued to be almost the only nationally important daily which refused to print the details of sensational and scandalous events. A single murder case boosted the total circulation of the New York papers a million copies in a single day.[1]

One mushroom growth of American journalism made scandal its specialty and deliberately appealed to a type of reader who cared for nothing but headlines and illustrations. This was the "tabloid," first popularized in England by Lord Northcliffe and imported into the United States after the war for a new and more tropical flowering. The *Daily News,* fathered by the *Chicago Tribune* immediately after the war, was the first of the New York tabloids and the most successful. Hearst's *Mirror* and Bernarr Macfadden's *Evening Graphic* followed in close imitation.[2] As very little paper was re-

[1] Silas Bent, "Roller Coaster Journalism," *Sat. Rev. of Literature,* IV, 884 (May 19, 1928), reprinted in *Strange Bedfellows* (N. Y., 1928), chap. xii.

[2] O. G. Villard, "Sex, Art, Truth and Magazines," *Atlantic Mo.,* CXXXVII (1926), 388-398; and Jo Swerling, "The Picture Papers Win," *Nation,* CXXI, 455-458 (Oct. 21, 1925).

Daily Record

2 SHOT IN $204,500 HOLD-UP

Panic Reigns as Bandits Raid Armored Car in Yonkers

Armed with a sub-machine gun, repeating rifles and long-barreled automatics, from which slugs streaked and bullets rained, a band of desperate bandits today attacked a steel-armored money car in the very heart of Yonkers, wounded two men, threw hundreds into panic
and escaped with four
heavy canvas sacks con-
taining $104,500 in cash,
and securities valued at
another $100,000.

For technique and pure
recklessness the robbery
is without parallel in the
East, and the amount in-
volved is the largest ever
stolen in Westchester
county.

The wounded men are:
Adolph Kautter, a guard
on the truck, who was shot
after obeying the command
of the desperadoes to, raise
his arms.

Patrolman Patrick O'Keefe
of the Yonkers force, who
was riding on the front seat
with the driver and who
never had a chance to draw
his own revolver.

Two automobiles of the sedan
type were abandoned at the scene
of the crime and the other found
later at Jerome and Featal Ave-
nues. So far there are the only
clues authorities have succeeded in
unearthing and both these are expected to prove worthless, as has
been

Pandemonium Reigns

For five minutes shot rattled
against shot, bullets whined against
fronts as the bandits, seven in number, poured their fire from the varied assortment of weapons.

During that frightful period the
neighborhood of Jerome avenue and
Buena Vista Avenue was stripped
in a veritable rain of terror. Wom-
en fainted, children screamed,
momentarily. Pandemonium raged.
Before police reserve could ar-

Boy Shoots 9 Chicago Detectives

Three Girls Nabbed as Shoplifters

LOSE GAME OF "GRAB AND RUN"—Three east side girls are held in Flatbush court in $2,500 bail on
shoplifting charges, where the detective shows them with their attorney, who lost in plea for smaller bail. They
are, left to right, Mary La Rose, Mary Vallaro and Frances Corodentio.

(Daily Graphic)

Link Jersey Child Slayer Fiend With Many Unsolved Murders

17 RIOT SQUADS HELD AT BAY IN 5-HOUR BATTLE

CHICAGO, Dec. 12 (By U.
P.).—Nine policemen were
wounded today, in attempting to capture a negro boy,
who had barricaded himself
in a two-story brick house on
the North Side.

The battle, which ended with the
killing of the youth, Frank Whithurst, 16, was one of the most spectacular in the long history of Chicago crime.

Seventeen police squads of five
men each, led by deputy commissioners of police and detectives, par-
ticipated in the affair. Metal washing machines, dressers and wicker
boards requisitioned from nearby
homes in the negro district were
used to build barricades in the
street. From behind these impro-
vised fortresses the police battled
for five hours.

Police Use All Their Armor

All of the Police Department's
riot armor was brought to the scene
of the conflict, along with a vast
strength of supply of machine guns,
rifles, etc.

At the end of the five hours of
fighting Sam Sloop, deputy commissioner of police, Detective Tom
Connolly and Sergeant Tom
Crisp forced their way to the door
of the room from which Whithurst
had held the police army at bay.
With Whithurst's sister, Mary, they
ordered the door. Her brother stood

Journalism at its worst

quired to print a tabloid—a small magazine-sized newspaper which could readily be held in his hand while the
reader was standing in a trolley car on his way home
from work—the financial problems which beset the
standard newspaper did not exist for it. All that was
necessary for success was to pile sensation on sensation
till the news-stand circulation would mount into the
hundreds of thousands. Many of these enterprises failed;
a few had the kind of success they desired. The tabloids
contained practically no general news, as their scant
space was crowded with pictures of fair criminals or
bathing beauties, sporting and theater gossip and the
like.

Humor, or well-meant attempts at it, occupied an
unwonted share of newspaper space. Formerly the
humorous part of a newspaper had usually consisted
of one political cartoon, a column of jokes and, on Sundays only, four pages of colored pictures for the children. But in postwar journalism there were often from
eight to twelve pages of colored comics on Sunday and
anywhere from two to ten daily "comic strips," which
were the same sort of thing without the color, quite
apart from joke columns or cartoons or the pleasant
facetiousness of the "column." Some column editors,
such as F. P. A. (Franklin P. Adams), Don Marquis
and Heywood Broun, were worthy to rank with the
Mr. Dooley (Finley P. Dunne) who had amused the
earlier years of the century or even with Mark Twain
on his more journalistic side: true satirists and ironists
posing as fools at the court of King Demos. "Yesterday the 'personal journalism' of those old giants,
Greeley, the Bennetts, Dana, Watterson, and their like
ruled the circus ring of journalism," wrote C. L. Edson.
"Today we see the grand entry of the clowns. . . .
The names of the newspaper clowns obscure the fame

of the editor and the owner. And thus we find that personal journalism is still with us." [1]

Almost as much might be claimed on behalf of the better comic-strip artists, some of whom were skilled draftsmen worthy of comparison with the classic caricaturists of *Punch,* and other satirists who could point a moral as effectively as Hogarth. [2] Fontaine Fox's sketches of Toonerville were a more genial and therefore more effective satire on American small-town life than Sinclair Lewis's *Main Street* or its hundred imitators. C. A. Briggs's "Mr. and Mrs." was a more searchingly realistic depiction of average married life than any novelist of the period was able to portray. When Andy Gump ran for Congress in 1922, the election-night crowds cheered him more than they did any of the real flesh-and-blood candidates. Some comic-strip artists even attempted, with less success, to be deliberately educational, and pictures of the "story of mankind," "the story of the Bible" and even "the story of philosophy" appeared on the same pages with "Mutt and Jeff" or "Our Boarding House." On the other hand, purely political cartooning was never, since the days of Nast, so little regarded by the public.

Though the influence of the press had largely passed from editorial to news columns, many newspapers still made history as well as recorded it. By giving publicity to local crime or municipal scandals on every day's front page, a paper could convince the voters that there was a "crime wave" or graft epidemic even if they disbelieved what the editorials might say about the administration. The influence of the press, however, was more

[1] C. L. Edson, *The Gentle Art of Columning* (N. Y., 1920), 119-120.

[2] Amram Schoenfeld, "The Laugh Industry," *Sat. Eve. Post,* CCII, 12 (Feb. 1, 1930), is a good account of the comic strips and their social significance.

effective in special crusades than in general politics. The political bias of a newspaper is always more or less discounted by its readers, but an appeal for clean streets or shade trees on the avenue enlists at once the civic patriotism of both Republican and Democrat. The establishment of the "safe and sane Fourth of July" by ordinances limiting the sale of fireworks was the result of a newspaper and periodical campaign which is estimated to have saved several hundred lives each year.[1] Similar crusades against the public sale of firearms, needless fire risks, reckless driving and unsanitary housing were among the most important factors in making the nation safe for its citizens. A very good idea of the range and variety of these civic services can be obtained from the prizes annually given since 1917 in honor of Joseph Pulitzer for the most meritorious service rendered during the year by any American newspaper (in addition to other prizes under the same will for various literary and journalistic achievements). Thus in 1921 the *Boston Post* was rewarded for exposing the financial swindles of Get-rich-quick Ponzi, in 1923 the *Memphis Commercial Appeal* got the prize for articles on the Ku Klux Klan, and in 1924 the *New York World,* Pulitzer's own paper, was honored for exposing the Florida peonage system.

This last instance may be taken as typical of a very rapid and successful newspaper crusade. In February, 1923, the state attorney of Cavalier County, North Dakota, asked the aid of the press in an investigation of the death of Martin Tabert, a Dakota boy flogged to death the previous year in a Florida prison camp. The *World* sent a staff reporter to the spot; within ten days a series of articles, syndicated among the newspapers of thirty-

[1] N. J. Radder, *Newspapers in Community Service* (N. Y., 1926), 123.

eight cities, began to appear and, in forty-seven days
from their first publication in the *World*, Florida had
abolished the existing system of convict leasing and the
lash as a means of discipline, the judge and sheriff involved in the Tabert case were removed from office, and
the whipping boss who killed him was brought to trial
for murder.[1] Nearly every great newspaper regularly
performed some special public-welfare service which
made it stand out from the rest, such as the annual collection of charity for "the hundred neediest cases" by
the *New York Times*, the *New York Tribune*'s "fresh-
air fund" for vacations for slum children, the campaigns
of the *Chicago Tribune* against accidents and crime, the
city-beautifying activities of the *Kansas City Star* and
the *Dallas Morning News*, and the good-roads agitation
of the *Milwaukee Journal*, the *Minneapolis Tribune*
and the *Atlanta Constitution*.[2]

But with all due credit to the publicity activities of
the daily newspaper, it must be conceded that its task of
influencing opinion by direct discussion had been largely
taken over by the weekly magazines. The ten and fif-
teen-cent monthlies, which had directed reform movements in the time of Roosevelt and Taft, had now
changed the character of their appeal and raised their
prices. The *American Magazine*, though perhaps more
prosperous than ever before, specialized in the biographies of successful men rather than in the exposure
of civic evils. *Everybody's* and *McClure's* joined the
ranks of the many fiction magazines. Among the weeklies the *Saturday Evening Post* and *Collier's*, with
greatly improved make-up and wider popular appeal,

[1] "The Tabert case is unique in the history of newspaper crusades in
the swiftness with which public opinion was aroused." Radder, *Newspapers*, 159.

[2] Radder, *Newspapers*, 212-213. See also J. E. Drewry, "What Is the
Press Doing?," *Am. Rev. of Revs.*, LXXV (1927), 406-410.

very largely abandoned their radical crusades to become pillars of "Coolidge prosperity," but the *Nation*, under the editorship of Oswald Garrison Villard (separated from its union with the *New York Evening Post* in 1918), the *New Republic*, founded in 1914, and the *Freeman*, which ran a brief career for a few years after the war, were in some respects even more insurgent than the muckraking monthlies of the Roosevelt era. H. L. Mencken's *American Mercury*, a monthly established in 1924, followed a path of its own, specializing in acid criticism of all American life and institutions but having no positive gospel to present.[1]

Two weeklies of historic background dropped from the list of publications. *Harper's Weekly*, founded in 1857, merged with the *Independent* in 1916. The *Independent*, dating from 1848, had prospered during the war years under the editorship of Hamilton Holt, but the rising price of paper and a slump in advertising forced it in 1921 to sell out to the *Weekly Review*, a much more conservative publication started mainly to counteract the influence of the *Nation* and *New Republic*. After another change of ownership in 1924, the *Independent* lost its identity entirely four years later by being absorbed by its old friendly rival, the *Outlook*. The latter was now almost the sole surviving example of its type, the weekly which maintained a summary of current events and emphasized editorial comment as well.

Many periodicals were really newspapers issued at various intervals. The growing interest in convenient summaries of current events is indicated not only by the success of some established periodicals in the field, the

---

[1] Another interesting magazine enterprise of the time, Henry Holt's *Unpopular Review*, founded in 1914 and rechristened *Unpartizan Review* in 1919, was a quarterly of opinion, similar in general character to the older *Yale Review*, but having the unique feature of not printing the names of its authors until the next issue. It ceased publication in 1921.

circulation of the *Literary Digest* expanding from a quarter of a million in 1914 to over a million and a half in 1928,[1] but also by the launching of many new variants of the news-summary type, such as *Current History*, a monthly founded by the *New York Times* in 1914; *Time*, a Chicago weekly dating from 1923; the *United States Daily*, an accurate account without any comment of the official acts of the national government, published since 1926; and *Foreign Affairs*, a scholarly quarterly devoted to contemporary history outside the United States, started in 1922. The American of 1928 who read the right periodicals could far more accurately keep abreast of the really significant happenings of the day than the American of any previous period.

Ably edited as were the æsthetic *Dial*, the critical *Mercury*, the pacifist *Nation*, the liberal *New Republic*, the radical *Freeman* and the revolutionary *New Masses*, they failed somehow to make the contact with the liberal middle classes that the muckraking monthlies had done before the war, and still more failed to reach the working-man. If one were to judge by mass circulation the American mind was best represented and most influenced by the Curtis publications, such as the *Saturday Evening Post* and the *Ladies' Home Journal*, and by similar "home magazines" like *Collier's*, the *American*, *Woman's Home Companion*, *Pictorial Review*, *McCall's*, *Good Housekeeping*, *Delineator*, *Farm and Fireside*, *Liberty* (a *Chicago Tribune* enterprise) and the *Literary Digest*. These periodicals were as a class admirably printed and edited and often beautifully illustrated, but tended towards colorlessness in opinion, giving to the critic's litmus paper a neutral reaction, neither radical nor conservative. Their articles and stories were often very good, for they could afford the highest prices in

[1] *American Newspaper Annual and Directory* (1914, 1922).

the market, but they suffered a tendency towards standardization. The all-fiction magazines also flourished,
but rarely attained the circulation heights of the family
periodicals. The most interesting tendency among the
fiction magazines was towards extreme specialization.
From a single news-stand one could pick up such differ-
entiated fiction as *Sport Stories* (wholly devoted to athletic tales), *Amazing Stories* (all having a "scientific"
motive), *Love Stories, Ranch Romances, Spy Stories,
Sea Stories, Detective Stories, Far West Stories, Flying
Stories, Fire Fighters* and at least a dozen periodicals
given over entirely to moving-picture novelizations.

One group of these, devoted to the exploitation of
sex, corresponded to the tabloids among the newspapers.
They were of three kinds.[1] Two require little comment:
the jest book, such as has always dwelt in the journalistic
slums, and the "art magazine," which confined itself to
more or less undraped "studies" of the female form and
circulated among all classes except artists. More novel
was the "true-story" type, which owed its origin to a
venture of Bernarr Macfadden, long editor of *Physical
Culture*, a somewhat faddy but reputable health magazine. In 1919 he started *True Story*, a magazine of nar-
ratives of betrayed virgins, unhappy wives and narrowly averted sex tragedies, said to be based on the actual
experiences of the contributors. In 1923 he followed this
venture with *True Romances*. Many other publishers
imitated him, and the magazine stands blossomed—or
blushed—with *I Confess, True Confessions, Secrets* and
the like. The common characteristic of nearly all the sex
magazines was to pretend to much greater daring in
title and cover than the contents ventured to live up to;
a European student of bookstalls would have been
more bored than shocked by them. One may venture to

[1] See Villard, "Sex, Art, Truth and Magazines," 388-398.

doubt also if their "truth" were not as much a sham as their naughtiness.

One thing may be said of all the magazine world: from the aristocracy of the self-styled "quality group" —*Atlantic, Harper's, Scribner's, Century, Review of Reviews, World's Work, Golden Book*—through the middle class of the *Red Book, Cosmopolitan* and *Collier's* down to the mental bottoms of the "true-story" type, all strove to win attention by attractive presentation of material and economy of the reader's time. It was an age when few had leisure to read without running, and it is significant that *Liberty,* a weekly very much in the spirit of the period, put above each story or article an estimate of "reading time" required, so as to warn away those too busy to take twenty-two minutes or attract those who might spare eighteen! Equally typical was the experiment of *Collier's* with the "short short-story," a dramatic narrative that reached its point within a single page. Articles, too, however abstruse their topic, followed the example of the newspapers by summarizing their conclusions within the first two or three paragraphs, using titles more striking than descriptive, and increasing the space devoted to more or less relevant photographic illustration.

No longer decorously shoved to the rear of the magazine, but flanking the stories and articles on the same page, stood the advertisements. They deserved their promotion, for however impatient the reader might be at having to search remote corners of his magazine for the end of a story, he was pleasantly entertained on the way by the attractive display of advertising matter competing for his attention. "Advertising," declared a student of the time, "has ceased to be a modest invitation to buy, and has become an extraordinarily cunning exemplification of practical psychology, forming national habits of thought and action." [1] The art and science of commercial advertisement were so wholly American that a textbook on the subject could state, as a mere matter of course, that "other countries may practically be ignored in a book of this kind." [2] Indeed, with but few and minor exceptions, it was only in the United States that text-books on advertising were written, or courses on "the psychology of advertising" offered in reputable univer-sities, or advertisement copy writers leagued to defend the "ideals of the profession."

The magnitude of the advertising business was most imposing. "Measured in dollars and cents, advertising is the most important form of education in the United States," one economist asserted. [3] According to the state-ment of Francis H. Sisson, a New York banker, the annual volume of advertising in 1927 was over a billion and a half dollars: $800,000,000 to the newspapers, $200,000,000 to the magazines, $200,000,000 for out-door display and more than $300,000,000 in campaigns conducted through the mail. [4] Experience demonstrated that this apparently reckless expenditure paid the manu-facturers, since they must win new markets as well as hold their own against competitors in familiar fields. Moreover, new inventions were constantly placing com-modities on the market never known before, and with-out extensive sales campaigns they would have reached the consumer too slowly. A man accustomed for thirty years to an old-fashioned razor would think twice be-fore buying the new-fangled "safety." But the adver-tiser made him think not twice but fifty times, placing the idea before him in every trolley car and every news-

[1] R. L. Duffus, "1900-1925," *Century*, CIX (1925), 487.
[2] E. E. Calkins, *The Business of Advertising* (N. Y., 1915), 3.
[3] N. H. Comish, *The Standard of Living* (N. Y., 1923), 110.
[4] *N. Y. Times*, July 11, 1928.

paper and every drug-store window until at last he ventured the experiment. The Society of American Florists and Ornamental Horticulturalists presented a gold medal to Major P. F. O'Keefe for inventing a four-word slogan, "Say It with Flowers," which helped double the flower business between 1921 and 1924 and increased it a fourth again the following year.[1]

Because of the incessant appearance of new products and new methods the American advertiser had to obtain favorable publicity not for his own product alone but equally for the whole class of commodities which it represented. The man with California oranges to sell had first to make oranges the favorite fruit at the breakfast table before he could give much attention to explaining the particular merits of fruit grown in his own locality. The Postum manufacturer prepared the way for his own product by undermining the established position of coffee. Bread, meat and milk were praised in general as well as in particular. Rivals interested in the same commodity had to league together in common defense; there were two thousand trade associations in 1927. "Oil and gas and coal are fighting for the job of heating the country," wrote Merle Thorpe. "Electric refrigeration and ice are fighting for the job of cooling it. . . . You are besieged, not so much by men seeking to sell the same product as by those who urge concrete against brick, asbestos against cedar shingle, metal lath against wood, wallboard against plaster, linoleum against oak." [2]

The history of the wars and alliances of the "Great

---

[1] *Golden Book*, IV (1926), 402. For criticism of advertising from the consumer's standpoint, see esp. Stuart Chase and F. J. Schlink, *Your Money's Worth* (N. Y., 1927).

[2] Merle Thorpe, "The Business Revolution of 1927-1937," *Nation's Business*, XV (1927), 27. See also Chase and Schlink, *Your Money's Worth*, 33; and W. A. White, *Masks in a Pageant* (N. Y., 1928), 445.

Powers" of American industry is a curious one. As one
writer pointed out,

> The carpet-tack industry grapples with the oriental
> rug industry, because nobody who uses oriental rugs
> needs carpet tacks. The oriental rug interests ally them-
> selves with their old-time enemy the domestic rug mak-
> ers, to attack the Brussels carpet people. Whereupon
> Brussels carpets appeal for help to carpet tacks, which in
> turn persuade linoleum to fall into line.[1]

Surely, a diplomatic complication worthy of the days
of Kaunitz and Talleyrand!

The methods used by the American advertiser, while
interesting in themselves, are even more significant as
witnesses to the tastes and standards of the time, for the
whole success of the copy writer depended on his ability
to understand the psychology of the potential consumer.
A Berlin professor pointed out that, "while European
business men still look upon producers and upon material production as the aim of modern economics, their
American colleagues have realized . . . that the key to
modern business life is held by the Honorable Mr. Consumer." [2] Because of this anxious study of the whims and
humors of the buying market, the advertisers are almost
our best source as to the actual aspirations, standards
and ideals of the masses of the nation. Let us consider
what the historian of some distant future might reasonably conclude as to the American people of the war and
reconstruction years from their advertisements.

First, and most confidently, he would conclude that
the American people were free spenders. Advertisements
said little about low price and very much about "the

---

[1] Philip Wagner, "Cigarettes vs. Candy," *New Republic*, LVII, 343-
345 (Feb. 13, 1929).
[2] M. J. Bonn, "The American Way," *Atlantic Mo.*, CXLII (1929),
304.

best is cheapest in the long run," or "you may pay a little more, but—" followed by a panegyric on the commodity in question. A French perfume failing to sell at ordinary rates, its price was raised, the advertising slogan became: "It costs a little more but Milady deserves the best," and a fortune was made. When shoes of identical make, in one experiment, were displayed in the windows at six dollars and at twelve dollars a pair, the twelve-dollar pairs sold out the more quickly.[1] One firm sold bedding from the same grade of feathers under five trade names and at five prices to reach different markets.[2] Finding that nearly every home had its automobile, advertisers strove to widen their market by pointing out the desirability of an extra car for the wife and children, and watchmakers succeeded in impressing their public with the need for both a wrist watch in the daytime and a pocket watch in the evening.[3]

Closely related to the premium on costliness as a positive advantage in goods was the emphasis on social competition—"keeping up with the Joneses." Social standards were fixed not by the economic class in which the consumer lived but by the class immediately above. An "aristocratic" cigarette or piano or automobile, something "exclusive," used by "men and women of discriminating taste" or by "the crowned heads of Europe," was sure of success in the American democracy. Once upon a time a certain hotel was sneered at as "providing exclusiveness for the masses," but that would be a literal description of half the advertising of the period. Millions of people bought clothes advertised as "different," or beauty secrets alleged to be hitherto known only to nobility, or books advertised to appeal only to "the

[1] Chase and Schlink, *Your Money's Worth*, 48.
[2] Chase and Schlink, *Your Money's Worth*, 83.
[3] "The Double Standard," *N. Y. Times* (editorial), Jan. 11, 1929.

emancipated few," or the particular brand of cigarette patronized by a movie star or a baseball hero. Advertisers subtly flattered the reader by always depicting scenes of comfort or luxury in their illustration; if the goods were as commonplace as oilcloth or kitchen furniture they would be attractively shown in the pictured interior of a grand mansion.

That success in life was the same as material success our historian would also rightly conclude. In nearly all advertising copy the possible consumer was vaguely placed in some "office" and assumed to be a business man. Except in farm journals, the out-of-door worker rarely appeared on the page, and the professional man and the factory operative were almost equally neglected. Success was depicted in terms of being a business manager; failure was being "a clerk at fifty." Health was advertised not so much for its own sake as being a business asset; education treated as a question of being able to "get on" in life; even "personality" considered merely as a means to "success," not as being success in itself. One typical advertisement may stand as a sample of many thousands: "This Singular Book Wields a Strange Power Over Its Readers, giving them a Magnetic Personality almost instantly! Will you read it 5 days free—to prove it can multiply *your* present income?" [1] Testimonials from successful people seemed to give a business guarantee as well as a social hall mark. The degree of sincerity of most of these "voluntary indorsements" can be judged from the following trade notice: "For those of your organization who require testimonials or special posing of moving picture players, operatic or theatrical stars, famous athletes, society people, and other famous personalities, there is vailable a new service called Famous Names, Inc., Chicago (branches in New York and

[1] *Collier's* (advertising pages), LXXXIII, 25 (Feb. 2, 1929).

Hollywood, Calif.). The fee for the exclusive use of a star is between $150 and $2500." [1]

Another safe induction from the mass of advertising evidence would be the charm of novelty, the love of efficiency, and the indiscriminate but genuine interest in the triumphs of inventive science. Goods were sold as novelties under manufactured trade names instead of, as in the previous generation, an imitation of something older. "Rayon" rather than "artificial silk" sold dress goods. Old-fashioned laundry or bathroom fittings were sneeringly dismissed as comparable with corsets, crino-lines, kerosene lamps and buggies. The phrases of science helped sell all kinds of commodities. Foods were discussed in terms of "calories," "vitamins" and the "fuel value" of so many pounds of beefsteak. Pictures of a scientist examining a test tube replaced the sometime Indian herb doctor in advertisements of patent medicines and cosmetic lotions and notions. Even the sheerest quacks and frauds had to assume the verbiage of the laboratory. The swindler "may aver that if you lie on a large electric warming pad worth $15, but sold under a fancy name at $100, you may invigorate your entire organism by currents of magnetic vibration operating directly through the iron of your blood. . . . Each one of these statements has, in fact, drawn crowds and convinced them, in a city infested with authentic scientists of the best (hence most inarticulate) quality." [2]

Two other aspects of latter-day advertising warrant some attention: the indirect approach and the appeal to the sense of beauty.[3] In the more costly display advertising, in high-grade magazines or on the billboards,

[1] Chase and Schlink, *Your Money's Worth*, 24.
[2] T. S. Harding, "Swindling the Public in the Name of Science," *Current History*, XXIX (1929), 609.
[3] Thus an incinerator, instead of talking about itself, bore the appeal, "Plant a rose-bush where your garbage pail now stands!"

the name of the advertiser was not rudely intruded; the indirect, implicit appeal to the wary customer proved more effective than a direct attack. The reader might obtain the general impression from automobile advertisements, for instance, that the sole function of the machine was to provide an unobtrusive background for a bevy of charming bathing girls. Not goods, but social values and "service," were sold in the advertiser's copy; not clothes, but the advantages of neat appearance; not foods, but health; not labor-saving devices in the home, but visions of leisured women engaged in sports; not dancing or saxophone lessons as such, but social popularity.

Perhaps as a result of keen competition, perhaps because women did so large a share of American buying, the æsthetic appeal of manufactured goods was stressed more than ever before. "Women are making men style-conscious," declared the chairman of the fashion board of the National Association of Merchant Tailors. "To-day style is the compelling sales factor in every line of merchandise from automobiles to pajamas; even dish-washing machines are being offered in pastel shades to harmonize with the wall tones of the kitchen." [1] The sweeping lines of an automobile, the colored tiles of a bathroom, the increasingly attractive window dressing of the main avenue shops, the "cabinet" phonograph in place of the old trumpet, the less obtrusive heating and lighting fixtures in the living room, the improved designs of the kitchen sink and the bright aluminum ware above it, the French designs of perfume bottles [2]— these merely illustrate the freer use of color and more

[1] N. Y. Times, Feb. 1, 1929.
[2] "Future connoisseurs may collect the perfume bottles of the twentieth century as they now collect the snuffboxes of the eighteenth." E. E. Calkins, "Beauty the New Business Tool," Atlantic Mo., CXL (1927), 148. The article is an excellent summary of the wedding of art and commerce.

tasteful employment of line in the newer manufacture. If in any respect the United States of 1928 was beyond question superior to the nation of 1914, it was in the comparative decrease of industrial ugliness.

Advertising commodities was, of course, but one phase of the general industry of publicity. The science of propaganda, so greatly developed during the war, found much employment in time of peace. Press-agenting of individuals, propaganda for causes, campaigns for charitable work, and many other occupations where an understanding of the arts of persuasion was important, enlisted numerous trained workers.[1] By 1927 more than a hundred cities were advertising their advantages at an estimated total cost of ten million dollars a year.[2] As in China, the American public authorities have not thought it beneath their dignity to appeal to their public and not merely command it. There is a winsomeness about "This is your park, please keep it in order," not to be found in the older signs "Persons littering the park will be prosecuted to the full extent of the law"; wastepaper receptacles labeled "Please stuff me with paper" obtain results not reached in the mere command not to throw rubbish into the street; and the touch of comradely humor in "Go slow and see our town; go fast and see our jail" proved often more effective than the bare information, "Speed limit—15 miles an hour."

Another influence of advertising psychology on national customs was euphemism, the practice of wording a familiar idea in a more attractive way. In commerce

[1] A study of the earnings of the graduates of the school of journalism of Columbia University showed that the average income of those who stuck to strictly journalistic work was about $6000 a year a decade after graduation, while those who went in for advertising or publicity work were averaging over $10,000. *Columbia Alumni News*, XVIII, 145 (Nov. 19, 1926).

[2] Merle Thorpe, "Cities Enter the New Competition," *Nation's Business*, XV (1927), 15-17.

"second-hand cars" became "used" or "rebuilt" cars, "installment plan" became "deferred-payment plan," the real-estate agent became a "realtor," and the undertaker a "mortician" in charge of a "funeral home." In politics the attractive phrase "short ballot" was used for the plan of making most offices appointive instead of elective, and woman suffrage was called by its advocates "equal suffrage," by its opponents "double suffrage," the former phrase stressing the idea of democratic right, the latter the unwelcome enlargement of the vote. The publisher Haldemann-Julius discovered that by manipulating the titles of his "little blue books" (paperbound classics and best sellers) he could increase the sale of any given volume several fold.[1]

Still another effect of advertising technique was the concentration of civic-welfare crusades into brief "drives," conducted in much the same way as the liberty-loan drives of war time. Between April, 1924, and April, 1925, in a single Mid-Western city over thirty special days and weeks were set aside for community observance,[2] among them: suburban day, home-sewing week, ice-cream week, truth week, father's day, mother's day, boy's day, thrift week (with seven special days inside it), home-beautiful week, education week, art week, music week, joy week, go-to-church Sunday, labor Sunday, golden-rule Sunday, child-health week, fire-prevention week, courtesy week, defense day, "buddy-poppy" day (for aid to the veterans) and a dozen more. America was not far from the calendar of the French Revolution with each day, week and month consecrated to some special civic virtue.

[1] "That Which We Call a Rose," New Republic, LVII, 206-207 (Jan. 9, 1929).
[2] R. S. Lynd and Helen M. Lynd, Middletown (N. Y., 1929), 491.

CHAPTER XIV

SCIENCE, MISTRESS AND HANDMAID

BY EDWIN E. SLOSSON

IN the early years of the nineteenth century Americans, though awakening to full national consciousness with all its multiform ambitions, had been able to make little or no contribution to the world's stock of scientific knowledge. A hundred years later there were hundreds of research workers in various parts of the country whose occasional monographs were watched for by scholars everywhere. Before reviewing their typical achievements and their influence it might well be pointed out that in the world's opinion neither as yet bore a proper ratio to the population or to the economic power of the country. The Nobel Institute of Stockholm, which was founded by the inventor of dynamite for the appraisement and reward of contemporary achievements without national bias, awarded, between 1901 and 1928, eighty-three prizes in science of which five came to the United States.[1] During this period France had nearly six times as many as America, if proportionate population is reckoned, England nearly eight and Germany more than eight, while the Netherlands had twenty and Denmark had thirty-four times as many.[2] Furthermore,

---

[1] It is interesting to note in this connection that the United States up to 1929 had received none of the twenty-six Nobel Prizes in literature but had been awarded four of the thirty-one for the promotion of peace: Theodore Roosevelt, 1905; Elihu Root, 1912; Woodrow Wilson, 1919; and C. G. Dawes, 1925.

[2] These computations are made from the *World Almanac for 1928*, 305, 551-554, 893.

if one were to judge only by these data, there was no acceleration in the relative accomplishment of Americans after 1914.

A. A. Michelson of the University of Chicago, who had received the prize in 1907, added to his laurels during this later period by measuring the diameter of Betelgeuse with his interferometer, by determining the velocity of light with unprecedented accuracy, and by repeating with the same negative result his historic experiment of 1887 to determine ether drift, an experiment which gave rise to Einstein's theory of relativity. Alexis Carrel of the Rockefeller Institute for Medical Research, who had been so honored in 1912, continued his surgical successes in suturing blood vessels and transplanting organs. During the fourteen years covered by this volume, to cite one "miracle" among his many, he kept alive a dissevered fragment of chicken heart.

The Nobel Prize for chemistry was given in 1914 to Thomas W. Richards of Harvard for his life-long labors in determining atomic weights. Robert A. Millikan of the California Institute of Technology, Nobel prize winner in 1923, determined the weight of the minutest particle of matter, the electron, and later measured the length of the shortest waves, the cosmic rays. Arthur H. Compton of the University of Chicago was rewarded in 1927 for his discovery that X-rays scattered by reflection from an electron were reduced in frequency, showing loss of energy. New evidence that the wave theory and the corpuscular theory of radiation, formerly thought incompatible, are both in some sense true was adduced by C. J. Davisson and L. H. Germer of the Bell Telephone Laboratories when they showed that a stream of electrons is reflected and diffracted from the face of a nickel crystal like X-rays.[1] A unique contribution to

[1] Franklin Institute, *Journ.*, CCV (1928), 597.

our knowledge of the earth's magnetism was made by the nonmagnetic ship *Carnegie,* which voyaged all the oceans making observations.

When the rise of the curtain of censorship at the conclusion of the war revealed Einstein's general theory of relativity, the American people showed keen curiosity to know what it meant. Although in the subsequent development of mathematical theory and philosophical speculation resulting from these new conceptions American names were not conspicuous, the two great observatories in California, Mt. Hamilton and Mt. Wilson, supplied the most substantial evidence on the astronomical questions which Einstein suggested as decisive tests of the correctness of his hypothesis: the displacement of star images during the sun's eclipse, and the shift of spectral lines toward the red.[1] Of other achievements of American astronomers it will suffice here to mention the theory of dwarf and giant stars of Henry Norris Russell of Princeton and the calculations of the size of the universe by Harlow Shapley of Harvard.

Chemistry, in harmony with what was thought to be the American genius for the practical, made comparatively little advance in determining the fundamental nature of matter, though the discovery of illinium by B. S. Hopkins of the University of Illinois in 1926 gave America the honor of one of the ninety-two chemical elements. Extraordinary progress was made, however, in applying to the convenience of man the chemical knowledge already possessed. As far as materials were concerned the country gained immensely by the war; the German patents on coal-tar dyes and drugs, which had well-nigh

---

[1] Mt. Hamilton answered the former question and Mt. Wilson the latter. W. W. Campbell in Lick Observatory, *Bull.,* nos. 348, 397 (Univ. of Calif., *Publs. in Astronomy*); C. E. St. John and W. S. Adams, *Convection Currents in Stellar Atmospheres* (Mt. Wilson Observatory, *Contribs.,* no. 279).

dominated the American market, were now placed at the disposal of manufacturers on this side of the sea by the alien-property custodian, Francis P. Garvan. When peace was restored the needs of the country were being fully supplied by domestic production in most chemical commodities, and dyes that formerly had been imported were being exported.

Industry and invention in this field were stimulated to intense activity by the manufacture of munitions and poison gases. In the fabrication of defense masks for use against the latter attention was directed to absorptive surfaces in general. As the carbon compounds in the masks absorbed the poison discharged against the soldier, so certain gases inserted in a bulb, Irving Langmuir and his coworkers discovered, would themselves absorb the heat from a tungsten filament and make it possible to develop a greater intensity of electric light than the old vacuum lamp had allowed. The effect of this illumination throughout the country was second only in importance to Edison's fundamental invention of the lamp nearly forty years before.[1]

Chemistry made possible the production of artificial silk or "rayon," which, though developed first in England and Italy, reached its greatest proportions in the United States. In chemical laboratories, also, was found the method which doubled the strength of wrapping paper so that the carton made of this light material could supplant the wooden box in the transportation of groceries and many other commodities at reduced freight cost.[2] Among the new respects in which American chemists led the world was in the development of lacquers

[1] W. J. Bartlett, "Chemistry in Incandescent Lamp Manufacture," *Industrial and Engineering Chemistry*, XXI, 970-973.
[2] F. Reinthaler, *Artificial Silk* (F. M. Howe, tr., N. Y., 1929) ; J. N. Stephenson, ed., *The Manufacture of Pulp and Paper* (N. Y., 1925), V, sec. v.

composed of nitrated cellulose dissolved in various products of fermentation. Since these could be made in any color and be sprayed on automobiles in a few minutes, instead of the weeks formerly required for painting and varnishing, they satisfied two of the desires of the American people, for speed and gayety. These instances, taken almost at random, illustrate the innumerable services which chemistry in this era was performing for the life of society.

In the field of biology perhaps the most distinctively American line of research was the experimental study of the mechanism of heredity and sex linkage carried on at Columbia by Edmund B. Wilson, T. H. Morgan and their associates.[1] In this work the fruit fly, *Drosophila,* was found particularly available since a large population of them could be raised in a glass jar on a bit of rotting banana and generations follow in quick succession. In these little insects it was found possible to recognize over one hundred distinctive variant features and in many cases to identify the invisible factors (genes) that control their inheritance, even to map them as though they were arranged like beads on a string in the chromosomes of the cell. That exposing the fruit flies to X-rays would multiply the number of their mutations a hundredfold was discovered by H. J. Muller of Texas in 1927. By chopping up flatworms C. M. Child of Chicago developed his hypothesis of metabolic gradients to explain the directions and rate of growth.[2]

From the study of twin calves from the Chicago stockyards Frank R. Lillie showed how the male may repress the female even in embryo. At the Rockefeller Institution for Medical Research, Jacques Loeb con-

[1] T. H. Morgan, *The Physical Basis of Heredity* (N. Y., 1919); E. B. Wilson, *The Cell in Development and Heredity* (N. Y., 1925).
[2] C. M. Child, *Senescence and Rejuvenescence* (Chicago, 1915).

tinued till his death in 1924 his researches on the border-land of chemistry and biology in support of his mechanistic conception of life.[1] Of American researches on the hormones, the mysterious substances which, secreted in the blood by the ductless glands, regulate our bodily and mental balance, it must suffice to mention but two: the isolation of thyroxine, the active principle of the thyroid gland, by E. C. Kendall of the Mayo Clinic in 1915; and the experiments of W. B. Cannon of Harvard on the relations of the hormones to the emotions.[2]

The standards of the medical schools were constantly raised in the face of a growing number of eager applicants for admission. A growing proportion of the staff were full-time men, finding their career in the classroom and particularly in the laboratories. At the same time that specialization went steadily forward, illustrating the old law of general progress through differentiation, the specialists realized their dependence upon each other. "Pathological bacteriologists," wrote a leader in medical education, "are not only using chemical and physiological technic, but chemists and physicists are working in bacteriological and medical laboratories." [3] With infinite pains, on such experiment tables, bacteriological cultures were developed which came into wide use as curative aids; in general the drug list was substantially cut down. The dentist and the medical doctor came in this period to realize their interdependence more completely than at any time since the former branched off from the latter a century before.[4] Indeed, the extraction

[1] Jacques Loeb, *Forced Movements, Tropisms and Animal Conduct* (N. Y., 1918).

[2] W. B. Cannon, *Bodily Changes in Pain, Hunger, Fear and Rage* (N. Y., 1915).

[3] William Darrach, "Medicine," D. R. Fox, ed., *A Quarter-Century of Learning, 1904-1929* (N. Y., 1930).

[4] D. R. Fox, *The Completion of Independence* (*A History of American Life*, V).

of diseased teeth as a means of restoring health became for a time almost a professional fad.

It was this sort of interpretation of special interests, however, which moved toward the establishment of medical centers where various schools, institutes and hospitals could be brought into touch and coöperation. In this development the great achievement of the twenties was the Medical Center in New York, formed around the Columbia University School of Medicine and the Presbyterian Hospital. This tendency reflected the trend in industry to merge complementary enterprises. In part, too, it accorded with the tendency to concentrate cultural enterprises in large cities; but Emerson's dictum that the world would make a beaten path to the door of any man, wherever he might live, who could meet its wants, was strikingly illustrated in the importance of the Mayo Foundation for Medical Education and Research which Dr. Charles H. Mayo and Dr. William J. Mayo established in 1915 in connection with their clinic at Rochester, Minnesota.

Physics contributed mightily to medicine in the perfection of the electrocardiograph and the increased employment of the X-ray. By the use of barium or bismuth, as had become common by the middle twenties, a meal could be followed for days as X-ray observations from time to time revealed its diffusion through the body. Though the cause and cure of cancer remained a tragic mystery, X-ray therapeutics along with radium proved able to dispel minor or incipient tumors. It was a sad circumstance of this advance that in the earlier stages some experimenters with this agent unwittingly induced in their own bodies fatal forms of the same disease they sought to conquer in others. American surgeons, like those of European countries, profited greatly by the experience of the World War. In some concerns surgery tended to supplant the older methods of treatment as, for example, in orthopedics, where operations came to be esteemed more efficacious than straps and braces.[1]

In the study of the diseases of plants and in the fight against their insect enemies the United States, as might be expected, led the world. The large and pernicious family of mosaic diseases, which cause the mottling or distortion of the leaf, were found to be due to some virus, too small to be filtered off by porous porcelain, which was carried by insects from the infected plant to a healthy one; but whether the agency belonged to the animal, vegetable or chemical kingdom was not determined by the time this volume closed. Much work was done on the effects of light alterations on plant growth, among which may be mentioned the discovery of W. W. Garner and H. A. Allard, of the United States department of agriculture, that the growth and flowering of plants could be regulated by changing the length of their day by artificial lighting. The application of the principles of heredity to the human race, eugenics, excited wide popular interest and considerable research, of which one of the centers was at Cold Spring Harbor, New York, with its Carnegie Station for Experimental Evolution and Eugenics Record Office under C. B. Davenport.

The dietary habits of the American people underwent two marked alterations during this period, one sudden and temporary, the other gradual and lasting. The former was due to the patriotic appeals of the federal food administrator, Herbert Hoover, to the American people to eat less and scrape their plates in order to save food for overseas. "It is my belief," he said, "that food will win this war—starvation or sufficiency will

[1] Darrach, "Medicine."

in the end mark the victor." [1] Many of those who then acquired the habit of "hooverizing" from patriotic principles kept it up afterwards for hygienic reasons. The other change in food habits is shown chiefly in the decreased use of beef and the increased use of milk, fresh fruit and salads. The per-capita consumption of beef, which stood at 77.5 pounds in 1907, declined to 54.5 in 1915, and though it rose somewhat after the war, it was down by 1928 to a lower level, 51.7 pounds. [2] The citrus fruits from Florida and California, facilitated by coöperative marketing and skillful advertising, jumped into unprecedented popularity. The output of oranges rose from about fifteen million boxes in 1919 to over thirty-nine million in 1926. Of grapefruit only about a million boxes were marketed in 1909, but by 1926 the consumption had risen to eight million seven hundred thousand boxes. [3]

The outlying territories of the United States contributed increasingly to the needs of our people, thanks chiefly to the application of American capital and skill in the growth and preservation of perishable products. For instance, between 1913 and 1926 the importation of canned pineapples from Hawaii leaped from four million dollars' worth to thirty-four million; of canned salmon from Alaska from twelve million dollars' worth to over forty-eight million; of the oil and dried meat of the coconut from the Philippines from two million dollars' worth to twenty-five million; of sugar from Porto Rico from twenty-five million dollars' worth to forty-six. [4]

The American public, as usual, was quick to catch and try to utilize every new discovery of science, some-

[1] *Independent*, XCII, 510 (Dec. 15, 1917). See earlier, chap. ii.
[2] Department of Agriculture, *Circular*, no. 241.
[3] *Yearbook of Agriculture for 1927*, 841.
[4] *Commerce Yearbook for 1926*, II, pt. ii, *passim*.

times indeed before the scientists themselves were agreed upon it or had worked out its bearings and limitations. This eagerness in application was especially conspicuous in the sciences most closely concerned with human conduct, such as health, nutrition and psychology. In these fields the rewards of research were particularly rich, and any fragment of fact was likely to be found sufficient to support a new fad or cult. It was during this period that experiments with restricted diets on animals and men showed that certain factors in some foods were essential in minute amounts for health, growth and fertility. These unknown ingredients were provisionally designated as Vitamins A, B, C, D, E and F and, although they had not been isolated and their chemical constitution determined when this volume closes, enough was known about which foods contained them and which were deficient in them to make a marked change in the food habits of the nation. The increased use of fresh fruits, green leaves and milk was doubtless due largely to the belief that they were rich in certain of the vitamins. The effects were shown most convincingly in the cure of pellagra by fresh meat and milk and the cure of rickets by cod-liver oil or ultraviolet rays.[1]

In no field was the influence of science more marked than in public health and sanitation. As the doctors proved that they deserved more confidence, they got it. Their advice on sanitary questions was more willingly listened to and more obediently followed by individuals and official bodies. Owing to the introduction of better systems of water supply and sewage disposal, to the pasteurization of milk and to vaccination, typhoid fever was nearly conquered by 1925; its share in the death

[1] Among the many workers in this field there is room here to mention only a few: T. B. Osborne, L. B. Mendel, E. V. McCollum, H. C. Sherman, W. H. Eddy, H. M. Evans, B. Sure, Alfred F. Hess, A. Seidell. See Julius Stieglitz, ed., *Chemistry in Medicine* (N. Y., 1928), chap. iv.

rate was only a twentieth of what it had been forty years before. Diphtheria and scarlet fever also declined. Tuberculosis, formerly figuring in the mortality statistics at the top of the list of diseases causing death, showed, during the first quarter of the century, a decided and almost continuous decline, which by 1927 had reduced the death rate from this cause to less than half what it was in 1900. This meant that the victims of tuberculosis in 1926 were one hundred and thirty thousand fewer than they would have been if the mortality from this disease had continued at the same rate as at the opening of the century.[1] The average length of life was greatly extended, so that a baby born in 1927 could look forward to living 59.1 years, while a baby born in 1901 had the expectation of only 49.24 years. But this gain was due chiefly to greater control of infantile diseases and epidemics. Infant mortality was cut down by half in the first quarter of the century though centenarians were probably no more numerous.[2] As the population on the average grew older, the diseases characteristic of advanced years increased, such as cancer and heart disease.[3]

During the fourteen years following 1914 the study of psychology underwent striking changes in America. It was in that year that John B. Watson of Johns Hopkins published his book on *Behavior;* before the period concluded a considerable number of psychologists had

[1] L. I. Dublin, *Health and Wealth* (N. Y., 1928), 84.
[2] Dublin, *Health and Wealth*, 182, 183.
[3] The changes during the period of this book are indicated by the following figures from *Mortality Statistics for 1925*, Part II (Bureau of the Census, Washington). The figures give the death rate per 100,000 in the registration area of 1910, comprising nearly 60 per cent of the population in that year. Total death rate was 1359 in 1914, 1203 in 1925; from typhoid, 12.3 in 1914, 4.0 in 1925; from diphtheria, 17.2 in 1914, 8.1 in 1925; from scarlet fever, 7.2 in 1914, 3.9 in 1925; from tuberculosis, 121.5 in 1914, 74.6 in 1925; from cancer, 83.4 in 1914, 105.1 in 1925; from heart disease, 168.4 in 1914, 210.4 in 1925.

abandoned the time-honored conception of the "mind" and maintained that human beings like other animals had only reactions of nerves, muscles, secretory glands and the like, and that what had been called thought was only the subvocal pronunciation of words customarily associated with these reactions. This was, of course, an extreme position, which its critics charged was too mechanistic even for America; but it was true that most psychologists of whatever school no longer sat and thought about thinking; rather, they worked out objective studies of behavior by laboratory experiment, a development which owed much to the pioneer work in the previous period of Professor Edward L. Thorndike of Columbia. Popular interest centered in psychoanalysis, imported from Austria, in whose name were made far-reaching therapeutic claims, many of them undoubtedly reckless. Psychology, indeed, now seemed to be a concern of everybody: the parent, the doctor, the penologist, the lawyer, the safety expert, the personnel manager, each sought to enlist it in solving his problems.[1] Certainly business attempted to make ample use of the "new" science; it was perhaps significant that in 1924 Watson himself became vice-president of the country's leading advertising agency.

In the so-called social sciences two tendencies were at work, one in method and one in administration. In all fields there seemed a preference for the inductive use of statistics wherever it was practicable. Whereas in previous periods individual scholars had usually gone each his own way, scholarship in many instances now

[1] J. M. Cattell, *Psychology in America* (Garrison, N. Y., 1929); Gardner Murphy, *Historical Introduction to Modern Psychology* (N. Y., 1929), *passim;* S. W. Feinberger, "Statistical Analyses of the Members and Associates of the American Psychological Association," *Psychological Rev.*, XXXV (1928), 447-465; E. L. Thorndike, *The Measurement of Intelligence* (N. Y., 1926), *passim;* R. M. Yerkes, *Psychological Examining in the United States Army* (Natl. Acad. of Sci., *Memoirs*, XV).

organized upon the team plan, with elaborate coöperative projects. If these enterprises seemed less personal than formerly they were likewise impersonally financed, much of their cost being met by research grants from educational foundations set up by American millionaires. Sometimes such an organization directed the research itself.[1] In other cases individuals or groups were given subsidies by the advice of a board such as the Social Science Research Council, incorporated in 1925, which itself represented seven learned societies and virtually administered a considerable appropriation from the Rockefeller Foundation. A Dr. Johnson of the new age desiring aid for a great project like his dictionary did not have to depend upon the capricious favors of a noble lord, but had rather to organize a staff of workers and interest the administrative council of a research fund.[2] The fact that so much scholarship in this country was coöperative with, as a result, less conspicuous individual achievement, may account in part for the small number of Nobel Prizes for science awarded to Americans, as noted at the beginning of this chapter.

In practical affairs science continuously increased its influence over the American people. The newspapers

[1] For example, E. R. Johnson and others, *History of Foreign and Domestic Commerce in the United States* (Wash., 1915); V. S. Clark, *History of Manufactures in the United States before 1860* (Wash., 1916); C. E. MacGill and others, *History of Transportation in the United States before 1860* (Wash., 1917); P. W. Bidwell and J. I. Falconer, *History of Agriculture in the Northern United States, 1620-1860* (Wash., 1925). All these were published by direction and support of the Carnegie Institution. Similar coöperative studies went forward under the direction of the Brookings Institution, founded in Washington in 1922 by Robert S. Brookings; and the Pollak Foundation for Economic Research, founded in 1920, etc.

[2] An excellent example of this kind of coöperation and this kind of support in providing a serviceable aid to scholarship was seen in the *Social Science Abstracts* (N. Y., 1929-   ), a function of the Social Science Research Council. This did for social science what *Chemical Abstracts*, *Medical Abstracts*, *Psychological Abstracts*, etc., had done for their respective fields.

gave more space to it, and more often gave it correctly. The value of scientific research in agriculture and manufacturing became widely recognized and substantially supported. The latest discoveries in medicine, hygiene and dietetics were eagerly welcomed and often exaggerated. In the schools textbooks and methods of instruction improved. Even more was accomplished for the spread of scientific principles among the people in the field of mechanics by their daily familiarity with automobiles, radios and electrical appliances in the home.

Science really enters human history not when a discovery is first announced to the inner circle of scientists or when the first patent on some of its applications is granted, but at some later and more indefinite date when the conception begins to modify public opinion and conduct or when inventions involving it enter the common life. This latent period between the inception of an idea and its general utilization, which in other times and countries has extended to years or centuries, has been extremely short in the United States. This, very probably, has been due to unprecedented facilities for bringing words and pictures to so many millions without impeding political or language frontiers. The diffusion of wealth in America made it possible to take advantage of every practical idea almost immediately; machinery, buildings, vehicles, clothing, furniture, all could, if desired, be scrapped and replaced without delay. Labor, no matter how highly organized, welcomed rather than hindered those discoveries which cut down the need for human handiwork; it encouraged every increase of production, confident, on the basis of precedent, that it would share in a consequent prosperity. Science, then, as far as its useful application might be concerned, worked in a most favorable environment.

Agriculture, with its immense voting strength in a

democracy but with meager individual resources, had long since turned to the governments, federal and state, for scientific advice.[1] But such systematic research was not generally applied to manufacturing until the World War disclosed to an astonished and affrighted world that the issue would not be determined, as heretofore in history, by the massing of men, but more by the management of machinery; that inventive skill and factory methods were more important in the conflict than mere numbers and individual valor. When the United States became a belligerent, the immediate demand was for men who knew how to apply scientific principles to new situations, and not enough of them were to be found. As the National Academy of Sciences was founded by President Lincoln to give scientific counsel to the government during the Civil War, so the National Research Council, a daughter of the Academy, was also a war child, born of the needs of 1918.

After the war many more corporations made definite provision for investigation of the problems of their business, either in their own plants or by supporting fellows in such establishments as the Mellon Institute of Pittsburgh. By 1928 such industrial research laboratories numbered more than a thousand, not including those connected with federal, state or municipal governments or with educational institutions, and they were expending at the rate of about twenty-five million dollars a year.[2] The natural scientists preceded the social scientists in making effective use of the coöperative method. The new strategy bore an interesting analogy to the new

[1] See, for example, Allan Nevins, *The Emergence of Modern America* (*A History of American Life*, VIII), 272-276. The federal and state appropriations for agricultural research aggregated approximately thirteen and a half million dollars for the year 1928. R. W. Trullinger in *U. S. Daily* (Wash.), July 14, 1928.

[2] "Industrial Research Laboratories of the United States," Natl. Research Coun., *Bull.*, no. 60.

methods of warfare. As individual raids of intrepid warriors gave way to systematic siege operations, so the struggles of individual inventors, like Palissy in pottery or Goodyear in rubber, were displaced by a corps of coöperating experts in all the various sciences involved, equipped with the necessary apparatus and power machinery. The electrical industries were the most liberal in their support of research in pure science. Frequently the investigations seemed without regard to usefulness, but in time they richly justified themselves on the ledger. As a consequence of laboratory research the progress in the use of electrical appliances was most rapid. By 1928 the American Telegraph and Telephone Company employed two thousand research workers at an annual cost of about fifteen million dollars.

The achievements so far recounted were impressive and in many instances dramatic, yet probably there were comparatively few who realized their social significance. Very different was the case with certain discoveries and their application in the fields of physics and engineering. An entirely new factor in human affairs sprang into existence during the latter half of this period and within five years was exerting a conspicuous influence toward the unification and the simultaneity of American thought. Wireless telephony made it possible for a tenth of the United States to listen to the voice of a single man at the time of delivery. This was accomplished by the invention by Lee De Forest in 1906 of the audion, or vacuum-tube valve, in which a wire grid was inserted in the electron stream passing from the hot filament to the plate of opposite polarity.[1] Slight fluctuations in the potential of the grid caused large changes in the plate current so that a weak series of electric waves could be amplified as much as desired. By this means messages

[1] H. L. Jome, *Economics of the Radio Industry* (N. Y., 1925), 14.

could be reënforced and relayed, thus making it possible to talk by wired telephone across the continent or by wireless waves halfway around the world.

Communication by wireless telegraphy and telephony was developed during the World War in strict secrecy and under government control. In Europe broadcasting remained a government monopoly. But in the United States, after the ban was removed in 1919, the field was open to amateurs and became an amazingly popular pastime among those fond of tinkering with scientific apparatus.[1] Any ingenious schoolboy could make a receiving set out of a couple of ear phones, a crystal of galena and a few coils of wire with which he could "listen in" on song and speech from miles away. Encouraged by this, he was often led to build up more elaborate apparatus and to devise new "hook-ups" in the effort to reach more distant broadcasting stations. Constructing sending apparatus was not much more difficult. Newspapers issued weekly radio supplements and more than thirty periodicals devoted to the new art flourished during this chaotic period. In so free an atmosphere the inventive genius and love of novelty of the American people had full scope, and progress was unprecedented. Every few months brought out new and improved apparatus and the radio "fan" was quick to scrap his antiquated equipment of the year before. In 1921 the sales of radio apparatus were ten million dollars; by 1925 they had reached one hundred and seventy-eight million dollars.[2]

The manufacturers of radio supplies soon found it to their interest to provide something worth listening to, and they began to broadcast programs on a definite wave length at regular hours. The first broadcasting sta-

[1] Jome, *Radio Industry*, 166.
[2] *Commerce Yearbook for 1926*, I, 419.

tion in the world was KDKA at East Pittsburgh, Pennsylvania, where the Westinghouse Electrical and Manufacturing Company on November 2, 1920, started a daily schedule with the returns of the presidential election.[1] In order to assure an adequate audience the company had given away a number of simple head-phone listening sets. The broadcasting was effected by a transmitter of one hundred watts housed in a rough box upon the roof of one of the taller buildings of the plant, and phonograph records furnished most of the music for the early programs. Time signals from the government station at Arlington were retransmitted every night at ten o'clock.

The pioneer ventures in the use of the new medium for entertainment and instruction were made mostly in Pittsburgh.[2] Free from the government monopoly of control of broadcasting and from the tax imposed on receiving sets in other countries, the radio expanded in America with the greatest rapidity and to the greatest extent. By 1928 it was estimated that about ten million receiving sets were in use in the United States and, since many of them were equipped with loud speakers, the listeners to each included, willy-nilly, a large part of the household and near neighbors. Multiplying the ten million by whatever factor might be allowed for the number of listeners and dividing by whatever factor

[1] H. P. Davis, *The History of Broadcasting in the United States* (Address at Graduate School of Business Administration, Harvard Univ., 1928).

[2] The church led, the first religious service broadcast being that conducted by Dr. E. J. van Etten, rector of the Calvary Episcopal Church, on January 2, 1921. The first public address to go "on the air" was the appeal of Herbert Hoover for funds to support European relief work, made at a dinner at the Duquesne Club about two weeks later, while the first program from the stage came from the Davis Theater on May 9. It was hailed as a striking achievement of science when on New Year's Eve, 1923, the British public listened and danced to American jazz transmitted by short waves from Pittsburgh and rebroadcast from Manchester. A year later South Africa and Australia had the same privilege.

might be allowed for the hours of disuse, the result will show that a very large proportion of the population of the United States was making use of this new channel of communication. As with automobiles, there were at that time about as many receiving sets in this country as in the whole outside world counted together.[1]

The first attraction of any novelty is the novelty of it. The early patrons of the motion picture were thrilled by seeing on the screen ocean waves beating on a coast or a locomotive coming head-on at them; later they demanded a story. So too the pioneer devotees of the radio got sufficient excitement in their ability to hear unexpected voices from distant states or foreign lands, regardless of the value of what was said. Soon, however, this experience palled, and at the same time advertisers perceived the value of entertaining the radio audience if allowed to mention at the opening and close of the program the name and product of the company, or allude more or less adroitly to its slogan or trademark. Consequently the American people were provided at all hours in their own homes with concerts and other amusements ranging from vocal vaudeville to high-class symphonies, at the expense of those who wished to sell tooth paste, cough drops, watches, coffee, carpets, ginger ale, mattresses, life insurance, typewriters, motor fuel and so forth.

As the audience became more critical and competition more intense, the programs became more costly and attractive. Any household in the vicinity of New York with a receiver of moderate capacity could, for example, choose its entertainment from the programs of forty or fifty different stations if they did not conflict in time and wave length. The leading stations in 1928 were giving

[1] "Radio Markets of the World," Dept. of Commerce, *Trade Information Bull.*, no. 600.

from twenty-five to thirty-five numbers beginning with setting-up exercises at 6:45 A. M. and closing with jazz at midnight. After that hour, if the appetite of the listener continued and his instrument was of sufficient intensity, he could pick up western stations as far as the Pacific. Light is thrown on the leisure interests and tastes of the American public by the fact that the distribution of the time of the programs broadcast from all the New York City stations during the month of February, 1927, averaged as follows: dance music 26.2 per cent; other music 48; educational 9.3; religious 5.3; news, market and other information 2.8; drama and readings 2.6; sports 1.8; children's program 1.1; miscellaneous 2.6.[1]

In 1926 the chain system of broadcasting was developed by which two companies sent out by wire features furnished by advertisers or arranged by the companies to be broadcast by two of the local stations in leading cities. This increased the trend toward uniformity, for a large part of the radio listeners in all parts of the country were hearing the same songs or speeches at the same moment. By 1928 Henry Ford found it worth while to spend a thousand dollars a minute over such a chain in announcing his new model with an hour's entertainment of popular singers and speakers.

The political power of the radio came prominently into play in the national election of 1924 when the citizen had the opportunity to contrast the conduct of the two great party conventions, whichever form he might favor—the Republican at Cleveland, which ran as smoothly and swiftly as a well-oiled machine to its foreordained conclusion, and the Democratic convention from which he could hear the former favorite of

[1] G. A. Lundberg, "The Content of Radio Programs," *Social Forces*, VII (1928), 59.

the party, William Jennings Bryan, shouted down by
Smith sympathizers in the gallery, the eloquent but futile
defense of Woodrow Wilson by his devoted secretary of
war, Newton D. Baker, and in later days the tedious
roll calls of the one hundred and three ballots for a
presidential nominee. In the campaign of 1928 both parties made extensive use of the radio, and most of the
voters had opportunity to hear in their own homes the
presidential candidates and to compare their style of
talking, mode of thinking and method of argumen-
tation.

One of the incidental, but probably influential, effects
of the rise of the radio was that of broadening the minds,
or at any rate enlarging the contacts, of the American
people. Persons who from inertia or social standing
would never think of attending a mass meeting, certainly
of the opposing political party, or the services of various
churches or a concert of classical music, were undoubtedly
led to listen when the sound was brought into their very
homes. At the inauguration of President Hoover one
hundred and twenty broadcasting stations were hooked
up in continental chains and a large part of the American
people could hear the addresses, the oath of office (including a mistake by Chief Justice Taft in administer-
ing the presidential oath), the bands of the procession
(as well as the remarks of spectators standing in the
rain), and the description of the spectacle as seen by the
airmen overhead.

The framers of the United States Constitution of
1787, though credited by pious patriotism with almost
superhuman foresight, did not make specific provision
for the regulation of radio, and the American people
had been conversing with one another by this new art
of communication for five years before Congress awakened to the need of action. By mutual agreement and by

arrangement with the department of commerce, under the shadowy authority of a law of 1912, the broadcasting stations, so long as they were few, divided among themselves the thousand kilocycles of available wave bands and the twenty-four hours of the day. But as the number of stations and their power increased, the competition for favored time and space became so close that chaos reigned in the ether. A symphony was liable to be choked off by jazz, a speaker in Washington might be interrupted by a market report from Dakota, and the howling of the heterodyning interfered with them all. The number of stations had risen to seven hundred and thirty-two by March, 1927, when the federal radio commission was established by Congress, and there were only eighty-nine wave lengths to be divided between them.[1] A separation of ten kilocycles was then adopted as essential to avoid serious interference, with six channels reserved for Canada.

The two complementary forms of dramatic art, the pantomime of the screen and the dialogue of the radio, the one appealing exclusively to the eye and the other exclusively to the ear, developed simultaneously. The motion picture as a factor in American life had an influence difficult to overestimate. It became during this period one of the most popular pastimes in all parts of the country, and one of the weekly habits of a large portion of the population. By the middle 1920's it had become the fourth largest industry in the country, representing a capital investment of more than one and a half billion dollars.[2] By 1927 there were twenty thou-

[1] Federal Radio Commission, *Report for 1927*, 2.
[2] Jewish Americans took a leading part in its development. "In terms of the uppermost strata of control, the motion picture industry in the United States is now 90 per cent Jewish." In 1926 the motion-picture industry was said to be practically in the control of about four men: Adolph Zukor of Famous Players-Lasky, Marcus Loew of Metro-Goldwyn-Mayer, William Fox of Fox Pictures, and Carl Laemmle of Uni-

sand five hundred motion-picture theaters with a seating capacity of some eighteen million. In these were shown daily about twenty-five thousand miles of celluloid film, and to these resorted weekly about a hundred million of the American people, counting the many who habitually went more than once a week.[1] About half of these theaters were in towns of less than five thousand inhabitants, and they extended about as far out into the suburban fringe of the cities as groceries and drug stores. Only the most remote localities were beyond easy reach of the movies and only the most exclusive individuals failed to patronize them occasionally.

The small, unattractive and often unsafe halls which served well enough in the earlier years of the century now developed into gorgeous and gigantic theaters designed especially for the purpose, equipped with pipe-organ and symphony-size orchestra, and providing elaborate divertissements involving soloists, ballet and chorus, in addition to the pictures, which, it must be confessed, did not improve in proportion to their setting, except in photographic technic. The turning point in this development of building and program may be dated as 1914 when Samuel L. Rothafel, known to millions as "Roxy," who not many years before in a little Pennsylvania mining town had had to give his show behind a barroom on such days as he could borrow chairs from an undertaker, opened the Strand Theater in New York and developed a form of entertainment more akin to the opera than to the old "nickelodeon."

Meantime the art of the silent drama was showing steady improvement. Those actors who possessed the

versal Pictures. Terry Ramsaye, "The Motion Picture," Am. Acad. of Polit. and Social Sci., *Annals,* CXXVIII, 15, 19.

[1] Alice M. Mitchell, *Children and Movies* (Chicago, 1929), 17-66.

peculiar power to impress their personality on the public through pantomime rose speedily to prominence and attained, what previously had been an exaggeration, world-wide celebrity. Among the first to become such popular favorites were three young girls: the Gish sisters, Lillian and Dorothy, and Gladys Smith (better known as Mary Pickford) in pathetic and sentimental rôles; and, among the men, Charlie Chaplin in comedy and Douglas Fairbanks in romantic drama.

In 1913 Charles Spencer Chaplin was an inconspicuous vaudeville actor, playing a character part that he had picked up as a boy from observing an old man who had been reduced to holding horses in front of a London public house. Michael Simm Sinnot (Mack Sennett) offered him $150 a week to play in his Keystone Comedies. Two years later another company was glad to take him over at $1250 a week, and the next year he was getting more than ten times that salary. Before he had been in the movies ten years Charlie Chaplin was known by name and sight to more of his contemporaries in all lands than any man who had ever lived. This unique position was due to the unprecedented opportunity afforded by the invention of the motion picture and to his being particularly clever in a field and in a rôle of perennial popularity. The slap-stick farce had been a favorite from the earliest ages of acting, and no plot in folk tales had made a wider appeal than that of the underdog who by some surprising turn came out on top. Charlie Chaplin's customary make-up, his tiny mustache, his ill-fitting shoes, suit and hat, his air of injured innocence under unmerited misfortunes, and his quick "comeback," aroused amusement and subconscious sympathy in all lands and classes.

The first photoplay to develop the dramatic capabilities of the film was "The Birth of a Nation," produced in 1915 by David Wark Griffith from *The Clansman* by the Reverend Thomas Dixon, a novel of Reconstruction days in which the Ku Klux Klan was presented as the defender of white supremacy and feminine virtue. Though the play aroused the bitter resentment of the Negroes and their Northern sympathizers, and though it was the first motion-picture show for which the full theater price of two dollars was charged, it was an immediate and long-continued popular success. It was perhaps no mere coincidence that a few years later the K. K. K. was revived and became an active factor in American politics. "The Birth of a Nation" was an epoch-making work in the history of the motion picture, because Griffith had the courage to cut loose from the conventions and limitations of the stage and to employ the technic peculiar to the screen, such as flight and pursuit, mobs and battles, distant views and close-ups, the fade-out and the switch-back, and by the alternation of views of simultaneous events in distant places to keep the attention of the spectator on their interaction, as, in this case, the extremity of the besieged and the approach of the rescuers.

Griffith's production also demonstrated the value of the photoplay in the depiction of historical events, and established the supremacy of the feature film. The feature film ordinarily ran from one to two hours and cost to prepare from ten thousand dollars to several millions. Between seven and eight hundred feature films were produced in America annually. Among the most successful were: several of pioneer days, "The Covered Wagon," "The Iron Horse" and "The Pony Express"; war plays, "The Big Parade," "The Four Horsemen of the Apocalypse" from the story of Blasco Ibañez, and "What Price Glory"; religious dramas, "The Ten Commandments," "The King of Kings," "Quo Vadis" and "Ben Hur";

Griffith productions, "America" and "The Orphans of the Storm"; North African plays, such as "The Sheik" and "Beau Geste"; romantic dramas in which Douglas Fairbanks starred, such as "The Three Musketeers," "Robin Hood" and "The Thief of Bagdad."

Hollywood, California, as we have seen elsewhere, became the world center of motion-picture production on account of its brilliant sunshine, mild winter weather and diversified scenery. After the war American films largely monopolized the field in Europe, Asia and South America, often constituting from eighty-five to ninety per cent of the pictures exhibited. This aroused patriotic opposition which took the form of protests against the pernicious influence of the spread of American luxury, manners, morals and ideals as portrayed, oftentimes with great want of fidelity, in the pictures. Finally, France and other European governments imposed restrictions, requiring the exhibit of a certain quota of homemade films.

By the end of the period methods of synchronizing voice, music and other incidental sounds with the film were perfected so that dramas and operas were heard as a whole. The achievement was first demonstrated by the sudden success of "The Jazz Singer" in which Al Jolson, a Jewish black-face favorite, sang his characteristic "Mammy" songs. This was in October, 1927, and within two years the leading theaters of the country had remodeled their mechanism so as to use sound.[1]

In the field of aviation America got a long start but failed to hold the lead.[2] "At the time of our entry into

---

[1] R. E. MacAlarney, "The Noise Movie Revolution," *World's Work*, LVIII (1929), no. 4, 48.

[2] The achievements of American pioneers in the field of aviation are discussed in H. U. Faulkner, *The Quest for Social Justice* (*A History of American Life*, XI), chap. vi. See also Mark Sullivan, *Our Times* (N. Y., 1927), II, 604.

the War we had no combat planes and only a few planes for training and scouting purposes." [1] The World War forced the art of flying into a sudden prematurity as soon as it was discovered that the airplane was not merely "the eyes of the army" but a most effective fighting machine. All the European powers spent money and sacrificed lives without stint, so both the science and the art of aviation developed more rapidly in four years than it normally would have in forty. In this development Americans took no part at first except for the gallant young men who volunteered in French and British flying corps and for the planes made in the United States to fill orders of the belligerent powers. But when at last we entered the war the American people had high anticipations of what they would achieve in aviation. We were confessedly unfamiliar with the methods of modern warfare, and it was uncertain how our hastily levied troops and new-made officers would compare with the seasoned soldiery of Europe, but in a field like this, where inventive genius, industrial organization and mass production were the important essential factors, everyone expected that the nation would achieve notable success.

The first rumors allowed to leak through the veil of the volunteer censorship confirmed public confidence. A little group of engineers, it was said, within a week of arrival in Washington had evolved a "Liberty" engine of eight cylinders adapted to immediate mass production. But before it was even tested, advice from the front had compelled a twelve-cylinder model. Actually it was nearly a year before American battle planes began to arrive in France. Twenty-four million dollars were spent on planes that had to be discarded; most of our

[1] "The Hughes Aircraft Report," *Aerial Age Wkly.*, VIII, 511 (Nov. 18, 1918).

young aviators had to train in France in French machines.

As these facts became known, public opinion shifted from impossible anticipations to unfounded suspicions. It was alleged that half a billion dollars had been wasted, that colossal graft had marked the whole enterprise, that Germans and traitors in the shops had cramped and blocked production, and much more. These charges were referred by the president for investigation to the attorney-general with the coöperation of Charles E. Hughes. After the examination of some three hundred witnesses and the taking of seventeen thousand pages of testimony, the report was made on October 25, 1918.[1] No member of the aircraft boards or signal corps was found guilty of any dishonesty or intentional delay or disloyalty, though Hughes added dryly, "The provisions of the criminal statutes do not reach inefficiency."

There was ample evidence of extravagance and confusion. "Wasteful conditions were permitted to exist that were wholly inexcusable." "In the labor market the Government was largely competing with itself." The sabotage was insignificant; in spite of widespread suspicion only seven persons were indicted out of one or two hundred thousand laborers. The delay and loss were chiefly caused by frequent changes in design after manufacturing was under way, by conflict and confusion due to duplicated and undefined authorities, and by the constant friction between civilian zeal and military red tape. But when the great apparatus was in order production leaped to almost incredible proportions. Let us give the last word to the official side of it: "Up to the Armistice, 15,700 training engines and 13,396 Liberty engines had

[1] The findings were published in full in the *Aerial Age Wkly.*, VIII (Nov. 11, 1918-Jan. 20, 1919). They are summarized under "Aeronautics" in the *New International Yearbook for 1918.*

been produced. The Liberty engine development, in point of view of rapidity, cost and quality, was one of the most strikingly successful projects of the War." [1] And from the oversea aspect: "At the cessation of hostilities, we had a total of forty-seven squadrons in active service at the front, eleven of which were equipped with the American plane and Liberty motor. The total number of planes in our forces on the front at this time was 860." [2]

When the war stopped abruptly there were twenty-four aircraft plants in the United States capable of turning out twenty-one thousand airplanes annually, and no market for them, for the government contracts amounting to a million dollars were immediately canceled.[3] In Europe a network of regular airlines for passengers, mail and express developed, chiefly supported by government subsidies, but in America it was not until 1926 that commercial aviation began to prove profitable. Little was done except through the efforts of the United States post office, which started with a daily air-mail service between New York and Washington in 1918 and gradually extended it until by 1924 a regular day-and-night service was established between New York and San Francisco via Chicago and Cheyenne. The postage, at first twenty-four cents for a one-ounce letter, was reduced to five cents in 1928.

In the matter of airships the United States had bad luck. The government after the war, determined to get

[1] Rear-Admiral W. A. Moffett, Chief of U. S. Bur. of Aeronautics, "Air Forces," *Encyclopedia Britannica* (suppl. to thirteenth edn.), I, 68.
[2] Lieut.-Col. L. H. Brereton, Chief of Air Service Operations, in T. M. Knappen, *Wings of War* (N. Y., 1920), 74.
[3] Howard Mingos, "America Takes the Lead in Aviation," *World's Work*, LI (1926), 633-644; G. K. Spencer, "1926—A Turning Point in American Aviation," *Current History*, XXV (1927), 465-479. W. J. Davis, *The World's Wings* (N. Y., 1927), shows how far the United States was behind Europe in aviation, except for our continental air mail.

the biggest and best, ordered four dirigibles from different sources, but three of them were destroyed.[1] The chief danger of the dirigible is from fire on account of the inflammability of hydrogen that inflates it, but safety from this cause was insured by a discovery made in America during the war. This was that helium, a rare element, first found by spectroanalysis in the sun and then not known to exist on earth, was contained in considerable proportions in certain gas wells in Texas and Oklahoma. Since helium is next to hydrogen in lightness, it is almost as good for filling balloons and has the great advantage of being unburnable.

Another American contribution to the science of aviation was the invention of the earth-inductor compass which enables the pilot to steer a straight course in fog or darkness, since its coil rotating on a vertical axis shows any deviation in relation to the lines of force about the globe. Another of a different type was the metallurgical achievement of Sylvanus A. Reed in developing a metal propeller which made possible an increase of twenty per cent in speed.

The American people appreciated the privilege of saving three days in sending a letter across the continent, but flying did not appeal to them as a business proposition. They took no interest in it as a speculation but much interest as a spectacle. It was the adventure rather than the invention that attracted the public. Measuring public interest by inches of newspaper space no event of the fourteen years covered by this volume was so notable as

[1] The *Roma* bought from Italy burned up a few months later, with 44 lives lost. The *ZR-2* built by the British broke down on her trial trip shortly before starting oversea and 62 persons perished. The *Shenandoah*, made in America after the Zeppelin design, was wrecked in a Mid-West storm in September 1925. The fourth, built at the Zeppelin works at Friedrichshafen by special permission of the council of ambassadors in 1919, was sailed over the ocean by a German crew in 1924 and christened the *Los Angeles*. She was still intact at the time this record closed.

Charles A. Lindbergh's flight from New York to Paris on May 20-21, 1927. More space was given to it in some of the papers than to the premature or the correct announcement of peace. During the first four days, according to a clipping bureau, 27,000 columns were published about it in the American papers, and the number of the "stories" ran 220,000 above those published when Woodrow Wilson died.[1] New York papers sold from 40,000 to 100,000 extra copies a day.

The unprecedented popularity of Lindbergh arose partly from the fact that he was the ideal object of American hero worship. His youth and ingenuousness and his modest demeanor unspoiled by world-wide adulation prevented his popularity from coming down quickly like a rocket stick as happened with previous heroes of the American people. His courage won him at first the nickname of the "Flying Fool," then his success won him the nickname of "Lucky Lindy," but later he was recognized as an unusually careful and skillful mechanic and competent aviator. He had been an air-mail pilot when he made up his mind to enter the competition for the $25,000 Orteig prize for the transatlantic flight. Using up all his savings, two thousand dollars, in buying an airplane, he got enough to pay the balance from St. Louis men. He reconstructed the machine according to his own ideas and flew from San Diego, California, to New York in record time. On Friday morning, May 20, a little before eight o'clock, he set out alone in his single-motored monoplane the *Spirit of Saint Louis* and landed on the field of Le Bourget thirty-three hours and a half later (10:42 Paris time), where he was received by such a throng that he considered it "the most dangerous part of the trip," and the canvas of his

[1] Silas Bent, "The Art of Ballyhoo," *Harper's Mag.*, CLV (1927), 485-494.

Douglas Fairbanks in his motion picture
"The Thief of Bagdad."

Charles A. Lindbergh with some of his St. Louis backers after
his flight to Paris.

precious plane was cut to pieces by indomitable souvenir hunters.

The officials and French people gave him a warm and enthusiastic welcome, although they were still sad over the loss of two of their favorite flyingmen, Coli and Nungesser, who had set out for New York two weeks before and never been heard of afterward. A week later Lindbergh flew to Brussels and next day to Croydon, England, then back to France, whence he was brought to Washington as the guest of the nation in the cruiser *Memphis*. His receptions here and at New York, St. Louis and other cities were such as had never been given to a private citizen before.[1] The rest of the year he spent in touring the country in the *Spirit of Saint Louis* under the auspices of the Daniel Guggenheim Fund for the Promotion of Aeronautics. He visited every state in the Union. In the *Spirit of Saint Louis* he spent two hundred and sixty hours in the air and flew 22,350 miles, visiting eighty-two cities in the forty-eight states, always on time or ahead of time. Then he flew to Mexico and various Central American and South American and Caribbean countries as an "unofficial ambassador of good-will."

Lindbergh's exploit was so conspicuous because he carried it out by himself and without a slip, while equally daring ventures of the time met with various misfortunes. A longer nonstop flight to Europe was made shortly after by Clarence D. Chamberlin and C. A. Levine, who started for Berlin on June 4, but were forced to land a hundred miles away when their fuel ran out after they had made 3911 miles in forty-two hours and a half. Four men, Richard E. Byrd, G. O. No-

[1] For a summary of Lindbergh's flight and receptions, see *Current History*, XXVI (1927), 512-538; and C. A. Lindbergh, "We" (N. Y., 1927).

ville, Bert Acosta and Bernt Balchen, attempted to repeat Lindbergh's feat in the three-motored monoplane *America,* but after flying over France in the fog for hours and failing to find Paris, came down in the English Channel, narrowly escaping with their lives. The flight from Oakland, California, to Hawaii was accomplished in 1927 by eight persons in four planes, but nine men and one woman lost their lives in the attempt.

In the midst of the excitement over these direct flights to Europe many recalled that the first transatlantic air voyage had been achieved some years before and was "not a sporting proposition but a naval manœuver planned and executed with all the scientific preparation and care that characterizes any other operation in our navy." [1] Three of the navy seaplanes first flew from Rockaway to Trepassy, Newfoundland, on May 15, 1919, then to the Azores. One of them, the *NC-4,* with Commander Read and Lieutenant Walter Hinton, went on to Lisbon, then to Ferrol, Spain, and reached Plymouth, England, on May 31. The American navy also has the honor of the first flight to the North Pole, accomplished on May 9, 1926, by Lieutenant Commander Richard E. Byrd and Floyd G. Bennett, who flew from Spitsbergen to the pole and returned without landing in sixteen hours, having traveled sixteen hundred miles. Byrd later added the South Pole to his collection, and mapped wide regions of the Antarctic in 1929.

Once awakened by Lindbergh's flights and similar feats to the practical possibilities of aviation, the American people made up for the time lost by their reluctance to enter this field. By the end of 1928, the twenty-fifth anniversary of Wright's first flight, there were forty-

[1] Lieut. Walter Hinton, "The First Transatlantic Flight," *Current History,* XXVI (1927), 548.

eight airways in the United States, with a combined length of twenty thousand miles, linking three hundred and fifty-five cities which had municipal airports. Licensed aviators increased from fifteen hundred to more than eleven thousand.[1]

In 1928, whether one surveyed the production of airplanes or any other branch of manufacturing, it was apparent that more respect was being paid the expert than had been the case in 1914. The "practical" man who had nothing but his own experience to stand on was being supplanted by the university-trained man who had mastered the underlying principles that governed the work at hand. The laboratory had become appurtenant to the shop. There were many who smiled a little when some scientist pronounced *ex cathedra*, as though the truth as to any natural phenomenon had been all and finally ascertained, but it can still be said that the average man felt more respectful and more grateful to the scientist, whether in the field of research or that of useful applications, in 1928 than he had ever felt before.

[1] *Aircraft Year Book for 1929*, 1.

CHAPTER XV

THE MIND OF A NATION

THE æsthetic side of American civilization has usually been its weakest. In the new arts created by science, such as the motion picture, the radio and the phonograph, the United States did indeed play the leading part, but perhaps this may be attributed rather to inventive skill than to artistic sense. As we have seen, after 1914 there also occurred a marked improvement in artistic appreciation and a demand for greater beauty in household equipment and advertised commodities. It was no less true that American architecture was almost revolutionized in every category from the bungalow to the skyscraper, and that civic-welfare movements made the average small town a far more attractive home for its citizens. Even coins and medals were more pleasingly designed; even billboards less offensive; even boxes and bottles and binding twine in better taste. Women's clothing— though this reflected a world-wide tendency—was perhaps more beautiful, from an artistic point of view, than at any previous time in American history, graceful in line and rich in color.

But the great improvement in popular taste during the period by no means implied any corresponding development of popular craftsmanship. It remained true, as it has elsewhere been pointed out,[1] that the modern American creative instinct "finds expression in changing the washers on the faucets or tinkering with the Ford."

[1] J. T. Adams, *Provincial Society* (*A History of American Life*, III), 140.

More than ever goods were made in the factory and distributed to the consumer through the channels of trade. The suburbanite meekly accepted a good house design from his architect and less than ever ventured to interject his amateur fancies into the architect's plans. The feminine arts of needlework and cooking were less emphasized; the tendency to leave the plan of a room to a professional decorator and the garden to a landscape designer increased. There was, indeed, less artistic *self*-expression than even in the tasteless Victorian days when the lady of the house was painting china badly, making pyrographic mottoes for the bedroom wall and fixing up absurd museums of shells and starfish for the parlor curio cabinet but, at all events, creating something with however little skill. In artistic creation, as in amusements, the American had never before been so well served and never before done so little to serve himself. Pampered by machinery and surrounded by its often excellent products, the Yankee had almost forgotten how to whittle.

When massed together in a civic regiment under expert direction, however, the American found it possible to participate in an æsthetic crusade. One of the first state-wide contests took place in Utah in 1914 and was repeated the following year. Residences were inspected by local committees, and towns by state judges, a prize being given the town showing greatest civic pride in each of six classes according to size.[1] In many other instances a local newspaper fostered "city-beautiful" contests. Elsewhere a chamber of commerce or a Rotary, Lions or Kiwanis club, or a woman's civic group took the movement under its wing. Few communities alto-

[1] Seventy credits were granted for such practical matters as sewerage, stables (there were still stables then), garbage, water supply, sanitation, freedom from flies and the like; thirty credits for the beauty of streets and parks. *Survey*, XXXIV, 301-302 (July 3, 1915).

gether escaped, though the results were not always secure against backsliding.

In equal step with city beautifying went the movement for city planning. From 1914 to 1928, 570 cities
created planning commissions.[1] In 1916 only eight cities
were subject to zoning regulations, but by the end of
1928 over seven hundred cities, towns, villages, with a
total population of more than thirty-seven million, had
adopted the system.[2] The primary purpose of the zoning ordinances was to secure the pleasant residential sections of the towns from the possibility of being
swamped by the spreading business sections, but there
were many subsidiary regulations designed to secure the
maximum light and air to all parts of the community.
One aspect of these regulations had a remarkable effect on
the development of commercial architecture.

The skyscraper had been familiar for a generation to
the sight-seer in New York, Chicago and a few other
great cities when in 1913 the Woolworth Building in
Manhattan rose to a height of sixty stories, the tallest
inhabited structure in the world, 792 feet above street
level. For a long time that marked the limit of height,
though at the end of the period (1928) there were
several buildings in process of erection which would
outsoar it. The significant tendency during the interven-
ing years was not towards new records of height, but
towards multiplication of the skyscraper type and the
development, under the pressure of building regulations,
of a new style of structure. By 1925 there were over sixteen hundred buildings in New York City alone of more
than ten stories apiece, and Henry H. Curran, a member
of the municipal city-planning committee, was denounc-

[1] E. E. Calkins, "Beauty and the Booster," *Atlantic Mo.*, CXLV
(1930), 291.
[2] *U. S. Daily* (Wash.), April 11, 1929.

ing the congestion of mammoth buildings in lower Manhattan as a menace to public health and safety.[1] Yet the Manhattanites had the excuse of peculiar situation, an island of sturdy rock compressed between wide waterways almost to a pencil shape. Other cities on a loose earth soil with wide plains over which to expand took New York as the metropolitan model and out of imitative zeal copied the skyscraper in their own business districts. Very few followed Boston's example of placing an arbitrary limit to the height of buildings. More commonly the zoning laws followed the New York code of 1916 in limiting the height of vertical wall proportionately to the width of the streets but allowing additional towers where walls were set back from the limits of the lot.[2]

The new style, fostered and half compelled by the new building code, implied a massive tower burgeoning into a slenderer shaft, and this in turn into one still slighter, until the final pinnacle was reached. Instead of being a mere rectangular box set on end the typical skyscraper assumed a terraced or stepping-stone effect often compared to the Babylonian ziggurat. All problems of design were more carefully studied. Much impetus to the treatment of the skyscraper as an art form was given by the *Chicago Tribune* competition of 1922, which brought out two hundred and sixty designs from twenty-three countries.[3] The winning design, by John Mead Howells and Raymond Hood, was a graceful shaft flaming into pinnacles of Gothic treatment at its crest. Even more interest was aroused by the winner of the

[1] *N. Y. Times*, Sept. 5, 1926.
[2] C. H. Walker, "America's Titanic Strength Expressed in Architecture," *Current History*, XXI (1925), 555. See also T. E. Tallmadge, *The Story of Architecture in America* (N. Y., 1927), 288-289, for the effect on style of the New York and Chicago building codes.
[3] Tallmadge, *Story of Architecture*, 290.

second prize, a design submitted by Eliel Saarinen of
Finland, which gave an entirely new concept to the skyscraper. "It is the best design since Amiens!" exclaimed
one enthusiast.[1] In it the classic traditions of horizontal
lines and cornices were wholly abandoned and the vertical masses were given full scope without apology.
Saarinen was called to give instruction at the University
of Michigan, and his *Chicago Tribune* design was widely
imitated and adapted in the newer structures, which
relied entirely on mass and form for their effect, disdain-
ing superficial ornamentation. The skyscraper idea was
applied to other than office buildings. The Shelton Hotel
in New York (1925), the projected "cathedral of learning" of the University of Pittsburgh and the huge tower
of the new state capitol of Lincoln, Nebraska, illustrated
some of the diverse possibilities of the form. Churches,
apartment houses, university campaniles and war memorials also adapted suggestions from the new skyscraper.

But American architecture developed in more conventional ways as well. Purely classical buildings, such
as the Lincoln Memorial in Washington, and buxom
Roman structures, such as metropolitan railway terminals, won the praise of the severest foreign critics. In
domestic architecture the prewar tendencies continued
strong—colonial simplicity in new suburban homes in
the East and South, the cozy chalet, bungalow and
Elizabethan cottage patterns in the prosperous Middle
Western towns, the Spanish style in Florida, California
and sporadically elsewhere. The tasteful use of tinted
stucco, "tapestried" brick, varicolored slate or tile roofs
added the charm of color to that of design. Factories and
schools generally adopted a form of ground plan and an
extent of window space scientifically calculated to yield

[1] Tallmadge, *Story of Architecture*, 291.

the maximum amount of light and air to the occupants and, while thus seeking health and convenience, incidentally sometimes attained beauty also.

In painting, sculpture and the decorative arts generally the Americans were far less original than in architecture. Art exhibits showed a tendency to experiment with the new techniques of impressionism, cubism and futurism, but in all these movements the United States was a follower rather than a leader, and the permanent success of any of them was more than dubious. The war stimulated memorial sculpture, and it is encouraging to compare the free and bold sculptured groups which commemorated the battles of 1917-1918 with the stiff and formal "soldiers' monuments" that followed in the wake of the Civil War. Earlier history had its memorials too, notably the group of Confederate chieftains sculptured on the face of Stone Mountain, Georgia, begun by Gutzon Borglum but carried toward completion by other hands after that temperamental genius had quarreled with some of his sponsors. George Grey Barnard embodied in bronze a new conception of Lincoln, emphasizing his youthful ungainly angularity.[1]

Thanks to the radio and the phonograph the United States was quantitatively more musical than ever before, but the popular vogue of the crudest type of jazz casts some doubt on any improvement in taste.[2] At the same time it can be said that no previous generation had heard as much first-class orchestral music either at first

[1] It is not often that we have a popular referendum on a work of art. One may test the popularity of a book by noting how it sells, but the price of a statue or painting is more often fixed by a few admirers than by the verdict of the crowd. This gives interest to the votes of 1200 random magazine readers on the merit of six famous statues of Abraham Lincoln. St. Gaudens's statue in Lincoln Park, Chicago, had thrice the preferential vote of its nearest competitor and over eight times that of Barnard's ultrarealistic version, the last of the six in favor. *Independent*, XCII, 591 (Dec. 29, 1917).

[2] For popular music in the United States, see earlier, pp. 282-284.

hand or as brought to them by Victrola and radio. Most opera presented in American cities was European in both music and libretto, but in the early months of 1927 "The King's Henchman," with a "book" by Edna St. Vincent Millay and music by Deems Taylor, was presented successfully in New York and hailed by the critics as the best effort in grand opera that America had thus far produced. Of course, many American singers had an international reputation. Particularly noteworthy was the meteoric career of Marion Talley, a young Missouri girl who joined the Metropolitan Opera Company in 1925, rose in the following year to a star of the first magnitude, taking twenty curtain calls at her début in grand opera, and retired from the stage in 1929.

The theater generally was hard hit by increasing costs of production and by the competition of the moving pictures. Though vaudeville, musical comedies, "follies" and "vanities" flourished, the old-time melodrama of the Bowery type practically disappeared. "Nellie, the Beautiful Cloak Model," and her sisters had to get a job with the movies or else accept the offer of the villain millionaire—the stage had no place for them. At the other extreme of the spoken drama, and allowing for certain "revivals" by Walter Hampden and others, Shakespeare fared almost as badly. More than ever the stage tended to become a monopoly of the metropolis in contrast to the movies which were equally at home in New York and in the remotest prairie hamlet. In the attempt to hold the fickle public some producers overdid the emphasis on sex and frightened moralists into a campaign of repression. Of course nearly every play is based on sex by its traditional trade name of "the love interest," but the critics meant that some of the new plays went farther in disrobing bodies, and others in disrobing minds, than had hitherto been considered tolerable. Fortunately, the

objectionable plays were neither the most numerous nor
the most popular. "Abie's Irish Rose," by Anne Nichols,
held the boards longer than any other play of the postwar decade, and while the critics scorned it as machine-
made art no moralist objected to it; on the contrary
the plot was a regular Sunday-School lesson in racial
and religious tolerance. There was still in the American
audience a sentimental fondness for lovable, eccentric
characters; and Frank Bacon in "Lightnin' " (1918)
repeated the success of Joseph Jefferson's "Rip Van
Winkle" of a former generation, while Don Marquis's
"The Old Soak" (1921) was popular with readers as
well as with spectators.

The most powerful original force in American drama
was Eugene O'Neill, considered by many the foremost
of all American dramatists. His "Emperor Jones"
(1921) was an imaginative masterpiece depicting the
quicksands of superstition and terror engulfing the
masterful personality of a Negro dictator as he lived over
again in vision the tragic chapters of the history of his
race. "Anna Christie" (1922) was an equally effective
triumph of relentless realism; "The Hairy Ape"
(1922), a symbolic play of a primitive mind bewildered
by the complexity of life; "Desire under the Elms"
(1924) verged on the morbid with its sultry atmosphere
of tension and repression; and "The Great God Brown"
(1925) carried symbolism to such a degree of complexity as completely to bewilder even the most intelligent audiences. Always, whether as realist or fantasist, he
wrote in the minor key, tragedy minus romance, with a
sense of doom that was more Russian than Greek; it was
a tribute to his genius that he was so greatly admired in
the most optimistic country in the world. Perhaps continental European influences had in some degree prepared
the public for him. On the metropolitan stage, and in

university and other amateur performances, the plays of such continental dramatists as Molnar and Capek rivaled the Irish drama of Yeats and Dunsany and the English plays of Galsworthy and Milne. The Theater Guild, organized in New York to promote appreciation of the drama, specialized in European plays. The Russian influence in music, dance and drama was strong, being much stimulated by the success of "Chauve-Souris" in 1922.

The weakness of the professional stage in most parts of the country was counterbalanced in no small degree by the popular interest in amateur and experimental playwriting and acting. In colleges, universities and high schools, where literary and debating societies and literary magazines languished in neglect, there were often several dramatic societies producing successfully different types of drama. "Little theaters" and small traveling companies, such as the Jitney or the Rockford players, specialized in symbolic and intellectual plays that might not tempt the Broadway managers. Some Broadway successes, indeed, were first launched by artists in Provincetown, Massachusetts, or in New York's "ghetto" of the lower East Side. Courses in playwriting were popular in many universities, and when in 1925 Yale won Professor George P. Baker, director of "47 Workshop" (a student class in the technique of playwriting), from Harvard, the alumni of both institutions were almost as stirred as over a football triumph. In North Dakota and in North Carolina the country folk, under intelligent direction, wrote, staged and acted plays dealing with their own life on Dakota plains or in Carolina hills with almost as much simple and earnest effectiveness as the peasant religious drama of Oberammergau.[1]

[1] See the introduction to *Carolina Folk Plays* (N. Y., 1922), edited by F. H. Koch.

Verse in the United States had a new blooming, a
silver age that remotely suggested the golden day of Poe,
Whitman, Emerson, Lowell, Longfellow, Bryant,
Whittier and Lanier.[1] Which, if any, of the new poets
will be ranked with the giants of the middle third of the
nineteenth century cannot at present (1930) be guessed;
they still "abide our question" and criticism has not yet
given them their respective ratings. But if there be no
gold among them, at any rate their silver is ore fresh
from the mine, not old coins a hundred times rehandled
like the conventional magazine verse which passed current for lack of better during a great part of the period
from the Civil War to the World War. The rugged free
verse favored by the new American poets was more often
a promise than an achievement, but it is something that
experiments were being made. Except for a common dis-
dain of conventional rules and poetic traditions there is
not much one can say about the new poets as a group.
They were all individual, in a sense they were all "exceptions."

For instance, Edgar Lee Masters, whose *Spoon River
Anthology* (1915) took the country by storm even
while filling it with consternation, was often bracketed
with Nicholas Vachel Lindsay, whose *Congo* (1914)
aroused a similar furor of praise and bewilderment. But
while the two poets broke bounds with equal audacity
they made their escape in opposite directions. Masters
disdained rime and rhythm; his verse was really ironic
prose. Lindsay, on the contrary, outdid Chesterton or
Kipling in his fondness for rhythm, alliteration, asso-
nance and every other device that can make words sound
like a military band marching in full blast down the
street. All his verse had music, though sometimes it

[1] See C. R. Fish, *The Rise of the Common Man* (*A History of American Life*, VI), 245-254.

might be the music of his own favorite circus "kallyope" rather than that of the traditional lute and lyre. Carl Sandburg, exponent of the "barbaric yawp" of Chicago, combined something of the zest and gusto of Lindsay with the harshness, irony and unmusical verse of Masters. All three took their themes from the common life of the Middle West and used the language of everyday with a nonchalant frankness that would have driven even Wordsworth to protest.

Other poets had a more self-conscious craftsmanship. Robert Frost in *North of Boston* (1914), *New Hampshire* (1923) and most of his other work painted with unsparing realism the dour lives of the Yankee farmers, but there was no such harshness in his method as marked the satire of Masters and Sandburg. Every touch of his pen showed both tenderness and humor, the twin offspring of human sympathy. Edwin Arlington Robinson, a poet's poet, was sterner in mood but equally austere and restrained in his art. His *The Man against the Sky* (1916), *The Man Who Died Twice* (1924) and *Tristram* (1927) won more general critical approval than any other verse of the period, though many poets had a wider popular audience. William Ellery Leonard in *Two Lives* (1925) [1] wrote the tragedy of his own life much more effectively and with no less realism than in his prose autobiography *The Locomotive God* (1927). The vehicle he chose was the traditional sonnet sequence, a conventionality of form that added to the effect of its stark modernism of theme. Amy Lowell, chief of the imagists, practically abandoned subject matter for pure decoration. Her verses, like the paintings of Whistler, were combinations of form and color rather than stories told in art. Shortly before her death in 1925 she completed an excellent biographical study of Keats, a poet

[1] Printed privately in 1922.

with whose ideal of abstract beauty, unrelated to theme, she had so much natural sympathy. Among the minor lyricists Edna St. Vincent Millay deserves a special word of praise for sheer beauty of expression. Some poets, such as Louis Untermeyer, Witter Bynner and the veteran Edwin Markham, lent occasional aid to humanitarian propaganda, and one must not forget the martyr poets of the war, Joyce Kilmer and Alan Seeger, nor the few journalistic humorists, such as T. A. Daly and Arthur Guiterman, who were able to put real wit into real verse.

The most interesting tendency in the fiction of the period was towards what might be called the self-criticism of the small town. We are, as Bernard Shaw once called us, a "nation of villagers," not of peasants, like Russia, and only by exception metropolitans. The widest and most populous section of the nation was now the Mississippi Valley—appropriately celebrated in Meredith Nicholson's *Valley of Democracy* (1918)—and as the center of population moved westward this section increasingly became the norm of American life, with New England, New York, the old South and California as its marginal variations. The rather standardized small-town life on the flat plains, with its universal public-school system, its ubiquitous commercial clubs and secret societies, its competitive Protestant sects, its combination of Yankee business ruthlessness on week days with sentimental aspiration on Sundays and civic holidays, became the target for a score of literary archers. Not all Americans, to be sure, were so unfortunate as to live by the *Spoon River* of Edgar Lee Masters, or with Sherwood Anderson in *Winesburg, Ohio* (1919), or *West of the Water Tower* (1923) with Homer Croy, or on *Main Street* (1920) with Sinclair Lewis. The novels of Booth Tarkington and the stories of William

Allen White painted a better balanced picture of contrasted light and shade than these rather one-sided indictments. But it is significant that most of these grim realists were themselves of the Western small town by birth and residence, not merely literary slummers from the metropolis. The Middle West, or one layer of it, was indulging in the wholesome diversion of self-disparagement. Boosterism led to equal exaggeration on the opposite side.

Sinclair Lewis's *Main Street* might be called from the historian's point of view—though emphatically not from that of the literary critic—the most important book written in the United States in the postwar decade. Stuart P. Sherman, whose own viewpoint was widely different, declared that "more thoroughly than any novel since *Uncle Tom's Cabin*, it has shaken our complacency with regard to the average quality of our civilization." [1] In a little over two months it sold fifty thousand copies and in eight years eight hundred thousand. [2] It created, or ushered in, a whole school of fiction. "The appetite of Americans for hearing themselves abused may well take rank in history as the eighth wonder of the world," declared Henry Sydnor Harrison. [3] Some critics, such as Simeon Strunsky, interpreted the movement as but another form of the old Mid-Western sport of muckraking, with "the Shame of Kiwanis" taking the place of the "Shame of the Cities" and the "Treason

[1] S. P. Sherman, *Points of View* (N. Y., 1924), 191.
[2] *N. Y. Times*, March 17, 1929.
[3] "Let the reader as an exercise begin, say, with *Main Street* and *These United States*, and . . . count his way out to the newest collection of *Americana, The Great American Band-Wagon*, or such later contributions as may by this time have appeared. Let him by no means forget the historical and biographical works of the 'debunkers.' . . . we Americans have rolled up a literature of self-depreciation of absolutely staggering proportions." H. S. Harrison, "Last Days of the Devastators," *Yale Rev.*, XVIII (1928), 88-103.

of the Senate" in prewar days.[1] An anonymous correspondent in *Harper's* wittily represented the avidity with which the American public devoured the most hostile criticisms of itself as a case of inferiority complex.[2] There was, however, ample evidence of resentment at the acidity of the Lewisite school of social criticism.[3]

The attack on the small town was but one aspect of a general school of mordant naturalism. Sinclair Lewis showed that he was not a champion of the "city slickers" against the "hicks" by treating prosperous Zenith City in *Babbitt* (1922) even more severely than he had the village backwater of Gopher Prairie. His real enemy was commercialism and its ideals, whether in town or country, and his journalistic photography was often excellent though it never rose to portraiture. *Arrowsmith* (1925), his critique of the medical profession, contained his most nearly heroic hero and his only attractive heroine. *Elmer Gantry* (1927), which aimed to perform a similar service for the clergy, fell rather flat because Lewis hated the church and divided his pastors into fools and rogues only, whereas his physicians had included fools, rogues and sages. *Dodsworth* (1929) put the more selfish sort of American merchant princess in her place, a very low one; Dodsworth himself is a Babbitt to whom is added a code of honor and a gleam of culture. Booth Tarkington's *The Plutocrat* (1927) is another Babbitt, one wholly without culture but with real qualities of power, decision and energy, an interesting suggestion that even if the American business man fails as a Greek he may succeed as a conquering Roman.

The greatest of the novels of realistic naturalism in

[1] See H. U. Faulkner, *The Quest for Social Justice* (*A History of American Life*, XI), chap. v.

[2] *Harper's Mag.*, CLVII (1928), 395.

[3] For one example from hundreds, see Struthers Burt, "These Standardized United States," *Sat. Eve. Post*, CCI, 10 (May 11, 1929).

American life was probably Theodore Dreiser's *An American Tragedy* (1925), which succeeded in making an impression by sheer brute force in spite of an almost willful clumsiness of style. It attracted the unfavorable attention of the Boston police authorities and, along with a number of other current novels, was banned from the bookstalls under the amazing legal principle that, if a jury finds a single passage in a book objectionable, without reference to the tenor of the book as a whole, it is subject to prosecution.[1] Floyd Dell's *Moon-Calf* (1920), Zona Gale's *Miss Lulu Bett* (1920), John Dos Passos's pacifist novel *Three Soldiers* (1921), Sherwood Anderson's *Poor White* (1920), Edith Summers Kelly's *Weeds* (1924) and G. D. Eaton's *Backfurrow* (1925) are other typical reflections of discontent with the America that emerged from the war.

Another phase of cynicism and disillusionment was the jest at ancient ideals. John Erskine began it with his *Private Life of Helen of Troy* (1925) and *Galahad* (1926), followed later by restatements in the modernist vein of *Adam and Eve* (1927) and *Penelope's Man* (1928). His books had both popular and literary success and of course had imitators, such as Elmer Davis's *Giant Killer* (1928) "debunking" the reputation of King David, with the usual implication that, as a Frenchman put it, "Plutarch lied"—in other words, all the world's heroes were merely adventurers and the world's statesmen merely dead politicians. Biography, though very popular, was most relished when slightly acidulous, stressing the human character of the great man and especially his human weaknesses.

The fact that Thornton Wilder's *The Bridge of San Luis Rey*, a story of the mellow richness of an old Latin-American scene, became a best seller in 1928 was hailed

[1] F. L. Bullard in the *N. Y. Times*, April 28, 1929.

as a revulsion of taste alike from formlessness, from un-
distinguished, journalistic style and from cynical naturalism, but in truth at no period had the "debunkers" occupied the whole literary stage. Joseph Hergesheimer
and Willa Cather ranked equal with them in popular
approval and perhaps rather more highly in artistic
merit. Willa Cather's *One of Ours* (1922) and *Death
Comes for the Archbishop* (1927) entitled her to be
considered queen of the novel, but her court had many
accomplished maids or matrons of honor, such as Edith
Wharton, Corra Harris, Edna Ferber, Dorothy Canfield
and Mary Roberts Rinehart. James Branch Cabell stood
a little apart in this period—romantic and even fantastic
in theme, but allied to the cynics by a certain disdainful
attitude towards moral idealism. His preoccupation with
sex in *Jurgen* (1919) won for him the hostility of self-
appointed book censors and along with it the exaggerated praise of insurgents against all censorship.

The dominant figure in American criticism was unquestionably Henry Louis Mencken, critic for the *Baltimore Sun* and, after 1924, editor of the *American Mercury*. Although sometimes grouped with the "radical"
critics of American institutions, his point of view was
essentially that of the disdainful aristocrat, as his ultra-
reactionary *Notes on Democracy* (1926) should have
made plain to his admirers as well as his enemies. The
confusion probably arose from the fact that he joined the
radical onslaught on prohibition, Puritanism and the
Anglo-Saxon tradition in literature. Just because he disliked nearly everything in the United States he became
the more valuable as a balance wheel to keep national
pride in bounds, to remind America that its greatness is
but mortal and sometimes absurd into the bargain. In the
Mercury, which advertised itself as a "magazine with no
dreams of reform; it is concerned only with setting up

America as a puppet-show for the entertainment of its civilized inhabitants," he collected all he could find of the crack-brained deeds and words that crept into the press and called it "Americana." Unsophisticated college boys delighted to sip his sophistication, and a whole generation of them tried to imitate his style. For the rest, he was a good philologist,[1] a clever critic and a "bonny fechter."

But however great might be Mencken's services to American criticism, two major defects threatened to outweigh all his virtues. One was that he scorned so much and admired so little that he lacked the sympathy necessary to an understanding of other men and their institutions and opinions. Timon of Athens is not the best man to give a comprehending account of the great Athenian civilization! His other fault was that, being confined by temperament to the single field of satire, he used his weapons clumsily. Jonathan Swift was equally scornful of the world, but his subtle Irish rapier could get under the shield and between the ribs of the man he wished to wound, whereas the best Mencken could do was to rap him over the skull with bludgeoning epithets of "boob" and "moron" and "yokel."

To the historian of civilization what the American reads is more important than what he writes, for in the nature of things there must be several thousand who listen to each prophet who speaks. A study of the "mind of a nation" is very different from the study of a few exceptional minds in a nation, in much the same way that a study of the national standard of living differs from an account of a millionaire's colony in Newport or Palm Beach. The United States as a whole may safely be set down as a reading nation but not a bookish

[1] Note his dialect studies on *The American Language* (N. Y., 1919; rev., 1921, 1923).

nation. It led the world in the circulation of periodicals and newspapers but lagged behind all the countries of northern Europe in the number of books published in ratio to population and apparently (though here statistics are often incomplete) in the proportionate number of copies sold. Bookstores were less in evidence in American cities than in almost any European capital, though this deficiency was partly made good by the number of public libraries and by the sale of books through mail-order houses, department stores, newsstands and other channels. The chief novelty in book distribution was the club which offered its subscribers at stated intervals, usually of one month, a new book selected by a committee of expert critics. By the end of this period the Book-of-the-Month Club had about a hundred thousand subscribers.[1] The activity of the Literary Guild and the Book-of-the-Month Club held first place in the news of publishing during 1927 and 1928, "for the choice of a book by either board puts it in the best seller class immediately."[2]

The number and type of books published remained remarkably constant during the changeful years of 1914-1928. During the war the high cost of printing and paper, and perhaps the popular preoccupation with newspapers, cut down the number of new titles in nearly every class of work except those, such as history and books on military affairs, which dealt directly with the events of the day. But after the war the normal production and the normal distribution were restored. In proportion to the growing population slightly fewer

[1] Similar organizations included the Literary Guild, the American Bookseller's Association, the Religious Book Club, the Book League of America, the Catholic Book Club, the Detective Story Club, the Poetry Clan and the Freethought Book Club.

[2] W. B. Pressey in the *New International Year Book for 1927*, 470. For attacks on the book-of-the-month clubs by publishers, see *Lit. Digest*, CI, 27 (June 1, 1929).

books of nearly all kinds were being printed in the 1920's than during the three or four years just before the war.[1] This did not imply that the public was doing less reading. On the contrary, the total output of books and pamphlets increased from one hundred and seventy-five million copies in 1914 to almost four hundred and twenty-four million in 1925,[2] an increase from about two to nearly four per capita.[3] As nearly half these works were pamphlets, however, it would be safe to say that even by the latter date book circulation was barely two books a year to each American, or ten a year for a typical family of five. The tendency was evidently towards fewer books but a greater circulation for the average book.

The question of quality is always more important than that of quantity. What was the American asking for at his bookstall on the rather infrequent occasions when he visited it? E. Haldeman-Julius, who sold about twenty million "little blue books" a year, believed that, in relative demand, sex books and love stories and books on self-improvement stood first.[4] Certainly the advertising pages of all the periodicals corroborate his belief. Books on roads to success, on efficiency in business, on the making of "personality," on etiquette, and "outlines" of science, art, letters, history, philosophy and knowledge in general were ubiquitous. A sociological study of a Mid-Western town showed that over a period of twenty years (1903 to 1923), while the population had doubled, the local library circulation of works of fiction had quadrupled; that of histories in-

[1] Tables of annual production are given in *Publishers' Wkly.*, CXV, 275-278 (Jan. 19, 1929).

[2] *Publishers' Wkly.*, CXV, 278.

[3] E. W. Burgess, "Communication," *Am. Journ. of Sociology*, XXXIV, 125.

[4] E. Haldeman-Julius, *The First Hundred Million* (N. Y., 1928).

creased eightfold; of religion, elevenfold; philosophy and psychology, twenty-six-fold; and useful arts (business, technology, automobiles, applied electricity, etc.), sixty-two-fold.[1] Here also the emphasis shifted increasingly to a study of the art of getting on in the world.

Another indication of national taste is the "bestseller" lists of individual titles. In 1913, which is a better index year than 1914 as it eliminates the ephemeral "war books," every one of the best fiction sellers was a romantic and more or less sentimental story. Winston Churchill's *The Inside of the Cup*, a plea for religious and moral reform sugar-coated with narrative, headed the list, followed by Henry Sydnor Harrison's *V. V.'s Eyes*, Gene Stratton-Porter's *Laddie*, Gilbert Parker's *The Judgment House*, John Fox's *Heart of the Hills*, Jeffery Farnol's *The Amateur Gentleman*, Hall Caine's *The Woman Thou Gavest Me* and Mrs. Eleanor H. Porter's *Pollyanna*, "the glad book," whose name became a byword for an omnivorous optimism.[2] In the list of nonfiction best sellers Gerald Stanley Lee's idealistic essays on *Crowds* stood first, followed by Price Collier's *Germany and the Germans*. President Wilson's *New Freedom*, Lord Bryce's *South America*, Arnold Bennett's courteous *Your United States* and Mary Antin's *The Promised Land*, an immigrant's view of America, stood high on the list, along with cookbooks and works on auction bridge. Both lists, fiction and nonfiction, reflect a cheerful, aspiring, unquestioningly patriotic and orthodox age.

The list of 1928 is harder to interpret. The current here flows in no one direction but seems troubled and turbid. The taste in fiction varies between realistic studies, grave and often sad, and the detective novel.

[1] R. S. and Helen M. Lynd, *Middletown* (N. Y., 1929), 237.
[2] *Publishers' Wkly.*, LXXXV, 404-405 (Feb. 7, 1914).

Thornton Wilder's *The Bridge of San Luis Rey* leads with the two English novels, Hugh Walpole's *Wintersmoon* and John Galsworthy's *Swan Song,* following. Just when we are about to conclude that the American people were a nation of highbrows, we meet next in line S. S. Van Dine's *The Greene Murder Case,* and are reminded of John C. Powys's statement that "during no age known to the history of our race has there been so immense a flood of crime literature as at the present day." [1] The list resumes with Vina Delmar's *Bad Girl,* Booth Tarkington's *Claire Ambler,* Warwick Deeping's *Old Pybus* and Anne Parrish's *All Kneeling.* The bestseller nonfiction list is strong on biography, mostly by Europeans, beginning with André Maurois's *Disraeli* and containing two biographies by the German Emil Ludwig, *Napoleon* and *Goethe,* besides the half-biographic *Trader Horn,* Lindbergh's account of his transatlantic flight, *"We,"* and a narrative of *Count Luckner, the Sea-Devil,* Katherine Mayo's *Mother India,* a mordant attack on Hindu civilization, stands second, and Eugene O'Neill's *Strange Interlude* holds sixth place, a rare tribute to the drama.[2] Two generalizations, at least, seem safe: a decline of popular affection for polite romance and comfortable sentiment in fiction, and a growing predilection for biography.

The presence among the best sellers of such books as

[1] J. C. Powys, "The Crime Wave in Fiction," *World's Work,* LVIII (1929), 66-69. From a brief examination of the most popular books of this sort, however, the conclusion arises that the taste for mystery tales is not a perverse taste for the morbid or even a romantic craving for excitement, but merely a liking for puzzles similar to that which created the cross-word-puzzle fad a few years earlier.

[2] *Publishers' Wkly.,* CXV, 267-268 (Jan. 19, 1929). The 1927 fiction list started with Sinclair Lewis's *Elmer Gantry* and Booth Tarkington's *Plutocrat,* followed by two books by Warwick Deeping, while Will Durant's *Story of Philosophy,* the best of the myriad "outline-of-everything" books, led the nonfiction. In library demand Theodore Dreiser's *An American Tragedy* held first place, though it did not do so well on the bookstands. *Publishers' Wkly.,* CXIII, 232-233 (Jan. 21, 1928).

Will Durant's *Story of Philosophy,* Lewis Browne's *This Believing World,* and Bruce Barton's *The Man Nobody Knows* and *The Book Nobody Knows,* interpretations of religious history in the terms of modern American commercial life, shows that popular interest in the problems of religion and the church was still active. The word "still" is used advisedly since the impression widely prevailed that the increasing pressure of secular interests was crowding religion out of American life. How far this impression was justified is impossible to say: the straws point simultaneously in too many directions. There was a large increase in church membership, considerably higher for most denominations than what might have been expected from the increase in population. On the other hand, there was some decrease in church building, especially in the rural districts, and a widely prevalent complaint that the use of the automobile on sunny Sunday mornings was reducing average attendance. Pulpit oratory, even now that the radio had extended its range, seems to have had less influence than in the days of Phillips Brooks and Henry Ward Beecher, and it is very doubtful if the partnership of "Billy" Sunday and H. A. Rodeheaver stirred the nation like the evangelistic campaigns of Moody and Sankey.[1] Yet church organizations and associations were never so active in projects of social welfare and civic reform and many complaints were heard, especially in connection with the prohibition question, that the United States was politically ruled by the churches.[2]

An increased tendency towards liberalism in the theological seminaries was balanced by the establishment of various "Bible Institutes" of impeccable orthodoxy.

[1] See Allan Nevins, *The Emergence of Modern America* (*A History of American Life,* VIII), 260, 345.

[2] See R. L. Hartt, "The Church in Politics," *World's Work,* L (1925), 299-304.

The number of books on philosophy, religion, the church and the Bible remained fairly constant and reached a wider circle of readers, but often took an unconventional turn. "Perhaps the most striking feature of the stream of new religious books," said Dr. Winfred E. Garrison in 1927, "is the number of them that deal directly with the personality and teaching of Jesus. It is literally true that there is never a week without a new one, and a dozen a month would be a fair average." Though many of these books were written by persons who had more zeal than historical or theological competence, and appealed chiefly to readers who were not ecclesiastically minded, "even so," he added, "it will be a sorry day when the experts get a corner on religion." [1]

According to the estimates of the department of commerce, based on denominational statements, the number of church members increased in the decade 1916 to 1926 from 41,926,854 to 54,624,976.[2] "Every prominent Protestant denomination stands today at the highest point of its history in respect to adherents," declared an observer in 1928. At the same time, in the decade following the armistice, "the Congregationalists 'dropped' 1046 organizations, the Presbyterians 'dismissed' 61 and 'dissolved' 1143, a total death list for the two denominations . . . of 2250 churches; while they had a net gain of 470,348 members. In the country districts the abandoned church edifice is becoming a common sight." [3] This does not mean that church rolls were increasingly padded; the real explanation seems to lie partly in the

[1] *Chicago Daily Tribune*, March 27, 1927.
[2] *U. S. Daily*, Sept. 28, 1928; *N. Y. Times*, same date. In what other country would the collection of religious data be done by the department of commerce?
[3] John Richelsen, "What's Happening in Protestantism," *Scribner's Mo.*, LXXXIV (1928), 93, 95.

community-church movement, combining several weak congregations into one strong one, especially in the villages and small towns, partly in the influence of the motor car in extending the size of the parish, and partly in the movement of population towards the great cities where the average congregation was larger than would be possible in a rural hamlet.

Nation-wide denominational union made little headway, though the idea was everywhere in the air.[1] The most radical step was taken in Canada where three major denominations, the Presbyterian, the Methodist and the Congregationalist, formed the United Church of Canada, the most considerable merger of Protestant sects since the Reformation. Promising negotiations were undertaken for bringing together in the United States those denominations with congregational government, such as the Congregationalists, the Universalists and the Disciples. On the other hand, a strong movement to reunite the northern and southern branches of the Methodist Church, divided since 1844,[2] failed to find sufficient support among the Southern membership. The Protestant Interchurch World Movement at the end of the World War attempted to bring about a spiritual, if not a political, federation of the churches and also, using the "drive" technique which the war had developed, to raise a great sum for religious and charitable work. A wearied public failed to respond financially in the degree that was hoped, but the interest of the churches in current social problems revealed by the movement strengthened their moral authority. The Interchurch report on the steel strike of 1919, for example, did much to swing public opinion to the support of labor's demand for an

[1] H. K. Rowe, *The History of Religion in the United States* (N. Y., 1924), chap. xii.
[2] See Fish, *The Rise of the Common Man*, 289-290.

eight-hour day in this basic industry.[1] The Federal Council of Churches, dating from 1908, and all the important denominations individually, have denounced war and advocated the peaceful settlement of all international disputes. The renewed vitality of the Roman Catholic Church in America was strikingly shown in the enthusiasm aroused by the Eucharistic Congress of 1926 near Chicago, which attracted a million pilgrims from all over the world.

New schisms in existing denominations were threatened as a result of the Fundamentalist movement. The Fundamentalists were the ecclesiastical party who proclaimed certain traditional doctrines as fundamentals of the Christian faith, particularly the virgin birth, bodily resurrection and substitutionary atonement of Jesus Christ, the inerrancy of the Bible and the literal truth of its miracles. They complained, not without reason, that the so-called "modernists" and "liberals" had sapped the literal meaning from the creeds by interpreting them in a purely symbolic sense never intended by the founders of the churches. The conflict was not primarily a theological one, like the old controversies between Calvinist and Arminian, Trinitarian and Unitarian. The issue lay rather in the field of history than that of philosophy: whether the scriptural records of the Old and New Testaments were to be taken as an unquestionable record of fact or as a body of ancient literature which had in it an element of legend.

The doctrine of biological evolution entered the conflict because the account of man's creation according to Darwin appeared to differ in several particulars from the account according to Genesis. Though this question had been fought out at a lofty intellectual level in the late nineteenth century, the battle was reopened and waged

[1] See earlier, p. 81.

with astounding bitterness now that the findings of science had come within the purview of the masses of the people. In the Presbyterian, Baptist and Methodist churches nearly every annual conference brought forth some trial of strength between modernist and Fundamentalist. Of course, there was also a large center party, which Professor Kirsopp Lake of Harvard christened "institutionalist," who cared more for the work of the church than for the prevalence of any doctrine, and this party remained strong enough to prevent the splitting of the old denominations into new sects.

The Fundamentalist cause found an eloquent and popular champion in William Jennings Bryan, who lectured much on the question in the postwar years.[1] At first the restrictive efforts of the Fundamentalists were confined to denominational schools, but later they appealed to the legislatures to prohibit the teaching of evolution in all public educational institutions on the ground that those who paid the taxes had the right to say what should be taught. Bills to this effect were introduced in many states year after year, but Tennessee was the first to make it

> unlawful for any teacher in any of the universities, normals, and all other public schools of the state, to teach any theory that denies the story of the divine creation of man as taught in the Bible, and to teach instead that man has descended from a lower order of animals.

This passed the lower house by a vote of seventy-one to five, the senate by twenty-four to six, and was signed by Governor Peay on March 13, 1925. Not long after, a test case was tried in Dayton, Tennessee, where a

[1] See his addresses: "The Origin of Man," in *In His Image* (N. Y., 1922); *The Bible and Its Enemies* (Moody Bible Institute, Chicago, 1921).

twenty-four-year-old teacher, John Thomas Scopes, consented to be arrested on the charge of teaching evolution in the county high school from a textbook prescribed by the state commission.[1] The cost of the defense was assumed by the American Civil Liberties Union of New York, and its chief spokesman was Clarence Darrow of Chicago, a well-known humanitarian and "pleader of lost causes." The most conspicuous figure on the side of the prosecution was Bryan.

The Dayton trial excited world-wide interest. The press representatives and special writers telegraphed from the town a daily average of one hundred and sixty-five thousand words during the trial. Since the men of science were not allowed to testify before the jury as to the truth of evolution, and since the defense admitted that Scopes had taught evolution, the trial resolved itself into a verbal duel between Darrow the agnostic and Bryan the Fundamentalist. This was the closing act of Bryan's varied and dramatic career, for he died at Dayton at the end of the trial, a martyr in defense of the faith, according to the estimation of his followers. Scopes was convicted and fined one hundred dollars.[2] The case was appealed to the supreme court of Tennessee which upheld the constitutionality of the statute but reversed the judgment on the technical ground that the judge had no right to impose a higher fine than fifty dollars. This prevented an appeal to the United States Supreme Court. Two other states followed the example of Tennessee. The Mississippi legislature in 1926 passed a law prohibiting the teaching in tax-supported institutions that "man ascended or descended from a lower order of animals" and the voters of Arkansas passed a

---

[1] A. G. Hays, *Let Freedom Ring* (N. Y., 1928), 25-89.
[2] Maynard Shipley, *The War on Modern Science* (N. Y., 1927), 211; L. H. Allen, ed., *Bryan and Darrow at Dayton* (N. Y., 1925).

similar statute by a referendum vote in the general election of 1928.

What was the actual status of religious faith among the American people? Here no census can serve us, as in the case of denominational affiliation, and one must trust to random samplings. A poll of two hundred and fifty thousand newspaper readers and thirty-six thousand college undergraduates in 1927 showed, first, a huge orthodox majority and, second, more orthodoxy among the college students than among the older generation.[1] Thus virtually all the students and ninety-one per cent of the newspaper readers admitted a belief in God; the divinity of Christ was affirmed by eighty-nine per cent of the students and eighty-five per cent of the others. Similar plebiscites taken at about the same period in England by newspapers and magazines revealed a much larger proportion of skeptics. In spite of the fantastic propaganda of the American Association for the Advancement of Atheism, chartered in New York in 1925, and the little groups of self-styled "Damned Souls" in a few colleges,[2] most observers agree that rarely in American history was there so little open hostility to the Christian faith. No one, not even Clarence Darrow, was quite big enough to inherit the mantle of Tom Paine or Bob Ingersoll as a popular American champion of anticlericalism. "No man today," say the historians of Middletown, "has his relatives announce over his open grave, as did more than one member of the Ethical Society [in the 1890's], that the deceased believed death to be the end."[3] Yet it is arguable that, in spite of Fundamentalism, Christian doctrines were more taken for granted and less a subject of earnest thought than in the earlier days of the repub-

[1] *Literary Digest*, XCIII, 28 (April 30, 1927).
[2] Homer Croy, "Atheism Beckons to Our Youth," *World's Work*, LIV (1927), 18-26.
[3] Lynds, *Middletown*, 321.

lic and, if there was less theological controversy, it was because there was less theological interest, many of the most active of the clergy and laity being "institutionalists" who viewed the church primarily as an engine of moral and social reform.

A survey of American folkways shows glaring contrasts in religious influence on daily life. The old sabbatarian "blue laws," if somewhat diluted, still remained on the statute books of many states, but were violated almost as a matter of course by every motorist who bought gasoline and every corner drug store that sold candy and magazines. Standards of personal conduct revealed interesting variations. In one Mid-Western city, probably fairly typical of others, about ten per cent of the families investigated had regular family prayers and Bible readings, and the majority of the children were permitted to attend the moving pictures on Sunday. "One family lets the children swim on Sunday . . . but not play golf; . . . others make popcorn on Sunday but not candy; others object to Sunday evening bridge but allow Mah Jong." [1] Some of the churches lost dignity in frantic efforts to show that they were abreast of the times and thoroughly understood the younger generation. One high-school girl boasted, "Our Sunday School class is *some class*. Our teacher . . . gives us some slick parties out at her place. Two of the girls in our class got kicked out of their clubs a year ago for smoking—*that's* the kind of class we have!" [2] There is something a little displeasing in the well-meant eagerness of the city clergy and the Y. M. C. A. workers to prove that they were no better than other men and much more interested in baseball, Rotary and city "booster" campaigns than in religious philosophy.

One cannot assert that America achieved .any na-

[1] Lynds, *Middletown*, 342.   [2] Lynds, *Middletown*, 399.

tional philosophy. Contemporary with the full blaze of modern science, "witches" were found in "Pennsylvania Dutch" communities, while Wilbur Glenn Voliva used the radio to broadcast from Zion City, Illinois, all round the terrestrial globe the news that it was flat. More students crowded the universities than ever before in human history, but, as we have seen, some of them were forbidden by law to learn modern biology. Harry Emerson Fosdick, most liberal of the modernists, and John Roach Straton, most unbending of the Fundamentalists, equally found home within the hospitable confines of the Baptist Church. In alternate Sunday newspapers, and apparently with equal belief, the American read eugenic articles on the omnipotence of heredity and "behaviorist" articles on the omnipotence of early environment.

With the more secular beliefs of the American of this period previous chapters have dealt. Usually he was a patriot, with a faith in the destiny of America almost religious in strength and character. The war had taught him that the nation held a claim on his life and property and labor superior to that of any private interest. What else to learn from the war he had not yet made up his mind. World peace was a good thing to affirm, but continuous association with European diplomacy seemed too high a price to pay and perhaps not the best means of getting it. Rather more than formerly he was on guard against the undue immigration of foreigners and of foreign ideas. This irritated defensiveness, embodied equally in the Senate and the Ku Klux Klan, made him seem narrowly chauvinistic. Yet he read copiously criticisms of his national folkways, and had acquired a wholly new taste for the more depressing sort of realistic fiction. With all his excess of public spirit he remained skeptical of politics and too cynical about politicians to be greatly

moved even by proved dishonesty. Not since the Bull
Moose days of 1912 had he taken part in a real political
crusade, and the "predatory interests" seemed more
harmless neighbors now that his own economic position
was improved.

The average American was more prosperous than ever
before and his conservatism and general optimism reflected this prosperity. The actual buying power of his
income was, allowing for the unequal progress of different classes, about a third greater than it had been in
1914. It is worth repeating, however, that nearly the
whole of this gain belonged to the last six or seven years
of the period. The years of uneasy neutrality, 1914 to
1916 inclusive, piled up great fortunes for holders of
"war-baby" stocks and somewhat helped the farmer
move his crops, but the rising prices depressed the real
income of the bondholder, the clerk, the teacher and the
policeman. The same was true in even higher degree of
the battle years, 1917 and 1918, and the big postwar
boom of 1919 and 1920. The swift depression that
followed stabilized prices, but it inflicted on the farmers
an injury from which, in this period, they never wholly
recovered. After about 1922 came real improvement in
the general welfare, the product not of the war but of
such factors as commercial combination, industrial
standardization, improved methods of production and
a more careful study of the consumer market. The stock
panic of 1929 brought a pause but, seemingly, not a
permanent check to this development. Hours of labor
decreased in spite of the weakness of trade unionism;
prices slowly fell while wages remained stable and
salaries rose, thus consolidating the earlier gains of the
manual laborers and pulling out of the slough of
despond the previously depressed middle classes. The
farmer remained the most aggrieved citizen; so, increas-

ingly, he moved to town and let the tractor make up for his going.

Increased prosperity brought increased luxury. The American became more self-indulgent, less inclined than in the past to think pleasure a sin. He motored on Sunday without shame or stint, played golf in Florida in winter, took holidays from his office to see the ball game, stayed up half the night to dance, bought goods on credit, gave generously to any cause that asked his help, sent his children to college as a mere matter of course, and perhaps spent his salary as soon as he got it. He was not a materialist or moneygrubber. "America is not dollar-mad," said one observer. "It is activity mad. . . . If the possession of money were the real end, America would be parsimonious." [1] The worship of activity and efficiency may be, of course, as damaging to the soul as the worship of money. If the better sort of American be depicted as Nietzsche's vehement *Ja-sager*, the affirmer of Life, the very phrase has an ironical echo in the "Yes-man," the obsequious lieutenant of the captain of industry.

The American's home had greatly changed. He had admitted his wife to full legal equality at the polls and accorded her better than equality in the courts of justice and in social affairs. He had almost abandoned parental control over his sons and daughters. His automobile enticed him more to travel, and the business of cooking and cleaning was passing from household to restaurant and laundry. Yet his house, though small in scale, was more costly and usually far more beautiful than the house where his father had dwelt. The city, too, was more attractive and improved in practically every respect except, sometimes, its government. He had, of course, a phonograph, a radio, an automobile, and went

[1] P. M. Mazur, *American Prosperity* (N. Y., 1928), 267.

about once a week to the .moving-picture palace, and therefore had a high opinion of applied science, which afforded so many mechanical pleasures.

Morally it would be hard to say whether the American was better or worse for the war and the national expansion of the postwar decade. He had abolished the saloon, a feat which few nations dared dream of attempting, but he had not altogether permitted public law to change his private habits. Professional vice had certainly decreased; amateur vice had possibly become more tolerated; divorce was clearly more favored. Business methods were, on the whole, more honest and decent. Theft remained common, and took the dangerous form of open brigandage in the largest cities, before which police and courts seemed almost powerless. Yet the American had been able almost wholly to abandon his national bad habit of lynching, and the general lawlessness stirred him to much protest and great, if often futile, legislative activity.

Often in history the acid test of wealth has been applied to a favored class; alone in all nations and all ages the United States of the 1920's was beginning to apply that test to a whole people. Applied science and business organization had made the test possible. Only a strong national morale could make it successful. Other nations, already greatly influenced by American methods, stood ready to shape their future according to the result.

"So This Is Progress!"

CHAPTER XVI

CRITICAL ESSAY ON AUTHORITIES

PHYSICAL SURVIVALS

THE nondocumentary materials of the period 1914-1928 have no greater promise of survival than those of earlier times. In an age in which ascending land rents cause great business blocks and apartment skyscrapers to be scrapped as ruthlessly as battleships, many of the architectural monuments of the era are certain to perish short of their natural lifetime. A useful guide to the unique architectural achievements of the generation is T. E. Tallmadge, *The Story of Architecture in America* (N. Y., 1927). The liberal policy followed by art museums of admitting contemporary paintings and sculptures makes it possible to compare the works of living American artists with those of earlier times in the galleries of New York, Boston, Washington and other cities. The patent office and the National Museum in Washington preserve models of mechanical inventions and other scientific apparatus. Charles A. Lindbergh's *Spirit of St. Louis,* for example, is kept in the latter institution.

World War mementos have actively engaged the attention of historical museums, and almost every village or city has at least one cannon on its public square. One of the best collections of war posters is that deposited by the Historical Commission of Ohio in the Ohio State Archeological and Historical Society museum in Columbus, Ohio. The influence of the war on sculpture has many illustrations in the war memorials erected in many cities. When properly assembled and made available to students, the motion pictures produced during these years, especially the current-events films, will prove a valuable source of information concerning many aspects of the life of the times. Another aid to the social historian, more important than in any earlier period because more highly developed, will be found in the great masses of phonograph records, which should be collected and classified for the uses of posterity. In general, pictorial reproductions of the significant industrial, agricultural and artistic contributions of the period can be found in R. H. Gabriel, ed., *The Pageant of America* (15 vols., New Haven, 1926-1929).

GENERAL TREATMENTS

The period was one of national self-examination and also of zeal for statistics. For both reasons, the material on the economic life of the time is voluminous. The World War also spawned official records, controversy and reminiscence and will doubtless continue to do so for many decades to come. To keep a bibliography within bounds it is necessary to select a few titles as representative of many others of their type. On many topics, however, the student of the time must do most of his reading in the periodical press. He will, for example, find dozens of good magazine or syndicated newspaper articles on such subjects as prohibition, feminism, family life, commercialized sport and criminal gangs to every book, good or bad.

Several general histories of the United States devote attention to the period since 1914. This is particularly true of C. A. Beard and Mary R. Beard, *The Rise of American Civilization* (2 vols., N. Y., 1927), which contains a thoughtful, though often ironical, analysis of recent trends in American life as affected by industrialism and capitalism. Other recent general surveys include: F. A. Ogg, *National Progress, 1907-1917* (A. B. Hart, ed., *The American Nation: a History*, N. Y., 1904-1918, XXVII) ; J. S. Bassett, *Expansion and Reform, 1889-1926* (A. B. Hart, ed., *Epochs of American History*, rev. edn., N. Y., 1925-1929, IV) ; C. R. Lingley, *Since the Civil War* (rev. edn., N. Y., 1926) ; F. L. Paxson, *Recent History of the United States, 1865-1927* (rev. edn., Boston, 1928) ; L. B. Shippee, *Recent American History* (N. Y., 1924) ; and P. L. Haworth, *The United States in Our Own Times* (N. Y., 1924).

A considerable number of descriptive accounts of various aspects of modern civilization, especially American, appeared in symposium form. F. H. Hooper, ed., *These Eventful Years* (N. Y., 1924), consists of a series of encyclopedic articles on the war and subsequent events in the United States and in Europe. Fuller and more frankly personal are the articles in *Whither Mankind* (N. Y., 1928), edited by C. A. Beard; *Recent Gains in American Civilization* (N. Y., 1928), edited by Kirby Page; *These United States* (2 vols., N. Y., 1923-1924), edited by E. H. Gruening; *Civilization in the United States, an Inquiry by Thirty Americans* (N. Y., 1922), edited by H. E. Stearns, a study notable for the highly critical, almost hostile, attitude assumed by the majority of the contributors. By far the best type study was R. S. Lynd and Helen M. Lynd, *Middletown: a Study in Contemporary American Culture* (N. Y., 1929), an intensive analysis of a Middle Western city selected for its strikingly "American" character.

Individual studies both by Americans and Europeans were numerous. Perhaps André Siegfried, *America Comes of Age* (N. Y., 1927), a cool and skeptical French view, was most noticed by the critics. Others of note are Hilaire Belloc, *The Contrast* (London, 1923), emphasizing the differences between America and Europe; Bernard Faÿ and Avery Claflin, *The American Experiment* (N. Y., 1929); E. A. Mowrer, *This American World* (N. Y., 1928); Waldo Frank, *The Rediscovery of America* (N. Y., 1929); E. A. Ross, *What Is America?* (N. Y., 1919); F. E. Smith (first Earl of Birkenhead), *America Revisited* (London, 1924); J. A. Spender, *Through English Eyes* (N. Y., 1928); James Truslow Adams, *Our Business Civilization: Some Aspects of American Culture* (N. Y., 1929); and Ramsay Muir, *America the Golden* (London, 1927). Extremest hostility to American life and ideals appeared in C. E. M. Joad, *The Babbitt Warren* (N. Y., 1927); J. F. C. Fuller, *Atlantis* (London, 1926); and C. H. Bretherton, *Midas, or the United States and the Future* (N. Y., 1926). On the other hand, foreign books devoted wholly to American economic life were, as will be later noted, almost fulsome in their tributes. References to other general estimates of American civilization will be found under the heading, Periodical Literature.

PERIODICAL LITERATURE

Aside from the official yearbooks and annual reports of the executive departments, later noted, some privately published annuals are useful, notably the *American Year Book* (1910-1919; 1925-   ); the *New International Year Book* (1908-   ) and the *Americana Annual* (1923-   ), current-events supplements to encyclopedias; the *American Labor Year Book* (1916-   ); and, for a miscellaneous compilation of statistics, the newspaper *Almanacs*, particularly that of the *New York World* (1891-   ).

In July, 1928, the *American Journal of Sociology* (XXXIV) printed a series of articles on various aspects of American life for the year 1927, and in May, 1929 (XXXIV), for the year 1928, and the editors held out a promise that this might become a regular annual feature. The contributors dealt with such topics as population, resources, inventions, production, labor, wages, employment, social legislation, public health, communications, rural life, the family, crime, education, race relationships and religion, in addition to political affairs. The published *Annals* of the American Academy of Political and Social Science (Phila., 1890-   ) contain essays by specialists on matters of current interest. The proceedings of the national government in all its branches can be followed from day to day in the columns of the *United States Daily* (Wash., 1926-   ). The *American Political Science Review* (Balt., 1906-   ), the *Political Science Quarterly* (N. Y., 1886-   ) and *Social Forces* (Chapel Hill, N. C., 1922-   ) are also of substantial value.

The journalism of opinion had probably less influence than during the preceding decade (1903-1913), the "age of the muckrakers." Several of the monthlies then prominent ceased publication or shifted their interest from social analysis to fiction and "inspirational" articles. Their place was taken partly by such older critical weeklies as the *Nation*

(N. Y., 1865-   ), which turned to radicalism under the editorship of O. G. Villard; the *Survey* (N. Y., 1897-   ); and the *Independent* (N. Y., 1848-1928), which absorbed *Harper's Weekly* (N. Y., 1857-1916) and was later merged with the *Outlook* (N. Y., 1870-   ); and partly by such newer ones as the *Weekly Review* (N. Y., 1919-1921), conservative; the *Freeman* (N. Y., 1920-1924), ultraradical; and the *New Republic* (N. Y., 1914-   ), a severe and independent critic of conservatism and radicalism alike.

By far the most valuable of the current-events periodicals was the monthly *Current History* (N. Y., 1914-   ), sponsored by the *New York Times*. The magazine *Time* (N. Y., 1923-   ) digested current happenings weekly. The *Literary Digest* (1890-   ) is useful chiefly as convenient summary of press comment, and *Collier's* (N. Y., 1888-   ) and the *Saturday Evening Post* (Phila., 1821-   ) for special articles by high-priced popularizers. The *American Mercury* (N. Y., 1924-   ), a monthly edited by H. L. Mencken, was the most outspoken periodical opponent of current American ideas and ideals, but is even more useful for its collection of "Americana," absurdities clipped from the press. The *Unpopular Review,* rechristened in 1919 the *Unpartizan Review* (N. Y., 1914-1921), reflected the views of the editor Henry Holt and a group of contributors, temporarily anonymous, from the academic and literary worlds. The older literary monthlies, such as the *Atlantic Monthly* (Boston, 1857-   ), published many articles on sundry aspects of contemporary civilization. The *Nation's Business* (Wash., 1912-   ), monthly, had important brief articles on economic trends. Specialized periodicals are noted under appropriate headings later.

Of the daily newspapers the *New York Times* was by far the most valuable because it printed in full documentary material which most other newspapers were content to summarize. The *Christian Science Monitor* (Boston) had singularly good correspondence service. The *New York World* had an exceptionally brilliant editorial staff and the *New York Tribune* maintained its influence as an orthodox exponent of Republican doctrine. The most influential Western newspaper, the *Chicago Tribune*, may profitably be studied for its chauvinistic "hundred-per-cent Americanism." The *Kansas City Star*, the *Milwaukee Journal*, the *Des Moines Register* and William Allen White's achievement in personal journalism, the *Emporia Gazette*, better reflected the mass of moderate liberal opinion of the inland states. Allan Nevins, ed., *American Press Opinion* (N. Y., 1928), 519-591, contains extracts on many topics from the press of 1914-1927.

W. A. Dill, *Growth of Newspapers in the United States* (Lawrence, Kansas, 1928), is useful for the quantitative aspects of journalism, as N. J. Radder, *Newspapers in Community Service* (N. Y., 1926), and Silas Bent, *Ballyhoo, The Voice of the Press* (N. Y., 1927), are for evaluating it. C. L. Edson, *The Gentle Art of Columning* (N. Y., 1920), treats of the most novel development in personal journalism. See also *Publishers' Weekly* (N. Y., 1872-   ), the *American Newspaper Annual and Directory* (Phila., 1869-   , title varies) and J. L. Woodward, *Foreign News in American Morning Newspapers* (N. Y., 1930).

PUBLIC DOCUMENTS

GENERAL: The publications of the executive branch of the federal government are far more extensive and, on the whole, better edited than for any previous period. Particular note should be made of the excellent *Yearbooks* of the departments of commerce and agriculture. The *Bulletins* of these departments, and those of labor and of the interior, contain indispensable statistical material on the national standards of life. On the other hand, the *Congressional Record* is perhaps of less interest than usual, as the emphasis in federal activity had shifted so greatly from debate and legislation to administration. The census of 1920 and the special studies which grew out of it, such as W. S. Rossiter, *Increase of Population in the United States, 1910-1920* (*Census Monographs*, I, 1922), are fundamental for statistical perspective, to be revised, of course, in the light of the results of the census of 1930 shortly to appear.

WORLD WAR: W. G. Leland and N. D. Mereness prepared

an invaluable *Introduction to the American Official Sources for the Economic and Social History of the World War* (New Haven, 1926) for the studies in the economic and social history of the war edited by J. T. Shotwell. It would be impossible here to recapitulate all the bibliographical data to be found in its 532 crowded pages, but one might cite its estimate of the importance of the material which it catalogues: "of more than administrative interest is the correspondence of those branches of the government that come in closest contact with the individual citizen, particularly of such units as the Food Administration and the Council of National Defense. For the future historian, however, perhaps the most valuable category of material includes the great mass of statistical information that was assiduously gathered in many offices of the government. These compilations bear upon all phases of economic life and activity; they show the stocks of commodities on hand at different periods, the varying rate of production, the movement of raw materials, the supply of labor, the state of the crops, the movement of money, and many other important states and processes" (xliii-xliv).

More than half the states of the Union published formal *Reports* of their state councils of defense (sometimes called commissions or committees of public safety) prior to 1926. State war histories and war records were also numerous. See F. F. Holbrook, "The Collection of State War Service Records," *Am. Hist. Rev.*, XXV, 72-78; N. D. Mereness, ed., "American Historical Activities during the World War," Am. Hist. Assoc., *Ann. Rep. for 1919*, I, 204-294; and Leland and Mereness, *Introduction*, 439-484.

The *Final Report* of General John J. Pershing (Wash., 1919) is of essential importance for any study of America at war. The official statistics of organization, supply and mobilization can be conveniently obtained from L. P. Ayres, *The War with Germany* (Wash., 1919). The council of national defense issued *Reports* of its activities for 1917, 1918, 1919 and 1920. The *Reports* for 1917, 1918 and 1919 of the director of the states-relations service of the department of agriculture give surveys of war-time agricultural stimulation by public and private agencies. The department of agriculture also sent out numerous bulletins, pamphlets and printed and mimeographed circulars of information for farmers and home gardeners during the war. Particular attention should be called to the *War Work of the Bureau of Standards* (Department of Commerce, Wash., 1921), which seems "most likely to result in permanent benefit not only to the military departments but also to the industries and public"; to the account of the national war labor board (Bureau of Labor Statistics, *Bull.,* no. 287, 1922), a description of its formation and activities accompanied by the more important documents; to the *Reports* of the director-general of railroads for 1918, 1919, 1920 and 1921; to the *Reports* of the United States shipping board for 1917, 1918, 1919 and 1920; to the *Reports* of the war trade board in 1918 and 1920, especially the latter, which reviews the work of the board; to the *Report* of the United States housing corporation (2 vols., Wash., 1919-1920); to the navy department's account of the *Activities of the Bureau of Yards and Docks* (Wash., 1921); and to the reports of the historical branch of the general staff, including *Economic Mobilization in the United States for the War of 1917* (Wash., 1918); *A Handbook of Economic Agencies of the War of 1917* (Wash., 1919); and *Organization of the Services of Supply* (Wash., 1921).

Of a semiofficial character are certain accounts of governmental activities reviewed by responsible officials. Particularly valuable are B. M. Baruch, *American Industry in the War* (Wash., 1921), a report of the war industries board; W. L. Chenery, *The War Labor Administration* (Wash., 1918); and C. G. Dawes, *A Journal of the Great War* (2 vols., Boston, 1921), the second volume of which contains the final report of the general purchasing agent for the American expeditionary force. Other works of a somewhat similar nature are listed under the heading, World War: General.

During the war the government issued an official *United States Bulletin,* giving a daily summary of war news and of federal activity, and three series of propagandist pamphlets, the *War Information Series* (Wash., 1917-1918), the *Red,*

White and Blue Series and the *Loyalty Leaflets*, besides preparing all sorts of miscellaneous matter for "four-minute" orators and for distribution in enemy ranks. For a summary of this work, see George Creel, *How We Advertised America* (N. Y., 1920). The army had its own press, notably the soldier newspaper *The Stars and Stripes*.

WORLD WAR: GENERAL

Aside from official publications in regard to the World War, the subject was treated from many different points of view by historians, economists, publicists and others. Only some of the more significant works can be named here. America's participation received general treatment in J. B. McMaster, *The United States in the World War* (2 vols., N. Y., 1918-1920); J. S. Bassett, *Our War with Germany* (N. Y., 1919); Charles Seymour, *Woodrow Wilson and the World War* (Allen Johnson, ed., *The Chronicles of America Series,* New Haven, 1918-1921, XLVIII), particularly useful for the political background; R. J. Beamish and F. A. March, *America's Part in the World War* (Phila., 1919); T. G. Frothingham, *The American Reinforcement in the World War* (Garden City, 1927); Shipley Thomas, *The History of the A. E. F.* (N. Y., 1920); Frederick Palmer, *America in France* (N. Y., 1918); and Major-General F. V. Greene, *Our First Year in the Great War* (N. Y., 1918), a half-way-through-the-war viewpoint. Two valuable French works are *The American Army in the European Conflict,* by Colonel de Chambrun and Captain de Marenches (N. Y., 1919), and Edouard Réquin, *America's Race to Victory* (N. Y., 1919).

For war-time preparation behind the line, see especially the six volumes of *How America Went to War,* edited by Benedict Crowell and R. F. Wilson (New Haven, 1921), including *The Armies of Industry* (2 vols.), *The Giant Hand, The Road to France* (2 vols.) and *Demobilization*. The activity of the federal government is treated in W. F. Willoughby, *Government Organization in War Time and After* (N. Y., 1919), and F. L. Paxson, "The American War Government, 1917-1918," *Am. Hist. Rev.,* XXVI, 54-76.

Other useful studies include the symposium on *Mobilizing America's Resources for the War* in the *Annals* of the American Academy of Political and Social Science, LXXVIII (1918); G. B. Clarkson, *Industrial America in the World War* (Boston, 1923); E. A. Powell, *The Army Behind the Army* (N. Y., 1919); Isaac Marcosson, *S. O. S.* (N. Y., 1919); E. N. Hurley, *The Bridge to France* (Phila., 1927); and General Johnson Hagood, *The Services of Supply* (Boston, 1927).

The interaction of public policy and private business is considered in J. A. Emery and N. B. Williams, *Governmental War Agencies Affecting Business* (N. Y., 1918); W. S. Culbertson, *Commercial Policy in War Time and After* (N. Y., 1919); *The Effect of the War on Business Conditions*, by the Blackman-Ross Company (N. Y., 1918); and F. H. Dixon, *Railroads and Government, Their Relations in the United States, 1910-1921* (N. Y., 1922). For the influence of war policy on agriculture, see C. R. Van Hise, *Conservation and Regulation in the United States during the World War* (Wash., 1917); F. M. Surface, *The Stabilization of the Price of Wheat during the War and its Effect upon the Returns to the Producer* (Wash., 1925), and his *The Grain Trade during the World War* (N. Y., 1928).

The working of the draft is treated in E. H. Crowder, *The Spirit of Selective Service* (N. Y., 1920). H. P. Davison gave a good account of *The American Red Cross in the Great War* (N. Y., 1919), and Katharine Mayo of the Y. M. C. A. in *"That Damn Y"* (Boston, 1920), incidentally an answer to many criticisms of its work. For American charitable work abroad, see especially G. I. Gay, *Statistical Review of Relief Operations* (Stanford Univ., 1925). *Rehabilitation of the Wounded* was discussed by several authorities in the *Annals* of the American Academy of Political and Social Science, LXXX (1918). American naval warfare is presented from the official admiralty point of view in W. S. Sims and B. J. Hendrick, *The Victory at Sea* (Garden City, 1920), and J. L. Leighton, *Simsadus: London* (N. Y., 1920).

Woman's share in war-time effort was the subject of much comment, notably in Harriet S. Blatch, *Mobilizing Woman*

Power (N. Y., 1918), and Ida C. Clarke, *American Women and the World War* (N. Y., 1918). For the share of the academic world, see P. R. Kolbe's judicious *The Colleges in War Time and After* (N. Y., 1919). Labor's part in the war brought forward some good monographic studies, such as Alexander Bing, *War-Time Strikes and their Adjustment* (N. Y., 1921); H. S. Hanna and W. J. Lauck, *Wages and the War* (Cleveland, 1918); and G. S. Watkins, *Labor Problems and Labor Administration in the United States during the World War* (Urbana, 1919).

Unquestionably the most significant running comment by American statesmen of the war period is to be found in the published correspondence of three associates of President Wilson: his secretary of the interior, his most influential personal friend, and the ambassador to Great Britain. See Franklin K. Lane, *Letters* (Anne W. Lane and Louise H. Wall, eds., Boston, 1922); E. M. House, *The Intimate Papers of Colonel House* (Charles Seymour, ed., 4 vols., Boston, 1926-1928); and B. J. Hendrick, *The Life and Letters of Walter Hines Page* (3 vols., Garden City, 1922-1925). The public addresses of President Wilson have been published in numerous settings, and his biography has been attempted by several writers. The most important biography, by R. S. Baker, is still unfinished, and the second best, that by W. E. Dodd, *Woodrow Wilson and His Work* (Garden City, 1920), is rather strongly partisan. For Wilson at Paris, see R. S. Baker, *Woodrow Wilson and World Settlement* (3 vols., Garden City, 1922-1923). Ex-President Roosevelt wrote copiously during the war, but his volumes, such as *Fear God and Take Your Own Part* (N. Y., 1916), *America and the World War* (N. Y., 1915) and *The Foes of Our Own Household* (N. Y., 1917), were hardly more than patriotic pamphlets.

Apart from the governmental series already noted, the literature of propaganda is endless. Little of it was ever important and most of it is now completely forgotten. The best summary is probably H. D. Lasswell, *Propaganda Technique in the World War* (N. Y., 1927). A typical plea for preparedness is W. H. Hobbs, *The World War and its Consequences* (N. Y., 1919), to which Roosevelt contributed a preface; and a radical plea for pacifism may be found in the *Untimely Papers* of R. S. Bourne (N. Y., 1919). Henry Ford's ill-starred venture in pacifism was chronicled by L. P. Lochner in *Henry Ford—America's Don Quixote* (N. Y., 1925). For the conscientious objector to military service, see C. M. Case, *Non-Violent Coercion* (N. Y., 1923), and N. M. Thomas, *The Conscientious Objector in America* (N. Y., 1923). J. A. B. Scherer, *The Nation at War* (N. Y., 1918), surveys the activities of state councils of defense and the varying local enthusiasm, indifference or covert hostility to the war; and J. P. Jones and P. M. Hollister, *The German Secret Service in America* (Boston, 1918), affords a fair idea of enemy activity. There is a considerable amount of pictorial material on the war in G. J. Hecht, *The War in Cartoons* (N. Y., 1919); L. N. Wilson, *Posters and Pictures Relating to the European War* (Worcester, Mass., 1917); and in the later chapters of William Wood and R. H. Gabriel, *In Defense of Liberty* (*The Pageant of America*, VII), 208-354.

THE CULT OF NATIONALISM

IMMIGRATION: The decision of the American nation to close the open door of foreign immigration was, next only to the war and prohibition, the most discussed public policy of the time. Among the general treatments of the immigration problem are: G. M. Stephenson, *History of American Immigration, 1820-1924* (N. Y., 1926); Edith Abbott, ed., *Immigration: Select Documents and Case Records* (Chicago, 1924); H. P. Fairchild, *Immigration, a World Movement and its American Significance* (N. Y., 1925); R. L. Garis, *Immigration Restriction* (N. Y., 1927), which contains both a history of restrictive legislation and an argument for the 1890 quota basis of limitation; J. W. Jenks, *The Immigration Problem* (N. Y., 1926); F. P. Cavanaugh, *Immigration Restriction at Work Today* (Wash., 1928), a study in administrative methods; C. M. Panunzio, *Immigration Crossroads* (N. Y., 1927); Edith M. Phelps, *Restriction of Immigration* (N. Y., 1924); and *Present Day Immigration,* a symposium in the *Annals* of the American Academy of Political and Social Science, XCIII (1921). I. A. Hourwich discusses with some optimism *Immigration and Labor* (N. Y., 1922); Clifford Kirkpatrick, on the basis of intelligence tests, treats of *Intelligence and Immigration* (Balt., 1926); and the army tests themselves are summarized in C. C. Brigham, *A Study of American Intelligence* (Princeton, 1923).

ASSIMILATION: R. E. Park, *The Immigrant Press and its Control* (N. Y., 1922), and Edward de S. Brunner, *Immigrant Farmers and Their Children* (Garden City, 1929), reveal certain aspects of national assimilation. The process known as Americanization provoked a large controversial literature, no doubt augmented by the war-time dread of "hyphenated Americans." E. H. Bierstadt, *Aspects of Americanization* (Cin., 1922), and B. K. Baghdigian, *Americanism in Americanization* (Kansas City, 1921), pleaded for a more tolerant attitude towards the bewildered foreigner; E. A. Steiner, *The Making of a Great Race; Racial and Religious Cross-Currents in the United States* (N. Y., 1929), hoped for much good to come from recent European contributions to the national life, while H. M. Kallen in *Culture and Democracy in the United States* (N. Y., 1924) went so far as to argue for a plurality of diverse national cultures instead of a common national tradition. On the other hand, L. F. Whitney and Ellsworth Huntington, *The Builders of America* (N. Y., 1927), are proud of the record of the older national stocks; T. L. Stoddard, *Re-forging America* (N. Y., 1927), and William MacDougall, *Is America Safe for Democracy?* (N. Y., 1921), are more definitely antialien, and such books as C. S. Burr, *America's Race Heritage* (N. Y., 1922), and C. W. Gould, *America a Family Matter* (N. Y., 1922), carry race pride to its limit, in spite of the proof afforded by Aleš Hrdlička, *Old Americans* (Balt., 1925), that the colonial stock was really a very mixed one.

KU KLUX KLAN: The revived Ku Klux Klan, as an extreme expression of American nativism, presents its own case in the pamphlet addresses of H. W. Evans, such as *The Klan of Tomorrow and the Klan Spiritual* (n. p., 1924), and is examined from the outside by J. M. Mecklin, *The Ku Klux Klan: a Study of the American Mind* (N. Y., 1924). The Klan had an extensive periodical literature including the *Dawn* (Chicago, 1922-1924), the *Fiery Cross* (Indianapolis, 1923-1925) and the *National Kourier* (1925-   ) which absorbed the *Fiery Cross* and sundry state and regional *Kouriers*. But the most radically chauvinistic periodical of the time was the *American Standard* (N. Y., 1924-1925) which specialized on the "Catholic menace."

INTOLERANCE: There were many studies of the intolerance of the time, of which the most important was Zechariah Chafee, jr., *Freedom of Speech* (N. Y., 1920), containing a bibliography of cases and decisions respecting radicals, conscientious objectors, etc. One might also mention Walter Lippmann, *American Inquisitors* (N. Y., 1928) ; Will Irwin, *How Red is America?* (N. Y., 1927) ; and A. G. Hays, *Let Freedom Ring* (N. Y., 1928), chronicling the activities of the American Civil Liberties Union. Maynard Shipley, *The War on Modern Science* (N. Y., 1927), deals with the attack on Darwinism and the evolutionary hypothesis. C. G. Miller, *The Poisoned Loving-Cup* (Chicago, 1928), is the fullest statement of the position of those who saw "United States School Histories Falsified through Pro-British Propaganda in Sweet Name of Amity" (subtitle). The whole subject of the relation of propaganda to history teaching is dispassionately canvassed in Bessie L. Pierce, *Public Opinion and the Teaching of History in the United States* (N. Y., 1926).

PROSPERITY, BUSINESS, LABOR

All study of the economic life of the period will begin with the two volumes on *Recent Economic Changes in the United States*, the report of the Committee on Recent Economic Changes (Herbert Hoover, chairman) of the President's Conference on Unemployment (N. Y., 1929), which came neatly at the end of the period and contains many important special articles and statistical estimates. Other useful official and semiofficial material may be found in the monthly *Bulletins* of the department of labor, valuable for price movements; the report of the federal trade commission on *National Wealth and Income* (69 Cong., I sess., *Senate Doc.*, no. 126, 1926); the report of the census bureau on *Wealth, Public Debt and Taxation, 1922* (Wash., 1924); the report of the National Industrial Conference Board on *Wages in the United States, 1914-1927* (N. Y., 1928); and the report of the National Bureau of Economic Research on *Income in the United States* (2 vols., N. Y., 1921-1923). Useful compilations also are the articles in the *Annals* of the American Academy of Political and Social Science on various economic problems: *Modern Manufacturing* (LXXXV, 1919); *National Industries and the Federal Government* (LXIII, 1916); *Personnel and Employment Problems* (LXV, 1916); *Standards in Industry* (CXXXVII, 1928); *The Price of Coal* (CXI, 1924); *Revival of American Business* (XCVII, 1921); on labor policy, *e.g.*, LXXXI (1919), LXIX (1917), CIII (1922), CXXIII (1926); on child welfare, XCVIII (1921) and CXXI (1925).

In the interpretation of contemporary American economic life special interest attaches to T. N. Carver, *The Present Economic Revolution in the United States* (Boston, 1925), which stated more clearly than any previous work the significance of the new standard of popular prosperity. Garet Garrett, *The American Omen* (N. Y., 1928), presents a similar point of view. Stuart Chase made an interesting blend of statistical estimate, interpretation and criticism of American business in *Men and Machines* (N. Y., 1929), *The Tragedy of Waste* (N. Y., 1925), and (with F. J. Schlink) *Your Money's Worth* (N. Y., 1927), an attack on high-pressure advertising. Other general studies worth noting are: E. L. Bogart and C. E. Landon, *Modern Industry* (N. Y., 1927); L. D. Edie, ed., *Current Social and Industrial Forces* (N. Y., 1920), a source book of current writings on the economic problems of war and reconstruction; W. R. Ingalls, *Wealth and Income of the American People* (York, Pa., 1922); F. R. Macaulay, *The Personal Distribution of Income in the United States* (N. Y., 1922); P. M. Mazur, *American Prosperity* (N. Y., 1928); Floyd Parsons, *Everybody's Business* (N. Y., 1923); H. H. Powers, *The Ameri-*

can Era (N. Y., 1920); R. G. Tugwell, *Industry's Coming of Age* (N. Y., 1927); R. G. Tugwell, Thomas Munro and R. E. Stryker, *American Economic Life and the Means of its Improvement* (N. Y., 1925); H. T. Warshow, *Representative Industries in the United States* (N. Y., 1928); F. W. Wile, ed., *A Century of Industrial Progress* (N. Y., 1928), a symposium on different factors in the American economic system; R. M. Keir, *Manufacturing* (N. Y., 1928); N. H. Comish, *The Standard of Living* (N. Y., 1923); E. W. Crecraft, *Government and Business* (Yonkers, 1928); and E. A. Filene, *The Way Out: a Forecast of Coming Changes in American Business and Industry* (Garden City, 1924).

Foreign students of American prosperity were numerous. The British department of overseas trade published a *Report on the Economic, Financial and Industrial Conditions of the United States of America in 1922* (London, 1923). Individual impressions of interest are: J. E. Barker, *America's Secret: the Causes of her Economic Success* (London, 1927); George Peel, *The Economic Impact of America* (London, 1928); G. K. Simonds and J. G. Thompson, *The American Way to Prosperity* (London, 1928); Albert Demangeon, *America and the Race for World Dominion* (N. Y., 1921), a French view; Kurt Hassert, *Die Vereinigten Staaten von Amerika als Politische und Wirtschaftliche Weltmacht* (Tübingen, 1922); Julius Hirsch, *Das Amerikanische Wirtschaftswunder* (Berlin, 1926); and Hermann Levy, *Die Vereinigten Staaten von Amerika als Wirtschaftsmacht* (Leipzig, 1923). The general character of these books is well reflected in their enthusiastic titles, and Americans needed the warning of W. C. Redfield, *Dependent America* (Boston, 1926), that no nation could be wholly self-sufficing.

For the problem of the merchant marine, see W. P. Elderton, *Shipping Problems, 1916-1921* (N. Y., 1927), and E. W. Zimmermann, *Zimmermann on Ocean Shipping* (N. Y., 1921). For the Esch-Cummins railroad legislation, see E. R. Johnson and T. W. Van Metre, *Principles of Railroad Transportation* (N. Y., 1921), and, for an unused alternative, see G. E. Plumb, *Industrial Democracy* (N. Y., 1923).

W. Z. Ripley, *Main Street and Wall Street* (Boston,

1927), contains interesting facts as to corporation ownership and control and, in particular, the growing divergence
between ownership and control as the former became widely
scattered and the latter remained centralized. In 1928 the
domestic-commerce division of the department of commerce
published a *Reading List on Installment Buying and Selling*
and a *Chain Store Bibliography* (Wash., 1928). Important books dealing with these new business trends were
E. R. A. Seligman, *The Economics of Installment Buying*
(N. Y., 1927); W. S. Hayward, *Chain Stores* (rev. edn.,
N. Y., 1929); and V. E. Pratt, *Selling by Mail* (N. Y.,
1924), concerned especially with the mail-order business.
E. L. Heermance raised some interesting questions in *The
Ethics of Business, a Study of Current Standards* (N. Y.,
1926). The activity of the business men's social and phil-
anthropic clubs can be followed in the monthly columns
of the *Rotarian* (Chicago, 1912-   ) and the *Kiwanis
Magazine* (Mt. Morris, Ill., 1923-   ).

Valuable for the achievements and problems of American labor are Selig Perlman, *A History of Trade Unionism
in the United States* (N. Y., 1922); V. W. Lanfear, *Business Fluctuations and the American Labor Movement,
1915-1922* (N. Y., 1924); Sylvia Kopald, *Rebellion in
Labor Unions* (N. Y., 1924), dealing with "outlaw" (un-
authorized) strikes; R. G. Fuller, *Child Labor and the Constitution* (N. Y., 1923); and the *Report on the Steel Strike
of 1919* by the Commission of Inquiry of the Interchurch
World Movement (N. Y., 1920). Other works on labor
conditions are cited under the heading, World War: General.

AGRICULTURE

The article on "Agriculture" by E. G. Nourse in *Recent Economic Changes*, cited earlier, is a good introduction to the subject, which may well be supplemented by
the report of the Chamber of Commerce on *The Condition of Agriculture in the United States and Measures for
its Improvement* (Wash., 1927), and E. R. A. Seligman,
The Economics of Farm Relief (N. Y., 1929). The stud-

ies of F. M. Surface on grain prices were mentioned among the books on the World War. The federal bureau of agricultural economics published a survey of *Changes in the Utilization of Land in the United States, 1914-1924* (Wash., 1926), which might be read in connection with C. O. Brannen, *Relation of Land Tenure to Plantation Organization with Developments since 1920* (Fayetteville, Ark., 1928; reprinted in U. S. Dept. of Agriculture, *Bull.,* no. 1269), and E. H. Wiecking, *The Farm Real Estate Situation* (Dept. of Agriculture, *Circular,* no. 377, 1927). E. C. Young, *The Movement of Farm Population* (Cornell Univ. Experiment Station, *Bull.,* no. 426, 1923); R. B. Forrester, *Report upon Large Scale Coöperative Marketing in the United States* (London, 1925); and the symposium on *The Agricultural Situation in the United States* in the *Annals* of the American Academy of Political and Social Science, CXVII (1925), are worth noting. Various aspects of the impact of industrialism on rural life are noted in E. R. Eastman, *These Changing Times* (N. Y., 1927); R. C. Engberg, *Industrial Prosperity and the Farmer* (N. Y., 1927); Macy Campbell, *Rural Life at the Crossroads* (Boston, 1927); and Arthur Williams, *Power on the Farm* (N. Y., 1927).

Arthur Capper, himself a senatorial leader of the bloc, wrote the history of the early days of *The Agricultural Bloc* (N. Y., 1922). The Nonpartisan movement, centering in North Dakota, was the subject of several studies: Andrew Bruce, *The Non-Partisan League* (N. Y., 1921), rather hostile; H. E. Gaston, *The Nonpartisan League* (N. Y., 1920), and C. E. Russell, *The Story of the Nonpartisan League* (N. Y., 1920), friendly; and A. S. Tostlebe, *The Bank of North Dakota* (N. Y., 1924), an interesting chapter in the history of state finance.

THE AUTOMOBILE

W. J. Cunningham's article on "Transportation" in *Recent Economic Changes,* cited earlier, emphasizes the part played by bus, coach and truck in the general traction problem. The annual *Facts and Figures of the Automobile Industry,* issued by the National Automobile Chamber of Commerce (1921-   ), performs the difficult task of keeping up-to-date the statistics of America's most rapidly growing major industry. For the history of the automobile, see especially R. C. Epstein, *The Automobile Industry* (Chicago, 1928); H. L. Barber, *The Story of the Automobile* (Chicago, 1927); E. G. Fuller, "The Automobile Industry in Michigan," *Mich. History Mag.,* XII, 280-296; and T. F. MacManus and Norman Beasley, *Men, Money and Motors* (N. Y., 1929).

Ford books and articles are multiplying almost as rapidly as the Fords themselves. The first choice from the group would be *My Life and Work* (Garden City, 1922), written by Henry Ford himself in collaboration with Samuel Crowther. Another useful biographical sketch is S. T. Bushnell, *The Truth About Henry Ford* (Chicago, 1922).

THE SOUTH AND THE RACE QUESTION

The annual *Blue Book of Southern Progress,* published by *Manufacturers' Record* (Balt., 1882-   ), is statistically useful. The best general account of recent Southern progress is Edwin Mims, *The Advancing South* (Garden City, 1926), which emphasizes both industrial and educational gains. W. J. Robertson, *The Changing South* (N. Y., 1927), is a less distinctive study along similar lines. H. W. Odum, *Southern Pioneers in Southern Interpretation* (Chapel Hill, N. C., 1925), discusses the work of leaders of enlightenment. Marjorie A. Potwin, *Cotton Mill People of the Piedmont* (N. Y., 1927), is an excellently written study in the life of the newly industrialized districts of South Carolina, not without a certain partisanship for the mill owners. Frank Tannenbaum, *Darker Phases of the South* (N. Y., 1924), on the other hand, emphasizes the seamy side of capitalistic paternalism. The extraordinary boom in Florida attracted national attention. The rise of the tourist industry and its economic consequences are optimistically depicted in F. P. Stockbridge and J. H. Perry, *Florida in the Making* (N. Y.,

1926), and in the *Business Survey of Florida* issued by the Florida Trust Company (Miami, 1926). J. H. Reese, *Florida's Great Hurricane* (Miami, 1926), relates the story of the storm which wiped out several new settlements in the farther South.

The *Negro Year Book* and the reports and bulletins of the National Association for the Advancement of Colored People are always useful for the life of Afro-America. There is a good select bibliography on the Negro in G. E. Haynes, *The Trend of the Races* (N. Y., 1922), a balanced and good-tempered study. The *Monthly Labor Review*, XXII (1926), 216-230, published a bibliography on the Negro in industry and the New York Public Library issued in December, 1925, a bulletin of *Books about the Negro*. The most comprehensive bibliography is M. N. Work, comp., *A Bibliography of the Negro in Africa and America* (N. Y., 1928). The wartime division of Negro economics (in existence 1918-1921) issued a report on *The Negro at Work during the World War and during Reconstruction* (Wash., 1921), and E. J. Scott prepared a useful study of *Negro Migration during the War* (N. Y., 1920). Useful general accounts are: H. J. Seligmann, *The Negro Faces America* (N. Y., 1920); E. B. Reuter, *The American Race Problem; a Study of the Negro* (N. Y., 1927); R. R. Moton, *What the Negro Thinks* (N. Y., 1929), by the head of Tuskegee; and C. H. Wesley, *Negro Labor in the United States* (N. Y., 1927).

PROHIBITION

The historical antecedents of national prohibition can be traced in earlier volumes of *A History of American Life*. The final drive that put the amendment across is best told in Peter Odegard, *Pressure Politics: the Story of the Anti-Saloon League* (N. Y., 1928). Justin Steuart, *Wayne Wheeler, Dry Boss* (N. Y., 1928), is rather prejudiced by an obscure factional quarrel with Mr. Wheeler, but it must serve until a better biography of the most prominent prohibition leader is written. Historical sketches by pronounced drys are E. H. Cherrington, *The Evolution of Prohibition in the United States of America* (Westerville, Ohio, 1920), and D. L. Colvin, *Prohibition in the United States* (N. Y., 1926). The federal prohibition bureau published a *Digest of Supreme Court Decisions Interpreting the National Prohibition Act* (Wash., 1927). The early days of the enforcement campaign are narrated by R. A. Haynes, *Prohibition Inside Out* (N. Y., 1923).

So much of the writing on prohibition is merely propagandist and controversial that we are exceptionally fortunate to possess any objective surveys of the results of the law. But the study of *The Prohibition Situation* (N. Y., 1925) put forth by the Federal Council of Churches of Christ in America, although brief and naturally predisposed in favor of prohibition, is remarkably careful to do justice to all factors of the situation. Treatments equally impartial and more full in detail may be found in Herman Feldman, *Prohibition, Its Economic and Industrial Aspects* (N. Y., 1927), and Martha B. Bruère, *Does Prohibition Work?* (N. Y., 1927). Irving Fisher, *Prohibition at Its Worst* (N. Y., 1926), and its supplement, *Prohibition Still at Its Worst* (N. Y., 1928), must be used with caution, because of the unfortunate mixture of exact statistics with mere "estimates"; yet the attempted reply by Clarence Darrow and Victor Yarros, *The Prohibition Mania* (N. Y., 1927), handles figures even more carelessly. Fabian Franklin, *The A B C of Prohibition* (N. Y., 1927), is written from a hostile viewpoint. A variety of aspects are considered in the *Annals* of the American Academy of Political and Social Science, CIX (1923).

CRIME AND CORRUPTION

For the Social Science Research Council, A. F. Kuhlman prepared *A Guide to Material on Crime and Criminal Justice* (N. Y., 1929). The publications of the state and national crime commissions are useful. See, for example, the Pennsylvania *Report to the General Assembly of the Commission Appointed to Study Laws, Procedure, etc., Relating to Crime and Criminals* (Phila., 1929). R. B. Fosdick, *American*

Police Systems (N. Y., 1920), is a standard treatment of the defects of American administration of the law. A. A. Bruce, *The Administration of Criminal Justice in Illinois* (Chicago, 1929), Herbert Asbury, *The Gangs of New York* (N. Y., 1928), and Lloyd Lewis and H. J. Smith, *Chicago: the History of its Reputation* (N. Y., 1929), give some glimpses of gangland. M. A. Kavanagh, *The Criminal and His Allies* (Indianapolis, 1928), and R. W. Child, *Battling the Criminal* (N. Y., 1925), afford illustrations of the many ways in which criminal justice breaks down, but are rather too alarmist in tone to be accepted uncritically. Prison reform is discussed in Frank Tannenbaum, *Wall Shadows: a Study in American Prisons* (N. Y., 1922); T. M. Osborne, *Society and Prison* (New Haven, 1924) and *Prisons and Common Sense* (Phila., 1924); H. E. Barnes, *The Repression of Crime* (N. Y., 1926); and S. S. Glueck, *Mental Disorder and the Criminal Law* (Boston, 1925). For a general symposium, see *Modern Crime* in the *Annals* of the American Academy of Political and Social Science, CXXV (1926). The complete transcript of the most famous trial of the period may be found in N. D. Baker and others, eds., *The Sacco-Vanzetti Case* (6 vols., N. Y., 1928); a select bibliography of the case appears in the *Lantern* (Boston), II (1929), 26.

All kinds of political chicanery of the day are illustrated in F. R. Kent's mordant study of *Political Behavior: the Heretofore Unwritten Laws, Customs and Principles of Politics as Practiced in the United States* (N. Y., 1928), and a typical incident is presented in lively fashion by M. E. Ravage, *Teapot Dome* (N. Y., 1924). The biographical sketches *Masks in a Pageant* (N. Y., 1928) by William Allen White, and the fictional presentation of the Harding administration in S. H. Adams, *Revelry* (N. Y., 1926), will suffice to complete the depression of the reader. A valuable picture of Chicago political life is afforded by C. E. Merriam's autobiographical *Chicago: A More Intimate View of Urban Politics* (N. Y., 1929).

EDUCATION

The *Bulletins* of the bureau of education are of particular value for elementary and secondary education. The student of rural education will find an account of the large new union schools in J. F. Abel, *Consolidation of Schools and Transportation of Pupils* (*Bull.*, no. 41, 1923), and *Recent Data on Consolidation of Schools* (*Bull.*, no. 22, 1925); the student of urban education will turn to W. S. Deffenbaugh, *Recent Movements in City School Systems* (*Bull.*, no. 8, 1927). For the reorganization of the grade system note may be made of H. B. Brunner, *The Junior High School at Work* (N. Y., 1925), and T. H. Briggs, *The Junior High School* (Boston, 1920).

For higher education during the period, see in general *American Universities and Colleges* (N. Y., 1928), edited by D. A. Robertson; E. R. Holme, *The American University; an Australian View* (Sydney, Aus., 1920); R. L. Kelly, *Tendencies in College Administration* (N. Y., 1925); P. R. Kolbe, *The Colleges in War Time and After* (N. Y., 1919); and E. H. Wilkins, *The Changing College* (Chicago, 1927). The existing system of college and university control is subjected to severe criticism in Thorstein Veblen, *The Higher Learning in America* (N. Y., 1918), and J. E. Kirkpatrick, *The American College and its Rulers* (N. Y., 1926). Reforms in teaching are considered in Alexander Meiklejohn, *Freedom and the College* (N. Y., 1923); R. C. Brooks, *Reading for Honors at Swarthmore* (N. Y., 1927); and Frank Aydelotte, *Honors Courses in American Colleges and Universities* (Natl. Research Council, *Bulls.*, no. 40, 1924; no. 52, 1925). But it is the undergraduate who received the lion's share of publicity. A few of the more important books dealing mainly with student life are: *Undergraduates; a Study of Morals in Twenty-three American Colleges and Universities* (N. Y., 1928), by R. H. Edwards, J. M. Artman and G. M. Fischer; R. C. Angell, *The Campus* (N. Y., 1928); F. P. Keppel, *The Undergraduate and His College* (Boston, 1917); Percy Marks, *Which Way Parnassus?* (N. Y., 1926); J. A. Benn, *Colum-*

bus-Undergraduate (N. Y., 1928); and J. A. Hawes, *Twenty Years among the Twenty Year Olds* (N. Y., 1929).

WOMEN, THE FAMILY AND RELIGION

The conquest of equal suffrage for women is related in the annual numbers of *The Woman Suffrage Year Book* (1917-   ) and in Carrie Chapman Catt, *Woman Suffrage and Politics* (N. Y., 1926). The more militant phases of feminism are presented in Inez H. Irwin, *The Story of the Woman's Party* (N. Y., 1921), and Doris Stevens, *Jailed for Freedom* (N. Y., 1920). The new economic position of woman attracted more attention than her political enfranchisement. In addition to the war-time studies already mentioned, the following should be noted: Elizabeth K. Adams, *Women Professional Workers* (N. Y., 1921); V. M. Collier, *Marriage and Careers* (N. Y., 1926), a volume of case studies; Catherine Filene, *Careers for Women* (Boston, 1920); Orie L. Hatcher, *Occupations for Women* (Richmond, 1927); Johanna Lobsenz, *The Older Woman in Industry* (N. Y., 1929); and Theresa Wolfson, *The Woman Worker and the Trade Unions* (N. Y., 1926).

Still more widespread was discussion of the weakening of the family tie and the alleged wildness of the oncoming generation. E. R. Groves and W. F. Ogburn, *American Marriage and Family Relationships* (N. Y., 1928); Anna G. Spencer, *The Family and Its Members* (Phila., 1923); Elizabeth Benson, *The Younger Generation* (N. Y., 1927); Miriam Van Waters, *Parents on Probation* (N. Y., 1927); *Our Changing Morality* (N. Y., 1928), a symposium, mainly radical in tone, edited by Freda Kirchwey; G. W. Fiske, *The Changing Family* (N. Y., 1929); and Margaret E. Rich, ed., *Family Life Today* (Boston, 1928), reflect the uneasy questionings of the age; but it was reserved for the "children's judge" of Denver, Benjamin B. Lindsey, to rouse the greatest sensation with his *The Revolt of Modern Youth* (N. Y., 1925) and *The Companionate Marriage* (N. Y., 1927), both written in collaboration with Wainwright Evans.

A thoughtful discussion of religious trends can be found in

the concluding chapters of H. K. Rowe, *The History of Religion in the United States* (N. Y., 1924). For denominational progress, note especially the *Handbook of the Churches* (named *Federal Council Year Book*, 1915-1916, and *Year Book of the Churches*, 1917-1925), issued by the Federal Council of the Churches of Christ and superseding the *Federal Council Year Book*, and the first volume of the two-volume *World Survey* made by the Interchurch World Movement (N. Y., 1920). One may note among individual studies W. A. Brown, *The Church in America; a Study of the Present Conditions and Future Prospects of American Protestantism* (N. Y., 1922); H. P. Douglass, *The Church in the Changing City* (N. Y., 1927); and A. B. Bass, *Protestantism in the United States* (N. Y., 1929), a canvass of the situation at the close of the period.

LITERATURE AND THE FINE ARTS

The Cambridge History of American Literature (4 vols., N. Y., 1917-1921), edited by W. P. Trent and others, is important as providing a background for an understanding of the intellectual life of the period. Van Wyck Brooks, *America's Coming of Age* (N. Y., 1915), and S. P. Sherman, *Points of View* (N. Y., 1924), estimate the current literature; L. R. Morris, *The Young Idea* (N. Y., 1917), is an anthology of new writers on their vocation; Norman Foerster, ed., *The Reinterpretation of American Literature* (N. Y., 1928), sets forth the newer tendencies in the study of American literature.

R. L. Duffus, *The American Renaissance* (N. Y., 1928), discusses the development of the drama and the fine arts in the United States. Burns Mantle, *American Playwrights of Today* (N. Y., 1929), is excellent for its theme. The dramatic revival is well reflected in the *Carolina Folk Plays*, edited by F. H. Koch (N. Y., 1922). Charles Merz, *The Great American Band Wagon* (N. Y., 1928), is a hash of current folly for the pleasure of the sophisticated. Considering the arts individually, first attention should go to architecture where the national achievement was unquestionably most important.

T. E. Tallmadge, *The Story of Architecture in America,*
cited before, and W. A. Starrett, *Skyscrapers and the Men
Who Build Them* (N. Y., 1928), are particularly worth
noting. Other arts are considered in Lorado Taft, *The
History of American Sculpture* (N. Y., 1924); Adeline V.
Adams, *The Spirit of American Sculpture* (N. Y., 1923);
Catherine B. Ely, *The Modern Tendency in American Paint-
ing* (N. Y., 1925); L. C. Elson, *The History of American
Music* (rev. by Arthur Elson, N. Y., 1925); and D. G.
Mason, *The Dilemma of American Music* (N. Y., 1928).
Popular music and the dance are represented by Paul White-
man and Mary M. McBride, *Jazz* (N. Y., 1926); H. O.
Osgood, *So This is Jazz* (Boston, 1926); and Mr. and Mrs.
Vernon Castle, *Modern Dancing* (N. Y., 1914). Gilbert
Seldes, *The Seven Lively Arts* (N. Y., 1924), treats of mu-
sic, dancing, the moving picture, the comic strip and other
frontier districts between art and commercial amusement.

SCHOLARSHIP, SCIENCE AND INVENTION

The creation of the National Research Council (for the
natural sciences), the Social Science Research Council and the
American Council of Learned Societies gave a great impetus
to organized scientific work in all these fields, and led to the
production of monographs defining and illuminating problems and methods of research, as well as works extending the
bounds of knowledge. F. A. Ogg, *Research in the Humanis-
tic and Social Sciences* (N. Y., 1928), is a valuable survey of
the scope and activities of existing research agencies, private
and governmental, prepared for the American Council of
Learned Societies. Such volumes as J. J. Jusserand, W. C.
Abbott, C. W. Colby and J. S. Bassett, *The Writing of History* (N. Y., 1926); H. E. Barnes, *The New History and the
Social Studies* (N. Y., 1925); Wilson Gee, ed., *Research in
the Social Sciences* (N. Y., 1929); and H. W. Odum and
Katharine Jocher, *An Introduction to Social Research* (N.
Y., 1929), discuss the newer trends of research, presentation
and methodology in the social sciences.

In addition to the scientific topics discussed under the heading, Prosperity, Business, Labor, one may mention R. T. Young, *Biology in America* (Boston, 1922); Julius Stieglitz, *Chemistry in Medicine* (N. Y., 1928); E. E. Slosson, *Creative Chemistry* (N. Y., 1921); L. I. Dublin, *Health and Wealth* (N. Y., 1928), statistical; and *Science in Modern Industry* (Am. Acad. of Polit. and Social Sci., *Annals*, CXIX, 1925). The development of aviation can be followed from the publications of the aeronautical branch of the department of commerce, and the *Aircraft Yearbook* put forth by the Aeronautical Chamber of Commerce of America, New York. C. A. Lindbergh, *"We"* (N. Y., 1927), is the narrative of the most famous flight of the period. The history of the motion picture is told in Terry Ramsaye, *A Million and One Nights* (N. Y., 1926); and various consequences of its development are discussed in *The Motion Picture in its Economic and Social Aspects* (Am. Acad. of Polit. and Social Sci., *Annals*, CXXVIII, 1926), Alice M. Mitchell, *Children and Movies* (Chicago, 1929), and H. B. Franklin, *Sound Motion Pictures* (Garden City, 1929). The story of another of the new scientific arts is recounted in Paul Schubert, *The Electric Word: the Rise of Radio* (N. Y., 1929), and Anton de Haas, ed., *The Radio Industry* (Chicago, 1928), a symposium by leaders of the industry.

INDEX

ACCIDENTS, increase of motor, 236.

Adams, F. P., journalism of, 355.

Adamson act, enactment of, 17.

Advertising, effect on fashions of, 155-156; tourism and, 238-240; volume of, 362-365; methods of, 365-371.

Agriculture, changes in, 190-191, 218; American type of, 191-193; mechanization of, 193-196; depression in, 199-204; coöperation in, 212-213; diversification in, 213-215; motor traction in, 234-235; Southern progress in, 265-266; bibliography, 455-456.

Airplanes. *See* Aviation.

Alabama, war committees in, 63.

Alcoholism, deaths from, 119-120.

Allard, H. A., discoveries of, 379.

Allen, Governor Henry, establishes industrial court, 85.

Amalgamated Clothing Workers, membership of, 174.

Amateur sports, vogue of, 272-276, 280. *See also* Sport.

American Association of University Professors, on football, 275; on academic freedom, 337.

American Civil Liberties Bureau, opposes draft, 69.

American Civil Liberties Union, activities of, 88.

American Cotton Association, established, 213.

American Defense Society, activity of, 24.

American Expeditionary Force ("A. E. F."), organized, 35-42; soldier life in, 42-49.

American Federation of Labor, favored by President Wilson, 17; supports war, 65-66; conservatism of, 85, 173; membership of, 174-175.

American League to Limit Armaments, activity of, 24.

American Legion, established, 78.

American Magazine, popularity of, 347, 358, 360.

American Mercury, character of, 359, 421-422.

American Relief Administration, activities of, 200, 291 *n.*

American Rights Committee, activity of, 24.

American Union against Militarism, activity of, 24.

American University (Washington, D. C.), in war time, 332.

Americanization, activities in, 302-304; bibliography, 451.

Amherst, President Meiklejohn at, 340.

Amusements, athletic, 271-281; parlor, 281-286, 342.

Anderson, Sherwood, fiction of, 417, 420.

Antioch College, educational experiments at, 341.

Anti-Saloon League, activities of, 109-112.

Anti-Semitism, 228, 314-315. *See also* Nativism.

Architecture, domestic, 138-141, 410; urban, 408-410.

Argonne, campaign in the, 49.

Aristocracy, in advertising, 366-367.

Arkansas, antievolution law in, 338, 432-433.

Armistice, celebrated, 71.

Art, tendencies in American, 406-414; bibliography, 463-464.

Ashland College, established, 340.

Astronomy, achievements in, 374.

Athletics. *See* Sport.

Atlanta Constitution, public services of, 358.

Atlantic, characterized, 362.

Smith-Hughes act, federal aid extended by, 328.
Smith-Lever act, federal aid extended by, 328.
Smuggling, liquor, 114-118.
Social Science Research Council, work of, 384.
Social sciences, taught in schools, 326; research in, 383-384.
Socialist party, divided on war issues, 29, 86; divided on communism, 87; declining strength of, 86-88.
Soft drinks, increased sale of, 126-128.
Soldier life, in barracks, 36-39; at the front, 42-49.
South, prohibition sentiment in, 108, 121-122, 252-253; sectional characteristics of, 251-253; race problem in, 253-262; industrial development of, 262-266; education in, 265-267; politics in, 267-269; bibliography, 457-458. *See also* Tourism.
Spanish, increased study of, 70, 327.
Spargo, John, leaves Socialist party, 29.
Speculation, in stock market, 180; in land, 198-201, 242, 246-247.
Spirit of St. Louis, flight of, 402-403.
Sport, popularity of, 270-272, 342, 437; varieties of, 272-281.
Stadium building, competition in, 274-275.
Stagg, A. A., on stadium building, 275.
Standard of living, enhancement of, 135-141, 162-204, 215-218, 270, 321-323, 336, 343-344, 436-437.
Standard Oil, stockholders of, 177.
Standardization, in retail trade, 183; in manufacture, 186-188; in automobiles, 228; in folkways, 251.
Stanley, Governor A. O., defies mob, 259.

Stars and Stripes, soldier newspaper, 45-46.
State councils of defense, organization of, 62-64.
Steel industry, strike of 1919 in, 80-82; hours of labor in, 80-82, 172; employee ownership in, 177.
Stephenson, D. C., in Klan politics, 312-314.
Stockholders, increase of, 176-179.
Stoddard, Lothrop, racial views of, 306.
Stokes, J. G. P., leaves Socialist party, 29.
Stone Mountain, Confederate war memorial at, 318-319, 411.
Straton, J. R., fundamentalism of, 435.
Strawn, S. H., on overproduction of laws, 102.
Strikes, during neutrality, 16-17; during war time, 65-68; in 1919, 80-81; in coal fields, 83-84; decrease after 1919, 82, 173.
Students' Army Training Corps, services of, 333.
Submarine, German underseas blockade by, 20-22; war against, 50-52.
Suburban development, increase of, 197.
Suffrage, for women, 157-161; for Negroes, 256.
Suicide, decrease of, 104.
Sunday, observance of, 434.
Sunday, Rev. William ("Billy"), as evangelist, 55, 427.
Superstition, persistence of, 435.
Surgery, development of, 378-379. *See also* Dentistry.
Sussex, sinking of, 22.
Swarthmore College, honors courses in, 340.
Sweetser, Arthur, international services of, 291 *n*.
Swimming, success of women in, 281.
Swindling, in advertising, 368.

TABERT, Martin, killing of, 357-358.